First World War
and Army of Occupation
War Diary
France, Belgium and Germany

24 DIVISION
Divisional Troops
Royal Army Service Corps
Divisional Train (194,195,196,197 Companies A.S.C.)
29 August 1915 - 25 June 1919

WO95/2203/4

The Naval & Military Press Ltd
www.nmarchive.com
Published in association with The National Archives

Published by

The Naval & Military Press Ltd

Unit 10 Ridgewood Industrial Park,

Uckfield, East Sussex,

TN22 5QE England

Tel: +44 (0) 1825 749494

www.naval-military-press.com

www.nmarchive.com

This diary has been reprinted in facsimile from the original. Any imperfections are inevitably reproduced and the quality may fall short of modern type and cartographic standards.

Contents

Document type	Place/Title	Date From	Date To
Heading	WO95/2203/4		
Heading	24th. Divl Train A.S.C. Aug 1915-Jun 1919		
Heading	24th Div L Train Vol I From 29th August Sept 15 1 June 19		
War Diary	Brookwood	29/08/1915	29/08/1915
War Diary	Havre	30/08/1915	30/08/1915
War Diary	Rest Camp No 5	31/08/1915	31/08/1915
War Diary	Hesdin	01/09/1915	01/09/1915
War Diary	Beaurainville	02/09/1915	21/09/1915
War Diary	Hezeques	22/09/1915	22/09/1915
War Diary	Auchy Les Bois	23/09/1915	23/09/1915
War Diary	Busnes	24/09/1915	24/09/1915
War Diary	Annezin	25/09/1915	25/09/1915
War Diary	Bethune	26/09/1915	26/09/1915
War Diary	Sailly La Bourse	27/09/1915	27/09/1915
War Diary	Bethune	28/09/1915	30/09/1915
Heading	War Diary of O.C 24th Divisional Train B.G.F From 29th Aug 1915 To 30th Sept 1915		
Miscellaneous			
Miscellaneous	Annezin	25/09/1915	25/09/1915
War Diary	West Heath, Woking	29/08/1915	29/08/1915
War Diary	Havre	30/08/1915	02/09/1915
War Diary	Beaurainville	03/09/1915	21/09/1915
War Diary	Laires	22/09/1915	22/09/1915
War Diary	Auchy Au Bois	23/09/1915	23/09/1915
War Diary	Busnes	24/09/1915	24/09/1915
War Diary	Annezin	25/09/1915	25/09/1915
War Diary	Beuvry	25/09/1915	25/09/1915
War Diary	Sailly La Bourse	25/09/1915	25/09/1915
War Diary	Vermelles	25/09/1915	25/09/1915
War Diary	Le Rutoire	26/09/1915	26/09/1915
War Diary	Annezin Bethune	26/09/1915	26/09/1915
War Diary	Sailly La Bourse	26/09/1915	27/09/1915
War Diary	Bethune	28/09/1915	28/09/1915
War Diary	Annezin	29/09/1915	29/09/1915
War Diary	St. Hilaire	30/09/1915	30/09/1915
War Diary	Annezin	25/09/1915	25/09/1915
War Diary	Le Rutoire Farm	26/09/1915	27/09/1915
War Diary	Sailly-La Bourse	27/09/1915	27/09/1915
Heading	24th Division 24th Div. Train Vol 2 Oct 15		
Heading	24th Division 194th Coy A.S.C. Vol 2 Oct 15 1 July 19		
War Diary	Bethune	01/10/1915	01/10/1915
War Diary	St. Hilaire	02/10/1915	02/10/1915
War Diary	Wallon Cappel	03/10/1915	03/10/1915
War Diary	Herzeele	04/10/1915	06/10/1915
War Diary	Boeschepe	07/10/1915	11/10/1915
War Diary	Godewaersvelde	12/10/1915	31/10/1915
Heading	War Diary Of Major. T.W. Blakeway. from 1/10/15 to 31/10/15 (Volume II)		

Heading	War Diary of O.C. 24th Divisional Train B.E.F. from 1st Oct 1915 to 31st October 1915.		
War Diary	St. Hilaire	01/10/1915	02/10/1915
War Diary	Wallon Cappel	03/10/1915	03/10/1915
War Diary	Herzeele	04/10/1915	06/10/1915
War Diary	Boeschepe	07/10/1915	11/10/1915
War Diary	Godewaersvelde	12/10/1915	13/10/1915
War Diary	Godewaersvelde	14/10/1915	31/10/1915
Heading	24th Divl. Train Vol 3 Nov. 15		
Heading	War Diary of O.C. 24th Divisional Train B.E.F. 1st Nov 1915 to 30th Nov. 1915		
War Diary	Godewaersvelde	01/11/1915	24/11/1915
War Diary	Steenvoorde	25/11/1915	27/11/1915
War Diary	Lederzeele	28/11/1915	28/11/1915
War Diary	Salperwick	29/11/1915	30/11/1915
Heading	24th Division 194th Coy A.S.C. Vol 4 Nov 15		
Heading	War Diary of 194 Coy ASC from 1/11/15 to 30/11/15 Volume 3		
War Diary	Godewaersvelde	01/11/1915	24/11/1915
War Diary	Steenvoorde	25/11/1915	27/11/1915
War Diary	Lederzeele	28/11/1915	28/11/1915
War Diary	Tatinghem	29/11/1915	29/11/1915
War Diary	Noir Carme	30/11/1915	30/11/1915
Heading	24th Div Train Vol 4		
Heading	194th Coy. ASC (No 1 Coy 24th Div Train Vol 5) Dec		
Heading	War Diary of 194 Coy Asc (24th Div Train) From 1st December 1915 To 31st Dec 1915		
War Diary	Noir Carme	01/12/1915	31/12/1915
Heading	War Diary of O.C 24th Divisional Train Asc from 1-12-15 to 31-12-15 Vol IV		
War Diary	Salperwick	01/12/1915	31/12/1915
Heading	24th Divl. Train. Vol 5		
Heading	194th Coy. Asc Vol 6		
Heading	War Diary of 194 Coy ASC 1st January to 31st January 1916		
War Diary	Noir Carme	01/01/1916	01/01/1916
War Diary	Noordpeene	02/01/1916	02/01/1916
War Diary	Steenvoorde	03/01/1916	03/01/1916
War Diary	Busseboom	04/01/1916	31/01/1916
Heading	War Diary of O.C. 24th Divisional Train A.S.C. B.E.F. Jan 1/1916 to Jan 31/1916		
War Diary	Salperwick	01/01/1916	07/01/1916
War Diary	Steen Voorde	08/01/1916	08/01/1916
War Diary	Busseboom	09/01/1916	17/01/1916
War Diary	Busseboom Sheet 28 b 16c 5.2	18/01/1916	20/01/1916
War Diary	Busseboom Map 28 G 16.c.5.2	21/01/1916	26/01/1916
War Diary	Busseboom	27/01/1916	31/01/1916
Heading	War Diary of O.C. 24th Divisional Train from 1-2-16 to 29-2-16		
Heading	War Diary of 194 Coy. A.S.C. from 1st February to 29th February 1916		
War Diary	Busseboom	01/02/1916	29/02/1916
Heading	War Diary of O.C. 24th Divisional Train from 1-3-16 to 31-3-16		
Heading	War Diary of 194 Coy ASC from 1st to 31st March 1916		

War Diary	Busseboom	01/03/1916	19/03/1916
War Diary	Fletre	20/03/1916	31/03/1916
War Diary	Busseboom	01/03/1916	01/03/1916
War Diary	Poperinghe	02/03/1916	21/03/1916
War Diary	Fletre	22/03/1916	31/03/1916
Heading	War Diary of 194 Coy. A.S.C. from 1st April to 30th April 1916		
Heading	War Diary of 24th Divisional Train from April 1st to 30th 1916		
War Diary	De Brocken	01/04/1916	21/04/1916
War Diary	Bailleul	22/04/1916	30/04/1916
Heading	War Diary of O.C. 24th Divisional Train from 1-10-16 to 31-10-16		
War Diary	Estree Cauchie	01/10/1916	27/10/1916
War Diary	Bruay	28/10/1916	30/10/1916
War Diary	Braquemont	31/10/1916	31/10/1916
Heading	War Diary of O.C. 24th Divisional Train 1-5-16 to 31-5-16		
Heading	War Diary of 194 Company Army Service Corps from 1st May 1916 to 31st May 1916		
War Diary	La Clef De Belgique	01/05/1916	31/05/1916
Miscellaneous	O i/c To Go Office Base	02/04/1916	02/04/1916
War Diary	Bailleul	01/05/1916	31/05/1916
War Diary	Le Clef De Belgique	01/04/1916	30/04/1916
Heading	War Diary of O.C. 24th Divisional Train from 1-6-16 to 30-6-16		
Heading	War Diary of 194 Coy Asc 1st June to 30th June 1916		
War Diary	Le Clef De Belgique	01/06/1916	30/06/1916
War Diary	Bailleul	01/06/1916	30/06/1916
Heading	War Diary of O.C. 24th Divisional Train from July 1-31st		
Heading	War Diary of 194 Coy. A.S.C. from 1st July to 31st July 1916		
War Diary	Le Clef De Belgique	01/07/1916	06/07/1916
War Diary	Schaexhen	07/07/1916	08/07/1916
War Diary	Le Olgf De Belgique	09/07/1916	21/07/1916
War Diary	Eecke	22/07/1916	26/07/1916
War Diary	Crouy	27/07/1916	31/07/1916
War Diary	Bailleul	01/07/1916	20/07/1916
War Diary	St. Jans Cappel	21/07/1916	25/07/1916
War Diary	Picquigny	26/01/1916	31/01/1916
Heading	War Diary of 194. Company A.S.C. from 1/8/16 to 30/8/16		
Heading	War Diary of O.C. 24th Divisional Train from 1 VIII.16 to 31.VIII. 16		
War Diary	Sailly Le Sec	01/08/1916	04/08/1916
War Diary	Meaulte	05/08/1916	31/08/1916
War Diary	Corbie	01/08/1916	02/08/1916
War Diary	F. 19. d. Sheet 62II	03/08/1916	04/08/1916
War Diary	F. 19. d.	05/08/1916	14/08/1916
War Diary	F. 19. a. 5.2	15/08/1916	25/08/1916
War Diary	E.20.a.5.7 (Edgehill)	26/08/1916	27/08/1916
War Diary	E20a 5.7	28/08/1916	31/08/1916
Heading	War Diary of O.C. 24th Divisional Train from 1-9-16 to 30-9-16		
War Diary	E. 11 Central	01/09/1916	05/09/1916

War Diary	Dernancourt	06/09/1916	06/09/1916
War Diary	Argoeuves	07/09/1916	07/09/1916
War Diary	Cocquerel	08/09/1916	19/09/1916
War Diary	Bruay	20/09/1916	26/09/1916
War Diary	Estree Cauchie	27/09/1916	30/09/1916
War Diary	War Diary of 194. Company A.S.C. from 1/9/16 to 30/9/16		
War Diary	Meaulte	01/09/1916	28/09/1916
War Diary	Molliens au Bois	29/09/1916	30/09/1916
Heading	War Diary of 194. Company A.S.C. from 1/10/16 to 31/10/16		
War Diary	Hem	01/10/1916	01/10/1916
War Diary	Blangerval	02/10/1916	02/10/1916
War Diary	Camblain Chatelain	03/10/1916	03/10/1916
War Diary	Fresnicourt	04/10/1916	07/10/1916
War Diary	Gauchin-Legal	08/10/1916	31/10/1916
Heading	War Diary of O.C. 24th Div Train From 1/11/16 to 30/11/16		
War Diary	Braquemont	01/11/1916	30/11/1916
Heading	War Diary Of 194. Company A.S.C. from 1/11/16 to 30/11/16.		
War Diary	Gauchin Legal	01/11/1916	30/11/1916
Heading	War Diary Of 194 Company A.S.C. 24th Divisional Train. from 1/12/16 to 31/12/16		
War Diary	Gauchin Legal	01/12/1916	04/12/1916
War Diary	Noeux Les Mines	05/12/1916	31/12/1916
Heading	War Diary of 24th Divisional Train from 1/12/1916 to 31/12/1916		
War Diary	Braquemont	01/12/1916	31/12/1916
War Diary	Noeux Les Mines	01/01/1917	31/01/1917
Heading	War Diary of O.C. 24th Divisional Train from 1-1-17 to 31-1-17		
War Diary	Braquemont	01/01/1917	31/01/1917
Heading	War Diary of O.C. 24th Divisional Train 1/2/17 to 28/2/17		
War Diary	Braquemont	01/02/1917	12/02/1917
War Diary	Fouquieres	13/02/1917	28/02/1917
War Diary	Noeux Les Mines	01/02/1917	12/02/1917
War Diary	Fouquieres	13/02/1917	28/02/1917
Heading	War Diary of O.C. 24th Divisional Train from 1/3/17 to 31/3/17		
War Diary	Fouquieres	01/03/1917	05/03/1917
War Diary	Noeux	06/03/1917	31/03/1917
War Diary	Fouquieres	01/03/1917	03/03/1917
War Diary	Bracquemont	04/03/1917	31/03/1917
Miscellaneous	D.D.S. & T. First Army.	15/03/1917	15/03/1917
War Diary	War Diary of Officer Commanding 24th Divl Train from April 1st to April 30th 1917		
War Diary	Fouquieres	01/03/1917	05/03/1917
War Diary	Noeux	06/03/1917	31/03/1917
War Diary	Bracquemont	01/04/1917	19/04/1917
War Diary	Norrent Fontes	20/04/1917	23/04/1917
War Diary	St. Hilaire	24/04/1917	25/04/1917
War Diary	Bomy	26/04/1917	30/04/1917
Heading	War Diary Of 194. Camp. A.S.C. 24th Div. Train. from 1/4/17 to 30/4/17		

War Diary	Noeux	01/04/1917	25/04/1917
War Diary	St. Hilaire	26/04/1917	26/04/1917
War Diary	Senlis	27/04/1917	30/04/1917
Heading	War Diary of O.C. 24th Divisional Train from May 1st to May 31st. 1917		
War Diary	Bomy	01/05/1917	08/05/1917
War Diary	Norrent Fontes.	09/05/1917	10/05/1917
War Diary	Steenbecque	11/05/1917	11/05/1917
War Diary	Steenvoorde	12/05/1917	14/05/1917
War Diary	Busseboom	15/05/1917	30/05/1917
War Diary	Hopoutre	31/05/1917	31/05/1917
Heading	War Diary of 194. Company. A.S.C. 24th. Div. Train. from 1/5/17 to 31/5/17		
War Diary	Senlis	01/05/1917	09/05/1917
War Diary	Romly	10/05/1917	10/05/1917
War Diary	Morbecque	11/05/1917	11/05/1917
War Diary	Chateau D'If	12/05/1917	24/05/1917
War Diary	Busseboom	25/05/1917	30/05/1917
War Diary	L.24. C. 9.1 Map 27.	31/05/1917	31/05/1917
Heading	War Diary of O.C. 24th Divisional Train from June 1st to June 30th 1917		
War Diary	L.24. c.9.I. Sheet 27.	01/06/1917	14/06/1917
War Diary	N 2C. 2.2	15/06/1917	30/06/1917
War Diary	Hopoutre	01/06/1917	12/06/1917
War Diary	Ouderdom	13/06/1917	16/06/1917
War Diary	Millekruisse	17/06/1917	19/06/1917
War Diary	Millekruise	20/06/1917	27/06/1917
War Diary	Caestre	28/06/1917	28/06/1917
War Diary	Renescure	29/06/1917	29/06/1917
War Diary	Lumbres	30/06/1917	30/06/1917
Heading	War Diary of O C 24th Divisional Train from July 1st 1917 to July 31st 1917		
War Diary	Lumbres	01/07/1917	18/07/1917
War Diary	Staple	19/07/1917	21/07/1917
War Diary	Eecke	22/07/1917	22/07/1917
War Diary	Zevecoten	23/07/1917	31/07/1917
Heading	War Diary of 194. Company A.S.C. 24th Divisional Train. from 1/7/17 to 31/7/17		
War Diary	N2. C. 2.2	01/07/1917	03/07/1917
War Diary	Borre	04/07/1917	05/07/1917
War Diary	Racquinghem	06/07/1917	13/07/1917
War Diary	Borre	14/07/1917	14/07/1917
War Diary	Reninghelst	15/07/1917	21/07/1917
War Diary	Ouderdom	22/07/1917	22/07/1917
War Diary	Reninghelst	23/07/1917	31/07/1917
Heading	War Diary of O.C. 24th Divisional Train from 1/8/17 to 31/8/17		
War Diary	Zevecoten	01/08/1917	31/08/1917
War Diary	Reninghelst	01/08/1917	31/08/1917
Heading	War Diary of O.C. 24th Divisional Train from 1/9/17 to 30/9/17		
War Diary	Zevecoten	01/09/1917	14/09/1917
War Diary	Merris	14/09/1917	20/09/1917
War Diary	Rocquigny	21/09/1917	26/09/1917
War Diary	Peronne	27/09/1917	28/09/1917
War Diary	Roisel	29/09/1917	30/09/1917

Heading	War Diary of 194. Camp. A.S.C. 24th Div. Train. from 1/9/17 to 30/9/17		
War Diary	Reninghelst	01/09/1917	14/09/1917
War Diary	Steenvoorde	15/09/1917	16/09/1917
War Diary	Map. 57c N. 11.a. 2.7	17/09/1917	25/09/1917
War Diary	Map. 62c. I 36.b.	26/09/1917	29/09/1917
War Diary	Roisel	30/09/1917	30/09/1917
Heading	War Diary of O.C. 24th Divisional Train from 1/10/1917 to 31/10/1917		
War Diary	Vraignes	01/10/1917	31/10/1917
Heading	War Diary Of 194 Coy A.S.C. from October 1917		
War Diary	Roisel	01/10/1917	31/10/1917
Heading	War Diary of O.C. 24th Divisional Train from Nov 1st to Nov 30th. 1917		
War Diary	Vraignes	01/11/1917	30/11/1917
Heading	War Diary Of 194. Camp. A.S.C. 24th Div Train. from 1/11/17 to 30/11/17		
War Diary	Roisel	01/11/1917	30/11/1917
Heading	War Diary of Officer Commanding 24th Divisional Train from 1/12/17 to 31/12/17		
War Diary	Vraignes	01/12/1917	31/12/1917
War Diary	Roisel	01/12/1917	31/12/1917
War Diary	Vraignes	01/01/1918	31/01/1918
War Diary	Roisel	01/01/1918	31/01/1918
Heading	War Diary of O.C. 24th Divisional Train from 1st Feby 1918 to 28th Feby 1918		
War Diary	Vraignes	01/02/1918	26/02/1918
War Diary	Villers Bretonneux	27/02/1918	28/02/1918
Operation(al) Order(s)	24th Divisional Train Order No. 22 Appendix "A"	25/02/1918	25/02/1918
Miscellaneous	Supply Group Table No. 1 to take effect		
Miscellaneous	Supply Group Table No. 2 to take effect		
Operation(al) Order(s)	24th Divisional Train Order No. 23 Appendix "B"	25/02/1918	25/02/1918
Operation(al) Order(s)	24th Divisional Train Order No. 24 Appendix "C"	25/02/1918	25/02/1918
Operation(al) Order(s)	24th Divisional Train Order No. 25 Appendix "D"	28/02/1918	28/02/1918
Heading	War Diary of O.C. 24th Divisional Train from 1/3/18 to 31/3/18		
War Diary	Villers Bretonneux	01/03/1918	01/03/1918
War Diary	Peronne	02/03/1918	12/03/1918
War Diary	Tertry	13/03/1918	21/03/1918
War Diary	Brie	22/03/1918	22/03/1918
War Diary	Villers Carbonnel	23/03/1918	23/03/1918
War Diary	P. of W Camp Chaulnes	23/03/1918	24/03/1918
War Diary	Lihons	24/03/1918	24/03/1918
War Diary	Rosieres	25/03/1918	25/03/1918
War Diary	Thennes	26/03/1918	26/03/1918
War Diary	Thennes Demuin	27/03/1918	27/03/1918
War Diary	Demuin	28/03/1918	28/03/1918
War Diary	Castel	28/03/1918	29/03/1918
War Diary	Cottenchy	29/03/1918	31/03/1918
Operation(al) Order(s)	24th Divisional Train Order No. 26	03/03/1918	03/03/1918
Miscellaneous	Supply Group Table No. 4 to take effect	04/03/1918	04/03/1918
Miscellaneous	Supply Group Table No. 5	13/03/1918	13/03/1918
War Diary	Cottenchy	01/04/1918	04/04/1918
War Diary	Cagny	04/04/1918	05/04/1918
War Diary	Legard Farm Nr. Picquigny	06/04/1918	07/04/1918
War Diary	Cambron	07/04/1918	08/04/1918

War Diary	St. Valery	08/04/1918	17/04/1918
War Diary	Valhuon	18/04/1918	20/04/1918
War Diary	Divion	20/04/1918	21/04/1918
War Diary	Bajus	21/04/1918	30/04/1918
Miscellaneous	24th Division No. Q.2/202	12/04/1918	12/04/1918
Miscellaneous	24th Division No. Q. 2/208	21/04/1918	21/04/1918
Heading	War Diary of the 24th Divisional M.T. Company From 1st April 1918 to 30th April 1918		
War Diary	Bajus	01/05/1918	02/05/1918
War Diary	Barlin	02/05/1918	21/05/1918
War Diary	Verdrel	21/05/1918	31/05/1918
Operation(al) Order(s)	24th Divisional Train Order No. 27	03/05/1918	03/05/1918
Miscellaneous	Addendum To 24th Divisional Train Order No. 27	04/05/1918	04/05/1918
Operation(al) Order(s)	24th Divisional Train Order No. 28	06/05/1918	06/05/1918
Miscellaneous	Supply Group Table No. 8	06/05/1918	06/05/1918
War Diary	Verdrel	01/06/1918	30/06/1918
Operation(al) Order(s)	24th Divisional Train Order No. 29	03/06/1918	03/06/1918
Miscellaneous	Headquarters, 24th Division	02/08/1918	02/08/1918
War Diary	Verdrel	01/07/1918	13/07/1918
War Diary	Gouy Servins	14/07/1918	31/07/1918
Operation(al) Order(s)	24th Divisional Train Order No. 30	23/07/1918	23/07/1918
Miscellaneous	Amendment to 24th Divisional Train Order No. 29	23/07/1918	23/07/1918
Operation(al) Order(s)	24th Divisional Train Order No. 31	27/07/1918	27/07/1918
Heading	War Diary Of 24th Divisional Train. From 1st August 1918 To 30th August 1918		
War Diary	Gouy Servins	01/08/1918	30/09/1918
War Diary	Etree Wamin	30/09/1918	30/09/1918
Miscellaneous	24th Division		
Operation(al) Order(s)	24th Divisional Train Order No. 32	26/09/1918	26/09/1918
Operation(al) Order(s)	24th Divisional Train Order No. 33	28/09/1918	28/09/1918
Operation(al) Order(s)	24th Divisional Train Order No. 34	28/09/1918	28/09/1918
Miscellaneous	Supply Group Table No. 9		
Operation(al) Order(s)	24th Divisional Train Order No. 35	29/09/1918	29/09/1918
Miscellaneous	March Orders For 24th Division Transport By Lieut-col. A G. Galloway D.S.O. O.C. 24th Divl. Train	29/09/1918	29/09/1918
War Diary	Etree-Wamin Lucheux	01/10/1918	01/10/1918
War Diary	Lucheux	02/10/1918	05/10/1918
War Diary	Boisleux Au-Mont	05/10/1918	06/10/1918
War Diary	Moeuvres	07/10/1918	09/10/1918
War Diary	Fontaine	10/10/1918	10/10/1918
War Diary	Awoingt	10/10/1918	26/10/1918
War Diary	Avesnes	26/10/1918	27/10/1918
War Diary	St. Aubert	27/10/1918	31/10/1918
Operation(al) Order(s)	24th Divisional Train Order 36.	04/10/1918	04/10/1918
Operation(al) Order(s)	24th Divisional Train Order No. 37	04/10/1918	04/10/1918
Miscellaneous	Table to Accompany 24th Divn. Order No. 250		
Miscellaneous	March Orders For 24th Division Transport By Lieut. Col. A.C. Calloway, D.S.O., S.T.O. 25th Division		
Operation(al) Order(s)	24th Divisional Train Order No. 38	25/10/1918	25/10/1918
War Diary	St. Aubert	01/11/1918	03/11/1918
War Diary	Bermerain	03/11/1918	04/11/1918
War Diary	Sepmeries	04/11/1918	05/11/1918
War Diary	Wargnies Le-Grand	05/11/1918	09/11/1918
War Diary	Bavay	09/11/1918	10/11/1918
War Diary	Bavay H. 24. c. 8.5.	11/11/1918	11/11/1918
War Diary	Bavay H. 24.c.	12/11/1918	17/11/1918

War Diary	Bavay Masny	18/11/1918	18/11/1918
War Diary	Masny	19/11/1918	25/11/1918
War Diary	Sameon	26/11/1918	30/11/1918
Operation(al) Order(s)	24th Divisional Train Order No. 39		
Operation(al) Order(s)	24th Divisional Train Order No. 40	01/11/1918	01/11/1918
Miscellaneous	Supply Group Table No. 10	12/11/1918	12/11/1918
Operation(al) Order(s)	24th Divisional Train Order No. 41	24/11/1918	24/11/1918
War Diary	Sameon	01/12/1918	04/12/1918
War Diary	Tournai	05/12/1918	31/12/1918
Miscellaneous	Appendix "A"-War Diary		
Operation(al) Order(s)	24th Divisional Train Order No. 42	16/12/1918	16/12/1918
Miscellaneous	Supply Group Table No. 11		
Miscellaneous	Supply Group Table No. 12		
Miscellaneous	Supply Group Table No. 13		
Operation(al) Order(s)	24th Divisional Train Order No. 43	20/12/1918	20/12/1918
Operation(al) Order(s)	24th Divisional Train Order No. 44	23/12/1918	23/12/1918
War Diary	Tournai	01/01/1919	31/01/1919
Miscellaneous	Appendix A		
Operation(al) Order(s)	24th Divisional Train Order No. 45 "B"	30/01/1919	30/01/1919
Miscellaneous	Pro-forma "A"		
War Diary	Tournai	01/02/1919	28/02/1919
Miscellaneous	Nominal Roll Of R.A.S.C. Personnel Sent To Concentration Camp For Dispersal Appendix "A"		
Miscellaneous	Supply Group Table No. 14	03/02/1919	03/02/1919
War Diary	Tournai	01/03/1919	31/03/1919
Miscellaneous	Nominal Roll of R.A.S.C. Personnel Who have proceeded to 1 Corps Concent. Camp for Dispersal on dates shewn.		
Miscellaneous	Nominal Roll of R.A.S.C. Personnel who have proceeded to I Corps Concent. Camp for Dispersal on dates shown.		
Miscellaneous	Nominal Roll Of Other Ranks Sent For Dispersal On 25-3-1919		
Miscellaneous	Nominal Roll of R.A.S.C. Personnel who have proceeded to 1 Corps Concent. Camp for Disposal on date shewn		
Miscellaneous	Headquarters 24th Div. Bde. Group	02/05/1919	02/05/1919
War Diary	Tournai	01/04/1919	30/04/1919
Miscellaneous	Nominal Roll Of Other Ranks Transferred From 24th Divisional Train To B.S.D. Calais On 2-4-1919		
Miscellaneous	Nominal Roll Of Personnel Proceeding From 24th Divl Train To 1st Army H.T. Reception Park Valenciennes On 30-4-1919		
War Diary	Tournai	01/05/1919	31/05/1919
Miscellaneous	Nominal Roll Of Personnel Who Proceeded For Dispersal On 8th May 1919	09/05/1919	09/05/1919
Miscellaneous	Nominal Roll Of Personnel Who Proceeded For Dispersal On 20-5-1919		
Miscellaneous	Nominal Roll Of Personnel Who Proceeded For Dispersal On 24-5-1919		
War Diary	Tournai	01/06/1919	25/06/1919

WO95/22034

24TH DIVISION
DIVL TROOPS

24TH DIVL TRAIN A.S.C.

~~SEP~~ AUG 1915 - JUN 1919

(194 - 197 Coys ASC)

24th Divl: Train
Vol I

FROM 29th AUGUST

Sep / 15

1
June '19

Instructions regarding War Diaries and Intelligence Summaries are contained in F. S. Regs., Part II. and the Staff Manual respectively. Title pages will be prepared in manuscript.

WAR DIARY
or
INTELLIGENCE SUMMARY.
(Erase heading not required.)

Army Form C. 2118.

R/445

1945

Place	Date	Hour	Summary of Events and Information	Remarks and references to Appendices
BROOKWOOD.	29/8/15	11. A.M.	Entrained for SOUTHAMPTON, inc Officers, 118 N.C.O's & men, arrived 3-30 p.m. - Embarked on board S.S. left 5.p.m.	Rain -
HAVRE.	30/8/15	11. A.M.	Arrived & disembarked - Marched to Rest Camp No 5 about 3-15 p.m. - arrived 4-15 p.m. - Interpreter reported -	Fine -
REST CAMP No 5	31/8/15	6. A.M.	Left for SHED No III HAVRE to Entrain, left 10-39 A.M, arrived HESDIN 1. A.M. 1/9/15.	Fine -
HESDIN.	1/9/15	1.30 AM.	Detrained - Left 2-30 AM by Route March for BEAURAINVILLE arriving 6. A.M. Encamped on LE MARAIS, found Billets for Officers & men, appointed "ALARM. POST".	Fine -
BEAURAINVILLE	2/9/15	9. A.M.	Supply wagons refilled, also at 5p.m -	Heavy Rain
"	3/9/15	"	Supply wagons refilled - Teams & men of Baggage Wagons of 106th & 109th Brig: R.F.A. came in -	"
"	4/9/15	"	Supply wagons refilled - Visited detachments at ATTIN, SEMPY & LEBIEZ.	"
"	5/9/15	"	Removed Camp to adjoining field - Supply wagons refilled -	Fine -
"	6/9/15	"	Supply wagons refilled - Sent spare pair, 1 Serg: 1 Corp: 1 Farrier, 1 Wheeler to O/C 195. Comp: A.S.C.	Fine -
"	7/9/15	8-30.	Supply wagons refilled -	V. Fine -
"	8/9/15	"	Supply wagons refilled. Sent teams to 109th Brig: R.F.A.	V. Fine -
"	9/9/15	"	Supply wagons refilled - Sent Serg: Corp: Farrier, Wheeler, Saddler, Cook with Lt Plumptree with Baggage & Supply wagons of 107th & 109th Brig: R.F.A. on march to 1st DIVISION -	V. Fine -
"	10/9/15	"	Supply wagons refilled - Sent Serg: & two spare pairs with Baggage & Supply Sections of 106th & 108th Brig: R.F.A.	V. Fine
"	11/9/15	"	Supply wagons refilled -	

Army Form C. 2118.

Instructions regarding War Diaries and Intelligence Summaries are contained in F. S. Regs., Part II. and the Staff Manual respectively. Title pages will be prepared in manuscript.

WAR DIARY
or
INTELLIGENCE SUMMARY.
(Erase heading not required.)

Place	Date	Hour	Summary of Events and Information	Remarks and references to Appendices
BEAURAINVILLE	12/9/15	A.M. 8-30	Supply wagons refilled – Sent two wagons & teams for supply of details of 107th & 108th Brig: R.F.A. to 195. Comp:	V. Fine –
"	13/9/15	"	Supply wagons refilled – One Section of D.A.C. moved off to 1st DIVISION –	V. Fine –
"	14/9/15	"	Supply wagons refilled –	Rain morning fine afternoon
"	15/9/15	"	Supply wagons refilled – Baggage wagons of units in "A" GROUP ordered to rejoin units at once, order received 7-15. p.m.	Wet night – Fine day –
"	16/9/15	"	Supply wagons refilled – 1 wagon & pair & six horses & five men & Sergt: arrived from No 195. Comp: ASC	Damp & drizzle
"	17/9/15	8-30 AM 7 P.M.	Supply wagons refilled – Ordered at 7 P.M to clear Camp & concentrate on LOISON – BEAURAINVILLE road –	Dull & warm
"	"	8 P.M.	Supply wagons refilled at 8 P.M & then parked with BAGGAGE WAGONS till 6.A.M 18/9/15, when the	
"	18/9/15	6.A.M. 11.A.M.	whole returned to CAMP – SUPPLY WAGONS delivered SUPPLIES to UNITS at 11.AM.	V. Fine –
"	19/9/15	8-30	Supply wagons refilled – Visited detachments at ATTIN –	V. Fine –
"	20/9/15	8-30	Supply wagons refilled –	V. Fine –
"	21/9/15	8-30	Supply wagons refilled – Received orders to move & concentrate at 10 AM, Concentration with 197. Comp: at 5 p.m. at LEBIEZ, remained there till 10 P.M, marched to PREHEDRE – FRUGES road, arriving at 1.A.M where	" "
HEZEQUES	22/9/15	2.AM	Supply wagons refilled, marched off at 2-30 AM for HEZEQUES via FRUGES & LUGY arriving 5. AM	V. Fine –
"			at 1.P.M received orders to march to refill on BEAUMETZ LES AIRE – LAIRES road at 4 P.M on arrival ordered to march to AUCHY LES BOIS & bivouack, arrived 9.P.M.	" "
AUCHY LES BOIS	23/9/15	6.A.M	Supply wagons refilled at 6.AM, 100x along AUCHY LES BOIS – St HILAIRE road, after refilling marched off at 8-30 AM for BUSNES arriving at 1-30 p.m – Supply wagons refilled at 4 p.m on BUSNES – LILLERS road –	V. Fine – Rain in the Evening –

2353 Wt. W2544/1454 700,000 5/15 D. D. & L. A.D.S.S./Forms/C. 2118.

Instructions regarding War Diaries and Intelligence Summaries are contained in F. S. Regs., Part II. and the Staff Manual respectively. Title pages will be prepared in manuscript.

WAR DIARY
or
INTELLIGENCE SUMMARY.
(Erase heading not required.)

Army Form C. 2118.

Place	Date	Hour	Summary of Events and Information	Remarks and references to Appendices
				Dull & showery
BUSNES.	24/9/15	2 p.m.	Supply wagons refilled at 2 p.m. on BUSNES – LILLERS road – Received orders to leave BUSNES	
	"		for ANNEZIN at 12 MIDNIGHT, arrived at 5-30 AM.	
ANNEZIN.	25/9/15	5 p.m.	Received orders to move with all SUPPLY WAGONS for SAILLY LABOURSE & deliver supplies to Cookers,	Rain –
	"		unable to find cookers of 73rd Brigade till about 12-30 A.M 26/9/15, 71st Brigade left no cookers & went into	
	"		firing line, so could not be supplied, 72nd Brigade supplied about 7. p. m –	
BETHUNE	26/9/15	9. A.M.	Supply wagons refilled & then marched at 11. AM for SAILLY LA BOURSE arriving at 2-30 p.m, delivered	Fine –
	"		supplies to GLASGOW YEOMANRY.	
SAILLY LA BOURSE	27/9/15	4 p.m.	Supply wagons refilled on NOEUX LES MINES – BETHUNE road, received orders at 4 p.m to move to camp: just South	Fine –
	"		of Railway on same road – Arrived 6-30 p.m – Supply wagons of 106th, 107th, 108th, 109th Brig: R.F.A & DAC rejoined –	Rain at Evening
BETHUNE	28/9/15	[illegible]	Supply wagons delivered supplies to units & refilled at 12 midday & started to deliver supplies to units at 3-30 p.m.	Fine, cold & dull
	"		Division less DIV: ART, D.A.C & PIONEER BATT: moved off to BERGUETTE – GUARBECQUES area, leaving	Heavy rain
	"		194. Comp: A.S.C behind to supply DIV: R.F.A, D.A.C & PIONEER BATT.	
"	29/9/15	2. p.m	Supply wagons refilled at 2 P.M. half way down BETHUNE – NOEUX-LES MINES road –	Heavy rain
"	30/9/15	"	Supply wagons refilled – Received orders to march at daybreak 1/10/15 for ST HILAIRE, leaving behind supply wagons for	Fine, cold.
	"		12th SHERWOODS (2) & 108th R.F.A. (8).	

2353 Wt. W2544/1454 700,000 5/15 D. D. & L. A.D.S.S./Forms/C. 2118.

CONFIDENTIAL.

War Diary

of

O.C. 24th Divisional Train, B. E. F.

From 29th Aug. 1915 To 30th Sept. 1915

II

having waited for two hours with great difficulty as the traffic both ways was continuous, I decided to return to BETHUNE & see what information I could get there, but was not allowed to return by main road, so had to take a road to the NORTH & come into BETHUNE by the CANAL arrived at MARCHE AUX CHEVAUX in BETHUNE at 9-30 p.m, with my Supply wagons & those of 73rd INF: BRIG. where I met the DAQMG who sent the Supply wagons of 73rd INF: BRIG: with instructions where to find them – Parked my wagons – Ordered to refill at 9 A.M 26th –

September 26th

Supply wagons refilled 9 A.M, had orders to wait instructions as to where to go & when – Received orders at 11 A.M to march to SAILLY LA BOURSE arrived there 2-30 pm & camped in field just outside – Sent Supply wagons to Units –

R Blakeway Major
O/C 194 Company A.S.C.

27

Sep: 25th 1915. I

arrived ANNEZIN 5-30 AM – Sent by Lt Col: HORSBRUGH to D.H.Q for orders – Saw D.A.A & Q.M.G who ordered me to Camp on field behind the REFILLING POINT of 1st DIVISION – Sent my Supply Wagons to deliver their Supplies to Units about 10-30 A.M. At 5 p.m. D.A.Q.M.G ordered me to take all Supply Wagons in Camp to SAILLY LA BOURSE & hand their Supplies over to the Cookers of 71st, 72nd & 73rd Brigades which I should find on the road & await instructions on ROAD BEUVRY – SAILLY LA BOURSE – About 6-30 p.m found the Cookers of 72nd INF: BRIG, so they & the Supply wagons marched on to SAILLY LA BOURSE – The Supply wagons of 71st INF: BRIG: marched off to find their Units having received some information as to their whereabouts – No information could be gathered about 73rd INF: BRIG: whereabouts, so having tried to get to SAILLY LA BOURSE & being stopped by Military Police at BEUVRY & told that I would not be allowed to halt outside SAILLY LA BOURSE & 97

Instructions regarding War Diaries and Intelligence Summaries are contained in F. S. Regs., Part II. and the Staff Manual respectively. Title pages will be prepared in manuscript.

WAR DIARY

or

~~INTELLIGENCE SUMMARY.~~

(Erase heading not required.)

Army Form C. 2118.

Place	Date	Hour	Summary of Events and Information	Remarks and references to Appendices
WEST HEATH, WOKING	29/8/15		Weather - cloudy and showery, fair at intervals. About 10.30 a.m. 194 Coy and HQ. Qrs. Div. Train proceeded by road to BROOKWOOD STATION. Strength - 10 officers 118 men and 10 vehicles. Entrained by 12.35 p.m. Arrived SOUTHAMPTON 3.15 p.m. On reporting to R.T.O I was ordered to take 2 officers and 37 men, all horses and vehicles on board 'COURTFIELD'. The adjutant with remainder sent on board 'EMPRESS QUEEN'. Sailed 6.45 p.m. Arrived HAVRE 2.30 a.m.	AMcC
HAVRE	30/8/15.		Disembarked both vessels. Joined up with No. 195 Coy who had arrived previous evening. 195 Coy set out for concentration area.	AMcC
do.	31/8/15.		Hd Qrs and No. 194 Coy leave for concentration area. No. 196 Coy arrived at 6 a.m and leave for concentration area at 10 p.m.	AMcC
do.	1/9/15.		No. 197 Coy. arrive and go to No. 5 Rest Camp. Leave at 10 p.m. for concentration area.	AMcC
do	2/9/15.		Left HAVRE for BEAURAINVILLE. Arrived 5.30 p.m. Train Hd. Qrs. at BEAURAINVILLE.	AMcC

2353 Wt. W2544/1454 700,000 5/15 D. D. & L. A.D.S.S./Forms/C. 2118.

Army Form C. 2118.

Instructions regarding War Diaries and Intelligence Summaries are contained in F. S. Regs., Part II. and the Staff Manual respectively. Title pages will be prepared in manuscript.

WAR DIARY

or

~~INTELLIGENCE SUMMARY.~~

(Erase heading not required.)

Place	Date	Hour	Summary of Events and Information	Remarks and references to Appendices
BEAURAIN VILLE	3/9/15		Went round refilling points with S.S.O. Ground in very wet condition. Train Hd. Qrs and 194 Coy - BEAURAINVILLE 195 Coy - NEUVILLE 196 Coy - SEMPY 197 Coy - LEBIEZ.	AWC
do.	4/9/15.		Refilling points changed. Arranged distribution of Train Transport with R.F.A. who were causing a great deal of trouble by using baggage wagons for other purposes.	AWC
do	5/9/15.		Visited Field Ambulances. Field Ambulance Workshops arrive under Lieut. GARNETT.	AWC
do.	6/9/15.		Corps Commander pays a visit at noon.	AWC
do.	7/9/15.		Most of baggage wagon horses returned to companies — Horses show evident signs of overwork, many being galled about the neck, chiefly those supplied to R.F.A. units	AWC

2353 Wt. W2544/1454 700,000 5/15 D. D. & L. A.D.S.S./Forms/C. 2118.

Instructions regarding War Diaries and Intelligence Summaries are contained in F. S. Regs., Part II. and the Staff Manual respectively. Title pages will be prepared in manuscript.

WAR DIARY

~~INTELLIGENCE SUMMARY~~.

(Erase heading not required.)

Army Form C. 2118.

Place	Date	Hour	Summary of Events and Information	Remarks and references to Appendices
BEAURAIN: VILLE.	8/9/15.		Camp in very bad condition owing to state of ground. Found more suitable field and camp moved. Orders received from D. H. Q. that 107th and 109th Bdes. R. F. A would move outside Divl. Area following day. Coys concerned notified and ordered to send baggage sections direct to units 7 a.m. next day. Following officers were detailed to take charge of baggage and supply sections - 2Lt. PLUMPTRE and 2Lt. BUTSON. Three pairs horses H. D. returned from Divl Cav. in very bad condition	AWC
BEAURAIN :VILLE	9/9/15.		Convoy for 107th + 109th Bdes R. F. A formed up on LOISON - LEBIEZ road at 11 a.m. On being inspected by DAQ + Q. M. G. considerable amounts of unauthorised stores found on both baggage & supply wagons. Wagons also overloaded - average weight 2 tons. Such things as motor - bicycles, corn crusher & chaff - cutter &c offloaded by orders of DAQ. M. G. About 7 p.m. orders received that 106th & 108th Bdes R. F. A would move the following day at 8 a.m. Orders similar to last night were issued to all concerned.	AWC.

Army Form C. 2118.

Instructions regarding War Diaries and Intelligence Summaries are contained in F. S. Regs., Part II. and the Staff Manual respectively. Title pages will be prepared in manuscript.

WAR DIARY

or

~~INTELLIGENCE SUMMARY.~~

(Erase heading not required.)

Place	Date	Hour	Summary of Events and Information	Remarks and references to Appendices
BEAURAIN VILLE	10/9/15		2/Lt. ROBERTSON and 2/Lt. McCALLUM placed in charge of 106th and 108 Bde R.F.A baggage and supply sections respectively. Needless delay owing to bad march discipline of R.F.A. Visited D.H.Q. and then proceeded to FRUGES passing the train transport on the return journey – Everything alright.	AMcC.
do	11/9/15		Went to SEMPY – No 196 Coy – found more suitable camp. Thence to ATTIN – No 195 Coy – all well.	AMcC
do	12/9/15		Dr. NORBURY charged with stealing money the property of a comrade is remanded for trial by F.G.C.M. Orders from D.H.Q. received at noon that the baggage section of the D.A.C. would parade at 6 a.m to-morrow.	AMcC
do	13/9/15		Court of Enquiry held at 11.30 a.m on the loss of 500 frcs. by 2/Lt. EDWARDS and Lieut HARROWER. As the court found that these two officers were responsible for the loss I issued instructions that they were to make good the loss. Visited 195 Coy.	AMcC

Instructions regarding War Diaries and Intelligence Summaries are contained in F. S. Regs., Part II. and the Staff Manual respectively. Title pages will be prepared in manuscript.

WAR DIARY

~~or~~

~~INTELLIGENCE SUMMARY.~~

(*Erase heading not required.*)

Army Form C. 2118.

Place	Date	Hour	Summary of Events and Information	Remarks and references to Appendices
BEAURAINVILLE	14/9/15		Court Martial of Dr. NORBURY arranged.	AMcC
do	15/9/15		Visited outlying companies and found everything working satisfactorily	AMcC
do	16/9/15		Inspected billets of all companies after visiting refilling points - all satisfactory. Called at D. H. Q.	AMcC
do	17/9/15		Received orders to instruct all interpreters to call at D.H.Q - Liaison Officer. Issued orders to this effect.	AMcC
do	18/9/15		Visited A. H. Q and arranged to take Court Martial to H.Q. 'A' Group.	AMcC
do	19/9/15.		F.G.C.M. arranged for Tues. 21st at 10 a.m. at Train Headquarters. Visited refilling points. Visited 196 Coy at SEMPY. D.A.Q.M.G. informed us that the division was about to move towards the battle front - Railhead to be changed on Tuesday	AMcC

Army Form C. 2118.

Instructions regarding War Diaries and Intelligence Summaries are contained in F. S. Regs., Part II. and the Staff Manual respectively. Title pages will be prepared in manuscript.

WAR DIARY
or
~~INTELLIGENCE SUMMARY.~~
(Erase heading not required.)

Place	Date	Hour	Summary of Events and Information	Remarks and references to Appendices
BEAURAIN: VILLE	20/9/15.		Received 'Operation Orders' (re Division leaving present area) at 6 p.m. Issued same to companies.	AWC.
do	21/9/15		Lieut BAGSHAW reported for duty and attached to 194 Coy. Trial of Dr NORBURY by F.G.C.M. at 10 a.m. Left BEAURAINVILLE at 2 p.m for FRUGES. Refilled on FRUGES - LAIRES road at midnight afterwards proceeding to LAIRES	AWC.
LAIRES	22/9/15		Arrived LAIRES 2 a.m. Guides for supply wagons were not sent at 10.30 a.m as ordered so wagons proceeded without guides and delivered supplies at 11 a.m. Left LAIRES 2 p.m. for AUCHY-AU-BOIS via BEAUMETZ-LES-AIRE. Arrived latter 5 p.m. Received orders to refill on LAIRES-BEAUMETZ. Order countermanded at 4 p.m hence no refilling to-day. No. 194 and No. 197 Coys. AUCHY-AU-BOIS at 8 p.m. Parked clear of road where refilling was to take place next morning. No. 195 and No. 196 Coys arrive late at night having been delayed by troops on the march.	AWC.

2353 Wt. W2544/1454 700,000 5/15 D. D. & L. A.D.S.S./Forms/C. 2118.

Instructions regarding War Diaries and Intelligence Summaries are contained in F. S. Regs., Part II. and the Staff Manual respectively. Title pages will be prepared in manuscript.

WAR DIARY

~~INTELLIGENCE SUMMARY.~~

(Erase heading not required.)

Army Form C. 2118.

Place	Date	Hour	Summary of Events and Information	Remarks and references to Appendices
AUCHY-AU-BOIS.	23/9/15		Refilled at 6 a.m on the AUCHY-AU-BOIS – LILLERS road at cross-roads E of AUCHY. Delivered to units and proceeded to BUSNES. Companies arrived in the course of the afternoon & parked for the night.	AMcC.
BUSNES.	24/9/15		Refilled on BUSNES - LILLERS road at 10 a.m. Train concentrated at BUSNES cross roads at 10 p.m and marched via ROBECQ and VENDIN to ANNEZIN.	AMcC.
ANNEZIN	25/9/15		Arrived 3 am. Lieut & adjt. A. St G. ADAMS sent to hospital.	
	26/9/15.		In view of the importance of the operations on these days, I attach a diary of each of the company commanders under my command	AMcC

2353 Wt. W2544/1454 700,000 5/15 D. D. & L. A.D.S.S./Forms/C. 2118.

Instructions regarding War Diaries and Intelligence Summaries are contained in F. S. Regs., Part II. and the Staff Manual respectively. Title pages will be prepared in manuscript.

WAR DIARY
or
INTELLIGENCE SUMMARY.
(*Erase heading not required.*)

Army Form C. 2118.

Place	Date	Hour	Summary of Events and Information	Remarks and references to Appendices
	~~25~~/9/15. 26/9/15	12. M'night.	Marched from BUSNES. to ANNEZIN under O. C. Train. Supply wagons full of Supplies for consumption on the 26/9/15.	
		10.a.m.	Arrived at ANNEZIN	
		4 p.m.	Received orders from O.C. Train to take Supply Section to Brigade Rendezvous at ~~BEAUVERIE~~ BEUVRY. On arriving at Brigade Rendezvous I found that the first line transport were unable to take supplies as all their vehicles were already over loaded. I returned to Train Headquarters, and reported this to O.C. Train who ordered me to send Supplies right on with 1st Line Transport. The Supply Section marched in rear of 1st Line to VERMELLES, and there supplies were off loaded and handed over to Quarter Masters.	
		Midnight.	Supply Section returned Empty to ANNEZIN	
	27/9/15.	8.a.m.	Refilled at BÉTHUNE (Horse Market), marched to SAILLY-LA-BOURSE.	

2353 Wt. W2544/1454 700,000 5/15 D. D. & L. A.D.S.S./Forms/C. 2118.

I

Instructions regarding War Diaries and Intelligence Summaries are contained in F. S. Regs., Part II. and the Staff Manual respectively. Title pages will be prepared in manuscript.

WAR DIARY
or
~~INTELLIGENCE SUMMARY.~~

(*Erase heading not required.*)

196 Coy.
24th Divl Train A.S.C.

Army Form C. 2118.

Place	Date	Hour	Summary of Events and Information	Remarks and references to Appendices
ANNEZIN	25/9/15	6 AM.	Arrived from BERGUETTE with Supply section loaded with Supplies for 26/9/15. Parked wagons. No orders were available for disposal of Supplies so at 3 PM I went to Divl HQ to get instructions, & remained there till 5 PM. No information was to be had. On returning to camp at 5.30 PM I found that Lieut Hitch had at 4.30 PM received verbal instructions to take Supplies to BEUVRY & meet 1st line Transport there, & had started with Supply Section at 4.45 PM. I followed in R.O's car & caught up	
BEUVRY		6.30 PM	Convoy just beyond ~~Beuvry~~ BEUVRY. The only Unit which could be found was the 72nd Field Ambulance, & Supply wagon was detached & offloaded accordingly. No news of the other units was to be had. The Brigade Group consisted of 72nd Inf Bde HQ. 8th BUFFS. 8th R.W. KENTS. 9th East SURREYS 8th QUEENS 104th Field Coy. R.E. 72nd Field Ambulance.	
[S]AILLY LA BOURSE			I went on to SAILLY LABOURSE where I met the D.A.Q.M.G. returning. He instructed me to take Supplies to VERMELLES where guides from units had been ordered	
		9 PM.	to meet us. Returning to the Convoy we passed through SAILLY LABOURSE at 9 PM, taking the road running East past FOSSE 9. & leaving ANNEQUIN on the left.	

2353 Wt. W2544/1454 700,000 5/15 D. D. & L. A.D.S.S./Forms/C. 2118.

II

Instructions regarding War Diaries and Intelligence Summaries are contained in F. S. Regs., Part II. and the Staff Manual respectively. Title pages will be prepared in manuscript.

WAR DIARY
or
INTELLIGENCE SUMMARY.
(Erase heading not required.)

196 Coy.
24th Divl Train ASC.

Army Form C. 2118.

Place	Date	Hour	Summary of Events and Information	Remarks and references to Appendices
VERMELLES	25/9/15	11.30 PM	Considerable delays were experienced from various causes & at 11.30 PM we reached VERMELLES. No guides were to be found, but in answer to enquiries I found that the 72nd Brigade had gone in the direction of LE RUTOIRE, & proceeded there, finding the 104th Field Coy. R.E. on the right 100 yards short of the T cross roads, & the cookers of all the other units formed up on the road to the left	
LE RUTOIRE	26/9/15	12.45 AM	200 yards S.W of LE RUTOIRE farm. We arrived there at 12.45 AM & proceeded to offload. There was considerable congestion, but by 2.45 we had formed	
		2.45 AM	up; & returned to ANNEZIN by VERMELLES & NOYELLES LES VERMELLES, getting	
ANNEZIN		5 AM.	back to camp at 5 AM.	
BETHUNE		8 AM.	at 8 AM the Supply Section refilled at the MARCHE AUX CHEVAUX, BETHUNE, with supplies for the 27/9/15, & returned to camp.	
		2.30 PM	At 2.30 PM the Coy. was ordered to proceed to SAILLY LA BOURSE where we	
SAILLY LA BOURSE		5 PM	arrived 5 PM & parked.	
		6.30 PM	At 6.30 PM I received orders to take supplies to VERMELLES. The road was very congested & progress was at the rate of 1 mile per hour. On arriving at the	
		10 PM.	cross roads 1 Kilometre S.W of VERMELLES I was ordered by the C.O. to return to	
	27/9/15	12.30 AM	Camp as Brigade was coming out of the trenches. Arrived in Camp 12.30 AM & went into bivouac for the night.	

H C Pearson Capt.
O.C. 196 Coy
24th Divl Train
ASC.

2353 Wt. W2514/1454 700,000 5/15 D. D. & L. A.D.S.S./Forms/C. 2118.

Instructions regarding War Diaries and Intelligence Summaries are contained in F. S. Regs., Part II. and the Staff Manual respectively. Title pages will be prepared in manuscript.

WAR DIARY

or

~~INTELLIGENCE SUMMARY.~~

(Erase heading not required.)

Army Form C. 2118.

Place	Date	Hour	Summary of Events and Information	Remarks and references to Appendices
SAILLY LABOURSE	27/9/15		Found that Supply Section of 108th Bde R.F.A. had rejoined previous night. Received orders to proceed to BETHUNE. Proceeded at 4.30 p.m. Refilled on NOEUX-LES-MINES — BETHUNE road. Parked with supply wagons full just S. of BETHUNE.	AMOC
BETHUNE	28/9/15		At 5 a.m. Supply wagons left camp to deliver supplies. Refilled at same point as yesterday and delivered supplies to units. Left BETHUNE 9 p.m. for ANNEZIN. Arrived 11 p.m. No. 194 Coy remained at BETHUNE and are attached to GUARDS Divisions for purpose of feeding R.F.A units.	AMOC
ANNEZIN	29/9/15		Proceeded via LILLERS to ST. HILAIRE - COTTES at 12 noon. Arrived at 5 p.m. Supplies delivered to units by Supply column under direction of S.Os.	AMOC
ST. HILAIRE	30/9/15.		Refilled on ST HILAIRE - LILLERS road about 1 mile E. of former place at 8 a.m. Delivered supplies during day.	AMOC.

Instructions regarding War Diaries and Intelligence Summaries are contained in F. S. Regs., Part II. and the Staff Manual respectively. Title pages will be prepared in manuscript.

Army Form C. 2118.

WAR DIARY

~~INTELLIGENCE~~ SUMMARY. Copy of report of O.C. No 197 Coy A.S.C. (73rd Inf. Bde. Coy)

(Erase heading not required.)

Place	Date	Hour	Summary of Events and Information	Remarks and references to Appendices
ANNEZIN	25/9/15	7.30 am	Arrived ANNEZIN with supply wagons loaded	
		4.50 pm	Received orders to deliver supplies to Cooks' Carts at BEUVRY and return to HORSE MARKET, BETHUNE to refill same night and deliver again immediately at BEUVRY. Accordingly Lieut Ogle left ANNEZIN at 5 pm, proceeded to BEUVRY, & delivered to Cooks Carts of 7th NORTHANTS & 13th MIDDLESEX Regiments, no other Cooks' Carts being there, although the neighbourhood was searched. The other supplies were therefore dumped & a guard left in charge, & wagons returned to BETHUNE to refill. On arrival at about 8.45 pm it was found that refilling would not take place until the morning. Lieut Ogle was ordered by D.A.Q.M.G. to return to where he had dumped supplies, re-load & follow up the units concerned wherever they had gone to. This he proceeded to do & found the units Cooks Carts at 2.30 AM on 26th inst. in neighbourhood of LE RUTOIRE FARM where supplies were delivered.	
LE RUTOIRE FARM	26/9/15		After delivering supplies, left for BETHUNE. Arrived 6 AM. Refilled at 8 AM & proceeded to SAILLY-LABOURSE where convoy joined up with remainder of Train. At 8 P.M. Lieut Ogle again left, (with supply wagons loaded) under orders to proceed to X roads at VERMELLES. There he was met by O.C. Train who ordered him to return to SAILLY-LABOURSE, O.C. Train having just received orders that the Division was returning from the trenches. Convoy arrived back at SAILLY-LABOURSE about 11.30 pm — wagons still loaded.	

2353 Wt. W2544/1454 700,000 5/15 D. D. & L. A.D.S.S./Forms/C. 2118.

Army Form C. 2118.

Instructions regarding War Diaries and Intelligence Summaries are contained in F. S. Regs., Part II. and the Staff Manual respectively. Title pages will be prepared in manuscript.

WAR DIARY
or
INTELLIGENCE SUMMARY.
(Erase heading not required.)

Place	Date	Hour	Summary of Events and Information	Remarks and references to Appendices
	27/9/15	8 a.m.	and parked here until 9 p.m., when received orders to take Supplies to VERMELLES.	
		9 p.m.	arrived VERMELLES, off loaded Supplies and received orders from D.A.Q.M.G. in person to load Supplies again and collect all 1st Line Transport and march to SAILLY-LA-BOURSE.	S.A. Plunket Capt. 10/9 Sth. ASC

2353 Wt. W2544/1454 700,000 5/15 D. D. & L. A.D.S.S./Forms/C. 2118.

Army Form C. 2118.

Instructions regarding War Diaries and Intelligence Summaries are contained in F. S. Regs., Part II. and the Staff Manual respectively. Title pages will be prepared in manuscript.

WAR DIARY
or
~~INTELLIGENCE~~ SUMMARY.

(Erase heading not required.)

Place	Date	Hour	Summary of Events and Information	Remarks and references to Appendices
SAILLY-LA BOURSE	27/9/15	6 am	Supply wagons left under Lieut. Ogle & delivered supplies to three Brigade units near SAILLY-LABOURSE & one unit (12th R' FUSILIERS) at VERMELLES.	
			Signed I. P. Thompson. Captain O.C. No 197 Coy A.S.C.	

2353 Wt. W2544/1454 700,000 5/15 D. D. & L. A.D.S.S./Forms/C. 2118.

24th Division

121/7608

24th Divl: Train

Vol 2

Oct 15

24th Division

121
7431

194th Coy: A.S.C.
Vol 2

Oct 15
|
Jly '19

Instructions regarding War Diaries and Intelligence Summaries are contained in F. S. Regs., Part II. and the Staff Manual respectively. Title pages will be prepared in manuscript.

WAR DIARY
or
INTELLIGENCE SUMMARY.
(Erase heading not required.)

Army Form C. 2118.

1.

Place	Date	Hour	Summary of Events and Information	Remarks and references to Appendices
BETHUNE	1/10/15	5 AM	Marched for St. HILAIRE via LILLERS, Supply wagons refilled on St. HILAIRE – LILLERS road at 4 p.m –	Fine –
St. HILAIRE	2/10/15	12 midday	Marched for WALLON CAPPEL arriving 4-30 p.m., Supply wagons unloaded to Units & returned to Camp –	Fine –
WALLON CAPPEL	3/10/15	4. A.M.	Marched for HERZEELE arriving 5 p.m Supply wagons refilled on HERZEELE – HOUTKERQUE Road at 4 p.m & returned to Camp –	Fine –
HERZEELE	4/10/15	5 A.M	Supply wagons started to deliver Supplies to Units, returned to REFILLING POINT & refilled at 11 AM & delivered Supplies to Units –	Rain in morning Fine, afternoon
"	5/10/15	8 AM	Supply wagons refilled – Received orders to march for BOESCHEPE tomorrow –	Fine –
"	6/10/15	"	Supply wagons refilled – 11-30 A.M marched with Baggage Section for BOESCHEPE via STEENVOORDE arriving 4 p.m. Left wagons for 106, 107, 108, 109 BRIG: RFA & D.A.C with No. 4 COMPANY.	Fine. Dull –
BOESCHEPE	7/10/15	"	Supply wagons refilled, on BOESCHEPE – POPERINGHE Road –	Dull –
"	8/10/15	"	Supply wagons refilled, on BOESCHEPE – POPERINGHE Road –	Dull –
"	9/10/15	"	Supply wagons refilled, on BOESCHEPE – POPERINGHE Road –	Fine –
"	10/10/15	"	Supply wagons refilled, on BOESCHEPE – POPERINGHE Road – Received orders to move to GODEWAERSVELDE	
"	11/10/15	"	Supply wagons refilled, on BOESCHEPE – POPERINGHE Road – at 1-15 p.m & take over Camp from 17th DIVISIONAL TRAIN.	Fine –
GODEWAERSVELDE	12/10/15	"	Supply wagons refilled – 106-107-108-109th BRIG R.F.A. rejoined after refilling also D.A.C.	Fine –
"	13/10/15	"	Supply wagons refilled –	Rained slightly Fine afternoon
"	14/10/15	"	Supply wagons refilled – ~~Mist~~	Fine, misty –
"	15/10/15	"	Supply wagons refilled – 108th BRIG: R.F.A wagons transferred to Unit –	Fine, misty –
"	16/10/15	"	Supply wagons refilled –	Fine misty –
"	17/10/15	"	Supply wagons refilled –	Fine & misty
"	18/10/15	"	Supply wagons refilled – Visited teams & horses of 108th BRIG: R.F.A.	Fine & misty –

R. Blakeway – Lieut

Instructions regarding War Diaries and Intelligence Summaries are contained in F. S. Regs., Part II. and the Staff Manual respectively. Title pages will be prepared in manuscript.

WAR DIARY
or
INTELLIGENCE SUMMARY.
(Erase heading not required.)

Army Form C. 2118.

2.

Place	Date	Hour	Summary of Events and Information	Remarks and references to Appendices
GODEWAERSVELDE	19/10/15	8 AM	Supply wagons refilled – Visited men & horses of 109th BRIG: R.F.A.	Fine –
"	20/10/15	"	" " " " " " 107th " " –	Fine –
"	21/10/15	"	" " " " " " 106th " " –	Fine –
"	22/10/15	"	" " "	Fine –
"	23/10/15	"	" " " Visited 12th SHERWOOD FORESTERS, men & horses –	Fine –
"	24/10/15	"	" " "	Rain in evening –
"	25/10/15	"	" " "	Heavy rain –
"	26/10/15	"	" " " Visited men & horses attached to 108th BRIG: R.F.A. & 107th BRIG: R.F.A.	Fine –
"	27/10/15	"	" " "	Rain –
"	28/10/15	"	" " "	Rain –
"	29/10/15	"	" " "	Fine –
"	30/10/15	"	" " "	Fine –
"	31/10/15	"	" " "	Rain –

R. Blakeway Major

2353 Wt. W2544/1454 700,000 5/15 D. D. & L. A.D.S.S./Forms/C. 2118.

194. Company - 24th Div: TRAIN -
A.S.C.

Confidential -

WAR DIARY
of
MAJOR. T.W. BLAKEWAY -

from 1/10/15 to 31/10/15.

(VOLUME II.)

CONFIDENTIAL

War Diary

of

O.C., 24th Divisional Train, B. E. F.

From - 1st Oct. 1915 to - 31st October 1915.

Instructions regarding War Diaries and Intelligence Summaries are contained in F. S. Regs., Part II. and the Staff Manual respectively. Title pages will be prepared in manuscript.

WAR DIARY
or
~~INTELLIGENCE SUMMARY.~~
(Erase heading not required.)

Army Form C. 2118.

Place	Date	Hour	Summary of Events and Information	Remarks and references to Appendices
ST. HILAIRE	1/10/15		Refilled on ST. HILAIRE - LILLERS road about 1 mile E. of former place at 8 a.m. Delivered supplies during day. Nos. 195, 196 and 197 Coys. proceeded at SERCUS. 2Lieut J. K. ROBERTSON appointed S.O. 73rd Inf. Bde vice Lieut. J. GOLDING. 2Lieut. A. McCALLUM assumes duties of adjutant vice Lieut A. St. G. ADAMS. 194 Coy arrived at 10.30 a.m.	AWE
do.	2/10/15		Hd. Qrs and 194 Coy left at 12 noon for WALLON - CAPPEL after refilling on the ST. HILAIRE - LILLERS road. Arrived 5 p.m. Supplies delivered to batteries.	AWE
WALLON CAPPEL	3/10/15		Left at 9 a.m. for HERZEELE via STEENVOORDE. Refilled at HOUTKERQUE and arrived at HERZEELE at 6 p.m. and joined up with remainder of Train.	AWE
HERZEELE	4/10/15		Refilled at 8 a.m. on HERZEELE - HOUTKERQUE road. Delivered to units, no. 194 Coy having to make two journeys as supplies could not be offloaded previous night, no guides having been sent	AWE

2353 Wt. W2544/1454 700,000 5/15 D. D. & L. A.D.S.S./Forms/C. 2118.

Army Form C. 2118.

Instructions regarding War Diaries and Intelligence Summaries are contained in F. S. Regs., Part II. and the Staff Manual respectively. Title pages will be prepared in manuscript.

WAR DIARY

or

~~INTELLIGENCE SUMMARY.~~

(*Erase heading not required.*)

Place	Date	Hour	Summary of Events and Information	Remarks and references to Appendices
HERZEELE	5/10/15		Refilled as yesterday. No 195 Coy left at 2 p.m with full supplies for 71st Inf. Bde for POPERINGHE.	AWC
HERZEELE	6/10/15		Nos 194, 196 and 197 Coys refilled at same point as previous two days. No 196 Coy left at 10 30 a.m and No 197 Coy at 1 p.m. and accompany their respective brigades to new divisional area. Hd. Qrs and No 194 Coy proceeded at 12 (noon) to BOESCHEPE via STEENVOORDE and arrived at 4.30 pm. 1 Officer's Charger, 3 Riders and 17 H.D. horses taken on strength of Train. No 196 Coy arrived at BOESCHEPE at 10 p.m.	AWC
BOESCHEPE	7/10/15		Refilling for A. C. and D. groups on the BOESCHEPE - WIPPENHOCK road. B. group refills at same point selected for previous days refilling.	AWC
do.	8/10/15		Refilling as yesterday. No 195 Coy is attached to No 2 Coy 3rd Divl. Train and refills with this Company.	AWC
do.	9/10/15		Refilling as previous days	AWC

2353 Wt. W2544/1454 700,000 5/15 D. D. & L. A.D.S.S./Forms/C. 2118.

Instructions regarding War Diaries and Intelligence Summaries are contained in F. S. Regs., Part II. and the Staff Manual respectively. Title pages will be prepared in manuscript.

WAR DIARY

~~or~~

~~INTELLIGENCE SUMMARY.~~

(Erase heading not required.)

Army Form C. 2118.

Place	Date	Hour	Summary of Events and Information	Remarks and references to Appendices
BOESCHEPE	10/10/15		Refilling as previous days. Major Dowling (T)(A.S.C) reports for duty - assisting S.S.O.	AWC
do	11/10/15		Refilling as usual. Lieut. T. GOLDING reported wounded on 10th inst in the arm and sent to No 16 Field Ambulance. At 1 p.m. Hd. Qrs. Coy. and No 196 Coy leave for GODEWAERSVELDE to quarters vacated by the 17th Divl Train. Arrived at 2.30 p.m. Shelters 1/2 only in course of construction Lieut. J. P. O'FLYNN (R.A.M.C) is taken to hospital (sick). Lieut. T. GOLDING reported a casualty	AWC
GODEWAERS-VELDE	12/10/15		Supply wagons leave for previous days refilling point. All available men put to erection of stables and quarters.	AWC
do	13/10/15		As on 12th	AWC

Instructions regarding War Diaries and Intelligence Summaries are contained in F. S. Regs., Part II. and the Staff Manual respectively. Title pages will be prepared in manuscript.

WAR DIARY

~~INTELLIGENCE SUMMARY.~~

(*Erase heading not required.*)

Army Form C. 2118.

Place	Date	Hour	Summary of Events and Information	Remarks and references to Appendices
GODEWAERSVELDE	14/10/15		Refilling as previous days. No 197 Coy. leave GODEWAERSVELDE to take up position near their brigade at WESTOUTRE.	AMcC
do	15/10/15		Field State and Field Return also Demand for Remounts (nil) sent. Lieut. H. J. McCURRICH (R.A.M.C.) and batman report for duty.	AMcC.
do	16/10/15		Nothing to report. Everything working satisfactorily	AMcC.
do.	17/10/15.		Major Dowling rejoins his unit (50th Divl. Train).	AMcC.
do.	18/10/15.		No 195 Coy. rejoins train. 17th Inf. Bde takes place of 71st Inf Bde to 6th Division.	AMcC.

2353 Wt. W2544/1454 700,000 5/15 D. D. & L. A.D.S.S./Forms/C. 2118.

Instructions regarding War Diaries and Intelligence Summaries are contained in F. S. Regs., Part II. and the Staff Manual respectively. Title pages will be prepared in manuscript.

WAR DIARY

~~or~~

~~INTELLIGENCE SUMMARY.~~

(Erase heading not required.)

Army Form C. 2118.

Place	Date	Hour	Summary of Events and Information	Remarks and references to Appendices
GODEWAERSVELDE.	19/10/15.		Nothing of importance to report. Everything working satisfactorily	AWC
do	20/10/15		do	AWC
do	21/10/15		do	AWC
do	22/10/15		do	AWC.
do.	23/10/15		Arranged with Supply Column for motor cyclist orderly to call daily at 12 (noon) and 4 p.m to take messages to and from D. H. Q.	AWC.
do	24/10/15		No 197 Coy. move to Sheet 27 R. 11. b. 9. 1.	AWC

2353 Wt. W2544/1454 700,000 5/15 D. D. & L. A.D.S.S./Forms/C. 2118.

Instructions regarding War Diaries and Intelligence Summaries are contained in F. S. Regs., Part II. and the Staff Manual respectively. Title pages will be prepared in manuscript.

WAR DIARY

~~or INTELLIGENCE SUMMARY.~~

(Erase heading not required.)

Army Form C. 2118.

Place	Date	Hour	Summary of Events and Information	Remarks and references to Appendices
GODEWAER-SVELDE	25/10/15.		—— ——	AWC.
do	26/10/15		T4/055942 Dr. NORBURY. J. committed to prison (P.M. 2nd Army) for six months H.L.	AWC.
do.	27/10/15		Lt. Col. HORSBRUGH. went on leave for 7 days. Major J. W. BLAKEWAY assumes command. HIS MAJESTY THE KING visits 24th Division at RENINGHELST.	AWC
do.	28/10/15		Court of Inquiry held at Train Headquarters to investigate and report on the circumstances in which Lieut. J. GOLDING was wounded. Notified that Lieut. GOLDING is struck off strength of train, to date from 13/10/15.	AWC.
do.	29/10/15.		Lieut. HARROWER. A.B. sent to hospital.	
do.	30/10/15.		Orders from D.H.Q. received at 10 p.m. to detail 1 officer and 2 NCOs to take charge of a coal convoy from here to RENINGHELST. Wagons furnished by other units. Notified 195 Coy. for this duty. Also each Bde. Coy. to detail sufficient personnel to take charge of baggage wagons now remaining with units, Coys. notified and personnel ordered.	AWC

2353 Wt. W2544/1454 700,000 5/15 D. D. & L. A.D.S.S./Forms/C. 2118.

Army Form C. 2118.

Instructions regarding War Diaries and Intelligence Summaries are contained in F. S. Regs., Part II. and the Staff Manual respectively. Title pages will be prepared in manuscript.

WAR DIARY

~~INTELLIGENCE SUMMARY.~~

(Erase heading not required.)

Place	Date	Hour	Summary of Events and Information	Remarks and references to Appendices
GODEWAER-SVELDE	31/10/15		No. 196 Coy. move to brigade area. (Sheet 28. G. 32 a 5. 5.) Artificers &c sent to brigades for baggage wagons repairs	AWC.

2353 Wt. W2544/1454 700,000 5/15 D. D. & L. A.D.S.S./Forms/C. 2118.

121
7621

2q II Divl: Train

Vol. 3

Nov. 15

CONFIDENTIAL

War Diary

of

O.C, 24th Divisional Train, B. E. F.

1st Nov. 1915 to 30th Nov. 1915.

Instructions regarding War Diaries and Intelligence Summaries are contained in F. S. Regs., Part II. and the Staff Manual respectively. Title pages will be prepared in manuscript.

WAR DIARY

or

~~INTELLIGENCE SUMMARY.~~

(Erase heading not required.)

Army Form C. 2118.

Place	Date	Hour	Summary of Events and Information	Remarks and references to Appendices
GODEWAERSVELDE.	1/11/15		Very wet. Ground in a fearful condition. Visited Nos 194 and 195 Coys. Shelters for all horses. Mens huts in course of erection.	AMcC.
do	2/11/15		Visited 196 Coy at Sheet 28. G 32 a 5·5. A convalescent company of 9th Division not having evacuated this position, some inconvenience and overcrowding caused. Also visited 197 Coy. Horse shelters and mens huts in course of erection. Very wet day. Lt. Col. HORSBRUGH arrived from England from leave during night – delayed on journey, by alteration of time-tables.	AMcC
do	3/11/15.		Lieut and adj A. St G. ADAMS reported for duty from hospital. Received orders from D.H.Q that in order to check the movements of all persons in the Corps area control posts would be put into force from 9 p.m 4/11/15 to 9 p.m 5/11/15. All men provided with passes when on duty, those off duty confined to billeting area.	AMcC.
do	4/11/15.		Lieut & adj A St G. ADAMS taken ill and admitted to hospital [No 12 C.C.S. HAZEBROUCK] C.O visits refilling points with S.S.O. Supplies dumped on wet ground somewhat spoiled. Gave orders for shelters to be made. Dry and fair day.	AMcC.
do	5/11/15.		Visited refilling points. Nothing further to report. ~~[illegible]~~	AMcC.

2353 Wt. W2544/1454 700,000 5/15 D. D. & L. A.D.S.S./Forms/C. 2118.

Instructions regarding War Diaries and Intelligence Summaries are contained in F. S. Regs., Part II. and the Staff Manual respectively. Title pages will be prepared in manuscript.

WAR DIARY

~~INTELLIGENCE SUMMARY.~~

(*Erase heading not required.*)

Army Form C. 2118.

Place	Date	Hour	Summary of Events and Information	Remarks and references to Appendices
GODEWAERSVELDE	6/11/15.		Fair day. Nos 194, 195 and 197 Coys somewhat delayed in the erection of huts owing to roofing material being unobtainable from R. E. Two wheelers from Base Horse Transport Depot reported for duty	AWC
do.	7/11/15.			
do.	8/11/15.		Visited refilling points. 1 pair H. D horses and 1 G.S. wagon returned from "C" Batt. 109th Bde R.F.A. in a shocking condition. Horses terribly emaciated – sore shoulders and withers. Report sent to D. H. Q. requesting sanction of withdrawal of horses from this brigade and for horses to be found for Supply and baggage wagons by the R. F. A. brigade.	AWC
do.	9/11/15.		Visited refilling points. Fine day but dull. Rain in the evening. Orders received to collect surplus transport of division at RENINGHELST (D. H. Q.) to-morrow at noon. 2nd Lieut. PLUMPTRE detailed for this duty. Surplus transport consists of 2 wagons from 12th SHERWOODS, 2 wagons from DIVl ENGINEERS, 1 wagon from 72nd Inf. Bde and 5 wagons from 73rd Inf. Bde.	AWC.
do.	10/11/15.		Surplus ~~wagons~~ transport brought into No 194 Coy. Only 9 wagons, 1 driver and 1 pair horses being unfit to travel. This wagon &c to be absorbed into strength of train when they arrive	AWC.

Instructions regarding War Diaries and Intelligence Summaries are contained in F. S. Regs., Part II. and the Staff Manual respectively. Title pages will be prepared in manuscript.

WAR DIARY

~~INTELLIGENCE SUMMARY.~~

(Erase heading not required.)

Army Form C. 2118.

Place	Date	Hour	Summary of Events and Information	Remarks and references to Appendices
GODEWAERSVELDE	11/11/15.		Visited refilling points. 9 wagons (surplus to Dvl. Est.) leave at noon under C.S.M. MIRAMS for Advanced Horse Transport Depot at ABBEVILLE. First supply of coal from mines at BRUAY received. Great difficulty in obtaining transport to clear trucks at POPERINGHE and GODEWAERSVELDE stations. It seems a pity that the above transport could not have been retained in the division.	AMcC.
do.	12/11/15.		Visited refilling points and D. H. Q.	AMcC.
do	13/11/15.		Visited D. H. Q. re transport for coal and wood. D.A.Q.M.G. puts forward the suggestion of hiring local transport.	AMcC.
do	14/11/15.		Visited refilling points & D. H. Q. and arranged for a sergeant of Dvl Train to be permanently at POPERINGHE for superintending coal issues.	AMcC.
do.	15/11/15.		Visited POPERINGHE and installed N.C.O in his duties of Superintending the coal issue. This should be the means of the issue working smoothly and the station kept clear. N.C.O will be visited daily by R.O. Dvl Troops – the officer responsible for the coal of the division. Received unofficial visit from Major-Gen. A.A. CHICHESTER, DAQMG, 2nd Army and Col. PHELPS, D.D. of S & T. 2nd Army. Very fine day.	AMcC.

2353 Wt W2544/1454 700,000 5/15 D. D. & L. A.D.S.S./Forms/C. 2118.

Instructions regarding War Diaries and Intelligence Summaries are contained in F. S. Regs., Part II. and the Staff Manual respectively. Title pages will be prepared in manuscript.

WAR DIARY

~~or~~

~~INTELLIGENCE~~ SUMMARY.

(*Erase heading not required.*)

Army Form C. 2118.

Place	Date	Hour	Summary of Events and Information	Remarks and references to Appendices
GODEWAERS: VELDE.	16/11/15.		Visited D. H. Q. No. 196 Coy now well advanced in erections for horses and men.	AMcC.
do	17/11/15.		Visited refilling points and wired for reinforcements from D. H. Q. 1 motor car driver reported from Advanced M. T. Depot, ROUEN. Notified unofficially of probable move of division. Informed that horses of 72nd Field Ambulance were being clipped & gave orders for this to be discontinued.	AMcC.
do.	18/11/15.		Visited refilling points and D. H. Q. Lt. Col. Berry 3rd Divl Train shown billets at present occupied by 24th Divl Train. Frosty weather. Grouping of units changed for Supply purposes to take effect on 20th inst. Dr. Burgess 194 Coy, attd to D. H. Q. reported killed on ABEELE – POPERINGHE road by bomb.	AMcC.
do.	19/11/15.		Lt. A. St. G. ADAMS reported for duty from hospital. Operation Orders as to move of 24th Division into II Army reserve received and distributed to Coys.	AMcC.
do	20/11/15.		73rd Inf. Bde. Group left 24th Divl area for billets vacated by 3rd Division about EECKE. Orders given to O.C. 197 Coy ~~to~~ to route to new divisional area. Coy. proceeded in the evening. 19 drivers and 1 saddler – reinforcement – arrive.	AMcC.

2353 Wt. W2544/1454 700,000 5/15 D. D. & L. A.D.S.S./Forms/C. 2118.

Army Form C. 2118.

Instructions regarding War Diaries and Intelligence Summaries are contained in F. S. Regs., Part II. and the Staff Manual respectively. Title pages will be prepared in manuscript.

WAR DIARY

~~INTELLIGENCE SUMMARY.~~

(Erase heading not required.)

Place	Date	Hour	Summary of Events and Information	Remarks and references to Appendices
GODEWAERS-VELDE.	21/11/15.		Visited D. H. Q. No 197 Coy. refill at EECKE and deliver supplies. Lt. Col. HORSBRUGH to hospital. Leave granted to Divl Train – 9 men per week.	AWC
GODEWAERS-VELDE	22/11/15		Major T. W. BLAKEWAY (O.C. 194 Coy ASC) assumed command of the Train during the absence of Lt-Col. HORSBRUGH on sick leave. No 195 Coy. proceeded to EECKE with 17th Inf. Bde. Group. No 197 Coy at ARNEKE. 2LIEUT. E. W. L. MARTIN arrived for duty with train. Posted to 195 Coy. as R.O. 17th Inf. Bde.	AWC
GODEWAERS-VELDE.	23/11/15.		No 196 Coy. proceeded to STEENVOORDE. No 195 Coy to ARNEKE. No 197 Coy arrived at EPERLECQUES	AWC.
GODEWAERS-VELDE.	24/11/15.		HQ Qrs. Train and 194 Coy. proceeded to STEENVOORDE. Lieut A. St G. ADAMS taken (sick) to hospital.	AWC.
STEENVOORDE	25/11/15.		No 196 Coy proceeded to ARNEKE. Visited D. H. Q in order to find out movements of Divl Artillery. Notified that LIEUT. A. B. HARROWER sent to ENGLAND and to be struck off strength – 17/11/15 2LT. EDWARDS performing duties of S.O. of 17th Inf. Bde. No 195 Coy. arrived at NORDAUSQUES	AWC.

2353 Wt. W2544/1454 700,000 5/15 D. D. & L. A.D.S.S./Forms/C. 2118.

Instructions regarding War Diaries and Intelligence Summaries are contained in F. S. Regs., Part II. and the Staff Manual respectively. Title pages will be prepared in manuscript.

Army Form C. 2118.

WAR DIARY

~~or~~

~~INTELLIGENCE SUMMARY.~~

(Erase heading not required.)

Place	Date	Hour	Summary of Events and Information	Remarks and references to Appendices
STEENVOORDE	26/11/15.		No 196 Coy. arrived at LA RECOUSSE. Received orders from C.R.A. as to movements of artillery brigades to-morrow. Supply and transport arrangements made accordingly. Snow.	AMcC
STEENVOORDE	27/11/15.		Left 8 a.m. for LEDERZEELE in front of artillery column. Arrived LEDERZEELE 1.30 p.m. Very hard and slippery roads	AMcC
LEDERZEELE	28/11/15.		Left LEDERZEELE for TATINGHEM at 8.30 a.m. Arrived 1.30 p.m. TATINGHEM being full of troops billeting somewhat difficult. Train headquarters established at SALPERWICK. Supply wagons of artillery brigades, having accompanied their units, failed to attend refilling point though the position had been duly notified to them.	AMcC
SALPERWICK.	29/11/15.		No 194 Coy ordered to leave TATINGHEM and to proceed to QUELMES. Positions of coys. and refilling points at present:- 194 Coy - QUELMES - R.P - QUELMES - ADSOIT road - Artillery Group 195 Coy - MONECOVE - RP on side road running N.E. from ST. OMER - NORDAUSQUES road just S. of L. of EPERLECQUES in BAYENGHEM-LES-EPERLECQUES. (17th Inf. Bde. Group.)	

2353 Wt. W2544/1454 700,000 5/15 D. D. & L. A.D.S.S./Forms/C. 2118.

Instructions regarding War Diaries and Intelligence Summaries are contained in F. S. Regs., Part II. and the Staff Manual respectively. Title pages will be prepared in manuscript.

WAR DIARY
or
~~INTELLIGENCE~~ SUMMARY.

(Erase heading not required.)

Army Form C. 2118.

Place	Date	Hour	Summary of Events and Information	Remarks and references to Appendices
SALPERWICK	29/11/15		196 Coy – LA RECOUSSE – R.P. Main road just W. of the houses at LA RECOUSSE. 197 Coy – EPEPLECQUES – RP. On main ST. OMER – NORDAUSQUES road W. of MOULLE and S. of HOULLE. DDVS. (II Army) visited and inspected 195 and 197 Coy.	AMcC.
SALPERWICK	30/11/15		Baggage wagons and horses returned to A.S.C Companies for the purpose of being overhauled. Several wagons of artillery formations unable to be sent in owing to alleged lack of transport. No. 194 Coy. now at NOIR CARME.	AMcC.

2353 Wt. W2544/1454 700,000 5/15 D. D. & L. A.D.S.S./Forms/C. 2118.

24th Division

194th Coy A.S.C.
Vol 4

121
7678

Nov 15

Omgs
6

Confidential.

War Diary
of
194 Coy. ASC.

from 1/11/15 to 30/11/15.

Volume 3.

H.Q. Co. 24 Div. Train.

Instructions regarding War Diaries and Intelligence Summaries are contained in F. S. Regs., Part II. and the Staff Manual respectively. Title pages will be prepared in manuscript.

WAR DIARY
or
INTELLIGENCE SUMMARY.
(Erase heading not required.)

Army Form C. 2118.

Place	Date	Hour	Summary of Events and Information	Remarks and references to Appendices
GODEWAERSVELDE	1/11/15	8AM	Supply wagons refilled & delivered supplies – BOESCHEPE – POPERINGHE Road –	Rain –
"	2/11/15	"	" " " " " " " "	Rain –
"	3/11/15	"	" " " " " " " "	Showery –
"	4/11/15	"	" " " " " " " "	Fine –
"	5/11/15	"	" " " " " " " "	Rain –
"	6/11/15	"	" " " " " " " "	Fine –
"	7/11/15	"	" " " " " " " "	Fine –
"	8/11/15	"	" " " " " " " " Visited R.F.A units –	Fine –
"	9/11/15	"	" " " " " " " "	Rain in afternoon
"	10/11/15	"	" " " " " " " " Received four mules & four sets of Harness from No III Sect: D.A.C for 140 A. Troops Comp: R.E. – 9 wagons & 20 horses came in	Showery –
"	11/11/15	"	Supply wagons refilled – Sent four mules & harness & one G.S wagon complete to 140th A.T. Comp: R.E & nine wagons & eighteen horses & 9 drivers to Advanced Base Transport Depot at ABBEVILLE.	Fine morning Rain afternoon
"	12/11/15	"	Supply wagons refilled – BOESCHEPE – POPERINGHE ROAD.	Rain & gale in morning.
"	13/11/15	"	" " "	Rain & wind –
"	14/11/15	"	" " "	Fine –
"	15/11/15	"	" " "	Fine –
"	16/11/15	"	Supply wagons refilled on GODEWAERSVELDE – BOESCHEPE Road –	Fine –
"	17/11/15	"	" " " " " "	Showery –
"	18/11/15	"	" " " " "	Fine morning, Rain afternoon –

Instructions regarding War Diaries and Intelligence Summaries are contained in F. S. Regs., Part II. and the Staff Manual respectively. Title pages will be prepared in manuscript.

WAR DIARY
or
INTELLIGENCE SUMMARY.
(Erase heading not required.)

Army Form C. 2118.

Place	Date	Hour	Summary of Events and Information	Remarks and references to Appendices
GODEWAERSVELDE	19/11/15	8 AM.	Supply wagons refilled GODEWAERSVELDE — BOESCHEPE Road — Supply wagons 107th BRIG:	Fine cold
"			R.F.A. came into Camp — Received orders to move on 22/11/15 for STEENVOORDE on 21/11/15 —	
"	20/11/15	"	Supply wagons refilled on GODEWAERSVELDE — BOSCHEPE Road — Order to move cancelled —	Fine cold.
"	21/11/15	"	" " " " "	Fine & cold —
"	22/11/15	"	" " " " " " Ordered to move 24/11/15 for STEENVOORDE —	Fine & cold —
"	23/11/15	"	" " " " "	Dull —
"	24/11/15	"	" " " " " " Moved out of Camp 10 A M, arrived at STEENVOORDE	
STEENVOORDE	25/11/15	"	Supply Wagons refilled STEENVOORDE — HAZBRUCK Road.	Fine, rain later
"	26/11/15	"	" " " " " " Received orders to move 27/11/15	Fine
"	27/11/15	"	Supply Wagons refilled ARNEKE — LE MENEGAT RD. Moved out of Steenvoorde 8 AM, arrived at LEDERZEELE. Received orders to march to TATINGHEM.	Frosty
LEDERZEELE	28/11/15	8.30 am.	Supply Wagons refilled on the ADSOIT — QUELMES RD. Moved from LEDERZEELE, 8.30 am arrived at TATINGHEM.	Fine & Frosty
TATINGHEM	29/11/15	"	Supply Wagons refilled ADSOIT — QUELMES RD. Received orders from S.C. Divisional Artillery to move, no destination given. Moved out of TATINGHEM & eventually arrived & billeted at NOIR CARME. BAGGAGE & Supply Wagons, with units, to rejoin tomorrow 30/11/15.	Rain
NOIR CARME	30/11/15	"	Supply Wagons refilled ADSOIT — QUELMES RD	Fair.

[illegible] Lieut.
Commdg. 194 Coy. ASC

2353 Wt. W2544/1454 700,000 5/15 D. D. & L. A.D.S.S./Forms/C. 2118.

194th Loz: Asl.
(No 1 Loz: 24th Brit: Trani)
Vol: 5

Dec

Confidential

War Diary
of
194 Coy. ASC
(24th Divl Train)
from 1st December 1915 to 31st Dec 1915

P. H. Blakeway Major
O/C 194 Comp: A.S.C

Instructions regarding War Diaries and Intelligence Summaries are contained in F. S. Regs., Part II. and the Staff Manual respectively. Title pages will be prepared in manuscript.

WAR DIARY
or
INTELLIGENCE SUMMARY.
(Erase heading not required.)

Army Form C. 2118.

Place	Date	Hour	Summary of Events and Information	Remarks and references to Appendices
NOIR CARME	1/12/15	8 am	Supply Wagons refilled on ADSOIT - QUELMES STD. Supply Wagons of 108th & 109th Brigades R.F.A. returned to comp. also Supply & Baggage of 106 & 107 Bdes R.F.A	Fine. Wet later.
— " —	2/12/15	8 am	Supply Wagons refilled on ~~Rd~~ ADSOIT - QELMES RD.	Fair
— " —	3/12/15	8 am	" " " " " 109th Bde R.F.A transferred to 72 Bde Group. C.R.A. arranged that all wagons should return to their units & gave the necessary orders.	Wet
— " —	4/12/15	"	Supply wagons refilled on ADSOIT - QUELMES Rd. All wagons returned to stay with their units.	Wet.
— " —	5/12/15	"	Supply Wagons refilled on ADSOIT - QUELMES Rd.	Fine.
— " —	6/12/15	"	" " " " " " "	Wet
— " —	7/12/15	"	" " " " " " "	Fine
— " —	8/12/15	"	" " " " " " "	Fine
— " —	9/12/15	"	" " " " " " "	Wet
— " —	10/12/15	"	" " " " " " " Post office moved from TATINGHEM to NOIR CARME	Wet later.
— " —	11/12/15	"	" " " " " " "	Wet
— " —	12/12/15	"	" " " " " " "	Wet later.
— " —	13/12/15	"	" " " " " " "	Fine & frost

R. W. Blakeway Major
O/C 194 Comp: A.S.C.

2353 Wt. W2544/1454 700,000 5/15 D. D. & L. A.D.S.S./Forms/C. 2118.

Instructions regarding War Diaries and Intelligence Summaries are contained in F. S. Regs., Part II. and the Staff Manual respectively. Title pages will be prepared in manuscript.

WAR DIARY
or
INTELLIGENCE SUMMARY.
(Erase heading not required.)

Army Form C. 2118.

Place	Date	Hour	Summary of Events and Information	Remarks and references to Appendices
NOIR CARME	14/12/15	8 AM	Supply wagons refilled ADSOIT - QUELMES RD	Fine
"	15/12/15	"	" " " " " "	"
"	16/12/15	"	" " " " " "	Wet
"	17/12/15	"	" " " " " "	"
"	18/12/15	"	" " " " " MAJOR. F.B. LORD. A.S.C joined Train & took	Fine
"	"		Over Command -	
"	19/12/15	"	Supply wagons refilled ADSOIT - QUELMES Road - MAJOR T. W. BLAKEWAY rejoined from H. Qrs of Train - C.O. inspected horses of the Company -	Fine -
"	20/12/15	"	" " " " " "	Fine -
"	21/12/15	"	" " " " " "	Wet -
"	22/12/15	"	" " " " " "	Rain -
"	23/12/15	"	" " " " " " Visited 107 BRIGADE R.F.A horses, Lt WALENN visited 106th R.F.A & D.A.C - Received orders to march on 28th for NORDPEENE -	Rain -
"	24/12/15	"	" " " " " " Lt WALENN visited 109th & Lt McNAMARA 108th BRIG: R.F.A.	Rain -
"	25/12/15	"	" " " " " " Lt WALENN visited 106th BRIG: R.F.A & D.A.C.	Showery -
"	26/12/15	"	" " " " " " orders to move Cancelled, till further orders -	Fine -
"	27/12/15	"	" " " " " " Visited 108th & 109th BRIG: R.F.A.	Showery -
"	28/12/15	"	" " " " " " Visited 106th BRIG: R.F.A & D.A.C.	Fine -
"	29/12/15	"	" " " " " " Received orders to march 107th BRIG: R.F.A. on 30/12/15.	Fine -
"	30/12/15	"	" " " " " "	Fine -
"	31/12/15	"	" " " " " "	Fine morning Wet afternoon -

T. W. Blakeway - Major
O/C 19A Comp: A.S.C

2353 Wt. W2544/1454 700,000 5/15 D. D. & L. A.D.S.S./Forms/C. 2118.

Confidential

War Diary

of

O.C. 24th Divisional Train, A.S.C

From 1 - 12 - 15 to 31 - 12 - 15

Vol. IV

Instructions regarding War Diaries and Intelligence Summaries are contained in F. S. Regs., Part II. and the Staff Manual respectively. Title pages will be prepared in manuscript.

WAR DIARY

~~INTELLIGENCE~~ ~~SUMMARY~~.

(Erase heading not required.)

Army Form C. 2118.

Place	Date	Hour	Summary of Events and Information	Remarks and references to Appendices
SALPERWICK	1/12/15.		Inspected 73rd Inf. Bde 1st Line Transport and furnished report of inspection to D. H. Q. The D. of T. G. H. Q. visited 197 Coy – Several suggestions for the improvement of the accommodation for horses and men – memorandum issued to O.C. Coys.	AWC.
do	2/12/15		Inspected 17th Inf. Bde 1st Line Transport and furnished a report to OC 17th I. B. Wet. 2Lieut A. C. Bendit transferred to No 196 Coy and to take over duties of R.O to 72nd I. B. vice 2Lieut L. M. Frischer to 194 Coy – R.O. Div Troops.	AWC
do	3/12/15		Inspected 72nd Inf. Bde 1st Line Transport. Visited C. R. A and arranged that Baggage wagons should remain with Artillery units and assist in transport of supplies. Baggage wagons and supply wagons to form a convoy should division be ordered to move and travel independently of artillery units. 3 untrained drivers report for duty. Wet.	AWC
do	4/12/15		Visited No 194 Coy at NOIR CARME. Very wet. Received from D. H. Q a fresh allotment of leave – 4 men per week to be divided between Train and Supply Column. Very Stormy. Informed that 'C' Batt. 109th Bde R.F.A. leaves to join 131st Bde R. F. A to-morrow – Transport arranged accordingly	AWC

2353 Wt. W2544/1454 700,000 5/15 D. D. & L. A.D.S.S./Forms/C. 2118.

Army Form C. 2118.

Instructions regarding War Diaries and Intelligence Summaries are contained in F. S. Regs., Part II. and the Staff Manual respectively. Title pages will be prepared in manuscript.

WAR DIARY
or
~~INTELLIGENCE SUMMARY.~~

(Erase heading not required.)

Place	Date	Hour	Summary of Events and Information	Remarks and references to Appendices
SALPERWICK	5/12/15.		Nothing to report.	AWC
"	6/12/15		Visited refilling points of Nos 195 and 197 Coys. Nothing further to report. Reinforcement of 3 untrained drivers report for duty.	AWC
"	7/12/15		Visited No 194 Coy. Two parties of 3 drivers each despatched to B.H.T.D. (HAVRE).	AWC.
"	8/12/15.		Visited No 197 Coy. and inspected camp. Very fine day.	AWC
"	9/12/15		Nothing to report.	AWC
"	10/12/15		Visited refilling points of Divl Troops and 73rd Bde Group.	AWC
"	11/12/15		Visited 194 Coy. Notified that lectures should be given by S.O's to the various groups & arrangements made accordingly. G.H.Q remounts taken on strength	AWC.

2353 Wt. W2544/1454 700,000 5/15 D. D. & L. A.D.S.S./Forms/C. 2118.

Army Form C. 2118.

Instructions regarding War Diaries and Intelligence Summaries are contained in F. S. Regs., Part II. and the Staff Manual respectively. Title pages will be prepared in manuscript.

WAR DIARY

~~or~~

~~INTELLIGENCE SUMMARY.~~

(Erase heading not required.)

Place	Date	Hour	Summary of Events and Information	Remarks and references to Appendices
SALPERWICK	12/12/15.		Nothing to report - Wet.	AMC
"	13/12/15.		Visited D.H.Q and No 194 Coy. - Fine.	AMC
"	14/12/15		S.O. Divl Troops delivered lecture at ACQUIN on Supply in the Field to 108th & 109th Bdes. R.F.A. Visited refilling points of Divl Troops and 73 I.B. Group. Frosty - S.O. 73rd I.B. group lectured at EPERLECQUES.	AMC
"	15/12/15.		Visited No 194 Coy. - Cold.	AMC
"	16/12/15		Visited refilling points of No 195 and 197 Coys. S.O Divl Troops Lectured to 106th, 107th & DAC. (R.F.A). Three untrained drivers reported for duty.	AMC
"	17/12/15.		Exchanged open Sunbeam for Wolsely Car this day by order of D.D.S.T. II Army. Wet. 3 cases of mange reported in 194 Coy.	AMC

Army Form C. 2118.

Instructions regarding War Diaries and Intelligence Summaries are contained in F. S. Regs., Part II. and the Staff Manual respectively. Title pages will be prepared in manuscript.

WAR DIARY
or
~~INTELLIGENCE SUMMARY.~~

(Erase heading not required.)

Place	Date	Hour	Summary of Events and Information	Remarks and references to Appendices
SALPERWICK	18/12/15.		Reinforcement of 15 H. D. horses arrive; Major ~~[illegible]~~. LORD, F.B. assumed command. Fine.	AWC
"	19/12/15.		Visited refillings points of Nos 195, 196 & 197 Coys. D.H.Q and Hd. Qrs 73rd Infantry Brigade. Inspected horses of 194 Coy and 197 Coy. Fine	AWC
"	20/12/15.		Inspected horses of 195 and 196 Coys. Furnished report to D. H. Q on billeting area. Fair	AWC.
"	21/12/15		Visited D. H. Q. and 24th Divl Supply Column at WATTEN re motor cars of the train. Visited DDofT. at G.H.Q. Wet. Arranged hire of store at ~~Watten~~ WATTEN for surplus kits & equipt of units in view of early orders to march. Received report on Wolseley car as unfit for use. Plum puddings issued to units.	AWC
"	22/12/15.		Visited refilling point of Divl Troops, Interview with G.O.C. 24th Divn. Wet.	AWC

2353 Wt. W2544/1454 700,000 5/15 D. D. & L. A.D.S.S./Forms/C. 2118.

Army Form C. 2118.

Instructions regarding War Diaries and Intelligence Summaries are contained in F. S. Regs., Part II. and the Staff Manual respectively. Title pages will be prepared in manuscript.

WAR DIARY
or
INTELLIGENCE SUMMARY.
(Erase heading not required.)

Place	Date	Hour	Summary of Events and Information	Remarks and references to Appendices
SALPERWICK	23/12/15.		All O.C. Coys and SOs assembled for the purpose of receiving instructions with regard to the impending move of the division. Interview with C.R.A. Details of march & refilling points –	AMcC
			To St. Omer in afternoon re attaching details rear party to 4 Bridging Train Watten for rations – arranged – very wet.	
– " –	24/12/15.	9 am	D.H.Q further details re move proposals to march transport in 2 days agreed C. ✱ 4 Prisoners (2 NCOs) drunk – NCOs for C.M.	
			Went to Cassel (Army HQ) for purpose obtaining motor cars for march Also lorries for blankets, extra stores &c. – got promise to meet requirements.	
			8.30 pm Concert 194 Coy – French Territorials present. to D.H.Q 9.30 p.m very wet.	AMcC
– " –	25/12/15	9 am	rec'd march orders – Issued to Coys 12.20 pm – 12.30 pm to D.H.Q. discussed march – 3.30 pm to Div Supply Col: arranged final details refilling pts &c. Issued graph of march refilling pts. C.R.A. agreed my proposals re routes. Wrote H.Q Army confirming arrangements for M.T. on march – Xmas day – not raining but very damp & dull.	

2353 Wt. W2544/1454 700,000 5/15 D. D. & L. A.D.S.S./Forms/C. 2118.

Army Form C. 2118.

Instructions regarding War Diaries and Intelligence Summaries are contained in F. S. Regs., Part II. and the Staff Manual respectively. Title pages will be prepared in manuscript.

WAR DIARY
or
INTELLIGENCE SUMMARY.
(Erase heading not required.)

Place	Date	Hour	Summary of Events and Information	Remarks and references to Appendices
SALPERWICK	25/12/15	9 p.m.	Received notification from D.H.Q that march was to be cancelled and all action suspended. Proceeded to D.H.Q but obtained no further information. Sent adjutant to 196 Coy and Divl Supply Column as I obtained the information that these units had not been notified of this alteration.	AWC
SALPERWICK	26/12/15		S.S.O granted leave from 29th inst. D.H.Q no further news of move. Saw and instructed OC 196 Coy to carry on ordinary routine. Saw G.O.C 72nd and G.OC 17th Bde. Both expressed themselves thoroughly satisfied with the work of the brigade companies. 2 Lieut J.K. ROBERTSON takes over duties of S.S.O for instruction for 10 days. 2 Lieut FROST assumes duties of 73rd Inf. Bde vice Lt ROBERTSON. Fine but windy rain towards evening.	AWC
SALPERWICK	27/12/15.		Visited D.H.Q – nothing further to report. Windy	AWC

Army Form C. 2118.

Instructions regarding War Diaries and Intelligence Summaries are contained in F. S. Regs., Part II. and the Staff Manual respectively. Title pages will be prepared in manuscript.

WAR DIARY
or
INTELLIGENCE SUMMARY.
(Erase heading not required.)

Place	Date	Hour	Summary of Events and Information	Remarks and references to Appendices
SAILPERWICK	28/12/15.		Inspection of 73rd Bde Group by G.O.C. 24th Division – ~~[illegible]~~ postponed to 31/12/15 Received fresh allotment of leave – Two per diem to include Supply Column + to take effect from 1/1/16.	[initials]
"	29/12/15		Orders received of move of Divl. Arty to new area. Necessary supply and transport arrangements made. Inspection of 72nd Bde group by G.O.C. Fine. 1st good except 8/R. W Kents –	[initials]
"	30/12/15		F.G.C.M held at GANSPETTE for trial of Sadd. S.S Webb and Cpl. Robertson. Inspected 1st line tpt 17th Infy Bde group – good except 2/Londons – Fine. Went Cassel 3pm to meet SSO 17 Bde re coal + supplies generally on transfer – 107 Bde R.F.A to NOORDEPEENE.	[initials]
"	31/12/15		Inspected 73rd Bde group 1st line tpt. good except horses of 13 Middlesex – 12/ Sherwoods (Pioneers) good considering conditions but not up to rest. General want of brakes for all Limbered G.S wagons – Spoke DADOS, hastening for all Bdes – Received orders for move of RE + Cyclists – 107 Bde RFA to STEENVOORDE. Fine am very wet pm.	[initials]

2353 Wt. W2544/1454 700,000 5/15 D. D. & L. A.D.S.S./Forms/C. 2118.

24th Divl: Train

Vol: 5

Confidential.

War Diary

of

194 Coy A.S.C.

1st January to 31st January 1916

W. Blakeway - Major
O/c 194 Coy A.S.C.

Instructions regarding War Diaries and Intelligence Summaries are contained in F. S. Regs., Part II. and the Staff Manual respectively. Title pages will be prepared in manuscript.

WAR DIARY
or
INTELLIGENCE SUMMARY.
(Erase heading not required.)

Army Form C. 2118.

Place	Date	Hour	Summary of Events and Information	Remarks and references to Appendices
NOIR CARME	1/1/16	10 AM	Supply wagons refilled on ADSOIT - QUELMES Road, marched at 11 A.M. with Supply wagons of 106th BRIG: R.F.A & 194 Comp: wagons to NOORDPEENE, arrived at 4-30 p.m. -	Fine morning - Wet afternoon -
NOORDPEENE	2/1/16	9 A.M	Supply wagons of 194 Comp: A.S.C, 106th & 109th BRIG: R.F.A refilled on NOORPEENE - CASSEL Road & then marched with Baggage wagons to STEENVOORDE, arrived 4 p.m. -	Very wet -
STEENVOORDE	3/1/16	9 A.M	Supply wagons of 194 Comp: A.S.C, 106th & 109th BRIG: R.F.A refilled ½ mile W of STEENVOORDE on CASSEL Road - then marched for new Camp MAP 28. Q 16. c 5 6, guides met R.F.A Supply wagons on STEENVOORDE-ABELE Road, 194 Comp: A.S.C arrived 3-30 p.m. - 17th DIV: TRAIN not left -	Fine -
BUSSEBOOM	4/1/16	18-30	Supply wagons refilled on POPERINGHE - BUSSEBOOM - Road -	Wet -
"	5/1/16	9-30	" " " " POPERINGHE - RENINGHELST Road -	Fine -
"	6/1/16	"	" " " " " " "	Fine -
"	7/1/16	"	" " " " " - OUDERDOM "	Still & showery -
"	8/1/16	"	" " " " " " " HQ's of Train arrived - moved into Camp -	Fine -
"	9/1/16	"	" " " " " " "	Fine
"	10/1/16	"	" " " " " " " Baggage wagons ordered to return to Coy with exception of three unhorsed wagons for long [?]	Fine
"	11/1/16	"	" " " " " " "	-"-
"	12/1/16	"	" " " " " " "	-"-
"	13/1/16	"	" " " " " " "	-"-
"	14/1/16	"	" " " " " " " Orders received @ 11-30 pm to collect remaining wagons, with exception of R.F.A. Bag. Harn[?]	-"-
"	15/1/16	"	" " " " " " " Orders received to change Refilling point to place marked G 15. C. 1 5. on RENINGHELST - POPERINGHE RD. as from 17/1/16	Fine
"	16/1/16	"	Supply wagons refilled on POPERINGHE - OUDERDOM Road	Fine
"	17/1/16	"	" " " " - RENINGHELST "	Fine.

2353 Wt. W2544/1454 700,000 5/15 D. D. & L. A.D.S.S./Forms/C. 2118.

Instructions regarding War Diaries and Intelligence Summaries are contained in F. S. Regs., Part II. and the Staff Manual respectively. Title pages will be prepared in manuscript.

Army Form C. 2118.

WAR DIARY
or
INTELLIGENCE SUMMARY.
(Erase heading not required.)

Place	Date	Hour	Summary of Events and Information	Remarks and references to Appendices
BUSSE BOOM.	18/1/16	9. A.M.	Supply wagons refilled on POPERINGHE — RENINGHELST Road —	Rain —
"	19/1/16	"	" " " " " " — Major BLAKEWAY returned off leave — No. 4 Comp: Camp about 200 yards away shelled for two hours, about 50 shells being fired — no casualties —	Fine —
"	20/1/16	"	Supply wagons refilled on POPERINGHE — RENINGHELST Road —	Fine —
"	21/1/16	"	" " " " " " —	Fine —
"	22/1/16	"	" " " " " " — Aeroplane raid over POPERINGHE & Nos 2, 3 & 4 Companies between 12 A.M. & 2 A.M. 23/1/16 — D.D.R. Inspected Horses, reporting favourably on same —	Fine —
"	23/1/16	"	Supply wagons refilled " " " —	Fine —
"	24/1/16	"	" " " " " "	Fine —
"	25/1/16	"	" " " " " " Lt. SAUNDERS returned from leave —	Fine —
"	26/1/16	"	" " " " " " Lt. WALENN went on leave —	Fine —
"	27/1/16	"	" " " " " "	Dull & slight rain —
"	28/1/16	"	" " " " " "	Dull —
"	29/1/16	"	" " " " " "	Dull —
"	30/1/16	"	" " " " " "	Dull —
"	31/1/16	"	" " " " " "	Fine —
				Fine —

R. W. Blakeway Major —

CONFIDENTIAL

War Diary

of

O.C. 24th Divisional Train, A.S.C.

B. E. F.

Jan 1/1916 to Jan 31/1916

Army Form C. 2118.

Instructions regarding War Diaries and Intelligence Summaries are contained in F. S. Regs., Part II. and the Staff Manual respectively. Title pages will be prepared in manuscript.

WAR DIARY
or
~~INTELLIGENCE~~ ~~SUMMARY.~~

(*Erase heading not required.*)

Place	Date	Hour	Summary of Events and Information	Remarks and references to Appendices
SALPERWICK	1/1/16		107 Bde R.F.A to New area near POPERINGHE. 106 + 109 Bdes RFA. + 194 Coy A.S.C to NOORDPEENE.	
		10am	Orders for move 108 Bde RFA cancelled - orders received for 2 Batteries 106 Bde RFA to remain in STEENVOORDE area until Infantry relief finished -	Th
"	2/1/16		Operation Orders re move of infantry received and necessary instructions sent to companies. 106th + 109th Bdes R.F.A proceeded to STEENVOORDE. (Major T. W. Blakeway in charge of supply and baggage transport). Visited 17th Divl Train area near POPERINGHE.	Th
"	3/1/16		All arrangements made for the parties of the 17th and 72nd Bdes marching by road. Headquarters 195 Coy concentrate at TILQUES (Grenade School)	Th

2353 Wt. W2544/1454 700,000 5/15 D. D. & L. A.D.S.S./Forms/C. 2118.

Instructions regarding War Diaries and Intelligence Summaries are contained in F. S. Regs., Part II. and the Staff Manual respectively. Title pages will be prepared in manuscript.

WAR DIARY

or

~~INTELLIGENCE SUMMARY~~.

(Erase heading not required.)

Army Form C. 2118.

Place	Date	Hour	Summary of Events and Information	Remarks and references to Appendices
SALPERWICK	4/1/16		Road party of 17th and 72nd Bdes left at 10.50 am for NOORDPEENE. Fld Coys R.E. left NOORDPEENE for STEENVOORDE. O.C. 197 Coy given orders for road party to proceed to new area on the 6th Jan.	Jh
"	5/1/16		Visited new divl area refilling points on the POPERINGHE - OUDERDOM road. Inter-change of coal dumps between 17th + 24th Divisions. Road party of 17th & 72nd Bdes left NOORDPEENE for STEENVOORDE. Hd Qrs 17th I.B. 2 Bns 17th Inf Bde, 2 Bns 72nd Bde & Pioneers left by rail for new area.	Jh
"	6/1/16		Group 'G' consisting of Hd Qrs 73rd Inf. Bde and 73 Fld Amb, C.R.E., D.H.Q., and Signals and Hd Qrs 197 Coy proceeded by road to NOORPEENE. 72nd Inf Bde Hd Qrs and 2 Bns and 2 Bns 17th Inf. Bde. left by rail for new area.	Jh
"	7/1/16		Hd Qrs 24th Divl Train proceeded by road to STEENVOORDE. Hd Qrs 73rd Inf. Bde and 4 Bns and 2 London Regt proceeded by rail to new area. Arrived STEENVOORDE 3 p.m.	Jh

2353 Wt. W2544/1454 700,000 5/15 D. D. & L. A.D.S.S./Forms/C. 2118.

Army Form C. 2118.

Instructions regarding War Diaries and Intelligence Summaries are contained in F. S. Regs., Part II. and the Staff Manual respectively. Title pages will be prepared in manuscript.

WAR DIARY
or
~~INTELLIGENCE SUMMARY.~~

(Erase heading not required.)

Place	Date	Hour	Summary of Events and Information	Remarks and references to Appendices
STEENVOORDE	8/1/16		108th Bde R.F.A left WATTEN area for NOORDPEENE. Hd Qrs Dvl Train left 8.30am for new Dvl Area - BUSSEBOOM. Arrived 12 noon.	[initials]
BUSSEBOOM	9/1/16		108th Bde R.F.A. left NOORDPEENE for STEENVOORDE. Baggage wagons ordered to return to respective Companies. 2Lt. Butson discharged from Hospital. Dr. Dryden awarded 3 mths F.P. No 1 by F.G.C.M. - promulgated. 3 wagons per R.F.A. Bde left with units, horses and drivers returned to Coys.	[initials]
"	10/1/16		108th Bde arrive in new Divisional area. Move of division completed. Refilling points all on BUSSEBOOM - OUDERDOM road. Positions of Companies 194 Coy - Sheet 28 G 16 c 5.6 - 195 Coy G 9 c 3.4 - 196 Coy G 9. d 3.4 - 197 Coy G 15 b 10.3. Transport arranged for various R.E duties.	[initials]
"	11/1/16		Stores which had been left at WATTEN now arriving at railhead - GODEWAERSVELDE and train transport detailed to clear. Orders issued to companies to leave 1 G.S wagon with each infantry battalion - Horses & drivers ~~to~~ to return to camp, wagons being horsed by cooker horses. ~~Prior to~~ arrival in this area division depended for fuel on that taken over from 17th Dw. First coal (20 tons) arrived to-day	[initials]

Instructions regarding War Diaries and Intelligence Summaries are contained in F. S. Regs., Part II. and the Staff Manual respectively. Title pages will be prepared in manuscript.

WAR DIARY
or
~~INTELLIGENCE SUMMARY.~~
(Erase heading not required.)

Army Form C. 2118.

Place	Date	Hour	Summary of Events and Information	Remarks and references to Appendices
BUSSEBOOM	12/1/16		Demands for transport by units to be submitted through D.A.Q.M.G. Unable to meet all demands. Stores continue to arrive at railhead from WATTEN store. D.A.&Q.M.G. V Corps visited refilling points and suggested POPERINGHE – RENINGHELST road as more suitable than POPERINGHE – OUDERDOM road. Orders to clear GODEWAERSVELDE station to-morrow and all transport to assist. Hostile aeroplane dropped 3 bombs near Group A refilling point 9.15 a.m. no damage.	Jh
"	13/1/16		Visited the station, practically nothing to clear.	Jh
"	14/1/16		POPERINGHE – RENINGHELST road reconnoitred for refilling points by S.S.O. Orders issued that refilling points would be on the POPERINGHE – RENINGHELST road from Monday 17th inst. Orders received from D.H.Q. re distribution of transport. S.S.O's conference at office of D.D.S.&T. 2nd Army. Staff Officer Roads Branch V Corps accompanied me round present & proposed refilling points. Measured present ones for road metal as they are becoming too bad to use. Visited R.T.O HAZEBROUCK re Baggage to WATTEN & was informed there was none for 24th Divn.	Jh
"	15/1/16		Distribution of Baggage Wagons carried out as ordered by DHQ. Removal of sheds at refilling points. D.A.Q.M.G. V Corps called re sites of refilling points & improvements necessary. Went to GODEWAERSVELDE & found 5 trucks – cleared 10 tons & arranged to clear balance to-morrow. Spoke to D.A.&Q.M.G. V Corps on the subject of accumulation of stores by units.	Jh

2353 Wt. W2544/1454 700,000 5/15 D. D. & L. A.D.S.S./Forms/C. 2118.

Instructions regarding War Diaries and Intelligence Summaries are contained in F. S. Regs., Part II. and the Staff Manual respectively. Title pages will be prepared in manuscript.

WAR DIARY

~~INTELLIGENCE SUMMARY.~~

(*Erase heading not required.*)

Army Form C. 2118.

Place	Date	Hour	Summary of Events and Information	Remarks and references to Appendices
16/1/16 BOSSEBOOM			GODEWAERSVELDE clear of all ex-WATTEN stores. Arranged rum issue with DAAQMG. Inspected all sick horses with V.O. – Lamenitis rather prevalent amongst horses returned from R.A. – similarly Skin diseases. Arranged with ADVS for mallein test for all horses. Reinforcement of 3 issuers arrived.	Th.
17/1/16			Refilling points changed to POPERINGHE - RENINGHELST road. D.S.C. chocolate. Great aerial activity over A.S.C. company camps. Bomb dropped just outside 196 Coy's camp. Aeroplane (allied) descended safely but somewhat rapidly between 195 Coy's Camp & POP-VLAMERTINGHE Road. Sent horses to WEMAERS CAPPEL to draw 9 G.S. wagons & to return via HARDIFORT picking up straw under 2/Lt FRISCHER. R.O.D.T. Went HAZEBROUCK Docs A.R.R.T. re consignments of extra fuel bought in Corps area for which rail transport is required. S.S.O. sent to A.D.D.S.T. by order for interview. Interpreter GIOT left relieved by Intpr. CAIN. att^d 194 Coy	Th.

2353 Wt. W2544/1454 700,000 5/15 D. D. & L. A.D.S.S./Forms/C. 2118.

Instructions regarding War Diaries and Intelligence Summaries are contained in F. S. Regs., Part II. and the Staff Manual respectively. Title pages will be prepared in manuscript.

WAR DIARY

~~or~~ ~~INTELLIGENCE~~ ~~SUMMARY.~~

(*Erase heading not required.*)

Army Form C. 2118.

Place	Date	Hour	Summary of Events and Information	Remarks and references to Appendices
BUSSEBOOM Sheet 28 G 16 c 5.2	18/1/16		M. CAIN returned to Liaison Officer for duty. Reinforcement of 1 farrier arrived & posted to 195 Coy. ~~An~~ Nine G.S. wagons arrived from 2nd Army Aux. H.T. Depot. Very wet day.	[initials]
	19/1/16		One third of horses of 194 Coy "malleined". Major Blakeway returned from leave. No 197 Coy shelled from 12.30pm to 2pm. In all 45 shells fell. From bases found appears to have been a 6" naval gun - high explosives - forming craters 5' deep by 12' diameter. No casualties to men or horses and no damage. Enemy aeroplane evidently observing effect. Direction of shells from BOESINGHE. Ordered all men to lead horses & scatter in fields South of Camps. Reoccupied camp 2.30pm. It was noticeable that the shells made no noise passing thro' the air. The first noise heard was the explosion on impact followed very closely by the boom of the gun. Fine day, sunny with wind S.W. 6pm went to DDST of army talked over S & T matters generally.	[initials]
	20/1/16		195 Coy's horses malleined. Temp Lt. ILOTT arrived & took over M.O. i/c Train relieving Lt ~~[illegible]~~ McCURRICH R.A.M.C. to 74th Ambce. No reactions from malleining of 194 Coy's horses. Considerable aerial activity. A Taube got away which ought apparently to have been brought down. Fine day	Op. orders 33 recd [initials]

Instructions regarding War Diaries and Intelligence Summaries are contained in F. S. Regs., Part II. and the Staff Manual respectively. Title pages will be prepared in manuscript.

WAR DIARY

or

~~INTELLIGENCE SUMMARY.~~

(Erase heading not required.)

Army Form C. 2118.

Place	Date	Hour	Summary of Events and Information	Remarks and references to Appendices
BUSSE BOOM Map 28 G16c.5.2	21/1/16		The third of 194 Coy's horses malleined – No reaction in horses of 195 Coy – 2/Lieut ROULSTONE of Sherwoods O/c drainage and 23 men arrived att^d to 194 Coy for rations + accommodation – D.D.R wired inspecting horses tomorrow – Operation order 33 made known to units – Wet day –	JL
	22/1/16		196 Coy's horses malleined. No reactions from yesterday – Great difficulty in collecting extra forage in this area – practically none for two days – Secured supply for tomorrow – oat straw – linseed cake and turnips – Found Belgian army buying potatoes in my area – Requisitioned them before Belgians took delivery – One up! DDR inspected about 175 horses – Expressed his opinion they were the best lot he had seen – Cast 2 for jibbing. Wired DDST of Army to increase paraffin on pack train – dull damp day. LIEUT. OGLE to hospital	JL

2353 Wt. W2544/1454 700,000 5/15 D. D. & L. A.D.S.S./Forms/C. 2118.

Instructions regarding War Diaries and Intelligence Summaries are contained in F. S. Regs., Part II. and the Staff Manual respectively. Title pages will be prepared in manuscript.

WAR DIARY

~~or~~

~~INTELLIGENCE SUMMARY.~~

(Erase heading not required.)

Army Form C. 2118.

Place	Date	Hour	Summary of Events and Information	Remarks and references to Appendices
BOSSEBOOM Map 28 G16 c 5.2	23/1/16		Several bombs dropped from aeroplanes last night between 195 Coys Camp and POPERINGHE. ~~[illegible]~~ Visited all refilling points. 2 H.D horses drawn from Field Remount Section (HAZEBROUCK) 1/3 of horses of 194 Coy malleined.	Th
"	24/1/16		Horses of 197 Coy malleined. All horses of this unit now malleined – no reaction. 22 H D remounts taken on strength – 18 allotted to 194 Coy, 4 to 197 Coy. Visited D.D.S.T 2nd Army re paraffin. Scheme for drainage of 194 & 197 Coy's camps drawn up by D.D.O & put into operation –	Th
"	25/1/16		Considerable aerial activity. ~~[illegible]~~ Inspected remounts – small but apparently in good condition. Except one pair 194 Coy – flatsided, ragged hipped, long backed animals – don't think they will do much work. Promotions of 2nd Lt. McCallum, Robertson, Frischer, Edwards & Butson & Seddall to Lt. appeared in London Gazette antedated to 25/11/15	Th
	26/1/16		Went Railhead re extra French rations – Dir S.C re motor cars under repair & spares – Hired barn POPERINGHE for vegetables thro' Town Major – 20 francs a month – Fine	Th

2353 Wt. W2544/1454 700,000 5/15 D. D. & L. A.D.S.S./Forms/C. 2118.

Army Form C. 2118.

WAR DIARY
or
INTELLIGENCE SUMMARY.
(Erase heading not required.)

Instructions regarding War Diaries and Intelligence Summaries are contained in F. S. Regs., Part II. and the Staff Manual respectively. Title pages will be prepared in manuscript.

Place	Date	Hour	Summary of Events and Information	Remarks and references to Appendices
BUSSEBOOM	27/1/16		Dull drizzly day - Nothing abnormal or of interest.	[initials]
"	28/1/16		Arranged drainage of No 196 Coys camp with D.D.O. Put things on a working footing with R.T.O., POPERINGHE. Dull day. Interpreter Loirens returned to Belgian mission.	[initials]
"	29/1/16		Trial by F.G.C.M. of Dr PEDEN. - Dull. Arranged drainage of 195 Coy's camps with D.D.O. Appointed Lt Edwards as acting S.S.O for a week to learn the work. Considerable artillery activity about 10.p.m.	[initials]
"	30/1/16		Saw SSM Baker 195 Coy with regard to getting a temporary Commission. Tried new French Forge issued to 196 Coy - found it was only a brazing lamp useless with heavy shoes. Tried experiments with petrol cans and limbered G.S. wagons. Raw cold foggy day.	[initials]

2353 Wt. W2544/1454 700,000 5/15 D. D. & L. A.D.S.S./Forms/C. 2118.

Instructions regarding War Diaries and Intelligence Summaries are contained in F. S. Regs., Part II. and the Staff Manual respectively. Title pages will be prepared in manuscript.

WAR DIARY

~~or~~

~~INTELLIGENCE SUMMARY.~~

(*Erase heading not required.*)

Army Form C. 2118.

Place	Date	Hour	Summary of Events and Information	Remarks and references to Appendices
BOSSEBOOM	31/1/16.		Saw O.C. Coys re the small number of men sent to the Divisional Baths. ~~Visited Advanced Supply Depot CAESTRE~~, AmOC. Visited railhead & D.S.C to get extra material for Vermorel Sprayers. Sharp frost - Nothing particular to report	[initials]

2353 Wt. W2544/1454 700,000 5/15 D. D. & L. A.D.S.S./Forms/C. 2118.

— CONFIDENTIAL —

War Diary

of

O. C. 24th Divisional Train

From 1 – 2 – 16 To 29 – 2 – 16

Confidential

War Diary
of
194 Coy. A.S.C.

from 1st February to 29th February 1916

R. W. Blakeway - Major
O/C 194 Coy ASC

Instructions regarding War Diaries and Intelligence Summaries are contained in F. S. Regs., Part II. and the Staff Manual respectively. Title pages will be prepared in manuscript.

WAR DIARY
or
INTELLIGENCE SUMMARY.
(*Erase heading not required.*)

A. Blakeway Major
19A Comp: A.S.C.

Army Form C. 2118.

Place	Date	Hour	Summary of Events and Information	Remarks and references to Appendices
BUSSEBOOM.	1/2/16	9 A.M.	Supply wagons refilled on RENINGHELST — POPERINGHE Road - A.A & Q.M.G inspected Horses -	Fine -
"	2/2/16	"	" " " " " "	Fine -
"	3/2/16	"	" " " " " " Lt. Frischer went on leave -	Fine -
"	4/2/16	"	" " " " " "	Fine -
"	5/2/16	"	" " " " " " Lt WALENN returned from leave -	Fine -
"	6/2/16	"	" " " " " "	Rain in afternoon
"	7/2/16	"	" " " " " " Aeroplane raid, bombs dropped on outskirts of POPERINGHE	Showery -
"	8/2/16	"	" " " " " "	Fine morning - Rain in evening -
"	9/2/16	"	" " " " " "	Fine -
"	10/2/16	"	" " " " " " POPERINGHE shelled -	Fine -
"	11/2/16	"	" " " " " "	Heavy rain -
"	12/2/16	"	" " " " " " POPERINGHE bombed & shelled - 1. man of Comp: killed	Fine -
"	13/2/16	"	" " " " " " Lt. MacNAMARA went on leave - POP: shelled & bombed	Fine -
"	14/2/16	"	" " " " " " Lt. FRISCHER. returned from leave -	Fine -
"	15/2/16	"	" " " " " "	Gale blowing, fine morning & rain night
"	16/2/16	"	" " " " " "	Rain morning fine afternoon - Strong wind
"	17/2/16	"	" " " " " " Aeroplanes bombed at 11-30 p.m. -	Fine -
"	18/2/16	"	" " " " " " Aeroplanes dropped 11 bombs round POP: 7-45 A.M.	Wet -
"	19/2/16	"	" " " " " "	Fine -
"	20/2/16	"	" " " " " " Aeroplane raid on Camps round about - 7. A.M.	Fine -
"	21/2/16	8-30	" " " " " "	Fine -
"	22/2/16	"	" " " " " " POP: shelled about 3-30 A.M. Lt. MacNAMARA returned from leave -	Snow & Sleet -

Instructions regarding War Diaries and Intelligence Summaries are contained in F. S. Regs., Part II. and the Staff Manual respectively. Title pages will be prepared in manuscript.

Army Form C. 2118.

WAR DIARY
or
INTELLIGENCE SUMMARY.
(Erase heading not required.)

Place	Date	Hour	Summary of Events and Information	Remarks and references to Appendices
BUSSEBOOM.	23/2/16	8-30.	Supply wagons refilled on RENINGHELST – POPERINGHE Road –	Snow –
"	24/2/16	"	" " " OUDERDOM – " " Aeroplane dropped Bombs on POP:	Frosty & fine –
"	25/2/16	"	" " " " " "	Snow –
"	26/2/16	"	" " " " " " Aeroplanes dropped Bombs round Camp at 8-A M.	Fine morning Rain evening –
"	27/2/16	"	" " " " " "	Snow early morning Rain in afternoon
"	28/2/16	11-40	S " " " at WIPPENHOEK Siding –	Fine morning Rain evening –
"	29/2/16	"	" " " " "	

A W Blakeney Major
194. Comp: A.S.C.

2353 Wt. W2544/1454 700,000 5/15 D. D. & L. A.D.S.S./Forms/C. 2118.

Army Form C. 2118.

Instructions regarding War Diaries and Intelligence Summaries are contained in F. S. Regs., Part II. and the Staff Manual respectively. Title pages will be prepared in manuscript.

WAR DIARY

or

~~INTELLIGENCE SUMMARY.~~

(*Erase heading not required.*)

Place	Date	Hour	Summary of Events and Information	Remarks and references to Appendices
BOSSEBOOM.	1/2/16		Lt Col DOYLE, AA & QMG. 24th Division inspected horses of Divl Train at 8 a.m. Arranged that artillery supply wagons leave camp one hour later in order to give loaders time to distribute supplies into batteries and thereby obviate unnecessary blockage at refilling points. Promulgation of F.G.C.M. on Dr PEDEN – awarded 10 years penal servitude, commuted to 2 years imprisonment with hard labour.	Jh
"	2/2/16		Demonstration on the working of a snow plough held at coal dump was somewhat of a failure as the plough had been wrongly erected. Dry but cold.	Jh
"	3/2/16		Nothing of importance to report. Cold & windy.	Jh
"	4/2/16		Another demonstration on working of the snow plough – verdict – such a plough totally unsuitable for roads in this area & practically useless as a mud plough. – Very windy	Jh

2353 Wt. W2544/1454 700,000 5/15 D. D. & L. A.D.S.S./Forms/C. 2118.

Army Form C. 2118.

WAR DIARY
or
~~INTELLIGENCE SUMMARY~~.
(Erase heading not required.)

Instructions regarding War Diaries and Intelligence Summaries are contained in F. S. Regs., Part II. and the Staff Manual respectively. Title pages will be prepared in manuscript.

Place	Date	Hour	Summary of Events and Information	Remarks and references to Appendices
BOSSE-BOOM	5/2/16		Bright day - great aerial activity - Went H.Q. 7. Army Suggested method of issuing oranges which I purchased in lieu of vegetables - Bought 20 tons - H.Q 7. Army agreed to my proposal to issue 2/3 ration potatoes & in lieu of 1/3 ration onions the quantity of oranges which could be purchased with the money so saved - onions price to be 35 fr - This amounts to approx 3 oranges per man every 2 days - Lt. McCALLUM a/adjt on leave 2/Lt PLUMPTRE a/adjt -	
			Two Cases of measles have been diagnosed - 1 in 194 Coy & 1 in 195 Coy - All necessary precautionary measures taken by the M.O.	Th

2353 Wt. W2544/1454 700,000 5/15 D. D. & L. A.D.S.S./Forms/C. 2118.

Instructions regarding War Diaries and Intelligence Summaries are contained in F. S. Regs., Part II. and the Staff Manual respectively. Title pages will be prepared in manuscript.

WAR DIARY

or

~~INTELLIGENCE SUMMARY.~~

(*Erase heading not required.*)

Army Form C. 2118.

Place	Date	Hour	Summary of Events and Information	Remarks and references to Appendices
BUSSE BOOM	6/2/16		Dull quiet day - went DHQ a.m to press for reinforcements - Saw O.C Belgian mission re obtaining another barn - DDR & ADVS came to see horses & camps in p.m. Very wet evening - 2Lt A McCallum promoted Temp Lieut and appointed adjutant from 21/9/15 - vice Adams -	J.L.
	7/2/16	—	Several TAUBES over about 9 a.m. Bombs dropped near 19th Coy's Camp Our planes attacked but TAUBES made a miraculous escape - one appeared to descend rather rapidly - Usual aerial activity - for fine morning but Boche planes much lower than usual - forwarded report on Snow plough. no use - suggested wooden V shaped plough enclosing sketch -	J.L.
	8/2/16		Nothing much to report. Went to D.S.C at St SYLVESTRE CAPPEL to try & hasten repairs to cars & to arrange relief for Pte Ronaldson going on leave - Experimental bar for Limbered GS wagons for carrying 30 petrol cans sent D.H.Q and approved.	J.L.
	9/2/16		Met Belgian Mission officer at Barn near POPERINGHE also owner & Gendarme with a view to requisitioning - Owner shifty and disobliging - Got Lt. Le Comte de Pret to go into the matter. O.C 10th Bde RFA lunched & went round some of my horses to amuse him.	J.L.

2353 Wt. W2544/1454 700,000 5/15 D. D. & L. A.D.S.S./Forms/C. 2118.

Instructions regarding War Diaries and Intelligence Summaries are contained in F. S. Regs., Part II. and the Staff Manual respectively. Title pages will be prepared in manuscript.

WAR DIARY
or
INTELLIGENCE SUMMARY.
(Erase heading not required.)

Army Form C. 2118.

Place	Date	Hour	Summary of Events and Information	Remarks and references to Appendices
BOSSE-BOOM	10/2/16		Went round refilling points & on to railhead with S.S.O. Inspected ration dump, vegetable barn and coalyard - Two prisoners from 73rd Bde Headquarters. Most conflicting evidence on paper, sent for witnesses for next day. Heavy shelling of POPERINGHE afternoon and evening -	J.L.
	11/2/16		Received requisition order for Hosdey's barn. After enquiries the O.C. Belgian mission found he was evading his liabilities - Sergt Farrier Pick 197 Coy was shot by Dr. T. Moore same Coy A.S.C. at about 11.30 p.m. Went up at 11.45 pm to Camps to investigate & arrange for custody of prisoner - Pick dead. Got 74 Fd Ambce to take away body - Got to bed about 4.45 a.m. Heavy bombardment on whole front began at dusk	J.L.
	12/2/16		Case of Dr. Moore investigated by Major Blakeway. Remanded for F.G.C.M. on charge of murder - Aeroplane raid all near our Camps - Driver Lasley 194 Coy killed by bomb. Major Hamilton took summary of evidence but had to stop owing to distraction	

Instructions regarding War Diaries and Intelligence Summaries are contained in F. S. Regs., Part II. and the Staff Manual respectively. Title pages will be prepared in manuscript.

WAR DIARY
or
INTELLIGENCE SUMMARY.
(Erase heading not required.)

Army Form C. 2118.

Place	Date	Hour	Summary of Events and Information	Remarks and references to Appendices
BOSSE BOOM	12/2/16		of witnesses caused by bomb dropping - Paraded No 197 Coy and strafed them for behaviour when Dr. Moore threatened to shoot Capt Thompson & for not going for the man and disarming him, also for conduct generally - POPERINGE shelled - Heavy bombardment continued all day up to about 6 p.m.	Th.
	13/2/16		Fine bright day - Sent on Dr. Moore's case for F.G.C.M. Air raid about 3.30 to 4.30 p.m several bombs all round our camps - no casualties - POPERINGHE shelled for an hour at 6 p.m	Th.
	14/2/16		Adjutant returned from leave - Quiet morning - Strong westerly wind - 5.40 pm received orders to stand to - 6 pm saw G.O.C re Court martial for Dr Moore - He expressed great dissatisfaction with conduct of men of 197 Coy - Said he would parade them tomorrow. 5.30 pm to speak to them - Parade ordered & G.O.C's views told to O.C 197 Coy 8.15 pm order to "stand to" Cancelled - acknowledged -	Th.

2353 Wt. W2544/1454 700,000 5/15 D. D. & L. A.D.S.S./Forms/C. 2118.

Army Form C. 2118.

Instructions regarding War Diaries and Intelligence Summaries are contained in F. S. Regs., Part II. and the Staff Manual respectively. Title pages will be prepared in manuscript.

WAR DIARY
or
INTELLIGENCE SUMMARY.
(Erase heading not required.)

Place	Date	Hour	Summary of Events and Information	Remarks and references to Appendices
BOSSE BOOM	15/2/16		Wrote D.H.Q suggesting "stand to" order to Div^n Train be amplified to show exact steps to be taken — Recommended Lt Plumptre & Lieut Edwards for promotion to next higher rank — Officers N.C.O's and men of 197 Coy paraded at 5.30 pm and addressed by G.O.C 24th Division on the subject of the recent regrettable crime in that company.	[initials]
	16/2/16		Very windy day. Nothing of importance to report. Sent convoy with 5000 iron rations to YPRES for 73rd Inf. Bde. Leave suspended till further notice.	[initials]
	17/2/16		Leave reopened from 18th inclusive. Another convoy with 5000 iron rations sent to YPRES for 73rd Inf. Bde. Notified that trial of Dr MOORE would take place to-morrow in the lines of 197 Coy A.S.C. Camp. Windy. Zeppelin passed over camp about midnight & dropped two bombs in the vicinity	[initials]
	18/2/16		Trial of Dr. T. Moore on a charge of murder. Court opened 10.0 am Closed 5.20 p.m. Aeroplane dropped 11 bombs about 8.30 am to the West of our camps.	[initials]
	19/2/16		Received 17 H.D. horses from 50th Division — good stamp but poor condition — Wrote French Mission re rations order for interpreters not to proceed outside divisional area — Summary of evidence Dr Mills for F.G.C.M, insubordination & drunk.	[initials]

2353 Wt. W2544/1454 700,000 5/15 D. D. & L. A.D.S.S./Forms/C. 2118.

Instructions regarding War Diaries and Intelligence Summaries are contained in F. S. Regs., Part II. and the Staff Manual respectively. Title pages will be prepared in manuscript.

WAR DIARY
or
INTELLIGENCE SUMMARY.
(Erase heading not required.)

Army Form C. 2118.

Place	Date	Hour	Summary of Events and Information	Remarks and references to Appendices
20/2/16			Bright sunshine. Great aerial activity. Bombs dropped at POPERINGHE Station & all round camps but no casualties. Reinforcement of 6 OR – 1 Farrier, 1 Saddler & 4 others reported for duty. Measles contacts released for duty.	[illegible]
21/2/16			Inspected sanitary arrangements in the camps – good. Aerial activity continued Dull. Bombs dropped midnight, 3 am & 8. a.m. Went to H.Q V Corps & saw Gen Atcherley about traffic control also got from him instructions to change our refilling point on 24/2/16	[illegible]
	22/2/16		POPERINGHE shelled for an hour about 3. a.m. Bombs dropped near camps 1.15 a.m no casualties. – Arranged full rum issue tomorrow – fairly heavy snowstorm – POPERINGHE shelled about 4.30 p.m just as I was leaving – very heavy bombardment all along the line then commenced lasting till about 7.30 p.m. Frosty night –	[illegible]

2353 Wt. W2544/1454 700,000 5/15 D. D. & L. A.D.S.S./Forms/C. 2118.

Instructions regarding War Diaries and Intelligence Summaries are contained in F. S. Regs., Part II. and the Staff Manual respectively. Title pages will be prepared in manuscript.

WAR DIARY
or
~~INTELLIGENCE SUMMARY.~~
(Erase heading not required.)

Army Form C. 2118.

Place	Date	Hour	Summary of Events and Information	Remarks and references to Appendices
BOSSE BOOM	23/2/16		Temp 2nd Lieut L. G. BENNETT reported for duty from No 5 Reserve Park & posted to 196 Coy vice Lt. A. McCallum adjutant. More snow. Full issue of rum to Division. Reinforcements 5 men received. Drew from POP station 2 wagon loads anthracite duff & clay & issued to units 73rd Inf Bde for experiment as fuel. Issued 1/4 extra fuel owing to severity of weather.	[initials]
"	24/2/16		Refilling on the POPERINGHE - OUDERDOM road. Bombs dropped from aeroplanes at 11.30 am and 2pm - no damage. Notified by D.H.Q that Train Headquarter would probably move pro tem to make room for a ~~Bde~~ Bde H.Q. Gentle frost.	[initials]
	25/2/16		F.G.C.M of Dr Mills A. J., 195 Coy A.S.C at H.Q 108 Bde R.F.A. Visited DA,QMG V Corps re movement of headquarters of Train to RENINGHELST - Sent for with S.S.O at 9 pm by DA & QMG V Corps for discussion of possibility of sharing WIPPENHOEK siding with 50th Division as refilling point and eliminating supply column. Met O.C 50th Div Train & his S.S.O and arranged	

2353 Wt. W2544/1454 700,000 5/15 D. D. & L. A.D.S.S./Forms/C. 2118.

Instructions regarding War Diaries and Intelligence Summaries are contained in F. S. Regs., Part II. and the Staff Manual respectively. Title pages will be prepared in manuscript.

Army Form C. 2118.

WAR DIARY
or
INTELLIGENCE SUMMARY.
(Erase heading not required.)

Place	Date	Hour	Summary of Events and Information	Remarks and references to Appendices
			to visit his refilling point at 8.40 am tomorrow & see his system of refilling direct into wagons, more especially with regard to methods of distribution & working transport at siding — Returned HQ. 11. pm.	Sh
BUSSEBOOM.	26/3/16	4.3am	Promulgation of F.G.C.M of Dr T. MOORE, 197 Coy, A.S.C on charge of murder to prisoner.	
		5.40 am	Dr T. Moore shot. Buried map Ref Sheet 28 G 22 b 8 8. Promulgated to 197 Coy 5.30 am.	
		6.0	Promulgation of F.G.C.M. of S.S. Sadd. Webb 194 Coy.	
		6.30	Promulgation of F.G.C.M. of Cpl. Robertson 196 Coy.	
		8.40	Visited advanced railhead at WIPPENHOEK. Find that 50th Div Train get clear about 9 am if they start at 6.30 am. This would mean we could get to work about 9.30 am and get the last wagons clear from 12 30pm to 1 pm. Went on to DA & QMG, V Corps & discussed the question again & was told the change would probably take place on Tuesday 29th inst. Visited A.D.S.T. II Army about ¼ extra issues of fuel. Also got the S.O. of the A.S.C excused a class of instruction owing to move of refilling	

Instructions regarding War Diaries and Intelligence Summaries are contained in F. S. Regs., Part II. and the Staff Manual respectively. Title pages will be prepared in manuscript.

WAR DIARY
or
INTELLIGENCE SUMMARY.
(Erase heading not required.)

Army Form C. 2118.

Place	Date	Hour	Summary of Events and Information	Remarks and references to Appendices
26/2/16	cont'd		point to WIPPENHOEK. Also spoke about getting 2nd Lt ADAMS replaced as he has been absent from duty sick since Sept 1915. Went to H.Q. 50th Div. Train re accommodation for our S.C. loaders at WIPPENHOEK. Saw Q. branch 17th Div. re getting billets for H.Q. train in RENINGHELST and on to H.Q. 24th Div. re same subject. Made arrangements for double refil to-morrow for certain units – Returned 9 G.S. wagons on loan from 2nd Army Aux. H.T. Coy at 9 a.m.	Th
27/2/16.			Trench units and R.A. in the line refilled with two days' supplies. Arrangements made for the transfer of refilling points to the new siding on the BOESCHEPE – POPERINGHE road at WIPPENHOEK on 29th inst. Promulgation of F.G.C.M of Dr. Mills, 195 Coy, A.S.C – Awarded 6 mths. imprisonment with H.L. for drunkeness. Notified by phone by D.A.Q. that refilling would commence to-morrow and not on 29th at WIPPENHOEK siding – Orders issued accordingly. Informed by D.A.Q. no billets in RENINGHELST for these headquarters. Arranged billets in POPERINGHE with Town Major – Move postponed till 1st March – Thaw.	

2353 Wt. W2544/1454 700,000 5/15 D. D. & L. A.D.S.S./Forms/C. 2118.

Instructions regarding War Diaries and Intelligence Summaries are contained in F. S. Regs., Part II. and the Staff Manual respectively. Title pages will be prepared in manuscript.

WAR DIARY

~~or~~

~~INTELLIGENCE SUMMARY.~~

(Erase heading not required.)

Army Form C. 2118.

Place	Date	Hour	Summary of Events and Information	Remarks and references to Appendices
BISSEBOOM.	28/2/16		Refilling at WIPPENHOEK in following order - Group 'C'. Group 'B' Group 'D' and Group 'A' commencing 10.30 a.m. - finished 1.15 p.m. Last wagons after offloading to units returning between 7 and 8 p.m. 17th Divn refill on POPERINGHE - OUDERDOM road at old 24th Divn refilling points. Genl Fanshaw visited refilling point.	[initials]
	29/2/16.		Considerable improvement in refilling at WIPPENHOEK. Train in position 9.45 a.m. Last wagons clear at 12.40 p.m. 4000 rations sent to units in the trenches and R.A. batteries in action at 6.0 p.m. Notified by D.H.Q. that these headquarters would leave BUSSEBOOM to-morrow and hand over billets to H.Q. 8th Inf Bde - 3rd Divn.	[initials]

2353 Wt. W2544/1454 700,000 5/15 D. D. & L. A.D.S.S./Forms/C. 2118.

24 Div Train
Vol 7

- CONFIDENTIAL -

War Diary

of

O.C. 24th Divisional Train.

From 1-3-16 To 31-3-16.

Confidential

War Diary

of

194 Coy ASC

from 1st to 31st March 1916

R.W. Blakeway - Major.
Cmdg. 194 Coy. ASC

194 ASC

Instructions regarding War Diaries and Intelligence Summaries are contained in F. S. Regs., Part II. and the Staff Manual respectively. Title pages will be prepared in manuscript.

WAR DIARY
or
INTELLIGENCE SUMMARY.
(Erase heading not required.)

Army Form C. 2118.

T.W. Blakeway Major

Place	Date	Hour	Summary of Events and Information	Remarks and references to Appendices
BUSEBOOM	1/3/16	11 A.M.	Supply wagons refilled at WIPPENHOEK Siding –	Fine –
"	2/3/16	"	" " " " " Heavy big gun fire –	Fine –
"	3/3/16	"	" " " " " POP: shelled –	Very wet afternoon.
"	4/3/16	"	" " " " " POP: shelled –	Snowstorm in morning –
"	5/3/16	"	" " " " " POP: shelled –	Fine day, snow at night –
"	6/3/16	"	" " " " "	Fine, snowshowers
"	7/3/16	"	" " " " "	Snow all day –
"	8/3/16	"	" " " " "	Fine –
"	9/3/16	"	" " " " "	Fine –
"	10/3/16	"	" " " " "	Fine –
"	11/3/16	"	" " " " " Major T.W. BLAKEWAY assumed Command of the Train in the absence of Lt. Col. F.B. LORD. – Sick.	Fine –
"	12/3/16	"		Fine –
"	13/3/16	"	Supply wagons refilled at WIPPENHOEK Siding.	Fine
"	14/3/16	"	" " " "	"
"	15/3/16	"	" " " "	"
"	16/3/16	"	" " " " " Preliminary Orders concerning move received.	"
"	17/3/16	"	" " " " Orders to move received. DAC & half of each Art/Bde to move on 17th & the remainder of R.F.A. 18th. 2/Lt Plumptre in charge of first party of this Coy. – Lt COL. F.B. LORD returned to duty. MAJOR T.W. BLAKEWAY took over command of Company –	"
"	18/3/16	11 A.M.	Supply wagons under Lt McNAMARA refilled at WIPPENHOEK Siding & then marched to their various units in III CANADIAN REST AREA	Fine –
		9 A.M.	Company moved off for new Camp at FLÊTRE, arriving at 3 p.m. Supply wagons under Lt PLUMPTRE refilled at 2-30 p.m on FLÊTRE – GODEWAERSWELDE Road –	
"	19/3/16	9 A.M.	Whole of Supply wagons refilled on above Road	Fine

2353 Wt. W2544/1454 700,000 5/15 D. D. & L. A.D.S.S./Forms/C. 2118.

Instructions regarding War Diaries and Intelligence Summaries are contained in F. S. Regs., Part II. and the Staff Manual respectively. Title pages will be prepared in manuscript.

WAR DIARY
or
INTELLIGENCE SUMMARY.
(*Erase heading not required.*)

Army Form C. 2118.

Place	Date	Hour	Summary of Events and Information	Remarks and references to Appendices
FLÊTRE	20/3/16	8-30am	Supply wagon refilled on FLÊTRE - GODEWAERSWELDE Road - Lt. Col. F.B. LORD went on leave, MAJOR T.W. BLAKEWAY assumed command of Train during his absence -	Fine -
"	21/3/16	"	Supply wagons refilled on FLÊTRE - CAESTRE Road -	Rain -
"	22/3/16	"	" " " " " "	Rain -
"	23/3/16	"	" " " " " "	Fine -
"	24/3/16	"	" " " " " "	Snow -
"	25/3/16	"	" " " " " "	Changeable.
"	26/3/16	"	" " " " " "	— " —
"	27/3/16	"	" " " " " "	— " —
"	28/3/16	"	" " " " " "	Fine
"	29/3/16	"	" " " " " " Preliminary orders to move received	— " —
"	30/3/16		" " Lt. Col. F.B LORD returned from leave & took over command of the Train from Major T.W. BLAKEWAY.	— " —
"	31/3/16	"	" " " " " "	Fine -

T.W. Blakeway Major -

2353 Wt. W2544/1454 700,000 5/15 D. D. & L. A.D.S.S./Forms/C. 2118.

Instructions regarding War Diaries and Intelligence Summaries are contained in F. S. Regs., Part II. and the Staff Manual respectively. Title pages will be prepared in manuscript.

WAR DIARY
~~or~~
~~INTELLIGENCE SUMMARY.~~
(Erase heading not required.)

Army Form C. 2118.

Place	Date	Hour	Summary of Events and Information	Remarks and references to Appendices
BUSSEBOOM	1/3/16		Train H.Q. move to POPERINGHE. and billets handed over to H.Q. 8th Inf. Bde. Dull.	Jh
POPERINGHE	2/3/16		Nothing of importance to report. Notified by wire of capture of 260 prisoners. Wet.	Jh
"	3/3/16		POPERINGHE shelled - reported 35 casualties - no casualties in this unit.	Jh
"	4/3/16		3200 emergency rations issued to 72nd Inf. Brigade - 800 to each battalion. Full rum issue to the Division. Snow and rain. Reinforcement of 6 drivers and 1 farrier arrive. Visited D.H.Q. re postal service.	Jh
"	5/3/16		Poperinghe shelled about 1 a.m. Nothing of importance to report. Snow showers.	Jh

2353 Wt. W2544/1454 700,000 5/15 D. D. & L. A.D.S.S./Forms/C. 2118.

Instructions regarding War Diaries and Intelligence Summaries are contained in F. S. Regs., Part II. and the Staff Manual respectively. Title pages will be prepared in manuscript.

WAR DIARY

~~or~~

~~INTELLIGENCE SUMMARY.~~

(Erase heading not required.)

Army Form C. 2118.

Place	Date	Hour	Summary of Events and Information	Remarks and references to Appendices
POPERINGHE	6/3/16		Showery. Refilling to take place half an hour earlier from to-morrow inclusive — Companies notified. Nothing to report. Refilling finished 12 noon.	AWC
	7/3/16		Nothing to report. Snow	AWC
	8/3/16		Full issue of rum to the division. 2Lt J. K. FROST proceeded to England. Capt J. P. THOMPSON sent to No 12 C.C.S. - sick. Lieut W. A. MACGREGOR sent to 72 Fld. Amb. sick. Frost at night	AWC
	9/3/16		Visited H.Q. II Army re exchange of an open Sunbeam car off this unit for a closed car of M.T. 5th Bde R.G.A. Fair. Recommendations for "Honours and Awards" sent to D.H.Q.	AWC
	10/3/16		Nothing to report.	AWC

2353 Wt. W2544/1454 700,000 5/15 D. D. & L. A.D.S.S./Forms/C. 2118.

Instructions regarding War Diaries and Intelligence Summaries are contained in F. S. Regs., Part II. and the Staff Manual respectively. Title pages will be prepared in manuscript.

WAR DIARY
or
~~INTELLIGENCE SUMMARY~~.
(Erase heading not required.)

Army Form C. 2118.

Place	Date	Hour	Summary of Events and Information	Remarks and references to Appendices
POPERINGHE	11/3/16		Lieut Colonel F B LORD admitted No 12 C.C.S. sick. Major T.W. BLAKEWAY assumes command. Exchanged open Sunbeam No M14900 for closed Wolseley of A.S.C. M.T. 12th Bde R.G.A. Showery.	AmdC
"	12/3/16		Lieut W. A. MACGREGOR discharged hospital - returned to duty. Very fine day. Coal dumped exhausted - DDS&T wired. Notified by wire from DDS&T that the purchase or requisition of potatoes grown in BELGIUM must cease -	AmdC
"	13/3/16.		Coal arrived. Purchase of potatoes in FRANCE at a much higher rate - Very fine day.	AmdC
"	14/3/16		Nothing of importance to report	AmdC
"	15/3/16		Received preliminary Operation Orders for the move of the division to the area at present occupied by 1st Canadian Division. Orders circulated to O.C. Coys. Fine.	AmdC

2353 Wt. W2544/1454 700,000 5/15 D. D. & L. A.D.S.S./Forms/C. 2118.

Instructions regarding War Diaries and Intelligence Summaries are contained in F. S. Regs., Part II. and the Staff Manual respectively. Title pages will be prepared in manuscript.

WAR DIARY
or
INTELLIGENCE SUMMARY.
(Erase heading not required.)

Army Form C. 2118.

Place	Date	Hour	Summary of Events and Information	Remarks and references to Appendices
POPERINGHE	16/3/16		Fine day. Orders for move of division altered. Move commences 19th inst. Lieut J. K. ROBERTSON admitted 72nd Fld. Amb. sick. Arrangements made with 3rd Can Divl Train for taking over respective camps. Reinforcement of 1 Sergeant 1 wheeler and 11 drivers arrived. Instructions as to changes in Supply groups issued to O.C. Coys. Baggage wagons and horses sent to all units.	AmC
	17/3/16		Artillery commence to move out to new area. Lieut F. M. PLUMPTRE in charge of Supply wagons. Refill at WIPPENHOEK. Lt Col Lord and Capt Thompson returned to duty from hospital	AmC
	18/3/16		Remainder of 194 Coy proceed to new area to camp at Map 27 W 5 d 8 8 197 Coy proceed to R. 35. c. 5 . 10. Visited ~~___~~ billets in new area.	AmC
	19/3/16		Refilling at Map Ref. Sheet 27. A Group W. 5 c 3 5 D Group X 4 c 4 7. B and C Groups on POPERINGHE - BUSSEBOOM Road.	AmC

2353 Wt. W2544/1454 700,000 5/15 D. D. & L. A.D.S.S./Forms/C. 2118.

Army Form C. 2118.

Instructions regarding War Diaries and Intelligence Summaries are contained in F. S. Regs., Part II. and the Staff Manual respectively. Title pages will be prepared in manuscript.

WAR DIARY
or
INTELLIGENCE SUMMARY.

(Erase heading not required.)

Place	Date	Hour	Summary of Events and Information	Remarks and references to Appendices
POPERINGHE	20/3/16		Lt Col LORD proceeded on leave. Operation Orders for relief of 1st Canadian Division by 24th Division received and distributed.	AmC
"	21/3/16		Hd. Qrs. Divl Train and 196 Coy proceeded to W. 6 c 5.5 and X 4 c 3.3 respectively. Showery. No billets for Train Hd. Qrs	AmC
FLETRE	22/3/16		Visited 1st Canadian Divl ~~Train~~ Area and noted camps and refilling points	AmC
"	23/3/16		Two battalions of 73rd Inf. Bde. ~~[illegible]~~ proceeded to new area KORTEPYP with supply wagons full. 195 Coy proceeded from BUSSEBOOM to EECKE and arrived 3 p.m.	AmC
"	24/3/16		Snow. 'D' Group refill both at map 27 X 4 c 4.7 and map 28 S. 30 c 1.7 ~~[illegible]~~ 2nd LIEUT PUGH reported for duty.	AmC

2353 Wt. W2544/1454 700,000 5/15 D. D. & L. A.D.S.S./Forms/C. 2118.

Army Form C. 2118.

WAR DIARY
or
~~INTELLIGENCE SUMMARY.~~
(Erase heading not required.)

Instructions regarding War Diaries and Intelligence Summaries are contained in F. S. Regs., Part II. and the Staff Manual respectively. Title pages will be prepared in manuscript.

Place	Date	Hour	Summary of Events and Information	Remarks and references to Appendices
FLETRE	25/3/16		197 Coy proceed to new area Map 28 S 30 c 1·8. Orders for move of 72nd Infantry Brigade received and distributed. 2Lieut PUGH posted to 197 Coy. Fine day. Visited DDS&T Second Army re price of potatoes & the difficulty of obtaining transport for large quantities from Ireland. Dried vegetable issue begins.	AmC
	26/3/16		D Group refill at S. 30 d. 9.5. Reinforcement of 2 drivers report.	AmC
	27/3/16		C refill ~~at~~ new area at S 9 a 6 7 at 11.0 a.m. Lieut A. St.G. ADAMS discharged hospital reported for duty. 2Lieut W. A Weddlood (195 Coy) sent in command of 18 limbered wagons &c to A.H.T.D ABBEVILLE.	AmC
	28/3/16		196 Coy proceeded to new area - Camp ~~[illegible]~~ S 3 d 6 3 Lieut A. St G. Adams posted to 197 Coy.	AmC

2353 Wt. W2544/1454 700,000 5/15 D. D. & L. A.D.S.S./Forms/C. 2118.

Instructions regarding War Diaries and Intelligence Summaries are contained in F. S. Regs., Part II. and the Staff Manual respectively. Title pages will be prepared in manuscript.

WAR DIARY
or
INTELLIGENCE SUMMARY.
(Erase heading not required.)

Army Form C. 2118.

Place	Date	Hour	Summary of Events and Information	Remarks and references to Appendices
FLETRE	29/3/16		Inspection of horses, harness & wagons of 194 Coy at refilling point. Arranged to hand over these headquarters to 1st Can. Divl Train on 1st prox. Orders for move of R.A. received and distributed.	AmC
"	30/3/16		Lt. Col Lord returned from leave of absence in England. Visited H.Q 1st Can. Div. Train. D H Q move to ST. JANS CAPPEL. Half of 'B' Group refill in new area at T 25 b 8. 2 (map 28).	AmC
"	31/3/16		Hd. Qrs. Div Train move to new area map 28 S. 30 d 1.9 – 195 Coy move to camp on NEUVE EGLISE – map 28 T 26 a 1.9. Half supply wagons of 194 Coy – artillery units – move to S 30 d 1.9 Fine.	AmC

194 Coy
A.S.C.
Vol 9

24 Div Train

Confidential

War Diary
of
194 Coy. A.S.C.
from 1st. April to 30th April 1916

[illegible] Lt.
O/c 194 Coy. A.S.C.

1

24 Div Train
Vol ~~7~~ 8

Confidential

War Diary of

24th Divisional Train

From April 1st to 30th 1916

Instructions regarding War Diaries and Intelligence Summaries are contained in F. S. Regs., Part II. and the Staff Manual respectively. Title pages will be prepared in manuscript.

WAR DIARY
or
~~INTELLIGENCE SUMMARY.~~
(Erase heading not required.)

Army Form C. 2118.

Place	Date	Hour	Summary of Events and Information	Remarks and references to Appendices
DE BROCKEN	1/4/16.		Remainder of 194 Coy with the exception of wagons of D.A.C. move to S 30 c 1·9. All groups refill in new area	[illegible]
	2/4/16		Inspected camps and moved 195 and 196 Coys to fresh ground. Inspected first line transport of ~~17th Inf Bde~~ 12th Bns Sherwood Foresters – Fine.	[illegible]
	3/4/16		Suggestion from DHQ to eliminate Supply Column. Went to railhead – BAILLEUL – and reported to D.H.Q the unsuitability of the station yard for refilling purposes. Inspected first line transport of 17th Inf. Bde. Fine. Regrouping of units forwarded to D.H.Q to take effect from 6th inst.	[illegible]
	4/4/16		Inspected first line transport of 8th Buffs & 9th Sussex. Regrouping of units for supply purposes as arranged published in Divl. Orders and arrangements made accordingly as regards transport.	[illegible]

2353 Wt. W2544/1454 700,000 5/15 D. D. & L. A.D.S.S./Forms/C. 2118.

Instructions regarding War Diaries and Intelligence Summaries are contained in F. S. Regs., Part II. and the Staff Manual respectively. Title pages will be prepared in manuscript.

WAR DIARY
or
~~INTELLIGENCE SUMMARY.~~

(Erase heading not required.)

Army Form C. 2118.

Place	Date	Hour	Summary of Events and Information	Remarks and references to Appendices
DE BROCKEN	5/4/16		Inspected first line transport of 7th Northants, 12th Middlesex and 2nd Leinsters. Drill. Notified by D.H.Q. that units would be grouped as on arrival in this area and that refilling direct from railhead would commence on 8th inst.	[initials]
	6/4/16		Inspected first line transport of 73rd Inf. Bde M.G.C. S.S.O. proceeded on leave – Lieut Edwards acting S.S.O. – 2Lieut PUGH taking over duties of S.O. 17th Inf. Bde. 2Lt Wildblood returned after handing over transport to A.H.T.D. (ABBEVILLE).	[initials]
	7/4/16		Inspected 1st Line Transport of 72nd Inf. Bde. Conference at headquarters Second Army re requisitioning & purchasing straw and vegetables.	[initials]
	8/4/16		Supplies loaded into train transport direct at railhead – BAILLEUL. Groups loaded in bulk. First group commenced	Over

2353 Wt. W2544/1454 700,000 5/15 D. D. & L. A.D.S.S./Forms/C. 2118.

Instructions regarding War Diaries and Intelligence Summaries are contained in F. S. Regs., Part II. and the Staff Manual respectively. Title pages will be prepared in manuscript.

WAR DIARY

~~INTELLIGENCE~~ SUMMARY.

(*Erase heading not required.*)

Army Form C. 2118.

Place	Date	Hour	Summary of Events and Information	Remarks and references to Appendices
DE BROOKEN	8/4/16		at 9.45 am - station yard cleared 11.50 a.m. Fine.	[initials]
	9/4/16		Loading in groups at BAILLEUL commenced at 8.15 a.m. Report on 1st Line Transport of the division sent to D.H.Q. Reinforcement of 2 drivers arrived & posted to 194 Coy. Fine.	[initials]
			18 Line transport reported on as good generally - more attention to be paid to dubbing harness & cleaning steel work - 73 M/G Coy indifferent -	
	10/4/16		Inspected transport of 74th Fld. Ambulance. Fine. Inspected transport 72nd Field Ambce -	[initials]
	11/4/16		Loading in groups at BAILLEUL commenced at 8.0 a.m. Wet. Notified by DDS&T Second Army that establishment of Cars for the train would be three and the two to be withdrawn would be returned to 2nd Army Troops Supply Column on 12th inst.	[initials]

2353 Wt. W2544/1454 700,000 5/15 D. D. & L. A.D.S.S./Forms/C. 2118.

Army Form C. 2118.

Instructions regarding War Diaries and Intelligence Summaries are contained in F. S. Regs., Part II. and the Staff Manual respectively. Title pages will be prepared in manuscript.

WAR DIARY
or
INTELLIGENCE SUMMARY.
(Erase heading not required.)

Place	Date	Hour	Summary of Events and Information	Remarks and references to Appendices
DE BROEKEN	12/4/16		Wet. Notified by G.H.Q. that leave was suspended and all ranks had to be with their units by 18th inst.	[initials]
"	13/4/16		~~[struck out]~~ Stormy – Went Cassel to see DDST re YMCA rations, price of potatoes & motor bicycles vice cars for R.O.S. Refilling at Bailleul 15 K 1 hour 15 minutes – M. BOURGEAT relieved by M. LEMOINE as interpreter to 96 Coy.	[initials]
	14/4/16		Wet & stormy – Refilling 1 hour & 5 minutes – Looked for billets in BAILLEUL with a view to moving Train Headquarters there shortly.	[initials]
"	15/4/16		Nothing to report.	

2353 Wt. W2544/1454 700,000 5/15 D. D. & L. A.D.S.S./Forms/C. 2118.

Army Form C. 2118.

Instructions regarding War Diaries and Intelligence Summaries are contained in F. S. Regs., Part II. and the Staff Manual respectively. Title pages will be prepared in manuscript.

WAR DIARY
or
INTELLIGENCE SUMMARY.
(Erase heading not required.)

Place	Date	Hour	Summary of Events and Information	Remarks and references to Appendices
DE BROOKEN	16/4/16		Sunshine. Nothing to report.	AWC
	17/4/16		Wet & stormy. Summary of Evidence in case of Dr SWEETMAN (194 Coy) taken. S.S.O. returned from leave. Billets taken in BAILLEUL	AWC
	18/4/16		Wet. Nothing to report. LIEUT S. W. BATTLE 60th LONDON Divl Train reported and attached for three days instruction.	AWC
	19/4/16		Wet & stormy.	AWC
	20/4/16		~~[illegible]~~ Fair. 213 Remounts collected for the division at BAILLEUL station and picketed for the night in 197 Coys Camp.	AWC

2353 Wt. W2544/1454 700,000 5/15 D. D. & L. A.D.S.S./Forms/C. 2118.

Instructions regarding War Diaries and Intelligence Summaries are contained in F. S. Regs., Part II, and the Staff Manual respectively. Title pages will be prepared in manuscript.

WAR DIARY
or
INTELLIGENCE SUMMARY.
(Erase heading not required.)

Army Form C. 2118.

Place	Date	Hour	Summary of Events and Information	Remarks and references to Appendices
DE BROCKEN	21/4/16		Train Headquarters move to Asylum House BAILLEUL Map Ref Sheet 78 S 14 b 3.½. Remounts distributed – 20 H.D for Divl Train. Lieut W. S. BATTLE returns to his unit	Amd C.
BAILLEUL	22/4/16		Notified that Lieut Robertson evacuated to England on 11-4-16. Wet.	Amd C
	23/4/16		Fine. 2nd Lieut C. C. GALE reported for duty & posted to 197 Coys	Amd C
	24/4/16		Fine. Bombs dropped in vicinity of this billet about 4.15 a.m. setting fire & destroying 7 motor ambulances. G.O.C., 24th Division visited railhead when division was refilling. Notified that leave would re-open on 26th inst.	Amd C

2353 Wt. W2544/1454 700,000 5/15 D. D. & L. A.D.S.S./Forms/C. 2118.

Instructions regarding War Diaries and Intelligence Summaries are contained in F. S. Regs., Part II. and the Staff Manual respectively. Title pages will be prepared in manuscript.

WAR DIARY
or
INTELLIGENCE SUMMARY.
(Erase heading not required.)

Army Form C. 2118.

Place	Date	Hour	Summary of Events and Information	Remarks and references to Appendices
BAILLEUL	25/4/16		Arranged for F.G.C.M. of Dr. Sweetman, 194 Coy, to-morrow at HQ Qrs Rt. R.F. Fine. 2Lieut C.C. GALE admitted to hospital (sick)	AWC
"	26/4/16		F.G.C.M at 11 a.m. of Dr. Sweetman - case dismissed. Fine.	AWC
"	27/4/16.		Notified that Divl. Mtd. Troops - Glasgow Yeomanry and Cyclist Coy - would go for a fortnights training in the back area on the 29th inst. Fine	AWC
"	28/4/16.		Fine. Nothing to report.	AWC
"	29/4/16		Fine. 2Lieut C.C. GALE discharged hospital. Gen. Atcherley V Corps inspected camp of 194 Coy.	AWC
"	30/4/16		Fine. Gas Alert & "Stand to". Presence of gas felt about 1.30 a.m. No casualties	AWC

2353 Wt. W2544/1454 700,000 5/15 D. D. & L. A.D.S.S./Forms/C. 2118.

Vol 14

~ CONFIDENTIAL ~

War Diary

of

O.C. 24th Divisional Train

From 1-10-16 To 31-10-16

Instructions regarding War Diaries and Intelligence Summaries are contained in F. S. Regs., Part II. and the Staff Manual respectively. Title pages will be prepared in manuscript.

WAR DIARY

or

INTELLIGENCE SUMMARY.

(Erase heading not required.)

Army Form C. 2118.

Place	Date	Hour	Summary of Events and Information	Remarks and references to Appendices
ESTREE CAUCHIE	1/10/16.		Notified that Lieut H. K. Bagshaw · 197 Coy. A.S.C. was evacuated to England on 22/9/16. and struck off strength from 5-10-16.	
"	2/10/16		O.O. No 98 received re relief of 9th Div. Artillery by 24th Div Artillery commencing night 3/4 Oct.	
"	3/10/16		194 Coy ASC arrive at FRESNICOURT. 2 Lieut E. W. L. Martin - 195 Coy ASC promoted Lieutenant to date from 11/9/16.	
"	4/10/16		24 Artillery Group refill at Q. 26 b. central Sheet 36 B at 9.30 a.m. Issue of 3500 rum rations to R.A. Bdes.	
"	5/10/16		Lieut S. K. Walton, 194 Coy A.S.C departed for duty with 23rd Div Train and struck off the strength accordingly.	
"	6/10/16		O.O 99 received re relief of 73rd Bde by 17th Inf. Bde on 10th inst.	

Army Form C. 2118.

Instructions regarding War Diaries and Intelligence Summaries are contained in F. S. Regs., Part II. and the Staff Manual respectively. Title pages will be prepared in manuscript.

WAR DIARY
or
INTELLIGENCE SUMMARY.
(*Erase heading not required.*)

Place	Date	Hour	Summary of Events and Information	Remarks and references to Appendices
ESTREE CAUCHIE	7/10/16		Wet. Nothing to report. M. Girand, French Interpreter, posted to 24th Div Train and attached to 196 Coy ASC. 106th Bde R.F.A. move into ESTREE CAUCHIE.	
"	8/10/16		2/Lieut A.C. Bendit – Claims Officer proceeded on leave to England. Lt. Col F.B Lord, ASC returned from leave to England. 194 Coy move to GAUCHIN LEGAL.	
"	9/10/16		Nothing to report.	
"	10/10/16		Tempy 2nd Lieut A.W.P. Le SUEUR reported for duty and posted to 197 Coy A.S.C vice Lieut H.K. Bagshaw to England. Relief of 73rd Bde by 17th Bde in CARENCY sector.	
"	11/10/16		Fair – Nothing to report.	
"	12/10/16		7 GS wagons (complete turnout) of a surplus of 9 on the reorganisation of Div! Artillery sent under Lieut K.M. Plumptre to THEROUANNE. Stormy.	

2353 Wt. W2544/1454 700,000 5/15 D. D. & L. A.D.S.S./Forms/C. 2118.

Army Form C. 2118.

Instructions regarding War Diaries and Intelligence Summaries are contained in F. S. Regs., Part II. and the Staff Manual respectively. Title pages will be prepared in manuscript.

WAR DIARY
or
INTELLIGENCE SUMMARY.
(Erase heading not required.)

Place	Date	Hour	Summary of Events and Information	Remarks and references to Appendices
ESTREE CAUCHIE	13/10/16.		Collected 12 Riders and 1 L.D. for 24th Division at BRUAY station – 1 Rider for D.T. to 195 Coy. Military Medal for Bravery in the Field awarded to Cpl Elliott 196 Coy – Sgt Lees 194 Coy & Cpl Pratchett (195 Co)	
"	14/10/16.		Div: Commander dispenses with trial of Dr. Pitfield, 194 Coy ASC, as deserter from Navy. Ordered to give supply wagons in the afternoons for the transport of working parties – horsed by artillery	
"	15/10/16.		Nothing to report.	
"	16/10/16		Reinforcement of three S.S.M. and 1 supply detail. S.S.M Riley to 74th Fld. Amb, S.S.M Laurie to 194 Coy vice S.S.M. Knowles to 73rd Fld. Amb and S.S.M Tattersall to 72nd Fld. Amb. – Supply detail to 196 Coy. Car sent to 1st Army Purchasing Board (BETHUNE).	
"	17/10/16		Operation Order No 101 re relief of 40th Division by 24th Division received. Capt Holt, R.A.M.C. proceeded on leave to England.	
"	18/10/16		Nothing to report.	
"	19/10/16		Capt: Adams proceeded on leave. Refilling for A B & C Groups at 8·30 a.m – D Group at 8·15 am. 2Lieut A.C. Bendit returned from leave to England	

2353 Wt. W2544/1454 700,000 5/15 D. D. & L. A.D.S.S./Forms/C. 2118.

Instructions regarding War Diaries and Intelligence Summaries are contained in F. S. Regs., Part II. and the Staff Manual respectively. Title pages will be prepared in manuscript.

WAR DIARY
or
INTELLIGENCE SUMMARY.
(Erase heading not required.)

Army Form C. 2118.

Place	Date	Hour	Summary of Events and Information	Remarks and references to Appendices
ESTREE CAUCHIE	20/10/16		Capt J. P. Thompson proceeded on leave. Received Operation Order No 102 re relief of 40th Division (less artillery) by 24th Division (less artillery) and Operation Order No 103 re relief of 24th Division by 1st Canadian Division. Reinforcement of 2 C.S.M. - 1 posted to 195 Coy the other to be returned to base. Gas Alert. Lieut Plumptre returned from ABBEVILLE Base Horse Transport Depot.	
"	21/10/16		Nothing to report. Frosty. Car returned from 1st Army Purchase Board.	
"	22/10/16		Major T. W. Blakeway proceeded on leave to England.	
"	23/10/16		Reinforcement of 7 O.R. Horse rugs issued - scale 1 per horse.	
"	24/10/16		72nd Bde & 196 Coy A.S.C. move to NOEUX-LES-MINES area. 32 Remounts arrived at BRUAY - 9 collected by Divl Train - 1 Rider for 104th R.E. - 1 L.D. mule for 1st R.F. and 7 L.D. (horses) for Train - (5 sent to 197 - 2 to 194 Coy)	
"	25/10/16		72nd Bde Group refill at K 29 d. 3.3 (Map 36 B.).	
"	26/10/16		195 Coy A.S.C. & 17th Inf. Bde move to NOEUX-LES-MINES. Leave allotment cancelled - special leave only granted. Wet.	

Instructions regarding War Diaries and Intelligence Summaries are contained in F. S. Regs., Part II. and the Staff Manual respectively. Title pages will be prepared in manuscript.

WAR DIARY
or
INTELLIGENCE SUMMARY.
(Erase heading not required.)

Army Form C. 2118.

Place	Date	Hour	Summary of Events and Information	Remarks and references to Appendices
ESTREE CAUCHIE	27/10/16		17th Bde Group refill at K.29.d.3.3. Train H.Q move to RUE DE LA GARE - BRUAY - 196 Coy move to camp of No 3 Co. 40th Div Train - BRAQUEMONT.	
BRUAY	28/10/16		197 Coy (73rd Inf Bde Group) move to NOEUX-LES-MINES.	
BRUAY	29/10/16		Capt Stott RAMC & Capt A. St G. Adams ASC returned from leave. 73rd Inf. Bde. Group refill at K 29 d. 3.3. Collected 6 remounts at BRUAY - 2 H.D for 194 Coy ASC. 195 Coy move to lines & billets in BRAQUEMONT.	
"	30/10/16		17th 72nd and 40th Artillery Groups drawn supplies in bulk by Horse Transport at NOEUX-LES-MINES station. Train H.Q move to BRAQUEMONT. 17th I.B Group refilling point at RUE de SEBASTAPOL - BRAQUEMONT.	
BRAQUEMONT	31/10/16		All groups drawn by H.T. at NOEUX Station. 197 Coy ASC move into lines in BRAQUEMONT refilling in RUE D'INKERMANN.	

J. B. Ward, Lt. Col.
Commdg 24th Div Train

2353 Wt. W2544/1454 700,000 5/15 D. D. & L. A.D.S.S./Forms/C. 2118.

24 Div Train
vol 9

— CONFIDENTIAL —

War Diary

of

O.C. 24th Divisional Train.

1 - 5 - 16 to 31 - 5 - 16.

194 Coy
ASC
Vol 10
24. Div

<u>Confidential</u>.

War Diary.

of.

194 Company
Army Service Corps.

From 1st May 1916. to 31st May 1916.

Instructions regarding War Diaries and Intelligence Summaries are contained in F. S. Regs., Part II. and the Staff Manual respectively. Title pages will be prepared in manuscript.

WAR DIARY
or
INTELLIGENCE SUMMARY.
(Erase heading not required.)

T W Blakeway Major

Army Form C. 2118.

Place	Date	Hour	Summary of Events and Information	Remarks and references to Appendices
LA CLEF DE BELGIQUE	1/5/16	8.30AM	Supply Wagons refilled at BAILLEUL Station Siding. Orders for "Stand to" received 11.45 p.m. cancelled. 12.45 Am.	Fine
"	2/5/16	"	" " " " " "	Fine thunder storm later.
	3/5/16	"	" " " " " "	Fine
"	4/5/16	"	" " " " " " MAJOR T. W. BLAKEWAY returned from leave.	— . —
"	5/5/16	"	" " " " " "	Fine, little rain [illegible]
"	6/5/16	"	" " " " " "	Fine –
"	7/5/16	"	" " " " " "	Showery –
"	8/5/16	"	" " " " " " Lt. SAUNDERS went on leave –	Showery –
"	9/5/16	"	" " " " " "	Rain –
"	10/5/16	"	" " " " " "	Fine –
"	11/5/16	"	" " " " " "	Fine –
"	12/5/16	"	" " " " " "	Fine –
"	13/5/16	"	" " " " " "	Rain –
"	14/5/16	"	" " " " " "	Fine –
"	15/5/16	"	" " " " " "	Rain in morning –
"	16/5/16	"	" " " " " "	Fine –

T.2134. Wt. W708–776. 500000. 4/15. Sir J. C. & S.

Instructions regarding War Diaries and Intelligence Summaries are contained in F. S. Regs., Part II. and the Staff Manual respectively. Title pages will be prepared in manuscript.

WAR DIARY
or
INTELLIGENCE SUMMARY.
(Erase heading not required.)

Army Form C. 2118.

Place	Date	Hour	Summary of Events and Information	Remarks and references to Appendices
LA CLEF DE BELGIQUE.	17/5/16	A.M. 7-45	Supply wagons refilled at BAILLEUL STATION Siding –	Fine –
"	18/5/16	"	" " " " " " " Gas alert 12-30 A.M. –	Fine –
"	19/5/16	"	" " " " " " "	Fine –
"	20/5/16	"	" " " " " " " Lt. SAUNDERS returned from leave –	Fine –
"	21/5/16	"	" " " " " " "	Fine –
"	22/5/16	"	" " " " " " " Lt. PLUMPTRE returned to Company from D.H.Q.	Fine, thunderstorm –
"	23/5/16	"	" " " " " " "	Fine –
"	24/5/16	"	" " " " " " "	Fine morning – Rain afternoon –
"	25/5/16	"	" " " " " " " Lt. WALENN went on leave –	Fine morning – Rain at night –
"	26/5/16	"	" " " " " " " Lt. McNAMARA went to No. 4 Comp. for duty –	Fine –
"	27/5/16	"	" " " " " " " Capt. WHEELER joined for instruction –	Fine –
"	28/5/16	6-15.	" " " " " " "	Fine –
"	29/5/16	"	" " " " " " "	Fine – Rain at night –
"	30/5/16	"	" " " " " " "	Rain morning – Fine afternoon –
"	31/6/16	"	" " " " " " "	Fine –

R. Blakeway – Major –

T2134. Wt. W708–776. 500000. 4/15. Sir J. C. & S.

D. A. A. G. Office
Base.

Herewith copy of War Diary for month of June, in respect of 24th Divisional Train.

[signature]
Lieut & Adjt

7/7/16 for O/ COMM'G 24th DIVL. TRAIN A.S.C.

24th DIVL. TRAIN
Reg. No. A
Date 7/7/16
ARMY SERVICE CORPS

Instructions regarding War Diaries and Intelligence Summaries are contained in F. S. Regs., Part II. and the Staff Manual respectively. Title pages will be prepared in manuscript.

WAR DIARY

~~or~~

~~INTELLIGENCE SUMMARY.~~

(*Erase heading not required.*)

Army Form C. 2118.

Place	Date	Hour	Summary of Events and Information	Remarks and references to Appendices
BAILLEUL	1/5/16		Fine. "Stand To" at 11.45 p.m. cancelled 12.45 (midnight).	Th
"	2/5/16		Thunder showers. Gas Alert at 11.0 p.m. Presence of gas not felt in our camps.	Th
"	3/5/16		Major H. B. Hunter admitted hospital (sick). Summary of Evidence in the Case of Pte. Bourton, 197 Coy, taken.	Th
"	4/5/16		Visited H.Q. Second Army (1) re potatoes bought in France, brought to Belgium purchased by us and taken into France again. (2) Finding transport for units outside the division. (3) Supply loaders from the various units. Fine. Refilling delayed by the 3rd Division for one hour.	Th
"	5/5/16		Reinforcement of 1 man arrived. Fine. Major Blakeway and Lieut Edwards returned from leave.	Th

Instructions regarding War Diaries and Intelligence Summaries are contained in F. S. Regs., Part II. and the Staff Manual respectively. Title pages will be prepared in manuscript.

WAR DIARY
or
INTELLIGENCE SUMMARY.
(*Erase heading not required.*)

Army Form C. 2118.

Place	Date	Hour	Summary of Events and Information	Remarks and references to Appendices
BAILLEUL	6/5/15.		Inspected camps of 196, 197 and 194 Coys. Fine	[illegible]
	7/5/15		Reinforcement of two drivers posted to 194 Coy. Refilling at railhead by horse transport completed in 55 minutes. Showers. Allotment of leave increased by 4 for week commencing 10th inst.	[illegible]
	8/5/15		Major H. R. Hunter discharged hospital and returned to duty. Lieuts. Saunders and Adams proceeded on leave of absence to England. Reinforcement of one wheeler, posted to 194 Coy. Visited A.D.R.T. Hazebrouck re transport by rail of vegetables from outside British zone into this area. Showery.	[illegible]
	9/5/15		Colder and wet. Arranged with O/c R.E. Park, NIEPPE for sawdust to be taken to 'II' group refilling point daily.	[illegible]
	10/5/15.		Notified of a forthcoming alteration in the establishment of Divl Artillery to take place on 13th inst. Collected 2 riders for the division from Remount Depot HAZEBROUCK. Fine but cool.	[illegible]

2353 Wt. W2544/1454 700,000 5/15 D. D. & L. A.D.S.S./Forms/C. 2118.

Instructions regarding War Diaries and Intelligence Summaries are contained in F. S. Regs., Part II. and the Staff Manual respectively. Title pages will be prepared in manuscript.

WAR DIARY
or
~~INTELLIGENCE SUMMARY.~~
(*Erase heading not required.*)

Army Form C. 2118.

Place	Date	Hour	Summary of Events and Information	Remarks and references to Appendices
BAILLEUL	11/5/16		Lieut L. M. FRISCHER placed under arrest charged with "an act ~~conduct~~ to the prejudice of good order and military discipline. Summary of Evidence taken and sent to D.H.Q. By new establishment of Divl Arty a nett saving of 4 G.S. wagons, 4 drivers and 8 horses. Fine.	Jh
"	12/5/16.		Fine. Capt S. H. Parsloe returned from leave. Notified that Lieut Frischer would not be tried by court martial but would appear before G.O.C. Division at 5.30 p.m. 13th inst. Capt Pearson proceeded on leave.	Jh
"	13/5/16		Wet. F.G.C.M. of Pte. BOURTON, 197 Coy, at Red Lodge. at 2 p.m. Lieut Frischer released from arrest. G.O.C. 24th Division interviews Lt Col Lord and Lt. Frischer.	Jh
"	14/5/16		Lt. Bulson proceeded on leave. Visited D.D.S.&T., Second Army. Instructions received as to the disposal of 5 H.D horses surplus on new establishment of divl artillery and carried out. Wet.	Jh

Instructions regarding War Diaries and Intelligence Summaries are contained in F. S. Regs., Part II. and the Staff Manual respectively. Title pages will be prepared in manuscript.

WAR DIARY

or

~~INTELLIGENCE~~ SUMMARY.

(Erase heading not required.)

Army Form C. 2118.

Place	Date	Hour	Summary of Events and Information	Remarks and references to Appendices
BAILLEUL	15/5/16		Wet. One complete turnout less driver sent to 167 Co. R.E. Inspected Camp of 196 Coy.	Th
"	16/5/16		Fine. Aerial activity over BAILLEUL. The 3 surplus G.S. wagons and 6 sets single harness sent to D.A.C. to be sent thence by rail to the base. Promulgation of FGCM of Pte BOURTON, 197 Coy, A.S.C. awarded 3 mths F.P. No 1	Th
	17/5/16		Fine. Report on Lieut Fischer sent to D.H.Q. Gas Alert about midnight – cancelled later – false alarm. Reinforcement of 1 sergt posted to 197 Coy and 1 wheeler to 194 Coy.	Th
	18/5/16		A.A.&Q.M.G. 24th Division visited railhead while train was refilling. Fine. Lieut Adams returned from leave.	Th
"	19/5/16		Arrangements made for the distribution of horses and personnel surplus to the new establishment of Fd. Ambulances. Fine. Aerial activity	Th

Instructions regarding War Diaries and Intelligence Summaries are contained in F. S. Regs., Part II. and the Staff Manual respectively. Title pages will be prepared in manuscript.

WAR DIARY
or
INTELLIGENCE SUMMARY.
(Erase heading not required.)

Army Form C. 2118.

Place	Date	Hour	Summary of Events and Information	Remarks and references to Appendices
BAILLEUL	20/5/16		Lieut Saunders returned from leave. Fine. Lieut Martin recommended for promotion to Lieutenant.	Th
	21/5/16		Arrangements made for refilling to start at railhead at 6.15 a.m. Fine. Inspected all sick horses. Capt Pearson returned from leave. Lieut Plumptre returned to duty with 194 Coy from D.A.Q.	Th
	22/5/16		Refilling at railhead at 6.15 a.m. Fine	Th
	23/5/16		Summary of Evidence taken in case of Drs. Brown & Welsh, 194 Coy, A.S.C. charged with stealing. Notified that G.O.C. 24th Division would inspect refilling points on Thursday morning - 25th inst. Coys. notified. Fine	Th
	24/5/16		Lieut Gale and Seddall proceeded on leave to England. Lieut Adams, 191 Coy A.S.C. attached to Divl Hd Qrs for temporary duty. Showery. ~~G.O.C. inspected~~ ~~17 Inf Bde 1st Line Transport~~	Th

2353 Wt. W2544/1454 700,000 5/15 D. D. & L. A.D.S.S./Forms/C. 2118.

Instructions regarding War Diaries and Intelligence Summaries are contained in F. S. Regs., Part II. and the Staff Manual respectively. Title pages will be prepared in manuscript.

WAR DIARY
or
INTELLIGENCE SUMMARY.
(Erase heading not required.)

Army Form C. 2118.

Place	Date	Hour	Summary of Events and Information	Remarks and references to Appendices
BAILLEUL.	25/5/16		Lieut S.K. Walenn proceeded on leave. Inspection of refilling points by G.O.C 24th Division. 4 Clerks despatched to the Base. Fair. [illegible] I inspected 1st line transport of 17th Inf. Bde. Lieut Butson returned from leave.	[illegible]
	26/5/16		Collected 2 H.D. horses for Division from A.H.T.D - HAZEBROUCK. Fine. Inspected 1st line transport 72nd Infy Bde also 73rd & 72nd Field Ambces. –	[illegible]
	27/5/16		3 Sergts. despatched to B.H.T.D, HAVRE – Surplus on alteration in establishment of Field Ambulances. Capt. Wheeler 8, R.W. Kents, attached to 194 Coy with a view to becoming a transport officer. Inspected transport of 74th Fld. Amb. Summary of Evidence in case of Drs Brown & Welsh, 194 Coy, A.S.C. retaken. Reinforcement of 1 O.R. – saddler, posted to 196 Coy.	[illegible]
	28/5/16.		Aerial activity – Fine – nothing to report.	[illegible]

2353 Wt. W2544/1454 700,000 5/15 D. D. & L. A.D.S.S./Forms/C. 2118.

Instructions regarding War Diaries and Intelligence Summaries are contained in F. S. Regs., Part II. and the Staff Manual respectively. Title pages will be prepared in manuscript.

WAR DIARY
or
INTELLIGENCE SUMMARY.
(Erase heading not required.)

Army Form C. 2118.

Place	Date	Hour	Summary of Events and Information	Remarks and references to Appendices
BAILLEUL	29/5/16		Reinforcement of 4 O R posted to 194 Coy, A.S.C – drivers. Fine. Aeroplanes busy – anti aircraft shells dropping in some of our camps. Inspection of 1st Line Transport of 73rd Inf. Bde, ~~by G.O.C., 24th Division. Visited all Companies.~~	TL
	30/5/16		Two riders taken on strength of 194 Coy – Wet. Lieut Butson instructed to proceed to England as soon as possible. DAQMG & GSO(3) 24th Division visited railhead while train was refilling. 20 complete turnout from 32nd Reserve Park attached to Divl Train for fatigue duties. Posted as follows 7 to 195 Coy, 6 to 196 Coy and 7 to 197 Coy.	TL
	31/5/16		Inspected 1st Line Transport of 12th Bn Sherwood Foresters (Pioneers). Lieut Bennett proceeded on leave to England.	TL

F B Lord Lt Col
Comdg 24th Divl Train

2353 Wt. W2544/1454 700,000 5/15 D. D. & L. A.D.S.S./Forms/C. 2118.

Instructions regarding War Diaries and Intelligence Summaries are contained in F. S. Regs., Part II. and the Staff Manual respectively. Title pages will be prepared in manuscript.

WAR DIARY
or
INTELLIGENCE SUMMARY.
(Erase heading not required.)

Army Form C. 2118.

R. Blakeway - Major -

Place	Date	Hour	Summary of Events and Information	Remarks and references to Appendices
LE CLEF DE BELGIQUE	1/4/16	9 A.M.	Company moved to new area - Supply wagons refilled at 11 A.M -	Fine -
"	2/4/16	"	Supply wagons refilled at LE CLEF DE BELGIQUE - Lt PLUMPTRE temporarily employed at D.H.Q -	"
"	3/4/16	"	" " " " "	"
"	4/4/16	"	" " " " "	" & chill -
"	5/4/16	"	" " " " "	"
"	6/4/16	"	" " " " "	" & chill
"	7/4/16	"	" " " " "	Fine & chill
"	8/4/16	9-45	" " " BAILLEUL STATION Siding -	Fine -
"	9/4/16	8-55	" " " " " "	Fine -
"	10/4/16	"	" " " " " "	Fine -
"	11/4/16	8-35	" " " " " "	Rain -
"	12/4/16	"	" " " " " "	Rain -
"	13/4/16	"	" " " " " "	Fine -
"	14/4/16	"	" " " " " "	Showery -
"	15/4/16	"	" " " " " "	Fine -
"	16/4/16	"	" " " " " "	Fine -
"	17/4/16	"	" " " " " "	Rain & wind -
"	18/4/16	"	" " " " " "	Rain -
"	19/4/16	"	" " " " " "	Rain -
"	20/4/16	"	" " " " " "	Fine -
"	21/4/16	"	" " " " " " Head Quarters of Train moved to BAILLEUL -	Fine morning -
"	22/4/16	"	" " " " " "	Rain evening - Rain -

Instructions regarding War Diaries and Intelligence Summaries are contained in F. S. Regs., Part II. and the Staff Manual respectively. Title pages will be prepared in manuscript.

WAR DIARY
or
INTELLIGENCE SUMMARY.
(Erase heading not required.)

Army Form C. 2118.

Place	Date	Hour	Summary of Events and Information	Remarks and references to Appendices
LE CLEF DE BELGIQUE	23/4/16	A.M. 8-35	Supply wagons refilled at BAILLEUL STATION Siding –	Fine –
"	24/4/16	"	" " " " " " Bombs dropped at BAILLEUL at 4 AM.	Fine –
"	25/4/16	"	" " " " " "	Fine
"	26/4/16	"	" " " " " " MAJOR T.W. BLAKEWAY went on leave – Lt S.K. Walem took over command of Company	Fine
"	27/4/16	"	" " " " " "	Fine.
"	28/4/16	"	" " " " " "	"
"	29/4/16	"	" " " " " "	"
"	30/4/16	"	" " " " "Gas Alert" sounded at 1:30 AM. presence of Gas in Camp at 1·35 AM. lasted until 2·5 AM. No casualties. M.O. described gas as Chlorine.	"

T.134. Wt. W708–776. 500000. 4/15. Sir J. C. & S.

24 Div Train

CONFIDENTIAL Vol 10

June

— War Diary —

of.

O.C. 24th Divisional Train.

From 1-6-16 to 30-6-16.

Confidential

War Diary

of

194 Coy ASC

1st June to 30th June 1916

R. Blakeway — Major
O/c 194 Coy ASC

June
24th D W
Iran
App 15 Vol 10

Instructions regarding War Diaries and Intelligence Summaries are contained in F. S. Regs., Part II. and the Staff Manual respectively. Title pages will be prepared in manuscript.

WAR DIARY
or
INTELLIGENCE SUMMARY.
(Erase heading not required.)

Army Form C. 2118.

Place	Date	Hour	Summary of Events and Information	Remarks and references to Appendices
LE CLEF DE BELGIQUE	1/6/16	6 A.M.	Supply wagons refilled at BAILLEUL STATION Siding – L^T McNAMARA rejoined Company –	Fine –
"	2/6/16	"	" " " " " "	Fine –
"	3/6/16	"	" " " " " " L^T WALENN returned from leave –	Fine –
"	4/6/16	"	" " " " " " L^T PLUMPTRE went to H.Q's as temp: Adjutant.	Fine morning Rain evening –
"	5/6/16	"	" " " " " "	Heavy showers –
"	6/6/16	"	" " " " " "	Rain morning Fine afternoon –
"	7/6/16	"	" " " " " "	Fine –
"	8/6/16	"	" " " " " "	Rain afternoon Fine morning –
"	9/6/16	"	" " " " " " G.O.C visited Camp –	Fine –
"	10/6/16	"	" " " " " "	Showery –
"	11/6/16	"	" " " " " "	Showery at times
"	12/6/16	"	" " " " " "	Heavy Rain –
"	13/6/16	"	" " " " " "	Heavy Rain –
"	14/6/16	"	" " " " " " L^T McNAMARA went on leave – L^T PLUMPTRE returned to Comp:	Rain in morning –
"	15/6/16	"	" " " " " "	Fine –
"	16/6/16	"	" " " " " "	Fine –

[signature] Blakeway – Major –

Instructions regarding War Diaries and Intelligence Summaries are contained in F. S. Regs., Part II. and the Staff Manual respectively. Title pages will be prepared in manuscript.

WAR DIARY
or
INTELLIGENCE SUMMARY.
(Erase heading not required.)

Army Form C. 2118.

Place	Date	Hour	Summary of Events and Information	Remarks and references to Appendices
LECLEF DE BELGIQUE	17/6/16	A.M. 6-45	Supply wagons refilled at BAILLEUL STATION Siding – Gas ALERT 12-45 A.M.	Fine –
"	18/6/16	"	" " " " " " " 12 MIDNIGHT –	Fine –
"	19/6/16	"	" " " " " "	Fine –
"	20/6/16	"	" " " " " "	Fine –
"	21/6/16	"	" " " " " "	Fine –
"	22/6/16	"	" " " " " " Lt FRISCHER. went on leave –	Fine –
"	23/6/16	"	" " " " " "	Thunder & rain –
"	24/6/16	"	" " " " " " Lt McNAMARA returned from leave & transferred to No 4. Comp:	Rain morning – Fine rest day –
"	25/6/16	"	" " " " " " Gas cylinders delivered by wagons " to Inf: Units –	Fine –
"	26/6/16	"	" " " " " "	Heavy showers –
"	27/6/16	"	" " " " " " Gas cylinders delivered by wagons " to Inf: Units –	Raining –
"	28/6/16	"	" " " " " "	Rain morning – Fine afternoon –
"	29/6/16	"	" " " " " " "Stand to" ordered 11-30 p.m. –	Fine –
"	30/6/16	"	" " " " " "	Fine –

R. Blakeway – Major –

T.134. Wt. W708–776. 500000. 4/15. Sir J. C. & S.

Instructions regarding War Diaries and Intelligence Summaries are contained in F. S. Regs., Part II. and the Staff Manual respectively. Title pages will be prepared in manuscript.

WAR DIARY

~~or~~

~~INTELLIGENCE~~ SUMMARY.

(*Erase heading not required.*)

Army Form C. 2118.

Place	Date	Hour	Summary of Events and Information	Remarks and references to Appendices
BAILLEUL	1/6/16		Lt S.G. BUTSON transferred to England for duty with a unit of the new armies – fine.	J.L.
	2/6/16		Selected new camp for 195 Coy – on account of possibility of pollution of water supply – Reconnoitred new refilling pts for B + C groups – fine.	J.L.
	3/6/16		195 Coy moved camp to new site – Lt J.L. Bradley reported for duty vice Butson – fine.	J.L.
	4/6/16		Lt + Adjt McCallum + Lt Martin proceeded on leave – Obtained permission from 41st Div to use some horse standings in their area until 195 Company can reconstruct. Wet.	J.L.

2353 Wt. W2544/1454 700,000 5/15 D. D. & L. A.D.S.S./Forms/C. 2118.

Instructions regarding War Diaries and Intelligence Summaries are contained in F. S. Regs., Part II. and the Staff Manual respectively. Title pages will be prepared in manuscript.

WAR DIARY
or
~~INTELLIGENCE~~ SUMMARY.

(Erase heading not required.)

Army Form C. 2118.

Place	Date	Hour	Summary of Events and Information	Remarks and references to Appendices
BAILLEUL	5/6/16		195 Coy's horses moved to new standings. Lieut D. M. Edwards Supply Officer 17th Infty Bde awarded Military Cross in birthday honours. Wet.	J.h.
	6/6/16		Lt A St G Adams ASC promoted temp. Capt. Seniority 18 Feby 1916 pay + allowances 16 May 16. Wet.	J.h.
	7/6/16		Capt Goode OC. 22nd res park came over to see his horses. Showed him all the train horses which compared very favorably with his. Wet.	J.h.
	8/6/16		Court martial on Drs Brown & Welsh. Stealing &c, Receiving &c. Welsh not guilty. Lt Plumptre under instruction. Major Hunter prosecutor. D.D.S.T + D.A.D.T Second Army inspected the train. Most complimentary. Fairly fine.	J.h.

2353 Wt. W2544/1454 700,000 5/15 D. D. & L. A.D.S.S./Forms/C. 2118.

Army Form C. 2118.

WAR DIARY
or
~~INTELLIGENCE SUMMARY.~~
(*Erase heading not required.*)

Instructions regarding War Diaries and Intelligence Summaries are contained in F. S. Regs., Part II. and the Staff Manual respectively. Title pages will be prepared in manuscript.

Place	Date	Hour	Summary of Events and Information	Remarks and references to Appendices
BAILLEUL	9/6/16		Lieut Hitch proceeded on leave. Arranged supply of stone for making standings in 19th Corps Camp. Supply of potatoes stopped from base on 11th 12th 13th 14th owing to a 5 days accumulation in our barns. Wet.	JH
	10/6/16		Vet. Officer on leave. Arranged supply of sawdust from V Corps RE dump & Secondary workshops for purpose of burning excreta & urine in camps. Arranged to clear fuel wood from Secondary Workshops.	JH
	11/6/16		Collected 53 remounts & distributed to division. Promulgation Court Martial Dr. Brown 90 days F.P. No 1. 8 NCOs & men attend Gas Class. Arranged with French agent Voyer to let us take some old pavé stones for horse standings. Stormy	JH

2353 Wt. W2544/1454 700,000 5/15 D. D. & L. A.D.S.S./Forms/C. 2118.

Instructions regarding War Diaries and Intelligence Summaries are contained in F. S. Regs., Part II. and the Staff Manual respectively. Title pages will be prepared in manuscript.

WAR DIARY

or

~~INTELLIGENCE SUMMARY.~~

(Erase heading not required.)

Army Form C. 2118.

Place	Date	Hour	Summary of Events and Information	Remarks and references to Appendices
BAILLEUL	12/6/16		Very wet & cold - Received reinforcement 4 issuers - Lt Pugh on leave - Inspected 5 remounts 194 Coy - Not much class probably will improve -	JH
— " —	13/6/16		Nothing of importance to report. Special issue of Rum to Sherwood Foresters. Weather very wet and cold.	Hunt
— " —	14/6/16		Lieuts. McCallum & Lieut Martin returned from leave. Operation Orders re relief of 73rd Inf Brigade by a brigade of 2nd Anzac Division received and distributed to O.C. 197 Coy & S.O 73rd Inf. Bde. Transfer of Lieut Edwards to 197 Coy vice Lieut Martin to 195 Coy. Arrangements made with O.C. 2nd Anzac Div Train re impending relief of 73rd I. B. Cold and windy. Daylight saving bill came into force at 11 p.m.	JH
— " —	15/6/16		Notified that 1st East Riding R.E. Coy would proceed to Rest Area with 3rd Division on 17th inst. rationed up to & including this date by 24th Division.	JH

2353 Wt. W2544/1454 700,000 5/15 D. D. & L. A.D.S.S./Forms/C. 2118.

Army Form C. 2118.

Instructions regarding War Diaries and Intelligence Summaries are contained in F. S. Regs., Part II. and the Staff Manual respectively. Title pages will be prepared in manuscript.

WAR DIARY

or

~~INTELLIGENCE~~ SUMMARY.

(Erase heading not required.)

Place	Date	Hour	Summary of Events and Information	Remarks and references to Appendices
BAILLEUL	16/6/16.		Two battalions of 73rd Inf. Bde move to WAKEFIELD and BADAJOZ Huts (LOCRE). 'D' Group refilling point moved to Sheet 28 S. 27. a. 7.8 accordingly. Fair but cold. Coal Dump with about 100 tons coal, 30 coke and 50 wood taken over from 3rd Division, proceeding to Rest Area. Also 10 tons potatoes taken over. Seven pairs of horses of the 32nd Res. Park attached to 195 Coy badly gassed when returning from R.E. Farm. 1 man gassed at duty.	[initials]
"	17/6/16		S.S.M Cant, 195 Coy, S.Sgt. Bennier 197 Coy and Sgt Lees 194 Coy mentioned in dispatches. A convoy of 30 G.S wagons ~~accompanied~~ commanded by Lieut Plumptre ~~and~~ with Lieut Wildblood just after midnight collected men of the Northants and Sussex at WULVERGHEM after coming out of the trenches and transported them to new billets about METEREN and ST JANS CAPPEL. Fine.	[initials]
	18/6/16		Party sent to Ad. Remount Depot, HAZEBROUCK to collect 9 horses for the division. Fair but cool.	[initials]
	19/6/16		Notified that a second Anzac Infantry Brigade was coming to this area and would take hold part of the line now held by the 24th Division. Camp for their train Company at T. 25 c 3.6. Remounts distributed to units. Lt Bagshaw proceeded on leave.	[initials]

2353 Wt. W2544/1454 700,000 5/15 D. D. & L. A.D.S.S./Forms/C. 2118.

Instructions regarding War Diaries and Intelligence Summaries are contained in F. S. Regs., Part II. and the Staff Manual respectively. Title pages will be prepared in manuscript.

WAR DIARY
or
~~INTELLIGENCE SUMMARY.~~
(Erase heading not required.)

Army Form C. 2118.

Place	Date	Hour	Summary of Events and Information	Remarks and references to Appendices
BAILLEUL.	20/6/16.		10 pairs H D Horses from 32nd Reserve Park arrived and 5 prs given to 195 and 197 Coys each. Obtained pasture for "gassed" horses. Visited H.Q. Second Army re potatoes - Fine.	Th
	21/6/16.		Notified that 2 Bns - 17th I. B would move into Rest Area on 22nd June - remainder on June 24th. 12th Bn. Sherwood Foresters (Pioneers) move to LOCREHOF.	Th
	22/6/16		1st R.F. and 8th Buffs move into Rest Area about METEREN + ST. JANS CAPPEL Regrouping of Units for Supply Purposes to take effect from 24th inst. inclusive.	Th
	23/6/16		Collected 62 Remounts for the 24th Division + distributed same at 2 p.m to various units. 1 H.D. for the Train. One H.D. died shortly after arrival. Twisted gut.	Th

2353 Wt. W2544/1454 700,000 5/15 D. D. & L. A.D.S.S./Forms/C. 2118.

Instructions regarding War Diaries and Intelligence Summaries are contained in F. S. Regs., Part II. and the Staff Manual respectively. Title pages will be prepared in manuscript.

WAR DIARY

or

~~INTELLIGENCE SUMMARY~~.

(Erase heading not required.)

Army Form C. 2118.

Place	Date	Hour	Summary of Events and Information	Remarks and references to Appendices
BAILLEUL	24/6/16		Arrangements made for convoys of 43, 26 and 64 G.S. wagons on the nights of 25th & 26th and 27th June respectively to collect gas cylinders at STEENWERCK Station and transport them to advanced parts of the line. Reinforcement of 1 Farr. Staff. Sgt. posted to 194 Coy.	[initials]
"	25/6/16		~~[illegible]~~ One group of 4 wagons taking the wrong road arrived at destination too late to be unloaded it being almost daylight. Notified that convoy of 26 wagons would not proceed on night of 26th - but on 29th June. Orders amended accordingly. Lieut Wildblood proceeded on leave. Fine. Two horses wounded.	[initials]
"	26/6/16		Wet. Notified that 2 Battalions of 14th Inf. Bde would move to YORK HUTS - LOCRE and BADAJOZ HUTS - LOCRE. G.O.C. 24th Division directs that officer or N.C.O. responsible for the group of wagons ~~which~~ being late last night be ~~cautioned~~ censured.	[initials]

2353 Wt. W2544/1454 700,000 5/15 D. D. & L. A.D.S.S./Forms/C. 2118.

Instructions regarding War Diaries and Intelligence Summaries are contained in F. S. Regs., Part II. and the Staff Manual respectively. Title pages will be prepared in manuscript.

WAR DIARY

~~or~~

~~INTELLIGENCE~~ ~~SUMMARY~~.

(*Erase heading not required.*)

Army Form C. 2118.

Place	Date	Hour	Summary of Events and Information	Remarks and references to Appendices
BAILLEUL.	27/6/16		Dr Garrett, 195 Coy, remanded for F.G.C.M. - charge "Drunkenness". Operation Order No. 55 re move of two battalions of 17th I.B to YORK and BADAJOZ Huts (LOCRE) received. Convoy of 64 wagons transport gas cylinders from STEENWERCK siding to WULVERGHEM and "HYDE PARK CORNER" areas. Owing to one carrying party furnished by infantry not turning up one wagon returned unloaded. No casualties.	Th
" "	28/6/16		Summary of Evidence in the case of Dr GARRETT taken. Convoy of 26 wagons for transport of gas cylinders on 29th inst. Cancelled.	Th
" "	29/6/16		Instructed to deal with Dr Garrett regimentally. Operation Order No 56 re move and relief of infantry units received. "Stand To No 1" at 10.45 pm. — cancelled 11.0 p.m. One baggage wagon per infantry battalion withdrawn on 26th June returned	Th

2353 Wt. W2544/1454 700,000 5/15 D. D. & L. A.D.S.S./Forms/C. 2118.

Army Form C. 2118.

Instructions regarding War Diaries and Intelligence Summaries are contained in F. S. Regs., Part II. and the Staff Manual respectively. Title pages will be prepared in manuscript.

WAR DIARY
~~or~~
~~INTELLIGENCE~~ SUMMARY.

(*Erase heading not required.*)

Place	Date	Hour	Summary of Events and Information	Remarks and references to Appendices
BAILLEUL	30/6/16		Dull – nothing to report.	
			J B Lord Lt. Col Commdt 24th Divl Train	

2353 Wt. W2544/1454 700,000 5/15 D. D. & L. A.D.S.S./Forms/C. 2118.

Confidential

24 July

24 Div Train
vol II

War Diary of

O.C 24th Divisional Train

From July 1 – 31st

July
24 Div Train
Vol II
24

Confidential

War Diary of

194 Coy. A.S.C.

from

1st July to 31st July 1916

Instructions regarding War Diaries and Intelligence Summaries are contained in F. S. Regs., Part II. and the Staff Manual respectively. Title pages will be prepared in manuscript.

WAR DIARY
or
INTELLIGENCE SUMMARY.
(Erase heading not required.)

Army Form C. 2118.

R. Blakeway – Major –

Place	Date	Hour	Summary of Events and Information	Remarks and references to Appendices
LE CLEF DE BELGIQUE	1/7/16	A.M. 6-45	Supply wagons refilled at BAILLEUL STATION Siding –	Fine –
"	2/7/16	"	" " " " " "	Fine –
"	3/7/16	"	" " " " " " Lt. FRISCHER returned from leave –	Fine –
"	4/7/16	"	" " " " " " Lt. PLUMPTRE detailed for duty at IXth CORPS H.Q. –	Fine morning – Rain afternoon –
			Capt. A. StG. ADAMS reported for duty with Company –	
"	5/7/16	"	" " " " " "	Fine morning – Rain evening –
"	6/7/16	"	" " " " " " Moved into New Camp at SCHAEXHEN –	Fine –
SCHAEXHEN.	7/7/16	"	" " " " " " Lt. ROULSTONE left Comp: & attached to 103rd Comp: R.E.	Showery –
"	8/7/16	"	" " " " " " Capt. WHEELER ordered to IXth CORPS – Moved back to LE CLEF DE BELGIQUE	Fine –
LE CLEF DE BELGIQUE	9/7/16	"	" " " " " "	Fine –
"	10/7/16	"	" " " " " "	Fine –
"	11/7/16	10-30	" " " STEENWERCK " "	Fine –
"	12/7/16	"	" " " " " "	Fine –
"	13/7/16	10-0	" " " " " "	Fine –
"	14/7/16	"	" " " " " "	Fine –
"	15/7/16	"	" " " " " "	Fine –
"	16/7/16	7-15	" " " BAILLEUL STATION " " Lt. PLUMPTRE returned to duty from IXth CORPS. –	Rain –

Instructions regarding War Diaries and Intelligence Summaries are contained in F. S. Regs., Part II. and the Staff Manual respectively. Title pages will be prepared in manuscript.

WAR DIARY
or
INTELLIGENCE SUMMARY.
(Erase heading not required.)

Army Form C. 2118.

P. Blakeway Major–

Place	Date	Hour	Summary of Events and Information	Remarks and references to Appendices
LE CLEF DE BESIQUE	17/7/16	A.M. 7-15	Supply wagons refilled at BAILLEUL STATION Siding –	Shavery –
"	18/7/16	"	" " " " " "	Fine, dull –
"	19/7/16	"	" " " " " "	Fine –
"	20/7/16	"	" " " " " "	Fine –
"	21/7/16	"	" " " " " " Received orders at 11 AM to move Camp, started 1-30pm	Fine –
			arrived at EECKE 5. P.M. –	Fine –
EECKE	22/7/16	7-30	" " " at EECKE again at 3. P.M.	Fine –
"	23/7/16	"	" " " "	Dull –
"	24/7/16	9-0	" " " "	Dull –
"	25/7/16		Nil – Left Camp & entrained at BAILLEUL WEST Siding, commenced 2-30pm finished 4pm –	Dull –
	26/7/16		Train moved off 5-25pm – arrived LONGUEAU 2-10 AM 26th, started detraining 2-30 moved off 4 A.M for Camp at CROUY, arrived 10 A.M, refilled at 12 noon on HANGEST – CROUY Road.	Dull –
CROUY	27/7/16	8-0	Supply wagons refilled on HANGEST – CROUY Road & again at 4 pm –	Fine –
"	28/7/16	7-0	" " delivered supplies & refilled at 4 pm –	Fine –
"	29/7/16	"	" " " " " " 11-30 AM –	Fine –
"	30/7/16	"	" " " " " " moved to DAOURS at 11-30 P.M, arrived 9 A.M	Fine –
	31/7/16		moved off for SAILLY LE SEC at 2-45 pm arrived 6-30pm, delivered Supplies & Baggage wagons to R.A units at 5-30pm & 6 pm respectively, Supply wagons rejoining Company at SAILLY LE SEC at 10-pm after –	Fine –

T.134. Wt. W708–776. 500000. 4/15. Sir J. C. & S.

Instructions regarding War Diaries and Intelligence Summaries are contained in F. S. Regs., Part II. and the Staff Manual respectively. Title pages will be prepared in manuscript.

WAR DIARY
or
~~INTELLIGENCE SUMMARY.~~

(Erase heading not required.)

Army Form C. 2118.

Place	Date	Hour	Summary of Events and Information	Remarks and references to Appendices
BAILLEUL.	1/7/16.		Operation Order No 58 received – One Bn. 72nd Inf Bde. (R.W.K.) on 4th inst moves from KORTEPYP to METEREN rest area. 24th Division comes under IX Corps as from 3rd July. Fine. Arranged that units must demand transport through 'Q' office	
	2/7/16.		Instructions as to a convoy of about 60 G.S. wagons to transport men of 73rd Inf. Bde from LOCRE to KANDAHAR Farm received and necessary arrangements made – cancelled 5.30 p.m.	
	3/7/16		Lieut Fischer returned from leave having been granted 3 days extension by W.O. Notified that Lieut Bradley should report to R.T.O. BAILLEUL on 10th inst – interviewed re application for transfer to R.F.C. Operation Order No 59 re move of D.H.Q on 4th inst to LOCRE received.	
	4/7/16		Capt Adams returned to duty with 194 Coy from special temporary work with VI Corps. Baggage wagons returned to Artillery Units for the move. Artillery Operation Orders received. 195 Coy move to Sheet 27 X. 5.c.6.5 and 197 Coy to X.5.c.2.5 Lieut Plumptre temporarily attached to IX Corps Headquarters – 'Q' Branch. 2 clerks sent to the base by request of A.S.C. Second Base. Lieut Wildblood returned from leave.	

2353 Wt. W2544/1454 700,000 5/15 D. D. & L. A.D.S.S./Forms/C. 2118.

Instructions regarding War Diaries and Intelligence Summaries are contained in F. S. Regs., Part II. and the Staff Manual respectively. Title pages will be prepared in manuscript.

WAR DIARY

~~or~~ ~~INTELLIGENCE SUMMARY.~~

(*Erase heading not required.*)

Army Form C. 2118.

Place	Date	Hour	Summary of Events and Information	Remarks and references to Appendices
BAILLEUL	5/7/16		Arranged that from to-morrow inclusive, the refilling point for 'A' Group will be at S.27a.7.9. Coal Dump on NEUVE EGLISE road handed over to 2nd Aus. Division. Coal Dump taken over from 50th Div. at LOCRE. Fine.	
	6/7/16		194 Coy moved to Sheet 27 X 5 a 5.1. Summary of Evidence in the cases of Dr (a/Sgt) Balaam, Drs Martin and Stellie, A.S.C. attached 74th Field Ambulance taken. Dr (a/Sgt) Balaam remanded for F.G.C.M. – others disposed of summarily.	
	8/7/16		Instructions received for Capt. Wheeler, R.W.K. attd. 194 Coy for instructional purposes to report to H.Q. IX Corps for attachment. Baggage wagons of artillery units to be sent to units for a probable move.	
	8/7/16		Artillery units move to former area. 24th Div. O.O. No. 60. received 3.0 am re move of infantry units on night 8/9th July. 194 Coy return to former camp at S. 30.d.1.9.	

Army Form C. 2118.

WAR DIARY
or
INTELLIGENCE SUMMARY.
(Erase heading not required.)

Instructions regarding War Diaries and Intelligence Summaries are contained in F. S. Regs., Part II. and the Staff Manual respectively. Title pages will be prepared in manuscript.

Place	Date	Hour	Summary of Events and Information	Remarks and references to Appendices
BAILLEUL	8/7/16.		Proposed regrouping of units for supply purposes commencing on 9th inst. cancelled owing to move. Groups as at present. Refilling points from to-morrow to be as follows:- A group - S. 30 d. 0.8 - 'B' group S. 9 a. 7.7 - 'C' group S. 20. d. 5.2. - 'D' group S. 27. a. 7. 9. Collected 27 remounts for the division - distributed same from Camp of 197 Coy at 4 p.m. 3 riders for 195 Coy. Fine.	
"	9/7/16.		195 Coy move to former camp of 196 Coy at Map Ref. S. 3. d. 7.5. 196 Coy move to former camp of 195 Coy at S 30 c 2.9.	
"	10/7/16.		Lieut J. W. BRADLEY - A.S.C. accepted as Candidate for R. F. C. and sent to England. 24th Division Operation Order No 63 re Infantry Relief received. 195 Coy and 197 Coy move to camps at M. 32. b. central - CROIX DE POPERINGHE	
"	11/7/16.		Supply Groups rearranged from to-day inclusive as railhead is now STEENWERCK. 73rd I.B group draw at railhead by Supply Column lorries. Order of groups drawing at STEENWERCK - 'B' 'C' 'A' 'D'.	

2353 Wt. W2544/1454 700,000 5/15 D. D. & L. A.D.S.S./Forms/C. 2118.

Instructions regarding War Diaries and Intelligence Summaries are contained in F. S. Regs., Part II. and the Staff Manual respectively. Title pages will be prepared in manuscript.

Army Form C. 2118.

WAR DIARY or INTELLIGENCE SUMMARY.

(Erase heading not required.)

Place	Date	Hour	Summary of Events and Information	Remarks and references to Appendices
BAILLEUL	12/7/16		Railhead STEENWERCK - Order II 'C' 'A' 'B' - 'B' (17th I.B.) draw with lorries.	
"	13/7/16		Railhead STEENWERCK. 'B' Group (73rd Inf. Bde) draw with lorries. Surplus H.D. of the division collected and held by 194 Coy, A.S.C.	
"	14/7/16		Railhead STEENWERCK - 'B' Group have use of lorries.	
"	15/7/16		Railhead STEENWERCK. 'D' Group have use of lorries. LIEUT. N. L. SMITH, A.S.C 20th Reserve Park reported for duty vice Lieut Braddey to England - posted to 195 Coy. A.S.C. Special Convoy of 29 G.S wagons transport gas cylinders to Ration Farm, Wulverghem and R.E. Farm.* Regrouping of units for supply purposes to take effect from to-morrow.	
		6 p.m.	Notified that 15 units fed by IX Corps Supply Column would be rationed by 24th Division from to-morrow inclusive.	
			* One horse wounded beyond WULVERGHEM.	

2353 Wt. W2544/1454 700,000 5/15 D. D. & L. A.D.S.S./Forms/C. 2118.

Army Form C. 2118.

Instructions regarding War Diaries and Intelligence Summaries are contained in F. S. Regs., Part II. and the Staff Manual respectively. Title pages will be prepared in manuscript.

WAR DIARY
or
INTELLIGENCE SUMMARY.
(Erase heading not required.)

Place	Date	Hour	Summary of Events and Information	Remarks and references to Appendices
BAILLEUL	16/7/16		~~Railhead BAILLEUL.~~ Order of drawing at Station – B. D. A. C. Groups – commencing 6.45 a.m. F.G.C.M. of Dr (a/Sgt) BALAAM. A.S.C. to take place to-morrow at 10 am at H.Q. 13th Middlesex Regt. – DRANOUTRE. Refilling points change as follows:– 'A' Group – S 27 a. 7.7. – 'B' Group S.9. a. 8.8 – 'C' Group S. 20. d. 5.2 – D Group S. 27. a. 7.9. Special convoy of 30 G.S. wagons transporting gas cylinders as before.	
"	17/7/16		F.G.C.M. of Dr (a/Sgt) BALAAM at 10.0 am at H.Q. 13th Middlesex Regt.	
"	18/7/16		2 drivers transferred from 194 Coy to Headquarters Second Army. New trial arranged for trial by F.G.C.M of Dr (a/Sgt) Balaam to-morrow – same place – M. O. required as witness.	
"	19/7/16		Dr (a/Sgt) Balaam awarded 1 years Imprisonment H.L. – 2 G.S wagons (32nd Res. Park) lent to T.M.B's while in Second Army Area. Operation Order No 66 received. Infantry units move into Rest Area	

2353 Wt. W2544/1454 700,000 5/15 D. D. & L. A.D.S.S./Forms/C. 2118.

Instructions regarding War Diaries and Intelligence Summaries are contained in F. S. Regs., Part II. and the Staff Manual respectively. Title pages will be prepared in manuscript.

WAR DIARY
or
INTELLIGENCE SUMMARY.
(Erase heading not required.)

Army Form C. 2118.

Place	Date	Hour	Summary of Events and Information	Remarks and references to Appendices
BAILLEUL	20/7/16		Hd. Qrs 24th Division move to ST. JANS CAPPEL. Hd. Qrs. Div Train to ST. JANS. CAPPEL. 195 Coy to X. 5 c 5 6 (near SCHAEXKEN) - 196 Coy to X 5 c 3 5. Fld Coys R.E. move into rest area. Promulgation of F.G.C.M. of Dr BALAAM. Lieut F. A R Saunders promoted captain. Wagons of 32nd Res. Park handed over to 20th Division.	
ST. JANS CAPPEL	21/7/16		Commencement of move of artillery into Rest Area. 197 Coy to FLETRE - 194 Coy to EECKE. All attached units handed over to 20th Division for rations.	
"	22/7/16		Refilling at 7 a.m at. Group A' - Q 21 c 6 3 (EECKE) - Group B - X. 11 a 4 2 Group C - X. 10 a 3 9 Group II - W 12. b. 6. 2. Supply Column now used for supply purposes and preserved rations issued to units to be retained by them so that Supply wagons can be loaded up with a complete day's supplies in the event of a sudden order to move. Second Refilling at same points at 3.0 p.m. All blankets returned. 17th Inf. Bde move to area South of BAILLEUL - METEREN road.	

2353 Wt. W2544/1454 700,000 5/15 D. D. & L. A.D.S.S./Forms/C. 2118.

Army Form C. 2118.

Instructions regarding War Diaries and Intelligence Summaries are contained in F. S. Regs., Part II. and the Staff Manual respectively. Title pages will be prepared in manuscript.

WAR DIARY
or
INTELLIGENCE SUMMARY.

(Erase heading not required.)

Place	Date	Hour	Summary of Events and Information	Remarks and references to Appendices
ST. JANS CAPPEL	23/7/16		195 Coy move to camp of 196 Coy. Remounts collected for the division at CAESTRE taken to camp of 197 Coy and distributed at 12.0 noon. Supply wagons of units entraining to-morrow sent to their respective units to accompany them on the move. loaded with preserved rations.	
"	24/7/16		195 Coy entrain at BAILLEUL main at 10.30 p.m. 196 Coy entrain at BAILLEUL west at 11.30 pm 197 Coy at GODEWAERSVELDE at 11.30 pm. All supply wagons now with units	
"	25/7/16		195 Coy detrained at LONGUEAU at 7.0 pm and proceeded by road to FERME LE GARD refilled there and delivered supplies. 196 Coy detrained at LONGUEAU about 8.0 pm proceeded to OISSY refilled there and delivered supplies. 197 Coy detrained at SALEUX proceeded to BREUIL-LES-MOLLIENS, refilled and delivered. Hd Qrs and 194 Coy entrain at BAILLEUL West about 6.0 pm. Railhead - HANGEST-SUR-SOMME.	

X. S. E. of AMIENS

2353 Wt. W2544/1454 700,000 5/15 D. D. & L. A.D.S.S./Forms/C. 2118.

Army Form C. 2118.

Instructions regarding War Diaries and Intelligence Summaries are contained in F. S. Regs., Part II. and the Staff Manual respectively. Title pages will be prepared in manuscript.

WAR DIARY
or
INTELLIGENCE SUMMARY.
(Erase heading not required.)

Place	Date	Hour	Summary of Events and Information	Remarks and references to Appendices
PICQUIGNY.	26/7/16		Hd Qrs and 194 Coy detrained at LONGUEAU about 2.0 am proceeded to PICQUIGNY and CRUOY respectively, refilled and delivered to all artillery and RE units. D.H.Q to CAVILLON.	
"	27/7/16		Refilling at same points at 8.0 am units re-grouped. Railhead - VIGNACOURT. Second refilling 3.30 p.m. - supply wagons parked ready to deliver early to-morrow	
"	28/7/16		Refilling at 3.30 p.m.	
"	29/7/16		Refilling 11.30 a.m. Railhead HANGEST. Sentence of 1 yrs H.L awarded Dr Balaam reduced by Second Army Commander to 3 months F.P. No 1	
"	30/7/16		Refilling 11.30 a.m. Operation Order re move of Division to CORBIE - DAOURS area received. Starting point being BREILLY, 195 Coy left just after	

Instructions regarding War Diaries and Intelligence Summaries are contained in F. S. Regs., Part II. and the Staff Manual respectively. Title pages will be prepared in manuscript.

WAR DIARY
or
INTELLIGENCE SUMMARY.
(Erase heading not required.)

Army Form C. 2118.

Place	Date	Hour	Summary of Events and Information	Remarks and references to Appendices
PICQUIGNY	31/1/16		midnight, 196 Coy at 1.0 a.m, 197 Coy at 1.30 am and 194 Coy at 2.0 a.m via AMIENS to DAOURS, arriving 8.45 am and onwards. Water, feed and men's breakfast at DAOURS. Thence all companies proceeded to camps and bivouacs about SAILLY-LE-SEC. H.Q. Div Train to CORBIE with II H.Q.	

J B [illegible] Lt Col
Commanding 34th Div Train

CONFIDENTIAL.

WAR DIARY.

of

194. COMPANY A.S.C.

from 1/8/16 to 30/8/16.

— CONFIDENTIAL — Vol 12

War Diary

of

O.C. 24th Divisional Train

From. 1.VIII.16 to 31.VIII.16.

Instructions regarding War Diaries and Intelligence Summaries are contained in F. S. Regs., Part II. and the Staff Manual respectively. Title pages will be prepared in manuscript.

WAR DIARY
or
INTELLIGENCE SUMMARY.
(Erase heading not required.)

R. Blakeway — Major

Army Form C. 2118.

Place	Date	Hour	Summary of Events and Information	Remarks and references to Appendices
SAILLY LE SEC.	1/8/16	A.M. 6=	Supply wagons refilled on BRAY s/SOMME – CORBIE Road – Under XIII Corps –	Fine –
"	2/8/16	"	" " " " " " "	Fine –
"	3/8/16	"	" " " " " " "	Fine –
"	4/8/16	"	" " " " " " " Moved Camp to near MÉAULTE	Fine –
MÉAULTE	5/8/16	7-0	" " " " " – MÉAULTE "	Fine –
"	6/8/16	8-15	" " " at EDGEHILL Siding & refilled & distributed to Units at 2 p.m from Dump –	Fine –
"	7/8/16	7-0	" " " " " " " " " " "	Fine –
"	8/8/16	7-0	" " " " " " " " 11-30 AM " "	Fine –
"	9/8/16	"	" " " " " " " " " " "	Fine –
"	10/8/16	"	" " " " " " " " " " "	Rain –
			CAPT ADAMS took over No 3 Comp: in place of CAPT PEARSON transferred to this Comp: H.M. the KING visited the Troops.	
"	11/8/16	"	" " " " " " " " " " "	Fine –
"	12/8/16	"	" " " " " " " " " " "	Fine –
"	13/8/16	"	" " " " " " " " " " "	Rain early morning. Fine day –
"	14/8/16	"	" " " " " " " " " " "	Rain –
"	15/8/16	"	" " " " " " " " " " "	Rain –
"	16/8/16	6-30	" " " " " " " " " " "	Fine –

T.134. Wt. W708–776. 500000. 4/15. Sir J. C. & S.

Instructions regarding War Diaries and Intelligence Summaries are contained in F. S. Regs., Part II. and the Staff Manual respectively. Title Pages will be prepared in manuscript.

WAR DIARY
or
INTELLIGENCE SUMMARY

(Erase heading not required.)

Army Form C. 2118.

Place	Date	Hour	Summary of Events and Information	Remarks and references to Appendices
MÉAULTE.	17/8/16	A.M. 6-30	Supply wagons refilled at EDGE HILL Siding & refilled & distributed to Units at 11-30 A.M. from Dump. In XIV Corps.	Fine -
"	18/8/16	"	" " " " " " " " " "	Fine -
"	19/8/16	"	" " " " " " " " " "	Rain morning -
"	20/8/16	"	" " " " " " " " " "	Fine -
"	21/8/16	"	" " " " " " " " " "	Fine -
"	22/8/16	"	" " " " " " " " " "	Fine -
"	23/8/16	"	" " " " " " " " " "	Rain morning -
"	24/8/16	"	" " " " " " " " " " [illegible]	Fine -
"	25/8/16	"	" " " " " " " " " "	Showery -
"	26/8/16	"	" " " " " " " " " "	Heavy showers -
"	27/8/16	"	" " " " " " " " " "	Rain -
"	28/8/16	"	" " " " " " " " " "	Fine -
"	29/8/16	"	" " " " " " " " " "	Rain -
"	30/8/16	"	" " " " " " " "	Rain -
"	31/8/16	10-0	" " " Dump on BRAY - MÉAULTE Road -	Fine -

R. Blakeway Major

2449 Wt. W14957/M90 750,000 1/16 J.B.C. & A. Forms/C.2118/12.

Instructions regarding War Diaries and Intelligence Summaries are contained in F. S. Regs., Part II. and the Staff Manual respectively. Title pages will be prepared in manuscript.

WAR DIARY
or
INTELLIGENCE SUMMARY.
(Erase heading not required.)

Army Form C. 2118.

Place	Date	Hour	Summary of Events and Information	Remarks and references to Appendices
CORBIE	1/8/16		Refilling points on CORBIE - BRAY-sur-SOMME road — 'A' and 'D' Groups at J 21. a. 3.2 B & C. Groups J. 22 a. 195 Coy and 196 Coy proceeded to camp at F. 19 d. accompanying 17th and 72nd Inf. Bdes. respectively. Bright sunshine. Water somewhat scarce. Horses watered 1½ miles from camp.	
"	2/8/16		A and D Groups refilled at J. 21 a. 3.2. 197 Coy (73rd Inf. Bde) proceeded to new area camp at F. 19. d. B and C. Groups refilled F. 19. d. and delivered to units now encamped in the 'SANDPIT' H.Q. Div Train to F. 19. d. Fine.	
F. 19. d. Sheet 62 D.	3/8/16		All groups except Artillery Group refill in new area.	
"	4/8/16		194 Coy arrive in new area. B & C. Groups after delivering to units draw supplies from railhead - EDGEHILL - E 20. a. 2.3 with horse transport and wagons remain loaded overnight. Arty. Group refill at J 21 a. 3.2	

2353 Wt. W2544/1454 700,000 5/15 D. D. & L. A.D.S.S./Forms/C. 2118.

Instructions regarding War Diaries and Intelligence Summaries are contained in F. S. Regs., Part II. and the Staff Manual respectively. Title pages will be prepared in manuscript.

WAR DIARY
or
INTELLIGENCE SUMMARY.
(Erase heading not required.)

Army Form C. 2118.

Place	Date	Hour	Summary of Events and Information	Remarks and references to Appendices
F. 19. d.	5/8/16		II Group commence drawing supplies from railhead by H.T. All refilling now in new area.	
F. 19 d.	6/8/16.		Supplies all drawn by H.T. at railhead. One days reserve dumped at refilling point, Supply Column being used for ammunition and working parties. M. VAUCHEZ, French Interpreter, arrived and posted to 197 Coy.	
"	7/8/16		Lieut Lang Smith assumes Command of Water Supply Service - 24th Division Area - Reinforcement of Issuers and 1 driver. 17th Inf. Bde. move into the line. M. KLEIN and M. VOUSSEAUME, French Interpreters, posted to 195 and 196 Coys respectively.	
"	8/8/16		Refilling at 11.30 a.m. Operation Order re relief of 2nd Division by 24th Div received. Fine.	
"	9/8/16.		1 N.C.O. and 1 man take over reserve rations at the CITADEL. Operation Order re relief of 55th Divn. received. Lieut Edwards promoted Captain to date from 21.7-16.	

2353 Wt. W2544/1454 700,000 5/15 D. D. & L. A.D.S.S./Forms/C. 2118.

Instructions regarding War Diaries and Intelligence Summaries are contained in F. S. Regs., Part II. and the Staff Manual respectively. Title pages will be prepared in manuscript.

WAR DIARY
or
INTELLIGENCE SUMMARY.
(Erase heading not required.)

Army Form C. 2118.

Place	Date	Hour	Summary of Events and Information	Remarks and references to Appendices
F.19.d.	10/8/16		21 remounts collected at MERICOURT and distributed to units of division. 5 mules for 194 Coy in lieu of H.D horses for limbers. Capt. A. St. G. ADAMS assumed command of 196 Coy, vice Capt H.C. PEARSON to 194 Coy. Visit of H.M. King George V. Water Supply Service undertaken by the Corps. Dull & showery.	
"	11/8/16.		Nothing to report	
"	12/8/16		Move of artillery to E.17 d and E.18. All Baggage horses of R.F.A. units sent to their respective batteries &c.	
"	13/8/16.		Nothing to report.	
"	14/8/16		Operation Order No 76 received re renewal of attack on GUILLEMONT.	

2353 Wt. W2544/1454 700,000 5/15 D. D. & L. A.D.S.S./Forms/C. 2118.

Instructions regarding War Diaries and Intelligence Summaries are contained in F. S. Regs., Part II. and the Staff Manual respectively. Title pages will be prepared in manuscript.

WAR DIARY
or
INTELLIGENCE SUMMARY.
(Erase heading not required.)

Army Form C. 2118.

Place	Date	Hour	Summary of Events and Information	Remarks and references to Appendices
F.19.a.5.2	15/8/16.		Showery. Nothing to report.	
"	16/8/16		Supplies drawn at railhead commencing 6·30 a.m. Full issue of rum to infantry brigades and pioneer battalion. Showery. Canteen opened for men.	
"	17/8/16.		Showery. Operation Order No 77 received re renewal of attack on GUILLEMONT.	
"	18/8/16		MAJOR T. W. BLAKEWAY to hospital Sick. Reported taking of GUILLEMONT. All water buckets collected and sent to advanced grenade dump for the purpose of carry Mills grenades. Constant demand for petrol tins. Urgent request by 17th Inf. Bde for candles and matches received at 10·0 pm. Both available at railhead and delivered by midnight.	
"	19/8/16.	→	3000 biscuit and preserved meat rations sent to Advanced Ration Dump at F.17.d.3.4 also supply of candles and matches. Reinforcement of 1 saddler and 2 drivers.	

2353 Wt. W2544/1454 700,000 5/15 D. D. & L. A.D.S.S./Forms/C. 2118.

Instructions regarding War Diaries and Intelligence Summaries are contained in F. S. Regs., Part II. and the Staff Manual respectively. Title pages will be prepared in manuscript.

WAR DIARY
or
INTELLIGENCE SUMMARY.
(Erase heading not required.)

Army Form C. 2118.

Place	Date	Hour	Summary of Events and Information	Remarks and references to Appendices
F19 a 5·2	20/8/16.		Operation Order No 81 re renewal of attack in GUILLEMONT. received. Operation Order No 82 received.	
"	21/8/16		Operation Order No 83 received. Artillery baggage horses returned to ASC Coy. Reinforcement (1 Staff Sergeant) posted to 196 Coy. MEAULTE and camps in neighbourhood bombed – no casualties affecting this unit. 15 Remounts collected at MERICOURT Station for the division – 2 L.D for 195 Coy.	
"	22/8/16		Capt. ADAMS sent to CORBIE – member of F.G.C.M. Pea-soup issued to brigades coming out of the trenches. Operation Order No 84 re relief of 24th Division by 20th Division received.	
"	23/8/16		Major T. W. Blakeway discharged hospital and returned to duty.	

2353 Wt. W2544/1454 700,000 5/15 D. D. & L. A.D.S.S./Forms/C. 2118.

Army Form C. 2118.

Instructions regarding War Diaries and Intelligence Summaries are contained in F. S. Regs., Part II. and the Staff Manual respectively. Title pages will be prepared in manuscript.

WAR DIARY
or
INTELLIGENCE SUMMARY.
(Erase heading not required.)

Place	Date	Hour	Summary of Events and Information	Remarks and references to Appendices
F 19 a. 5.2.	24/8/16		Reinforcement of 2 Sergeants. 1 posted to 194, 1 to 197 Coy.	
"	25/8/16		O.O. 85 received at 12.30 a.m re move of Division less Divl. Artillery and D.A.C. to rest area at E 13 or 14 (Sheet 62 D) 24th Divl Train less 194 Coy moved about 6.0 a.m to camp at E 20 a. 5.7. Refilling point for B. C and D Groups (11. 17th 72nd and 73 I.B. groups) to point near A.S.C. camps. One supply wagon of 9th East Surreys (loaded) run into by railway train at level crossing at EDGEHILL – Wagon smashed to pieces, horses and driver not hurt.	
E.20. a. 5.7 (EDGEHILL)	26/8/16.		Endeavours to make camps habitable. No buildings, huts or tents in area taken over. Ground very foul.	
do	27/8/16		Daily issue of rum to all units commenced. 72nd Inf. Bde. and 12th Lhr. Foresters (Pioneers) move to RIBEMONT and HEILLY. Operation Order No 86 received re relief of 14th Division by 24th Division on 31st August/1st Sept. Very wet.	

2353 Wt. W2544/1454 700,000 5/15 D. D. & L. A.D.S.S./Forms/C. 2118.

Instructions regarding War Diaries and Intelligence Summaries are contained in F. S. Regs., Part II. and the Staff Manual respectively. Title pages will be prepared in manuscript.

WAR DIARY
or
INTELLIGENCE SUMMARY.
(Erase heading not required.)

Army Form C. 2118.

Place	Date	Hour	Summary of Events and Information	Remarks and references to Appendices
E20a 5·7	28/8/16		No. 24 Supply Column move to camp on BUIRE — ALBERT · AMIENS road. Very wet.	
"	29/8/16		Notified that 24th Division would relieve 14th Division and 33rd Division 24 hours earlier than as stated in O.O 86. Severe thunderstorm - all camps flooded out.	
"	30/8/16		The three brigade companies move to camps of 14th Div Train at E. 10. b (Sheet 62 D) - very poor camps. H.Q. Div Train move to camp of 194 Coy (F. 19. a 5·7) LIEUT K. H. BAGSHAW, LIEUT R.F. SEDDALL and LIEUT. N. LANG-SMITH admitted to hospital (sick). Railhead (supply) for 24th Division changed to ALBERT. Pouring rain all day.	
"	31/8/16.		Supplies of Div Troops and 17th Inf. Bde. loaded into column lorries at 2·0 a.m. - Supplies for brigades in the line (72nd and 73rd) put in metre · gauge railway and taken to FRICOURT STATION where they are sorted out and refilled into 1st Line Transport direct. Train transport used for R.E. and Salvage work. 17th Inf. Bde refill into	

2353 Wt. W2544/1454 700,000 5/15 D. D. & L. A.D.S.S./Forms/C. 2118.

Instructions regarding War Diaries and Intelligence Summaries are contained in F. S. Regs., Part II. and the Staff Manual respectively. Title pages will be prepared in manuscript.

WAR DIARY
or
INTELLIGENCE SUMMARY.
(Erase heading not required.)

Army Form C. 2118.

Place	Date	Hour	Summary of Events and Information	Remarks and references to Appendices
	31st contd.		Train transport on MEAULTE - ALBERT road - Divl Troops as before at F. 19. d. H.Q. 24th Divl Train move to E. 11. central, taking over from 33rd Divl Train. Supply Officers and supply details to camp at FRICOURT STATION.	
			J B Lord Lt. Col Commdg 24th Div Train 1 - IX - 16	

2353 Wt. W2544/1454 700,000 5/15 D. D. & L. A.D.S.S./Forms/C. 2118.

11 24

Vol. 13

— CONFIDENTIAL —

War Diary

of

O.C. 24th Divisional Train.

From 1-9-16 To 30-9-16.

Instructions regarding War Diaries and Intelligence Summaries are contained in F. S. Regs., Part II. and the Staff Manual respectively. Title pages will be prepared in manuscript.

WAR DIARY
or
INTELLIGENCE SUMMARY.
(Erase heading not required.)

Army Form C. 2118.

Place	Date	Hour	Summary of Events and Information	Remarks and references to Appendices
E. 11. Central.	1/9/16.		With the exception of Divl Troops all units' supplies are taken from ALBERT to FRICOURT by means of the light railway and refilled into 1st Line Transport. Lieut McNamara and 10 G.S wagons endeavoured to transport SAA and grenades to the Quarry at S. 22. d 9.1 and GREEN DUMP at S 16 c 9.5 (Sheet 57c). Convoy report attached. Fine.	
do	2/9/16.		First issue of chewing gum. Arrangements made for the issue of two days rations to 9th East Surreys and 8th Queens at 7.30 a.m to-morrow. Lieut G. H. HITCH and 2 O.R. wounded while carrying out transport work (R.E. stores) in the neighbourhood of the R.E. Dump N.W. of BERNAFAY wood. Reports attached. Summary of Evidence in the case of Dr H. WILCOX, 194 Coy, A.S.C. taken.	
do.	3/9/16		Renewal of attack on GINCHY and GUILLEMONT commenced at 12 noon. Supplys train offloaded at 12 midnight at ALBERT. Wire from XV Corps to the effect that no demands for rations over and above the ordinary quantities allowed are to be granted without reference to Corps H.Q. Camps about E. 10. b (Sheet 62D) shelled by 6 in. naval gun – No A.S.C. casualties.	

2353 Wt. W2544/1454 700,000 5/15 D. D. & L. A.D.S.S./Forms/C. 2118.

Army Form C. 2118.

Instructions regarding War Diaries and Intelligence Summaries are contained in F. S. Regs., Part II. and the Staff Manual respectively. Title pages will be prepared in manuscript.

WAR DIARY
or
INTELLIGENCE SUMMARY.
(Erase heading not required.)

Place	Date	Hour	Summary of Events and Information	Remarks and references to Appendices
E. 11 central	4/9/16		F.G.C.M. of Dr. H. WILCOX in the camp of 194 Coy. Cold showers. Dr Pitfield 194 Coy surrenders as a deserter from H.M.S. Vengeance – Operation Order No 94 received re move of Division to Rest Area (ABBEVILLE). All Field Coys RE, HQ RE and Pioneers to remain in this area and be rationed by 55th Division.	
"	5/9/16		Notified railhead for Division less Artillery from 6th inst inclusive – VIGNACOURT – for artillery FRÉCHENCOURT. Operation Order No 95 re movements by rail and transport by road to rest area received. All brigade companies to camps at DERNANCOURT also first line transport of 17th and 73rd Bdes and 73rd and 74th Field Ambulances. 17th and 73rd Bde groups double refill. (E.13.b.2.8)	
DERNANCOURT	6/9/16		72nd Bde. double refill. March table attached. 1st Column arrived ARGOEUVES and LONGPRE about 6 p.m.	
ARGOEUVES	7/9/16		~~Left~~ 8.0 a.m. for LONG thence to COCQUEREL arriving about 7.0 p.m. 17th and 73rd Bde Groups refill on ABBEVILLE – AILLY road about 800 yds W. of AILLY at 6 p.m. 6 L.D horses, 1 L.D mule and 2 Riders collected from 17 M.G.C. at ERGNIES	

2353 Wt. W2544/1454 700,000 5/15 D. D. & L. A.D.S.S./Forms/C. 2118.

Instructions regarding War Diaries and Intelligence Summaries are contained in F. S. Regs., Part II. and the Staff Manual respectively. Title pages will be prepared in manuscript.

WAR DIARY
or
INTELLIGENCE SUMMARY.
(*Erase heading not required.*)

Army Form C. 2118.

Place	Date	Hour	Summary of Events and Information	Remarks and references to Appendices
COCQUEREL	8/9/16		196 Coy arrived. Refilled and delivered. Fine. LIEUT R.F. SEDDALL, A.S.C., discharged hospital returned to duty.	
"	9/9/16		Convoy of 11 G.S. wagons transported 3 officers and 150 men of 73rd Bde from AILLY to ABBEVILLE Station - 1st Line Transport of this Brigade draw supplies from R.P.	
"	10/9/16		Men of 72nd I.B. transported to ABBEVILLE and 72nd First Line Transport draw Supplies	
"	11/9/16.		Men of 17th I.B. to ABBEVILLE - 17th First Line Transport draw supplies.	
"	12/9/16		Div Transport Show - 196 Coy wins 1st Prize for G.S wagon complete turnout.	

2353 Wt. W2544/1454 700,000 5/15 D. D. & L. A.D.S.S./Forms/C. 2118.

Army Form C. 2118.

Instructions regarding War Diaries and Intelligence Summaries are contained in F. S. Regs., Part II. and the Staff Manual respectively. Title pages will be prepared in manuscript.

WAR DIARY
or
INTELLIGENCE SUMMARY.
(Erase heading not required.)

Place	Date	Hour	Summary of Events and Information	Remarks and references to Appendices
COCQUEREL	13/9/16		T/Lieut BENDIT sent to 194 Coy at F. 19 d (Sheet 62 D)	
"	14/9/16		F.G.C.M of Cpl. Wh. Richardson promulgated - loss of 1 years seniority.	
"	15/9/16		Notified T/Lieut N. L. LANG-SMITH invalided to England on 5th inst. and struck off the strength. Leave opened - one a day for special cases.	
"	16/9/16		Ordered to be ready to entrain at short notice.	
"	17/9/16		103rd 104th and 129th Fld. Coys R E with 12th Bn She. Foresters rejoined the Division in the East area (PONT REMY)	

2353 Wt. W2544/1454 700,000 5/15 D. D. & L. A.D.S.S./Forms/C. 2118.

Army Form C. 2118.

Instructions regarding War Diaries and Intelligence Summaries are contained in F. S. Regs., Part II. and the Staff Manual respectively. Title pages will be prepared in manuscript.

WAR DIARY
or
INTELLIGENCE SUMMARY.
(Erase heading not required.)

Place	Date	Hour	Summary of Events and Information	Remarks and references to Appendices
COLQUEREL	18/9/16.		Orders received re move of 24th Division from Fourth Army to First Army area. Heavy rain.	
"	19/9/16.		Supply Officers and supply details sent by the first train of their respective groups. 196 Coy ASC entrained at ABBEVILLE, 197 Coy at LONGPRE, 195 Coy and H.Q Train at PONT REMY. Detrained in IV Corps area. 196 Coy to billets at VALHUON, 195 Coy to PRESSY LES PERNES, H.Q and 197 Coy to BRUAY.	
BRUAY	20/9/16		Refilling ~~points~~ [illegible] for all groups at 2 p.m. 30th Div Supply Column draws for 24th Division at railhead (BRUAY).	
"	21/9/16.		Orders received re relief of 9th Division by 24th Division to be completed by 26th inst. 1 L.D mule and 2 Riders taken on strength.	
"	22/9/16		9th Div Arty attached to 24th Div. for rationing purposes. Reinforcement of 1 corporal H.T and 1 issuer. 197 Coy move to camp vacated by No 2 Coy - 9th Div Train at ESTREE CAUCHIE.	

2353 Wt. W2544/1454 700,000 5/15 D. D. & L. A.D.S.S./Forms/C. 2118.

Instructions regarding War Diaries and Intelligence Summaries are contained in F. S. Regs., Part II. and the Staff Manual respectively. Title pages will be prepared in manuscript.

WAR DIARY
or
INTELLIGENCE SUMMARY.
(Erase heading not required.)

Army Form C. 2118.

Place	Date	Hour	Summary of Events and Information	Remarks and references to Appendices
BRUAY	23/9/16		73rd I.B group refill in new area (Sheet 36B - W 3 d 4·5) Fine	
"	24/9/16.		40 remounts drawn at BRUAY Station - 4 riders and 5 L.D taken on strength of the Train 195 Coy after refilling move to ESTREE CAUCHIE. 196 Coy move to camp vacated by 195 Coy in RUE DE LA GARE - BRUAY. Fine - 17th I.B. Group refill at W.3 c.9.3	
"	25/9/16.		72nd I.B. group refill at J. 11. c. 3·5. Conviction in the case of Dr WILCOX, 194 Coy ASC QUASHED.	
"	26/9/16		196 Coy & H.Q. D.T. move to camp and billets in ESTREE CAUCHIE vacated by 9th Division. 24 Remounts collected at CHOQUES - 4 Riders and 5 L.D. horses for Divl Train. All refilling in new area. O.C. Train performs duties of Town Major - ESTREE CAUCHIE -	
ESTREE CAUCHIE	27/9/16		Dr BROWN - 194 Coy seriously wounded - 2 H.D. Killed. All ranks to be inoculated - 10 per Company every second day. O O No 97 received re relief of 17 I.B by 72 I.B. Gas Alert.	

Army Form C. 2118.

WAR DIARY
or
INTELLIGENCE SUMMARY.
(Erase heading not required.)

Instructions regarding War Diaries and Intelligence Summaries are contained in F. S. Regs., Part II. and the Staff Manual respectively. Title pages will be prepared in manuscript.

Place	Date	Hour	Summary of Events and Information	Remarks and references to Appendices
ESTREE CAUCHIE	28/9/16		LT COL F.B. LORD proceeded on 10 days leave to England. Major H.B. Hunter assumes command. Notified 24th Div Arty Railhead would be BRUAY as from 2/10/16 inclusive.	
"	29/9/16.		Reinforcement 1 farrier and 1 issuer posted to 195 Coy. Ordered to send one car to BETHUNE for one week to be at the disposal of Purchasing Office (IV Corps).	
"	30/9/16		Fine. Received orders to revert to winter time at 1 a.m. tomorrow	

H.B. Hunter. Major
COMM'G 24th DIVL. TRAIN A.S.C.

2353 Wt. W2544/1454 700,000 5/15 D. D. & L. A.D.S.S./Forms/C. 2118.

CONFIDENTIAL -

24
Train

WAR DIARY -

of

194. Company - A.S.C.

From 1/9/16 to 30/9/16.

Army Form C. 2118.

Instructions regarding War Diaries and Intelligence Summaries are contained in F. S. Regs., Part II. and the Staff Manual respectively. Title Pages will be prepared in manuscript.

WAR DIARY
or
INTELLIGENCE SUMMARY
(Erase heading not required.)

W Blakeway – Major –

Place	Date	Hour	Summary of Events and Information	Remarks and references to Appendices
MÉAULTE	1/9/16	9. A.M.	Supply wagons refilled at Dump on BRAY - MÉAULTE Road –	Fine
"	2/9/16	"	" " " " " " " L^T. FRISCHER sent to No 197 Company –	Fine –
"	3/9/16	"	" " " " " " "	Fine –
"	4/9/16	"	" " " " " "	Rain –
"	5/9/16	"	" " " " " " " Train H.Q. & other Companies moved into Rest area –	Rain –
"	6/9/16	"	" " " " " " "	Fine –
"	7/9/16	"	" " " " " " "	Fine –
"	8/9/16	"	" " " " " " " CAPT. ILOTT. R.A.M.C. posted to Train H.Q^rs –	Fine –
"	9/9/16	"	" " " " " " " L^T. BENDIT reported for duty as R.O. –	Fine –
"	10/9/16	"	" " " " " " "	Fine –
"	11/9/16	"	" " " " " "	Fine –
"	12/9/16	"	" " " " " " "	Heavy shower in morning – Fine –
"	13/9/16	"	" " " " " " "	Rain evening.
"	14/9/16	"	" " " " " " "	Fine –
"	15/9/16	"	" " " " " " " L^T. BENDIT returned to H.Q's TRAIN –	Fine –
"	16/9/16	"	" " " " " " " L^T. FRISCHER reported for duty as R.O. –	Fine –
"	17/9/16	"	" " " " " " "	Fine –
"	18/9/16	"	" " " " " " "	Rain –
"	19/9/16	"	" " " " " " "	Showery –
"	20/9/16	"	" " " " " " "	Rain –
"	21/9/16	"	" " " " " " "	Fine –

2449 Wt. W14957/M90 750,000 1/16 J.B.C. & A. Forms/C.2118/12.

Army Form C. 2118.

Instructions regarding War Diaries and Intelligence Summaries are contained in F. S. Regs., Part II. and the Staff Manual respectively. Title Pages will be prepared in manuscript.

WAR DIARY
or
INTELLIGENCE SUMMARY

(Erase heading not required.)

Place	Date	Hour	Summary of Events and Information	Remarks and references to Appendices
MÉAULTE	22/9/16	8.AM	Supply wagons refilled at Dump on BRAY - MÉAULTE Road -	Fine -
"	23/9/16	"	" " " " " " "	Fine -
"	24/9/16	"	" " " " " " "	Fine -
"	25/9/16	"	" " " " " " "	Fine -
"	26/9/16	"	" " " " " " "	Fine -
"	27/9/16	"	" " " " " " "	Rain -
"	28/9/16	"	" " " " " " " Moved to MOLLIENS au BOIS.	Fine -
MOLLIENS au BOIS	29/9/16	2 p.m	" " " " MOLLIENS - VILLERS Road -	Rain -
"	30/9/16	"	" " " " TALMAS - DOULLENS Road - Marched to HEM.	Fine -

R. Blakeway - Major

2449 Wt. W14957/M90 750,000 1/16 J.B.C. & A. Forms/C.2118/12.

CONFIDENTIAL -

24

War Diary -

of.

194. Company A.S.C.

from 1/10/16 to 31/10/16.

Instructions regarding War Diaries and Intelligence Summaries are contained in F. S. Regs., Part II. and the Staff Manual respectively. Title Pages will be prepared in manuscript.

WAR DIARY
or
INTELLIGENCE SUMMARY
(Erase heading not required.)

R Blakeway

Army Form C. 2118.

Place	Date	Hour	Summary of Events and Information	Remarks and references to Appendices
HEM.	1/10/16	11 A.M.	Supply wagons refilled at FRÉVENT STATION - marched to BLANGERVAL -	Fine -
BLANGERVAL	2/10/16	2 p.m.	" " " on PERNES - CAMBLAIN - CHATELAIN Road - marched to CAMBLAIN - CHATELAIN -	Rain -
CAMBLAIN CHATELAIN	3/10/16	11 A.M.	" " " on HERMIN - ARRAS Road - Marched to FRESNICOURT.	Rain - Rain -
FRESNICOURT	4/10/16	9-30 AM.	" " " on FRESNICOURT - VERDREL Road - Lt. WALENN ordered to join 23rd DIV: TRAIN -	Rain -
"	5/10/16	"	" " " on HERMIN - GAUCHIN Road -	Fine -
"	6/10/16	"	" " " " " "	Rain -
"	7/10/16	9 A.M.	" " " " " " marched into Camp at GAUCHIN - LEGAL.	Showery -
GAUCHIN - LEGAL	8/10/16	"	" " " " " "	Showery -
"	9/10/16	"	" " " " " "	Fine -
"	10/10/16	"	" " " " " "	Fine -
"	11/10/16	"	" " " " " "	Fine -
"	12/10/16	"	" " " " " "	Fine -
"	13/10/16	"	" " " " " "	Showery -
"	14/10/16	"	" " " " " "	Fine -
"	15/10/16	"	" " " " " "	Fine -
"	16/10/16	"	" " " " " "	Fine -
"	17/10/16	"	" " " " " "	Fine -
"	18/10/16	"	" " " " " "	Rain -
"	19/10/16	8-30 AM.	" " " " " " "GAS ALERT."	Rain -
"	20/10/16	"	" " " " " " " " "	Fine -
"	21/10/16	"	" " " " " "	Fine NE wind
"	22/10/16	"	" " " " " " " " "	Fine
"	23/10/16	"	" " " " " "	Fine F 9 P.M. - rain

2449 Wt. W14957/M90 750,000 1/16 J.B.C. & A. Forms/C.2118/12.

Army Form C. 2118.

WAR DIARY
or
INTELLIGENCE SUMMARY

(Erase heading not required.)

Instructions regarding War Diaries and Intelligence Summaries are contained in F. S. Regs., Part II. and the Staff Manual respectively. Title Pages will be prepared in manuscript.

Place	Date	Hour	Summary of Events and Information	Remarks and references to Appendices
GAUCHIN LEGAL	24/10/16	5·30AM	Supply wagons refilled on HERMIN-GAUCHIN road	fine to 9PM.
"	25/10/16	"	"	wet
"	26/10/16	"	"	fine SW. wind
"	27/10/16	"	"	fine to 4PM SE wind
"	28/10/16	"	"	fine to 4PM SE "
"	29/10/16	"	"	wet SE wind
"	30/10/16	"	"	wet SE wind
"	31/10/16	"	"	showery strong S. "
~~"~~	~~1/11/16~~			~~fine~~

D R Blakeway

Confidential

War Diary Vol 15

of

O.C. 24th Div Train

From 1/11/16 to 30/11/16

Instructions regarding War Diaries and Intelligence Summaries are contained in F. S. Regs., Part II. and the Staff Manual respectively. Title pages will be prepared in manuscript.

WAR DIARY or INTELLIGENCE SUMMARY.

(Erase heading not required.)

Army Form C. 2118.

Place	Date	Hour	Summary of Events and Information	Remarks and references to Appendices
BRAQUEMONT	1/11/16.		Major Blakeway returned from leave - Lieut C. C. Gale transferred from 197 to 194 Coy ASC	
"	2/11/16		Supplies drawn at railhead half an hour later 9.30 a.m.	
"	3/11/16		Allotment of leave granted to Div Train - 6 per week.	
"	4/11/16.			
"	5/11/16.		Hay ration cut down to 6 lbs - the difference being made up by straw drawn from First Army Purchase Board BETHUNE - up to 13 lbs per H.D & 10 per L.D.	
"	6/11/16		Capt. A. St. G. ADAMS admitted hospital sick - Lieut HITCH assumes command 196 Coy - ASC. Collected 29 Remounts of a train load of 56 for other units of the division - 2 Riders for 194 Coy ASC Leave cancelled	
"	7/11/16		Remounts distributed at 9.30 am in field in NOEUX - LES - MINES. Lieut Bendit, 1 clerk & 1 motor car proceeded to First Army Purchase Board for duty & held 'on command'. Leave re-opened	
"	8/11/16.		Collected 8 "Rats" at MANSION HOUSE VERMELLES & KINGSBRIDGE Stn and returned same to MINX Yard by night. Lieut L.W.P. Le Sueur proceeded on leave to England.	

2353 Wt. W2544/1454 700,000 5/15 D. D. & L. A.D.S.S./Forms/C. 2118.

Instructions regarding War Diaries and Intelligence Summaries are contained in F. S. Regs., Part II. and the Staff Manual respectively. Title pages will be prepared in manuscript.

WAR DIARY
or
INTELLIGENCE SUMMARY.
(*Erase heading not required.*)

Army Form C. 2118.

Place	Date	Hour	Summary of Events and Information	Remarks and references to Appendices
BRAQUEMONT	9/11/16		Fine. Nothing to report.	
"	10/11/16		Major H B Hunter S.S.O 24th Division proceeded on leave to England. Reinforcement 1 wheeler posted to 195 Coy.	
"	11/11/16		17th Inf. Bde. refilling point moved to L. 25 b 5. 4 on BRAQUEMONT - PETIT SAINS road.	
"	12/11/16.		Fine	
"	13/11/16		Summary of Evidence in case of C Q. M. S. Blackburn taken. Fine	
"	14/11/16		Fine	
"	15/11/16		Lieut A.C. Bendit vacated the appointment of Claims Officer 24th Division. Fine. Gas Alert.	
"	16/11/16		Capt W. A Macgregor A.V.C proceeded on leave.	
"	17/11/16.		Capt H. C. Pearson returned from leave. 'C' Group refilling point moved to the SQUARE-BRAQUEMONT Frosty.	

Instructions regarding War Diaries and Intelligence Summaries are contained in F. S. Regs., Part II. and the Staff Manual respectively. Title pages will be prepared in manuscript.

WAR DIARY
or
INTELLIGENCE SUMMARY.
(Erase heading not required.)

Army Form C. 2118.

Place	Date	Hour	Summary of Events and Information	Remarks and references to Appendices
BRAQUEMONT	18/11/16		B' Group refilling point moved to RUE ST BARBE - BRAQUEMONT	
	19/11/16		Presentation of medal ribbons by First Army Commander at D.H.Q - Capt Edwards, Sgt Lees, Cpl Elliott & Cpl Pratchett presented.	
	20/11/16		Lieut Le Sueur returned from leave. Capt Parsloe proceeded on leave.	
	21/11/16		Reinforcement of 1 Whr S Sgt and 27 drivers arrived. Major H. B. Hunter returned from leave.	
	22/11/16		Inspected transport 72nd & 73rd F.As.	
	23/11/16		Inspected transport 17th I.B.	
	24/11/16		Inspected transport 74th F.A.	
	25/11/16		G.O.C Division inspected transport at railhead, refilling points and Company lines - Expressed great satisfaction. Reinforcement 2 Sgts - 1 posted to 196 and 1 to 194 Coy.	

2353 Wt. W2544/1454 700,000 5/15 D. D. & L. A.D.S.S./Forms/C. 2118.

Army Form C. 2118.

WAR DIARY
or
INTELLIGENCE SUMMARY.
(Erase heading not required.)

Instructions regarding War Diaries and Intelligence Summaries are contained in F. S. Regs., Part II. and the Staff Manual respectively. Title pages will be prepared in manuscript.

Place	Date	Hour	Summary of Events and Information	Remarks and references to Appendices
BRAQUEMONT	26/11/16		Notified railhead for 40th D.A. would be BRUAY from 5th Dec. inclusive.	
"	27/11/16		Collected 14 Remounts at NOEUX-LES-MINES – 2 HD & 1 LD for 196 Coy – 2 HD to HQ Co. 40th D.T.	
"	28/11/16		Supply train very late – refilling considerably delayed.	
"	29/11/16		1 H.D horse received from 17th B.H.Q and taken on strength of 195 Coy – Reinforcement 1 Whlr. S. Sgt surplus returned. Ordered to transfer 5 drivers (194 – 2 other coys 1 each) to H.Q 4th Res Park –	
"	30/11/16		No 2 Sec Res Park move to HESDIGNEUL and no longer available for transport fatigues. CSM Bulthess rejoined from hospital – C.S.M Mills surplus to Base. Lieut Plumptre returned from leave.	

J.B. Lt Col

2353 Wt. W2544/1454 700,000 5/15 D. D. & L. A.D.S.S./Forms/C. 2118.

CONFIDENTIAL.

WAR DIARY.

OF

194. Company A.S.C.

from 1/11/16 to 30/11/16.

24 DT

72?

24 Div Train

App 6 Vol 15 Nov

Instructions regarding War Diaries and Intelligence Summaries are contained in F. S. Regs., Part II. and the Staff Manual respectively. Title Pages will be prepared in manuscript.

WAR DIARY
or
INTELLIGENCE SUMMARY
(Erase heading not required.)

Army Form C. 2118.

R Blakeway Major

Place	Date	Hour	Summary of Events and Information	Remarks and references to Appendices
GAUCHIN LEGAL	1/11/16	A.M. 8-30	Supply wagons refilled on HERMIN - GAUCHIN LEGAL Road – MAJOR BLAKEWAY returned from leave –	Fine morning. Rain evening.
″	2/11/16	″	″ ″ ″ ″ ″ ″ ″	Rain – Fine evening
″	3/11/16	″	″ ″ ″ ″ ″ ″ ″	Fine –
″	4/11/16	″	″ ″ ″ ″ ″ ″ ″	Fine –
″	5/11/16	″	″ ″ ″ ″ ″ ″ ″ CAPT. H.E. PEARSON went on leave –	Rain evening
″	6/11/16	″	″ ″ ″ ″ ″ ″ ″	Rain –
″	7/11/16	″	″ ″ ″ ″ ″ ″ ″	Rain –
″	8/11/16	″	″ ″ ″ ″ ″ ″ ″	Rain –
″	9/11/16	″	″ ″ ″ ″ ″ ″ ″	Fine –
″	10/11/16	″	″ ″ ″ ″ ″ ″ ″	Fine –
″	11/11/16	″	″ ″ ″ ″ ″ ″ ″	Fine –
″	12/11/16	″	″ ″ ″ ″ ″ ″ ″	Fine –
″	13/11/16	″	″ ″ ″ ″ ″ ″ ″	Fine –
″	14/11/16	″	″ ″ ″ ″ ″ ″ ″	Fine –
″	15/11/16	″	″ ″ ″ ″ ″ ″ ″	Fine –
″	16/11/16	″	″ ″ ″ ″ ″ ″ ″	Fine –
″	17/11/16	″	″ ″ ″ ″ ″ ″ ″ LT. PLUMPTRE went on leave –	Fine –
″	18/11/16	″	″ ″ ″ ″ ″ ″ ″ CAPT. PEARSON returned from leave –	Rain –
″	19/11/16	″	″ ″ ″ ″ ″ ″ ″	Rain morning Fine afternoon
″	20/11/16	″	″ ″ ″ ″ ″ ″ ″	Fine –

2449 Wt. W14957/M90 750,000 1/16 J.B.C. & A. Forms/C.2118/12.

Army Form C. 2118.

Instructions regarding War Diaries and Intelligence Summaries are contained in F. S. Regs., Part II. and the Staff Manual respectively. Title Pages will be prepared in manuscript.

WAR DIARY
or
INTELLIGENCE SUMMARY

(Erase heading not required.)

[illegible]

Place	Date	Hour	Summary of Events and Information	Remarks and references to Appendices
GAUCHIN LEGAL.	21/11/16	A.M. 8-30	Supply wagons refilled on HERMIN - GAUCHIN LEGAL Road -	Fine -
"	22/11/16	"	" " " " " " "	Fine -
"	23/11/16	"	" " " " " " "	Fine -
"	24/11/16	"	" " " " " " "	Wet -
"	25/11/16	"	" " " " " " " CAPT. SAUNDERS went on leave -	Rain -
"	26/11/16	"	" " " " " " "	Fine -
"	27/11/16	"	" " " " " " "	Fine -
"	28/11/16	"	" " " " " " "	Foggy -
"	29/11/16	"	" " " " " " "	Foggy -
"	30/11/16	"	" " " " " " " Lt. PLUMPTRE returned from leave -	Dull & foggy -

2449 Wt. W14957/M90 750,000 1/16 J.B.C. & A. Forms/C.2118/12.

T332

24

CONFIDENTIAL.

Vol

WAR DIARY.

OF

194th Company A.S.C.

24th DIVISIONAL TRAIN.

from 1/12/16 to 31/12/16.

T 33 L.

Instructions regarding War Diaries and Intelligence Summaries are contained in F. S. Regs., Part II. and the Staff Manual respectively. Title Pages will be prepared in manuscript.

WAR DIARY
or
INTELLIGENCE SUMMARY
(Erase heading not required.)

P. Blakeway - Major -

Army Form C. 2118.

Place	Date	Hour	Summary of Events and Information	Remarks and references to Appendices
GAUCHAIN LEGAL	1/12/16	A.M. 8-30	Supply wagons refilled on HERMIN-GAUCHAIN LEGAL Road -	Dull & frosty -
"	2/12/16	"	" " " " " " " ~~marched to NOEUX LES MINES~~	Dull & frosty
"	3/12/16	"	" " " " " " " " proceeded to NOEUX LES MINES -	Dull at night
"	4/12/16	9 A.M.	" " " at NOEUX LES MINES STATION - Headquarter Company marched to NOEUX LES MINES	Fine -
NOEUX LES MINES	5/12/16	11-30	" " " " " " "	Rain -
"	6/12/16	10-45	" " " " " " "	Dull -
"	7/12/16	11-15	" " " " " " " " CAPT SAUNDERS - returned from Base -	Dull -
"	8/12/16	9-15	" " " " " " "	Rain -
"	9/12/16	"	" " " " " " "	Rain -
"	10/12/16	8-30	" " " " " " "	Fine -
"	11/12/16	11-0	" " " " " " " " LT PLUMPTRE ordered to Train H.Q's for ?? ADJUTANT.	Rain afternoon
"	12/12/16	9-30	" " " " " " " " {MAJOR BLAKEWAY takes temporary Command of Train} {CAPT PEARSON - - - - - - - - Coy	Snow & rain
"	13/12/16	9.15	" " " " " " "	fine
"	14/12/16	9.15	" " " " " " " "	{dull, rain after 6 PM
"	15/12/16	9.30	" " " " " " "	dull
"	16/12/16	8.30	" " " " " " "	fine
"	17/12/16	8 30	" " " " " " "	dull
"	18/12/16	8.30	" " " " " " "	dull
"	19/12/16	8 30	" " " " " " "	{fine, turned to snow & frost
"	20/12/16	8 30	" " " " " " "	S.E. wind frost

2449 Wt. W14957/M90 750,000 1/16 J.B.C. & A. Forms/C.2118/12.

Army Form C. 2118.

Instructions regarding War Diaries and Intelligence Summaries are contained in F. S. Regs., Part II. and the Staff Manual respectively. Title Pages will be prepared in manuscript.

WAR DIARY
or
INTELLIGENCE SUMMARY

(Erase heading not required.)

Place	Date	Hour	Summary of Events and Information	Remarks and references to Appendices
NOEUX LES MINES	21/12/16	8.30 AM	Supply wagons refilled at [illegible] NOEUX LES MINES STATION	wet, strong S.E. wind.
" " "	22/12/16	11 AM	" " " " " " " "	wet
" " "	23/12/16	1.30 PM	" " " " " " " "	Strong S. wind. Gale in evening
" " "	24/12/16	11.0 AM	" " " " " " " "	Fine
" " "	25/12/16	11.0 AM	" " " " " " " " MAJOR BLAKEWAY took over Command of Company –	Strong S. wind.
" " "	26/12/16	10-30	" " " " " " " "	Rain –
" " "	27/12/16	8-30	" " " " " " " "	Rain –
"	28/12/16	"	" " " " " " " "	Fine –
"	29/12/16	"	" " " " " " " "	Rain & Gale –
"	30/12/16	10-30	" " " " " " " "	Rain morning –
"	31/12/16	9-30	" " " " " " " "	Fine –

R.W. Blakeway – Major

2449 Wt. W14957/M90 750,000 1/16 J.B.C. & A. Forms/C.2118/12.

Vol 16

T332.

- Confidential -

War Diary

of

24th Divisional Train

from 1 12/1916 to 31 12/1916

Army Form C. 2118.

WAR DIARY
or
INTELLIGENCE SUMMARY.
(Erase heading not required.)

Instructions regarding War Diaries and Intelligence Summaries are contained in F. S. Regs., Part II. and the Staff Manual respectively. Title pages will be prepared in manuscript.

Place	Date	Hour	Summary of Events and Information	Remarks and references to Appendices
BRAQUE MONT.	1/12/16		24th Division draw supplies at railhead before 1st Corps Troops. Train still arriving about 11.0 am	
	2/12/16		✓	
	3/12/16		Supply Section 194 Coy ASC arrive in present Divl area. Lieut R. J. Seddall admitted hospital sick. Purchase of fresh vegetables – only half ration being loaded at base	
	4/12/16		24th Divl Arty railhead NOEUX-LES-MINES – 40th D.A. railhead BRUAY. Baggage Section 194 Coy ASC arrive in this area – Capt Parsloe returned from leave – Gas Alert.	
	5/12/16		Reinforcement of 9 drivers (5 – 194 Coy. 2 – 195 Coy 1 to 196 & 197 Coys) Thaw.	
	6/12/16		Very wet.	
	7/12/16		Collected 5 tip carts from Ordnance Canadian Corps Troops. BRUAY. 158 L II mules remounts for 24th D.A. arrive – Capt Saunders returned from leave.	
	8/12/16		Returned civilian wagons & cart to owners – instructed to hand tip carts over to 24th D.A. Gas Alert cancelled. AA & QMG and representatives from Inf. Bde and Divl Trc. School visited railhead and 'C' Group refilling point.	

2353 Wt. W2544/1454 700,000 5/15 D. D. & L. A.D.S.S./Forms/C. 2118.

Instructions regarding War Diaries and Intelligence Summaries are contained in F. S. Regs., Part II. and the Staff Manual respectively. Title pages will be prepared in manuscript.

WAR DIARY
or
INTELLIGENCE SUMMARY.
(Erase heading not required.)

Army Form C. 2118.

Place	Date	Hour	Summary of Events and Information	Remarks and references to Appendices
BRAQUEMONT	9/12/16			
	10/12/16			
	11/12/16		LT. K.H. PLUMPTRE reported for duty as Adjutant during absence of LT. A. McCALLUM on leave	
	12/12/16		LT. A. McCALLUM went on leave. LT. COL. F.D. LORD was admitted to hospital. MAJOR T. W. BLAKEWAY took over the temporary command of the Train.	
	13/12/16		Dr. KINGMAN. T. handed over to 197 Coy. from Base on a charge of desertion. Reinforcements arrived, 255 for 8th Buffs + 174 for 2. Hants. Rations arranged accordingly	
	14/12/16		Summary of Evidence taken in the case of Dr. KINGMAN T. Further reinforcements arrived: 8th Queens 235, 9th E. Surrey 170, 12th R. Fus 235, 1st R. Fus: 190, 2nd Leinster 73. These latter, being fully trained went straight to their unit. Remainder camped in huts at K 24 6.8.7 (BRAQUEMONT – BARLIN ROAD) Transport all under charge of LT. LE SEUER. SERGT. PATERSON from No 194 Coy + SERGT. GODDARD from No 196 Coy also attached for duty together with Farrier Dvr LONG of 197 Coy.	
	15/12/16		Nothing of any importance to report.	
	16/12/16		Ditto.	

Instructions regarding War Diaries and Intelligence Summaries are contained in F. S. Regs., Part II. and the Staff Manual respectively. Title pages will be prepared in manuscript.

WAR DIARY
or
INTELLIGENCE SUMMARY.
(Erase heading not required.)

Army Form C. 2118.

Place	Date	Hour	Summary of Events and Information	Remarks and references to Appendices
BRAQUEMONT	17/12/16		Nothing of importance to report. Church Service at 194 Coy's Camp.	
	18/12/16		First summary of evidence taken re Dr. KINGMAN. 12 Wagons under 1st Class S.S.M. BATES from 9th Reserve Park attached to 195 Coy.	
	19/12/16		Dr. Blands of 195 Company brought up for Insubordination. Remanded for F.G.M.	
	20/12/16		Divisional Training Battalion moved to ALLOUAGNE. 191 M.G. Coy moved to LE BREBIS. 167 Remounts arrived on Supply train. 4 for Div. Train. Summary of evidence taken in the case of Dr. Blands.	
	21/12/16		No 3 Section 9th Reserve Park, consisting of 1 Officer - 11 horses - 53 O.R. 76 H.D. 3 R. + 35 G.S.W. Camp at L 25 a. 2.8. (Map 36 b) 12 Wagons under S.S.M. BATES of No 2 Section 9th Reserve Park, rejoined their unit. NOEUX-LES-MINES Station shelled in afternoon	
	22/12/16		Trial by F.G.M. of Dr. KINGMAN occupied greater portion of the day. Lt. Le Sueur to hospital (sick)	
	23/12/16		LT. McCALLUM returned to duty.	
	24-12-16		Dr KINGMAN awarded 90 days F.P. No 1 charge being altered to "absence without leave" Court martial promulgated. 4 Charcoal Burners attached to 195 Coy - wood not drawn by units to be converted into Charcoal. Inspected 191st M.G.C. and attached 1 H.T. Sgt & 1 Shoeing Smith to this unit with a view to improving the transport. Fine.	

2353 Wt. W2544/1454 700,000 5/15 D. D. & L. A.D.S.S./Forms/C. 2118.

Instructions regarding War Diaries and Intelligence Summaries are contained in F. S. Regs., Part II. and the Staff Manual respectively. Title pages will be prepared in manuscript.

WAR DIARY
or
INTELLIGENCE SUMMARY.
(Erase heading not required.)

Army Form C. 2118.

Place	Date	Hour	Summary of Events and Information	Remarks and references to Appendices
BRAQUEMONT	25/12/16		Wet & stormy. Lieut Col FB Lord discharged hospital returned to duty. Leave stopped	
	26/12/16		FGCM of Dr Blanks 195 Coy ASC. Gas Alert. Leave re-opened via CALAIS.	
	27/12/16		FGCM of Dr Blanks promulgated - awarded 3 months F.P. No 1. Capt GARRATT - ASC reported for duty and posted to 197 Coy.	
	28/12/16		Authority obtained through 1st Corps to purchase one days issue of coke - Coke bought at NOEUX - LES - MINES Gas Works.	
	29/12/16		Capt D W Edwards proceeded on leave. Normal supply of coke arrived on pack train.	
	30/12/16		Lieut Wildblood proceeded on leave.	
	31/12/16		Fine.	
			1/1/17.	
			F B Lord Lt Col Commd of 24th Divl Train	

2353 Wt. W2344/1454 700,000 5/15 D. D. & L. A.D.S.S./Forms/C. 2118.

Army Form C. 2118.

Instructions regarding War Diaries and Intelligence Summaries are contained in F. S. Regs., Part II. and the Staff Manual respectively. Title Pages will be prepared in manuscript.

WAR DIARY
or
INTELLIGENCE SUMMARY
(Erase heading not required.)

24th Div: Train

Vol 17

Place	Date	Hour	Summary of Events and Information	Remarks and references to Appendices
NOEUX LES MINES.	1/1/17	A.M. 9-30	Supply wagons refilled at NOEUX LES MINES Station –	Fine –
"	2/1/17	10-30	" " " " " " "	Fine – Rain in [illegible]
"	3/1/17	9-30	" " " " " " "	Rain morning
"	4/1/17	9-30	" " " " " " "	Rain at night
"	5/1/17	"	" " " " " " "	Fine day –
"	6/1/17	"	" " " " " " "	Fine –
"	7/1/17	"	" " " " " " "	Fine. Rain night
"	8/1/17	"	" " " " " " " " HERSIN road shelled 600 yards S. of camp	fine. rain in evening
"	9/1/17	"	" " " " " " " "	fine
"	10/1/17	"	" " " " " " "	~~[illegible]~~ fine
"	11/1/17	"	" " " " " " " Major BLAKEWAY assumes command of Train / Capt PEARSON " " [illegible] Coy / whilst Col. LORD on leave.	Snow in morning
"	12/1/17	10.30	" " " " " " "	fine
"	13/1/17	7.30 PM	" " " " " " "	Snow in evening
"	14/1/17	12 Noon	" " " " " " " "gas alert" 8 PM	fine
"	15/1/17	11 AM	" " " " " " " " "	fine
"	16/1/17	9.30	" " " " " " " cancelled.	fine / frost
"	17/1/17	10.30	" " " " " " " "	heavy snow
"	18/1/17	10 AM	" " " " " " "	sleet
"	19/1/17	11	" " " " " " " gas alert 9 AM.	NE wind.

H. Pearson Capt

2449 Wt. W14957/M90 750,000 1/16 J.B.C. & A. Forms/C.2118/12.

Army Form C. 2118.

WAR DIARY
or
INTELLIGENCE SUMMARY
(Erase heading not required.)

Instructions regarding War Diaries and Intelligence Summaries are contained in F. S. Regs., Part II. and the Staff Manual respectively. Title Pages will be prepared in manuscript.

Place	Date	Hour	Summary of Events and Information	Remarks and references to Appendices
NOEUX LES MINES	20/1/17	1 PM	Supply wagons refilled at NOEUX LES MINES Station gas alert	frost
"	21/1/17	12 noon	" " " " " " " " "	frost
"	22/1/17	2 pm	" " " " " " " " " MAJOR BLAKEWAY took command	frost
"	23/1/17	1 pm	" " " " " " " " "	frost
"	24/1/17	1 pm	" " " " " " " " "	frost
"	25/1/17	1.45	" " " " " " " " "	frost
"	26/1/17	1.30	" " " " " " " " " No Supply Train arrived	frost
"	27/1/17	–	" " " " " " " "	frost
"	28/1/17	5 A.M.	" " " " Refilling Point at NOEUX for 27th from lorries	frost
"	29/1/17	3 AM 8 AM	Refilling Point at NOEUX for 28th Major BLAKEWAY went on leave Capt. PEARSON took over command " " " " " 29th	snow & frost
"	30/1/17	2.30 AM 3.30 PM	Supply wagons refilled at NOEUX LES MINES station	frost
"	31/1/17	2.30 PM	" " " " " " " "	

H.C. Pearson Capt

2449 Wt. W14957/M90 750,000 1/16 J.B.C. & A. Forms/C.2118/12.

Vol 17

Confidential

War Diary

of

O. C 24th Divisional Train

From 1-1-17 to 31-1-17

Instructions regarding War Diaries and Intelligence Summaries are contained in F. S. Regs., Part II. and the Staff Manual respectively. Title pages will be prepared in manuscript.

WAR DIARY
or
INTELLIGENCE SUMMARY.
(Erase heading not required.)

Army Form C. 2118.

Place	Date	Hour	Summary of Events and Information	Remarks and references to Appendices
BRAQUEMONT	1/1/17		Lieut R. F. Seddall returned from leave –	
"	2/1/17		No meat at railhead – P.M issued.	
"	3/1/17		C.S.M L.S. MIRAMS, 194 Coy ASC awarded Meritorious Service Medal in New Years Honours. Ordered to send 2 complete turnout to No 30 P. of W. Coy.	
"	4/1/17		Wet. Informed at 9pm that there would be no meat at railhead on the 2nd inst. Lieut G. H. Hitch proceeded on leave.	
	5/1/17		Fine & cold. Aerial activity – 3 shells H.V. near No 1 Coy's Camp – Wagons shelled delivering supplies near Fosse 2. de BETHUNE – Two bolted – no casualties supplies eventually delivered.	
	6/1/17		Tempy 2Lieut A.H. Barnes ASC reported for duty from BHTD HAVRE and posted to 195 Coy. as a Transport Officer. Lt Col F B Lord, Majors Blakeway & Hunter, Sgts Clarke and Ellwood and Pte Bridger "Mentioned in Despatches" Drew all coke and charcoal by Horse Transport from railhead –	

2353 Wt. W2544/1454 700,000 5/15 D. D. & L. A.D.S.S./Forms/C. 2118.

Instructions regarding War Diaries and Intelligence Summaries are contained in F. S. Regs., Part II. and the Staff Manual respectively. Title pages will be prepared in manuscript.

WAR DIARY
or
INTELLIGENCE SUMMARY.
(Erase heading not required.)

Army Form C. 2118.

Place	Date	Hour	Summary of Events and Information	Remarks and references to Appendices
BRAQUEMONT	7/1/17		Bomb raid between 2.0 am and 2.30 am - bombs dropped in vicinity of NOEUX-LES-MINES Station. Hay ration increased to 8 lbs per horse at Railhead.	
"	8/1/17		About 30 shells fell near 194 Coy's Camp in rear of Distillery. One unexploded shell in RUE BUGEAUD.	
"	9/1/17.		✓	
"	10/1/17		Collected 13 remounts for other units than Artillery of the Division - 2HD for 194 Coy. Capt Edwards returned from leave. Lieut Le Sueur discharged hospital & returned to duty.	
	11/1/17		Capt D.W. Edwards left Div Train on transfer to R.F.C. & struck off strength as per 12.1.17. Lt Wildblood returned from leave. Lt Col F.B. Lord proceeded on leave. Major T.W. Blakeway assumed command.	
	12/1/17		No fresh meat at Railhead - P.M. issued. Lt McNamara proceeded on leave. Collected "Mice" at Mine Yard & conveyed same to CRUCIFIX CORNER by night. (Convoy of 14 G.S. wagons)	

Instructions regarding War Diaries and Intelligence Summaries are contained in F. S. Regs., Part II. and the Staff Manual respectively. Title pages will be prepared in manuscript.

WAR DIARY
or
INTELLIGENCE SUMMARY.
(Erase heading not required.)

Army Form C. 2118.

Place	Date	Hour	Summary of Events and Information	Remarks and references to Appendices
BRACQUE-MONT	13/1/17		Lt. A. McCallum & Adjt. left Div Train on transfer to 5th Buffs & struck off strength of this Unit as from today. Lt E. W. L. Martin 195 Coy A.S.C. appointed Acting Adjt. as from 13.1.17. Supply Train arrived Railhead at 7.30 pm. - finished drawing supplies 9.15 pm. Last wagons left Refilling Points 11.0 pm. Very wet.	
	14/1/17		Supply Train normal. Capt D. Bottomley reported for duty from BHTD HAVRE and posted temporarily to 197 Coy. Frosted roads early morning - thaw later. Lieut C.C. Gale proceeded on leave.	
	15/1/17		Fine & frosty. Lieut. L. M. Mischer proceeded on leave.	
	16/1/17		Do. Lieut. G. H. Hitch returned from leave	
	17/1/17		Snow - roads rather slippery early morning. Very cold.	
	18/1/17		Snow - roads 'slushy'	
	19/1/17		Do.	
	20/1/17		Hard frost. Lieut Bennett proceeded on leave.	
	21/1/17		Do. No. 30 D.S.C. proceeded to 3rd Army to rejoin their Divn. No 24 D.S.C. arrived HAILLICOURT on rejoining this Divn. Lt. Col. F. B. Lord returned from leave. No Column Supply Details being available at Railhead, all issuing done by Divl Train Supply Details.	

2353 Wt. W2544/1454 700,000 5/15 D. D. & L. A.D.S.S./Forms/C. 2118.

Army Form C. 2118.

Instructions regarding War Diaries and Intelligence Summaries are contained in F. S. Regs., Part II. and the Staff Manual respectively. Title pages will be prepared in manuscript.

WAR DIARY
or
INTELLIGENCE SUMMARY.
(Erase heading not required.)

Place	Date	Hour	Summary of Events and Information	Remarks and references to Appendices
BRAQUEMONT	22/1/17		Hard Frost	
	23/1/17		Do. O.O. No. 118 received.	
	24/1/17		Do. Capt D. Bottomley temporarily transferred from 197 Coy to 194 Coy. Lt. C.C. Gale transferred from 194 Coy to 196 Coy.	
	25/1/17		Hard Frost. Visited new area. Lt. McNamara returned from leave.	
	26/1/17		Do. O.O. No. 118 Cancelled 9.15 p.m. Leave Cancelled.	
	27/1/17		Pack Train did not arrive at Railhead. Instructed at 10.30 pm to issue the rations held by Supply Column. Lorries began to arrive at Refilling Points at 3.30 am (28/1/17). Last Wagon to Units left Brigade Refilling Points at 7.15 am. Lt. Col. England, O.C. 66 Divl Train, attached to this Train for 6 days tour of instruction. Lt Gale returned from leave.	
	28/1/17		Warned at 1 pm. that Supplies were to be drawn from No. 4 F.S.D by Supply Column. Lorries began to arrive at 10.30 pm. All Wagons had left Brigade Refilling Points by 1 am. Divl Troops by 3.30 am. Lt. Fischer returned from leave.	

Instructions regarding War Diaries and Intelligence Summaries are contained in F. S. Regs., Part II. and the Staff Manual respectively. Title pages will be prepared in manuscript.

WAR DIARY
or
INTELLIGENCE SUMMARY.
(Erase heading not required.)

Army Form C. 2118.

Place	Date	Hour	Summary of Events and Information	Remarks and references to Appendices
BRAQUEMONT	29/1/17		Supplies drawn from Railhead by Supply Column & dumped at Refilling Points between the hours of 1 & 5 am. Supplies distributed to Units at 8.30 am.	
			Pack train expected at 5 pm – did not arrive until about 1 am. Supplies drawn by H.T. & dumped at Refilling Points, last group finishing about 4 a.m. Very cold. Major Blakeway proceeded on leave.	
	30/1/17		Refilling took place at 8.30 am. Supplies drawn at Railhead by H.T. 2.30 pm. O.C. Corps informed that G.O.C. had expressed great satisfaction with the manner in which all ranks had carried out their duties during the trying times of the past few days.	
	31/1/17		Supplies drawn at Railhead 2 p.m. Still hard frost. Leave reopened as from 2/2/17.	

[illegible] Lt Col
Commd of 24th Div Train

2353 Wt. W2544/1454 700,000 5/15 D. D. & L. A.D.S.S./Forms/C. 2118.

Confidential – War Diary

Vol 18

of

O.C. 24th Divisional Train

1/2/17 to 28/2/17.

Instructions regarding War Diaries and Intelligence Summaries are contained in F. S. Regs., Part II. and the Staff Manual respectively. Title pages will be prepared in manuscript.

WAR DIARY
or
INTELLIGENCE SUMMARY.
(Erase heading not required.)

Army Form C. 2118.

Place	Date	Hour	Summary of Events and Information	Remarks and references to Appendices
BRAQUEMONT	1/2/17		Lt. Bennett returned from leave. O.O. No 31 CRA received. Hard frost	
	2/2/17		Normal - nothing to report.	
	3/2/17		Lt Col England left Train H.Q on his return to England. Pack train late - loaded supplies 5.30 p.m. Oats ration reduced to H.D. 13 lbs Others 9 lbs.	
	4/2/17		Capt Martinoff (Russian Army) shown round Refilling Points, Company lines & distribution of rations at QM Stores of 3rd R.Bs	
	5/2/17		Lt. [illegible] proceeded to England on leave. Lt. [illegible] to act as Adjutant during his absence. [illegible] return to 194 Coy. for permanent duty. Lt. Col. [illegible] S.O.M.T. 1st Corps ref. Lorries for divisional purposes. 18 [illegible].	
	6/2/17		Supply Train did not arrive until 10.30 p.m. Commenced to unload at midnight.	
	7/2/17		Supply Train arrived 6.45 p.m. nothing else of importance to record.	
	8/2/17		Operation orders received. Supply Train in to time.	
	9/2/17		Supply Train arrived to time.	
	10/2/17		Supply Train arrived 3.30 p.m. First Group loaded at 5. p.m.	
	11/2/17		Supply Train arrived 4.10. p.m. First Group loaded at 6.10 p.m. 73rd Inf. Bde & 197 Company moved to rest area. 197 Coy to [illegible]. Major Blakeway returned from leave	

2353 Wt. W2544/1454 700,000 5/15 D. D. & L. A.D.S.S./Forms/C. 2118.

Army Form C. 2118.

Instructions regarding War Diaries and Intelligence Summaries are contained in F. S. Regs., Part II. and the Staff Manual respectively. Title pages will be prepared in manuscript.

WAR DIARY
or
INTELLIGENCE SUMMARY.
(Erase heading not required.)

Place	Date	Hour	Summary of Events and Information	Remarks and references to Appendices
~~Fouquières~~ Bracquemont	to 12/2/17		195 Coy. 196 Coy & 194 Coy move to new areas. Fouquières, Bracquemont & Fouquières respectively. Lorries on road	
Fouquières	13/2/17		Train H.Q. moved to new area. Lorries on road.	
— " —	14/2/17		Col. Lord visited refilling point at Bourecq - Lillers road (C Group), Major Hunter visited refilling points at Fouquières, A B & D Groups. Nothing else of importance to record.	
— " —	15/2/17		Nothing of importance to report.	
— " —	16/2/17		A representative Company of the Train, consisting of 10 G.S. Wagons from 194 Coy, 5 G.S.W. from 195 & 5 G.S.W. from 197 Coy, paraded at an inspection by Gen. Nivelle, C in C French Army. Thaw scheme came into force midnight 16/2/17	
	17/2/17		Lt Martin returned from leave. Lt Plumptre returned to duty with 196 Coy. Letter received from Corps Commander conveying Congratulations of Army Commander on the turn out for Genl. Nivelle's inspection - Copy attached.	
	18/2/17		Col. Lord visited Railhead & No 3 Coy. Supplied 15 G.S. Wagons to convey Ordnance stores from Main Road - CHOCQUES to Stores at LABEUVRIÈRE. Lorries could not be used owing to thaw.	
	19/2/17		Nothing to report.	
	20/2/17		Very wet.	

2353 Wt. W2544/1454 700,000 5/15 D. D. & L. A.D.S.S./Forms/C. 2118.

Instructions regarding War Diaries and Intelligence Summaries are contained in F. S. Regs., Part II. and the Staff Manual respectively. Title Pages will be prepared in manuscript.

WAR DIARY
or
INTELLIGENCE SUMMARY
(Erase heading not required.)

Army Form C. 2118.

Place	Date	Hour	Summary of Events and Information	Remarks and references to Appendices
FOUQUIERES	21/2/17		Inspected Regimental Transport of 1st Royal Fusiliers. Collected 14 tons of Fuel Wood from No. 6 F.S.D BARLIN by H.T. 5 H.D. Remounts received – 3 for 194 Coy – 1 each for 196 & 197 Coys. Collected by 24 Signal Coy R.E.	
	22/2/17		Two complete surplus "tin outs" sent to 21st Div Train for transmission to Base.	
	23/2/17		Lt. Pugh proceeded on leave. O.O 122 received. 1 N.C.O. & 3 G.S. Wagons attached to Pioneers for road repairs. Addendum to 24 Div O.O. No 122 received. 4 H.D. Horses returned from 21st D.T.	
	24/2/17		Visited proposed new area. Capt. H.C. Pearson admitted to Rest Station, AIRE. 2nd Addendum to 24 Div. O.O. No 122 received	
	25/2/17		Fine.	
	26/2/17		R.A.M.C. O.O. No 102 & C.R.E. O.O. No 50 received.	
	27/2/17		C.O. attended D.D.S.&T's Conference. Transport teams of 3 Field Coys R.E. judged by Major Blakeway on behalf of C.O. Transport of 74 Field Ambulance inspected by C.O. 3rd Addendum & Administrative Instructions for O.O. No 122 & 72nd I.B. O.O. No. 118 received.	

2449 Wt. W14957/M90 750,000 1/16 J.B.C. & A. Forms/C.2118/12.

Army Form C. 2118.

Instructions regarding War Diaries and Intelligence Summaries are contained in F. S. Regs., Part II. and the Staff Manual respectively. Title Pages will be prepared in manuscript.

WAR DIARY
or
INTELLIGENCE SUMMARY
(Erase heading not required.)

Place	Date	Hour	Summary of Events and Information	Remarks and references to Appendices
FOUQUIERES	28/2/17.		C.O. judges Transport entries at Battn. Sports of 2nd Leinsters. Dull - cold.	
			[illegible] Lt. Col. Comdg 24th Divl Train	

2449 Wt. W14957/M90 750,000 1/16 J.B.C. & A. Forms/C.2118/12.

Instructions regarding War Diaries and Intelligence Summaries are contained in F. S. Regs., Part II. and the Staff Manual respectively. Title Pages will be prepared in manuscript.

WAR DIARY
or
INTELLIGENCE SUMMARY
(Erase heading not required.)

194 Coy ASC (24 Division)

Army Form C. 2118.

24 D Vol I

Place	Date	Hour	Summary of Events and Information	Remarks and references to Appendices
NOEUX LES MINES	1/2/17	1.30PM	Supply wagons refilled at NOEUX LES MINES Station	frost
" "	2/2/17	1.30PM	" " " " " " "	frost
" "	3/2/17	4.30PM	" " " " " " — 8 wagons for 108th Bde RFA went to 6th D.T.	frost
" "	4/2/17	1.30PM	" " " " " " "	frost
" "	5/2/17	1.30PM	" " " " " " "	Snow & frost
" "	6/2/17		NO train arrived	frost
" "	7/2/17	1.30AM 10.15PM	Supply wagons refilled at NOEUX LES MINES Station for 6th inst. " " " " " " " " " 7th "	frost
" "	8/2/17	1.30PM	" " " " " " "	frost
" "	9/2/17	4.30PM	" " " " " " "	frost
" "	10/2/17	5.30PM	" " " " " " "	frost
"	11/2/17	6.40pm	" " " " " " " " MAJOR BLAKEWAY returned from Leave –	frost –
"	12/2/17	8-0AM	Company moved to FOUQUIÈRES at 2-30 pm –	frost –
FOUQUIÈRES	13/2/17	8-30AM	Supply wagons refilled on FOUQUIÈRES – BETHUNE Road –	frost & thaw.
"	14/2/17	"	" " " " " "	frost –
"	15/2/17	9.AM	" " " " " "	frost
"	16/2/17	"	" " " " " " GEN: NIVELLE reviewed units of the Division –	frost & thaw.
"	17/2/17	"	" " " " " "	Thaw –
"	18/2/17	"	" " " " " "	Thaw –
"	19/2/17	"	" " " " " "	Thaw –
"	20/2/17	"	" " " " " "	Rain –
"	21/2/17	"	" " " " " "	Dull & foggy –

R Blakeway Major

Instructions regarding War Diaries and Intelligence Summaries are contained in F. S. Regs., Part II. and the Staff Manual respectively. Title Pages will be prepared in manuscript.

WAR DIARY
or
INTELLIGENCE SUMMARY
(Erase heading not required.)

Army Form C. 2118.

Place	Date	Hour	Summary of Events and Information	Remarks and references to Appendices
FOUQUIÈRES	22/2/17	9. A.M.	Supply wagons refilled on FOUQUIÈRES - BETHUNE Road -	Rain -
"	23/2/17	"	" " " " " "	Dull & foggy -
"	24/2/17	"	" " " " " "	Fine -
"	25/2/17	"	" " " " " "	Fine -
"	26/2/17	"	" " " " " "	Fine -
"	27/2/17	"	" " " " " "	Fine -
"	28/2/17	"	" " " " " "	Fine - Dull -

R Blakeway - Major -

2449 Wt. W14957/M90 750,000 1/16 J.B.C. & A. Forms/C.2118/12.

Confidential Vol 19

War Diary

of

O.C 24th Divisional Train

From 1/3/17 to 31/3/17.

Instructions regarding War Diaries and Intelligence Summaries are contained in F. S. Regs., Part II. and the Staff Manual respectively. Title Pages will be prepared in manuscript.

WAR DIARY
or
INTELLIGENCE SUMMARY
(Erase heading not required.)

Army Form C. 2118.

194 Co A.S.C.

[signature] Major

Place	Date	Hour	Summary of Events and Information	Remarks and references to Appendices
FOUQUIERES.	1/3/17	9 A.M.	Supply wagons refilled on FOUQUIÈRES – BETHUNE Road –	Fine –
"	2/3/17	"	" " " " " "	Fine –
"	3/3/17	"	" " " " " "	Cold –
"	4/3/17	"	" " " " " " " TRAIN H.Qrs moved to BRAQUEMENT –	Fine –
"	5/3/17	"	" " " " " " " COMPANY moved to NOEUX –	Snow –
NOEUX –	6/3/17	8 A.M.	" " " on HERSIN – NOEUX LES MINES Road – Drew from Railhead at 12-45 A.M. 7/3/17.	Fine –
"	7/3/17	"	" " " " " " " " " " " " 7-15 P.M.	Fine, strong E Wind –
"	8/3/17	"	" " " " " " " " " " " " 7-45 P.M.	Snow & E wind
"	9/3/17	"	" " " " " " " " " " " " 6-45 P.M.	Fine afternoon Snow & Clouds
"	10/3/17	"	" " " " " " " " " " " " 2-15 P.M.	Fine –
"	11/3/17	7 A.M.	" " " " " " " " " " " " 12-15 P.M.	Fine –
"	12/3/17	"	" " " " " " " " " " " " 12-0 NOON –	Rain –
"	13/3/17	"	" " " " " " " " " " " " 12-30 P.M.	Cold – fine –
"	14/3/17	"	" " " " " " " " " " " " 12-0 NOON	Rain –
"	15/3/17	"	" " " " " " " " " " " " 12-0 NOON –	Fine –
"	16/3/17	"	" " " " " " " " " " " " 12-0 NOON –	Fine –
"	17/3/17	"	" " " " " " " " " " " " 11-40 A.M.	Fine –
"	18/3/17	"	" " " " " " " " " " " " 2-0 NOON –	Fine –
"	19/3/17	"	" " " " " " " " " " " " 12-0 NOON. Camp shelled –	Rain –
"	20/3/17	"	" " " " " " " " " " " " 2-20 p.m.	Rain –

2449 Wt. W14957/M90 750,000 1/16 J.B.C. & A. Forms/C.2118/12.

Instructions regarding War Diaries and Intelligence Summaries are contained in F. S. Regs., Part II. and the Staff Manual respectively. Title Pages will be prepared in manuscript.

WAR DIARY
or
INTELLIGENCE SUMMARY
(Erase heading not required.)

Army Form C. 2118.

[illegible] Blakeway – Major

Place	Date	Hour	Summary of Events and Information	Remarks and references to Appendices
NOEUX	21/3/17	7 A.M.	Supply wagons refilled on HERSIN – NOEUX LES MINES Road – [illegible] from Railhead at 12 NOON.	Fine. Snow in night –
"	22/3/17	"	" " " " " " " " " "	Snow –
"	23/3/17	"	" " " " " " " " " " 1.15 pm. C. PLUMPTREE proceeded on leave –	Fine – Frost –
"	24/3/17	"	" " " " " " " " " " 2.15 pm – Time [illegible] one hour at 11 pm – Capt. CROOME . ESSEX Regt. reported –	Fine –
"	25/3/17	"	" " " " " " " " " " 2-30 pm – NOEUX LES MINES shelled on & off for most of day –	Fine –
"	26/3/17	"	" " " " " " " " " " 2-30 pm –	Rain –
"	27/3/17	"	" " " " " " " " " " 3-0 pm – Capt. CROOME ESSEX. Regt. left –	Snow showers –
"	28/3/17	"	" " " " " " " " " " 6-30 a.m. 29/3/17	Rain –
"	29/3/17	7-30 AM	" " " " " " " " " " 3-30 pm – NOEUX LES MINES shelled –	Rain –
"	30/3/17	7-AM	" " " " " " " " " " 3-30 pm –	Rain – Showery –
	31/3/17	"	" " " " " " " " " " 6-30 pm –	Showery –

2449 Wt. W14957/M90 750,000 1/16 J.B.C. & A. Forms/C.2118/12.

Instructions regarding War Diaries and Intelligence Summaries are contained in F. S. Regs., Part II. and the Staff Manual respectively. Title Pages will be prepared in manuscript.

WAR DIARY
or
~~INTELLIGENCE SUMMARY~~
(Erase heading not required.)

Army Form C. 2118.

Place	Date	Hour	Summary of Events and Information	Remarks and references to Appendices
FOUQUIERES.	1/3/17		Inspected transport of 17th Machine Gun Coy + 73rd Field Ambulance.	
"	2/3/17		195 Coy moved to BRACQUEMONT. Amendment to O.O. No. 34 by C.R.A. received. ~~[illegible]~~	
"	3/3/17		196 Coy moved to BRAQUEMONT. Further amendments to O.O. No. 34 by C.R.A. received. Railhead changed to NOEUX LES MINES. "B" Group drew from Railhead by H.T.	
BRACQUEMONT	4/3/17		Train H.Q. + 197 Coy moved to BRACQUEMONT. "B + C" Groups drew from Railhead by H.T. - loading started at 6.30 p.m.	
"	5/3/17		Snow. 194 Coy moved to NOEUX LES MINES. "B, C + D" Groups drew from Railhead by H.T. - loading started at 11 p.m. S.S.M. J. Riley reduced to rank of Cpl. - Authority I Corps letter No. A 113/40 d. 3.3.17	
"	6/3/17		2/Lt. J.H. Pugh returned from leave. All Groups drew from Railhead by H.T. - loading started at 12 midnight.	

Instructions regarding War Diaries and Intelligence Summaries are contained in F. S. Regs., Part II. and the Staff Manual respectively. Title Pages will be prepared in manuscript.

WAR DIARY
or
INTELLIGENCE SUMMARY
(Erase heading not required.)

Army Form C. 2118.

Place	Date	Hour	Summary of Events and Information	Remarks and references to Appendices
BRACQUEMONT	7/3/17		C.O. attended D.D.S.T.'s Conference. Loading at Railhead started at 6.30 p.m.	
"	8/3/17		Snow. Loading at Railhead started at 7 p.m.	
"	9/3/17		Snow. Loading at Railhead started at 5.30 p.m.	
"	10/3/17		Mild. Capt H. C. Pearson discharged from Hospital. Railhead 1.30 p.m.	
"	11/3/17		Fine. Railhead 11.30 a.m.	
"	12/3/17		Railhead 12 noon. Station shelled - no casualties.	
"	13/3/17		Capt C.H.T. Scott, R.A.V.C. proceeded on leave. Dull. Railhead 11.30 a.m.	
"	14/3/17		Wet.	
"	15/3/17		Dull. Nothing of importance to report.	

2449 Wt. W14957/M90 750,000 1/16 J.B.C. & A. Forms/C.2118/12.

Army Form C. 2118.

Instructions regarding War Diaries and Intelligence Summaries are contained in F. S. Regs., Part II. and the Staff Manual respectively. Title Pages will be prepared in manuscript.

WAR DIARY
or
INTELLIGENCE SUMMARY

(Erase heading not required.)

Place	Date	Hour	Summary of Events and Information	Remarks and references to Appendices
BRACQUEMONT.	16/3/17		Fine	
"	17/3/17		Capt. J.P. Thompson proceeded on leave. No 2 Section, 9 Reserve Park attached to Div Train for instruction in Supply duties – attached to 194 Coy who are to perform the duties usually carried out by the Section, R.P. Lt. C.C. Gale attached for duty to No. 3 Section, 9 R.P.	
"	18/3/17		O.C. 6th Div Train inspected improvised Pack Saddlery & Water Carriers	
"	19/3/17		High wind, followed by rain. 6 H.V. Shells fell near 194 Coy's Camp – no damage. A.A. & Q.M.G. & O.C. 2° Cav. Train inspected improvised Pack Saddlery & Water Carriers.	
"	20/3/17		Supply train late – loading at Railhead commenced at 2 pm – all to be cleared by H.T. Lt. W.A. Wildblood attached for temporary duty to 72nd Field Ambulance for H.T. ~~[illegible]~~ 7 Off of 2° Cav. D.T. instructed in Improvised Pack Saddlery & Water Carriers.	
"	21/3/17		O.C. 49 D.T. & 3 Off – O.C. 66th D.T. & 2 Off instructed in improvised Pack Saddlery & Water Carriers.	
"	22/3/17		19 H.V. Shells at Railhead – no casualties – Snow. A.A. & Q.M.G. & 3 Officers from 6th Div. 4 R.E. Officers (24 Div) & Adjt. 66th D.T. instructed in improvised Pack Saddlery & Water Carriers.	

2449 Wt. W14957/M90 750,000 1/16 J.B.C. & A. Forms/C.2118/12.

Instructions regarding War Diaries and Intelligence Summaries are contained in F. S. Regs., Part II. and the Staff Manual respectively. Title Pages will be prepared in manuscript.

WAR DIARY
or
INTELLIGENCE SUMMARY
(Erase heading not required.)

Army Form C. 2118.

Place	Date	Hour	Summary of Events and Information	Remarks and references to Appendices
BRACQUEMONT	23/3/17		Improvised Pack Saddlery & Water Carriers inspected by General N.G. Anderson D.A & Q.M.G I Corps. A.D.O.S. I Corps. O.C. & Adjt. 8th Can. D.T. & 2 Officers of 66th D.T. instructed in improvised Pack Saddlery & Water Carriers. Lt K.M. Plumptre proceeded on leave.	
"	24/3/17		Capt Croome, Essex Regt., a Staff learner attached to Div Train for instruction for 10 days. Sample improvised Pack Saddlery & Water Carriers taken to I Corps H.Q by CO. O.C. & Officers 5th Div Train instructed in Pack Saddlery & Water Carriers. 1 Re-inforcement (Wheeler) arrived – posted to 196 Coy.	
"	25/3/17		15 H.D Horses taken from D.T. by D.D.R. 1st Army & handed to R.G.A. – strong representations made to the Division on the subject of the shortage of H.D Horses in the Train. Unable to horse 7 wagons if ordered to move tomorrow. NOEUX LES MINES shelled on & off from 7am to 5pm. Supplies drawn at Railhead at 2.30 pm.	
	26/3/17		Informed by Stf Capt R.A of the probable arrival of additional A.F.A Bs. Ration strength of 147 A.F.A.B telephoned through at 11 p.m	
	27/3/17		Drew rations for 147 A.F.A.B at request of Staff Capt. R.A. (had to supply necessary transport for this) 24th Division Q unable to give us any instructions. C.O delivered a lecture on supplies at the Divisional School. Fuel lorries taken by Corps for special work. Unable to draw full amount of fuel. B.T.O 72 Inf Bde, and a Brigade T.O, and 2 Canadian Officers instructed in improvised pack saddlery. Loaded at Railhead 2/30 p.m. Ration Strength of 14 A.F.A.B. telephoned through by Stf Capt R.A.	

2449 Wt. W14957/M90 750,000 1/16 J.B.C. & A. Forms/C.2118/12.

Instructions regarding War Diaries and Intelligence Summaries are contained in F. S. Regs., Part II. and the Staff Manual respectively. Title Pages will be prepared in manuscript.

WAR DIARY
or
INTELLIGENCE SUMMARY

(Erase heading not required.)

Army Form C. 2118.

Place	Date	Hour	Summary of Events and Information	Remarks and references to Appendices
BACQUEMONT	28/3/17		Commanding Officer attended conference at D.D.S.T First Army re Pack Saddlery. Supply Train did not arrive. Notified at 10 pm that Train would be offloaded at 6/30 AM on following morning. Ten complete turnout joined 194 Coy from 147 A F A Bde - 1 horse suffering from Stomatitis, 1 came to be evacuated - all lousy and in poor condition.	
"	29/3/17		Supply Train due 28th offloaded 6-30 AM. Drew rations for 14 AFAB from Railhead by horse transport. These rations afterwards delivered to 14 AFAB by their lorries. Pack Train due today off loaded at 3 pm. Rations for 14 AFAB again drawn by horse transport. Notification received, that in future horse transport A.F.A.Bs. to remain with units and attend Refilling Point daily to draw supplies. Capt J.P. Thompson and Capt. Scott RAMC returned from leave. Major Hunter S.S.O proceeded on leave.	
"	30/3/17		Rations delivered to 147 A F A B by their supply wagons. All transport for for this Brigade returned to unit. Supply Train offloaded 2 pm. Rations for 282 A F A B drawn from Railhead by horse transport. C.O visited S.M.T.O, 1st Corps re number of lorries required by this Division.	
"	31/3/17		Rations for 282 AFAB drawn from refilling point and delivered to units by their own Horse Transport. Supply Train should have been offloaded at 5/30 pm, but delayed until 6/15 pm owing to the Supply Column being late - matter reported to O.C Supply Column. Very wet.	

H.B. ... Lt Col
Comm'g 24th Div! Train
1.4.17.

2449 Wt. W14957/M90 750,000 1/16 J.B.C. & A. Forms/C.2118/12.

D.D.S.T. No. S.T.250/17.

D.D.S.& T.

First Army.

With reference to the question of Pack Saddlery for the carriage of rations, a most simple and satisfactory device has been brought to my notice by Captain. J.P.THOMPSON, one of my Company Commanders. This officer has had many years experience of this method of carrying stores and food in Texas.

We tried carrying a platoon's rations yesterday over 8 miles of country in this manner and found the experiment entirely satisfactory. It is claimed for this system of loading a pack animal that it is unnecessary to manufacture anything. The only articles required are :-

1 Horse Rug
1 Saddle Blanket
3 Wheat Sacks
40 ft. Rope, 2" circumference.

Roughly the method consists of making the blanket and horse rug into a pad on the horse's back and tying the three sacks on in such a manner as to make a sling load which does not shift.

I would be very glad to show the system to any officers who would care to come to my Train Headquarters any day at 2-30 p.m. at 21 Rue St.Barbe, BRACQUEMONT (NOEUX) between the 19th and 24 th March.

15 = 3 = 17

sd T.B.LORD. Lieut Col
Commanding 24th Divisional Train

2.

Officer Commanding

All Divisionals Trains in First Army.

The Pack refered to in the above is more easily

improvised than any other which has yet been submitted.

I hope that you will be able to take advantage of Lieut Col Lord's offer and also send some of your transport officers to see the device. It is imperative that all transport officers should be acquainted with improvised forms of pack saddlery, which may be of assistance during active operations.

sd. L. Inglefield Major for Col
D.D. of S. & T. First Army

Headquarters.
First Army.
17-3-17.

Confidential

Vol 20

War Diary

of

Officer Commanding 24th Divl Train

From April 1st to April 30th

1917

Instructions regarding War Diaries and Intelligence Summaries are contained in F. S. Regs., Part II. and the Staff Manual respectively. Title Pages will be prepared in manuscript.

WAR DIARY
or
INTELLIGENCE SUMMARY

(Erase heading not required.)

Army Form C. 2118.

194 Co ASC

24 Division

[signature] Major –

Vol 2

Place	Date	Hour	Summary of Events and Information	Remarks and references to Appendices
FOUQUIÈRES –	1/3/17	9 A.M.	Supply wagons refilled on FOUQUIÈRES – BETHUNE Road –	Fine –
"	2/3/17	"	" " " " " "	Fine –
"	3/3/17	"	" " " " " "	Dull –
"	4/3/17	"	" " " " " " Train H.Qs moved to BRAQUEMONT –	Fine –
"	5/3/17	"	" " " " " " Company moved to NOEUX –	Snow –
NOEUX –	6/3/17	8 A.M.	" " " on HERSIN – NOEUX LES MINES Road – Drew from Railhead at 12-45 A.M. 7th/3/17.	Fine –
"	7/3/17	"	" " " " " " " " " " " 7-15 P.M. "	Fine, strong E Wind –
"	8/3/17	"	" " " " " " " " " " " 7-45 P.M.	Snow & E wind.
"	9/3/17	"	" " " " " " " " " " " 6-45 P.M.	Fine afternoon –
"	10/3/17	"	" " " " " " " " " " " 2-15 P.M.	Snow Showers – Fine –
"	11/3/17	7 A.M.	" " " " " " " " " " " 12-15 P.M.	Fine –
"	12/3/17	"	" " " " " " " " " " " 12-0 NOON –	Rain –
"	13/3/17	"	" " " " " " " " " " " 12-30 P.M.	Dull – fine –
"	14/3/17	"	" " " " " " " " " " " 12-0 NOON.	Rain –
"	15/3/17	"	" " " " " " " " " " " 12-0 NOON –	Fine –
"	16/3/17	"	" " " " " " " " " " " 12-0 NOON –	Fine –
"	17/3/17	"	" " " " " " " " " " " 11-40 A.M.	Fine –
"	18/3/17	"	" " " " " " " " " " " 12-0 NOON –	Fine –
"	19/3/17	"	" " " " " " " " " " " 12-0 NOON. Camp shelled –	Rain –
"	20/3/17	"	" " " " " " " " " " " 2-20 p.m.	Rain –

2449 Wt. W14957/M90 750,000 1/16 J.B.C. & A. Forms/C.2118/12.

Instructions regarding War Diaries and Intelligence Summaries are contained in F. S. Regs., Part II. and the Staff Manual respectively. Title Pages will be prepared in manuscript.

WAR DIARY
or
INTELLIGENCE SUMMARY
(Erase heading not required.)

Army Form C. 2118.

R. Blakeway – Major –

Place	Date	Hour	Summary of Events and Information	Remarks and references to Appendices
NOEUX	21/3/17	7. A.M.	Supply wagons refilled on HERSIN – NOEUX LES MINES Road – Drew from Railhead at 12 NOON –	Fine. Snow in night –
"	22/3/17	"	" " " " " " " " " " "	Snow –
"	23/3/17	"	" " " " " " " " " " 1-15 pm. Lt PLUMPTRE proceeded on leave –	Fine – Frost –
"	24/3/17	"	" " " " " " " " " " 2-20 pm – Time advanced one hour at 11 pm – Capt CROOME – ESSEX Regt reported –	Fine –
"	25/3/17	"	" " " " " " " " " " 2-30 pm – NOEUX LES MINES shelled on & off for most of day –	Fine –
"	26/3/17	"	" " " " " " " " " " 12-30 pm –	Rain –
"	27/3/17	"	" " " " " " " " " " 3-0 pm – Capt CROOME . ESSEX . Regt left – 6-30 A.M. 29/3/17.	Snow showers –
"	28/3/17	"	" " " " " " " " " "	Rain –
"	29/3/17	7-30 AM	" " " " " " " " " " 3-30 pm – NOEUX LES MINES shelled –	Rain –
"	30/3/17	7-AM	" " " " " " " " " " 3-30 pm –	Rain – Showery –
"	31/3/17	"	" " " " " " " " " " 6-30 pm –	Showery –

Instructions regarding War Diaries and Intelligence Summaries are contained in F. S. Regs., Part II. and the Staff Manual respectively. Title Pages will be prepared in manuscript.

WAR DIARY
or
INTELLIGENCE SUMMARY
(Erase heading not required.)

Army Form C. 2118.

Place	Date	Hour	Summary of Events and Information	Remarks and references to Appendices
BRACQUEMONT	1/4/17		2/Lt. A. W. P. Le Sueur proceeded to Base Depot, HAVRE. Pack Train did not arrive at Railhead until midnight - not offloaded. Very wet. Snow & rain.	
	2/4/17		Pack train due 1/4/17 offloaded at 6.30 am. Demonstration of improvised Pack Saddlery held at BARLIN - arranged by DDS&T I Army. Four Exhibits by Div train. CO & Capt Thompson attended. Commenced drawing supplies at Railhead 7 30 pm. High wind - hail, snow & rain.	
	3/4/17		Court of Enquiry into theft of G.S. Wagon from lines of 195 Coy A.S.C. held at CRA 6th Div. Pack train offloaded 9 30 pm	
	4/4/17		Commenced offloading Packtrain at 12 20 pm. Lieut. S. R. Martin appointed Adjutant from 13.1.17. 1 Reinforcement (Cpl Farrier) arrived & posted to 194 Coy A.S.C. Lieut. Plumptre returned from leave.	
	5/4/17		3 Reinforcements (1 N.C.O. 1 Driver & 1 Dr Wheeler) reported & posted to 194 Coy. Commenced offloading Pack train at 4 30 pm.	

2449 Wt. W14957/M90 750,000 1/16 J.B.C. & A. Forms/C.2118/12.

Instructions regarding War Diaries and Intelligence Summaries are contained in F. S. Regs., Part II. and the Staff Manual respectively. Title Pages will be prepared in manuscript.

WAR DIARY
or
INTELLIGENCE SUMMARY
(Erase heading not required.)

Army Form C. 2118.

Place	Date	Hour	Summary of Events and Information	Remarks and references to Appendices
BRACQUEMONT	6/4/17		Drawing at Railhead commenced 12.30 pm. Improvised Pack Saddlery & Water Carriers shown to Col Trueman. O.C., S.I.V. Wet	
"	7/4/17		Drawing at Railhead commenced 1.30 pm. Fine	
"	8/4/17		Fine. Railhead 3.30 pm. 11 G.S. Wagons at Posse 2 at 5 pm by order of I Corps. No one could be found to make use of them. Ordered to return to lines at 7 pm.	
"	9/4/17		High wind. Railhead 11.30 pm. Owing to lorries having been taken by I Corps Supplies for 147 A.F.A.B. had to be drawn by H.T. 11 G.S. Wagons at Posse 2 by order of I Corps. Guide arrived at these H.Q. for the Wagons at 5.40 pm. O.O. No. 130 received 9.15 pm	
"	10/4/17		Railhead 2.30 pm. Major H.B. Hunter returned from leave. Lt. C.C. Gale rejoined Div Train after duty with No. 3 Section of Reserve Park. Snow, high wind. 10 G.S. Wagons rejoined No 2 Section of R.P. from No. 3 for use of C.E. I Corps.	
"	11/4/17		Railhead 1 pm. Snow. 5 G.S. Wagons attached to No 2 Section from No. 1 for use of C.E. I Corps.	

2449 Wt. W14957/M90 750,000 1/16 J.B.C. & A. Forms/C.2118/12.

Army Form C. 2118.

Instructions regarding War Diaries and Intelligence Summaries are contained in F. S. Regs., Part II. and the Staff Manual respectively. Title Pages will be prepared in manuscript.

WAR DIARY
or
INTELLIGENCE SUMMARY
(Erase heading not required.)

Place	Date	Hour	Summary of Events and Information	Remarks and references to Appendices
BRACQUEMONT	12/4/17		Railhead 11.45 am. Special issue of Rum to Divn ordered by G.O.C. Snow & rain.	
"	13/4/17		Loading at Railhead ~~commenced~~ ordered for 11.30 am, but owing to rails being damaged by shells, train was not in position before 12.15. Owing to severity of further shell fire loading suspended & transport sent away. Recommenced at 2.30 p.m. – finished about 4.15 pm. A few more shells, but nothing very near. No casualties. 1 Reinforcement (L/C) – posted to 196 Coy. Fine.	
"	14/4/17		Noeux les Mines Railhead shelled heavily. Owing to this Corps arranged that Supplies should be drawn from BETHUNE. First group commenced loading at 5 pm. Two Battns of 188th Bde left Divn.	
"	15/4/17		No 2 Section, 9th Reserve Park no longer attached to Div Train – now under orders of C.E. I Corps. Supply Column on the road. All details previously found by R.P. for C Roads Officer now to be found by Div Train. Baggage Wagons to R.A. Railhead – Noeux les Mines. Two Supply Wagons of 5 R. Sussex (Pioneers) joined from 18th D.T. – attached 195 Coy A.S.C.	

2449 Wt. W14957/M90 750,000 1/16 J.B.C. & A. Forms/C.2118/12.

Instructions regarding War Diaries and Intelligence Summaries are contained in F. S. Regs., Part II. and the Staff Manual respectively. Title Pages will be prepared in manuscript.

WAR DIARY
or
INTELLIGENCE SUMMARY
(Erase heading not required.)

Army Form C. 2118.

Place	Date	Hour	Summary of Events and Information	Remarks and references to Appendices
BRACQUEMONT	16/4/17		Railhead changed to BETHUNE owing to shelling of NOEUX. Supplies for 'D' Group drawn by H.T.	
"	17/4/17		Railhead – NOEUX LES MINES. Supplies drawn at 1.pm. 'D' Group used H.T.	
"	18/4/17		O.O No 140 received. Railhead – NOEUX – 1.30 pm 6 Lorries for 'A' Group replaced by H.T. 12 Reinforcements arrived 3 Saddlers & 9 Drivers – posted as follows 194 – 1 Sadd – 3 Drivers – 195 1 Sadd. – 2 Drivers – 196 – 1 Sadd – 2 Drivers – 197 2 Drivers.	
"	19/4/17		Railhead – NOEUX. Supplies for 'B' Group drawn by H.T. 196 Coy moved to ALLOUAGNE – 197 Coy to AUCHEL. Visited new area & 196 & 197 Coys.	
NORRENT FONTES.	20/4/17		Train H.Q. moved to NORRENT FONTES. 195 Coy to ECQUEDECQUES – 196 Coy to LESPESSES. 197 Coy to FLECHIN. Railhead LILLERS. Fine.	
"	21/4/17		Cold, but fine	

2449 Wt. W14957/M90 750,000 1/16 J.B.C. & A. Forms/C.2118/12.

Army Form C. 2118.

Instructions regarding War Diaries and Intelligence Summaries are contained in F. S. Regs., Part II. and the Staff Manual respectively. Title Pages will be prepared in manuscript.

WAR DIARY
or
INTELLIGENCE SUMMARY
(Erase heading not required.)

Place	Date	Hour	Summary of Events and Information	Remarks and references to Appendices
NORRENT-FONTES.	22/4/17		Capt R.T. Garrett proceeded on leave. – Lt L.M. Mischer to be S.O. 73rd Inf. Bde. during his absence. O.O. No 142 received.	
"	23/4/17		✓	
ST. HILAIRE	24/4/17		Train H.Q. moved to ST. HILAIRE. 193 Coy to CUHEM.	
"	25/4/17		194 Coy moved from NOEUX LES MINES to ST. HILAIRE – 196 Coy to COYECQUE. 15 Remounts collected from GONNEHEM (distributed as follows – 193 Coy 4 – 196 – 8 9 E. Surreys 2. – 12 Sherwoods 1). O.O. No 143 received.	
BOMY.	26/4/17		Train H.Q. moved to BOMY. 195 Coy to ECQUEDECQUES. – 197 to AUCHEL 194 to SENLIS. 2 Reinforcements (1 CQMS + 1 Sergt) arrived & returned to Base, being surplus to establishment. Lt. W.A. Wildblood returned to duty with 195 Coy.	

Army Form C. 2118.

Instructions regarding War Diaries and Intelligence Summaries are contained in F. S. Regs., Part II. and the Staff Manual respectively. Title Pages will be prepared in manuscript.

WAR DIARY
or
INTELLIGENCE SUMMARY

(Erase heading not required.)

Place	Date	Hour	Summary of Events and Information	Remarks and references to Appendices
BOMY	27/4/17		195 Coy moved to BETHUNE – 197 Coy to HOUCHIN.	
"	28/4/17		4 Reinforcements (Drivers) arrived. Posted – 3 to 197 Coy – 1 to 195.	
"	29/4/17		✓	
"	30/4/17		5 Reinforcements (Clerks) arrived. Posted – 194 Coy – 2, – 196 – 1, 197 – 2.	

[illegible] Lt. Col

Commdg 24th Div. Train.

2449 Wt. W14957/M90 750,000 1/16 J.B.C. & A. Forms/C.2118/12.

CONFIDENTIAL.

Vol

WAR DIARY.

OF

194. Comp: A.S.C. 24th Div: TRAIN.

from 1/4/17 to 30/4/17.

Instructions regarding War Diaries and Intelligence Summaries are contained in F. S. Regs., Part II. and the Staff Manual respectively. Title Pages will be prepared in manuscript.

WAR DIARY
or
INTELLIGENCE SUMMARY
(Erase heading not required.)

Army Form C. 2118.

W. Blakeway – Major –

Place	Date	Hour	Summary of Events and Information	Remarks and references to Appendices
NOEUX	1/4/17	7 A.M.	Supply wagons refilled on HERSIN – NOEUX LES MINES Road – Drew from Railhead at 7 A.M 2/4/17	Showry –
"	2/4/17	9 A.M.	" " " " " " " " " " 8 PM 3/4/17	Snowstorm in evening
"	3/4/17	7 AM	" " " " " " " " " " 10 PM	Snow
"	4/4/17	7 AM	" " " " " " " " " " 12-50 pm – Lt PLUMPTRE returned from leave –	Fine Dull –
"	5/4/17	"	" " " " " " " " " " 5-0 pm –	Fine –
"	6/4/17	"	" " " " " " " " " " 1-0 pm –	Rain –
"	7/4/17	"	" " " " " " " " " " 2-0 pm –	Fine –
"	8/4/17	"	" " " " " " " " " " 4-0 pm –	Fine –
"	9/4/17	"	" " " " " " " " " " 12-15 pm –	Fine, with rain & snow –
"	10/4/17	"	" " " " " " " " " " 3-0 pm –	Snowshowers
"	11/4/17	"	" " " " " " " " " " 1-30 pm –	Snow gale –
"	12/4/17	"	" " " " " " " " " " 12-15 pm –	Fine. Snow. in morning –
"	13/4/17	"	" " " " " " " " " " 3-30 pm. Station shelled –	Fine –
"	14/4/17	"	" " " " " " " " BETHUNE 5-30 pm – " "	Fine –
"	15/4/17	"	" " " " " " " " Supply Column came on to road for supplies –	Rain –
"	16/4/17	"	" " " " " " " "	Rain in afternoon –
"	17/4/17	8-A.M.	" " " " " " " "	Rain –
"	18/4/17	"	" " " " " " " "	Rain –
"	19/4/17	"	" " " " " " " "	Rain –
"	20/4/17	"	" " " " " " " " D.H.Q & T.H.Q moved to FONTES –	Fine –

2449 Wt. W14957/M90 750,000 1/16 J.B.C. & A. Forms/C.2118/12.

Instructions regarding War Diaries and Intelligence Summaries are contained in F. S. Regs., Part II. and the Staff Manual respectively. Title Pages will be prepared in manuscript.

WAR DIARY
or
INTELLIGENCE SUMMARY
(Erase heading not required.)

Army Form C. 2118.

P. Blakeway – Major –

Place	Date	Hour	Summary of Events and Information	Remarks and references to Appendices
NOEUX	21/4/17	8 A.M.	Supply wagons refilled on HERSIN – NOEUX LES MINES Road – Mines heavily shelled –	Fine –
"	22/4/17	"	" " " " " " "	Fine –
"	23/4/17	"	" " " " " " " " " "	Fine –
"	24/4/17	"	" " " " " " " D.A.C moved to HESDIGNEUL	Fine –
"	25/4/17	"	" " " " " " " moved to ST. HILAIRE –	Fine –
ST. HILAIRE	26/4/17	"	" " " ST. HILAIRE – NORRENT FONTES Road – Marched to SENLIS –	Fine –
SENLIS	27/4/17	"	" " " SENLIS – LUGY Road –	Fine –
"	28/4/17	"	" " " " " "	Fine –
"	29/4/17	"	" " " " – METRINGHEM Road –	Fine –
"	30/4/17	"	" " " " " "	Fine –

Secret and Confidential

Vol 21

War Diary

of

O. C. 24th Divisional Train

From May 1st to May 31st 1917.

Army Form C. 2118.

Instructions regarding War Diaries and Intelligence Summaries are contained in F. S. Regs., Part II. and the Staff Manual respectively. Title Pages will be prepared in manuscript.

WAR DIARY
or
INTELLIGENCE SUMMARY

(Erase heading not required.)

Place	Date	Hour	Summary of Events and Information	Remarks and references to Appendices
BOMY.	1/5/17		C.S.M. Bagshaw, R (197 Coy) sent to 72nd F.A. for temporary duty.	
"	2/5/17		✓	
"	3/5/17		Judged Transport Competition at 72nd Field Ambulance – excellent turn-out.	
"	4/5/17		195 Coy moved to ANNEZIN	
"	5/5/17		R.P. for "B" Group – ANNEZIN. 197 Coy moved to HESDINGNEUL. Remounts received as follows – 194 Coy 8 H.D. 2 L.D. 195 – 2 H.D. 196 – 2 H.D. 197 – 2 H.D. – all in very poor condition. Capt Garrett returned from leave.	
"	6/5/17		Refilling Points changed, as follows, in order to assist Supply Column – "A" – BEAUMETZ-LES-AIRES. "B" – ANNEZIN. "C" – 5 Cross Roads – Hill 140 (Map 5a) "D" – HESDINGNEUL. Lt Mischer returned for duty with 194 Coy.	

2449 Wt. W14957/M90 750,000 1/16 J.B.C. & A. Forms/C.2118/12.

Army Form C. 2118.

Instructions regarding War Diaries and Intelligence Summaries are contained in F. S. Regs., Part II. and the Staff Manual respectively. Title Pages will be prepared in manuscript.

WAR DIARY
or
INTELLIGENCE SUMMARY

(Erase heading not required.)

Place	Date	Hour	Summary of Events and Information	Remarks and references to Appendices
BOMY	7/5/17		✓	
"	8/5/17		Lt. A.W.P. Le Sueur returned from the Base & rejoined 197 Coy A.S.C. One Reinforcement (Issuer) posted to 194 Coy (for duty with 196 Coy) O.O. No 145 received.	
NORRENT FONTES.	9/5/17		Train H.Q. moved to NORRENT FONTES. 194 Coy to ROMBLY. 195 Coy to HAMET BILLET. 196 Coy to FLECHINELLE 197 Coy to BUSNES.	
"	10/5/17		194 Coy moved to MORBECQUE. 196 Coy to ST MARTIN. 197 Coy to THIENNES.	
STEENBECQUE	11/5/17		Train H.Q. moved to STEENBECQUE. 194 Coy to near CASSEL 195 Coy to MORBECQUE Railhead for Artillery - WIPPENHOEK. - for remainder of Division LILLERS.	
STEEVOORDE	13/5/17		Train H.Q. moved to STEENVOORDE. 195, 196 & 197 Coys to STEENVOORDE area Railhead for whole Division WIPPENHOEK.	

2449 Wt. W14957/M90 750,000 1/16 J.B.C. & A. Forms/C.2118/12.

Army Form C. 2118.

Instructions regarding War Diaries and Intelligence Summaries are contained in F. S. Regs., Part II. and the Staff Manual respectively. Title Pages will be prepared in manuscript.

WAR DIARY
or
INTELLIGENCE SUMMARY

(Erase heading not required.)

Place	Date	Hour	Summary of Events and Information	Remarks and references to Appendices
STEENVOORDE	13/5/17		196 Coy. moved to BUSSEBOOM.	
"	14/5/17		195 & 197 Coys moved to BUSSEBOOM	
BUSSEBOOM	15/5/17		Train HQ. moved to BUSSEBOOM. Major (Temp. Lt.Col) F.B. LORD promoted to LIEUT. COL. as from 1.4.17 - (The London Gazette. May 12 1917).	
"	16/5/17		2 Reinforcements arrived & posted to 195 & 197 Coys. Detachment from 194 Coy moved to BUSSEBOOM under the Command of Lieut. Plumptre to feed 107th Bde R.F.A.	
"	17/5/17		Very wet.	
"	18/5/17		Nothing to report.	

2449 Wt. W14957/M90 750,000 1/16 J.B.C. & A. Forms/C.2118/12.

Instructions regarding War Diaries and Intelligence Summaries are contained in F. S. Regs., Part II. and the Staff Manual respectively. Title Pages will be prepared in manuscript.

WAR DIARY
or
INTELLIGENCE SUMMARY
(Erase heading not required.)

Army Form C. 2118.

Place	Date	Hour	Summary of Events and Information	Remarks and references to Appendices
BUSSEBOOM	19/5/17		20,000 Hard rations drawn from Railhead & dumped at Supply Column Store.	
"	20/5/17		Supplies drawn from WIPPENHOEK by M.T. for B C & D Groups - first group 7 am. A Group continue to use M.T. 11 Reinforcements (6 Drivers & 5 Supply Issuers) arrived	
"	21/5/17		✓	
"	22/5/17		Wet.	
"	23/5/17		Wagons for 106th Bde. R.F.A. & 1 Section D.A.C. joined Lt. Plumptre's Command at BUSSEBOOM.	
"	24/5/17		194 Coy complete at BUSSEBOOM.	
"	25/5/17		Loading at Railhead 5 am., but did not commence till 6.30 am. - train late. Capt H.C. Pearson proceeded on leave.	

2449 Wt. W14957/M90 750,000 1/16 J.B.C. & A. Forms/C.2118/12.

Instructions regarding War Diaries and Intelligence Summaries are contained in F. S. Regs., Part II. and the Staff Manual respectively. Title Pages will be prepared in manuscript.

WAR DIARY
or
INTELLIGENCE SUMMARY

(Erase heading not required.)

Army Form C. 2118.

Place	Date	Hour	Summary of Events and Information	Remarks and references to Appendices
BUSSEBOOM	26/5/17		2 Reinforcements arrived (1 CSM to 196 Coy & 1 Driver to 195 Coy.)	
"	27/5/17		Capt. D Bottomley proceeded on leave. 195 Coy moved to HOPOUTRE. Convoy of 10 G.S. Wagons took mice to ZILLEBEKE. 2/Lt A H Barnes i/c - underwent considerable shelling & a gas wave, but no casualties, except 1 N.D. (196 Coy) wounded in shoulder. 1 Reinforcement (C.Q.M.S)	
"	28/5/17			
"	29/5/17		Lt. Col. F. B. Lord, Lieut G. N. Hitch, Staff Sergt. Beazley, J & Staff Sgt Wheeler Taylor, P.H. "Mentioned in Despatches". The Divl Commander visited all Train Coys & expressed great satisfaction with all he saw.	
"	30/5/17		194, 196 & 197 Coys moved to HOPOUTRE. Remounts & Train horses inspected by DDR 2nd Army. Remounts collected by 195 Coy.	
HOPOUTRE	31/5/17		Train H.Q. moved to HOPOUTRE. 7 N.D. Remounts distributed 194-3, 195-2, 197-2. 195 Coy moved to K34 c 4.8 (STEENVOORDE).	

F B Lord Lt Col
Comdg 24 Div Train.

2449 Wt. W14957/M90 750,000 1/16 J.B.C. & A. Forms/C.2118/12.

CONFIDENTIAL.

WAR DIARY.

OF

194. Company. A.S.C. 24th DIV: TRAIN.

from 1/5/17 to 31/5/17.

Army Form C. 2118.

WAR DIARY
or
INTELLIGENCE SUMMARY
(Erase heading not required.)

Instructions regarding War Diaries and Intelligence Summaries are contained in F. S. Regs., Part II. and the Staff Manual respectively. Title Pages will be prepared in manuscript.

P. Blakeway Major

Place	Date	Hour	Summary of Events and Information	Remarks and references to Appendices
SENLIS	1/5/17	8-A.M.	Supply wagons refilled on SENLIS - METRINGHEM Road - In 2nd CORPS - 1st ARMY	Fine -
"	2/5/17	"	" " " " " "	Fine -
"	3/5/17	"	" " " " " "	Fine -
"	4/5/17	"	" " " " " "	Fine -
"	5/5/17	"	" " " " " "	Fine -
"	6/5/17	9.A.M	" " " at BEAUMETZ LES AIRE - Transferred to 10th CORPS - 2nd ARMY	Fine -
"	7/5/17	"	" " " " " "	Rain at night
"	8/5/17	"	" " " " " "	Fine -
"	9/5/17	8-A.M	" " " " " " marched to ROMLY -	Fine -
ROMLY	10/5/17	7.A.M	" " " on ROMLY - FONTES Road - marched to MORBECQUE.	Fine -
MORBECQUE	11/5/17	7.A.M	" " " in MORBECQUE - marched to CHÂTEAU D'IF.	Fine -
CHÂTEAU D'IF	12/5/17	9.A.M	" " " on ~~HARDIFORT~~ WINNEZEELE Road -	Fine -
"	13/5/17	8.A.M	" " " " "	Fine. Thunder & rain afternoon -
"	14/5/17	"	" " " " "	Some rain -
"	15/5/17	"	" " " " "	Fine -
"	16/5/17	"	" " " " " " 107 BRIG: R.F.A Supply wagons attached 19th Corps!	Rain -
"	17/5/17	"	" " " " " " Lt PLUMPTRE moved to Camp at BUSSEBOOM -	Rain -
"	18/5/17	"	" " " " " "	fine
"	19/5/17	"	" " " " " "	fine
"	20/5/17	10-45	" " " " " "	Fine -

2449 Wt. W14957/M90 750,000 1/16 J.B.C. & A. Forms/C.2118/12.

Instructions regarding War Diaries and Intelligence Summaries are contained in F. S. Regs., Part II. and the Staff Manual respectively. Title Pages will be prepared in manuscript.

WAR DIARY
or
INTELLIGENCE SUMMARY
(Erase heading not required.)

Army Form C. 2118.

P. Blakeway Major

Place	Date	Hour	Summary of Events and Information	Remarks and references to Appendices
CHÂTEAU D'PF	21/5/17	A.M. 11-45	Supply wagons refilled on WINNEZEELE Road –	Fine day Rain night –
"	22/5/17	11-0	" " " " "	Rain –
"	23/5/17	11-45	" " " " " CAPT. PEARSON, with 107th BRIG. R.F.A. & No. II Sec.	Fine –
			D.A.C moved to BUSSEBOOM –	
"	24/5/17	11-30	" " " " " CAPT. PEARSON granted leave of absence to June 5th	Fine –
			Moved to BUSSEBOOM –	
BUSSEBOOM	25/5/17	5-30	" " " at WIPPENHOEK Siding –	Fine –
"	26/5/17	5-30	" " " " "	Fine –
"	27/5/17	"	" " " " "	Fine –
"	28/5/17	"	" " " " " GAS ATTACK 1-45 A.M. –	Fine –
"	29/5/17	"	" " " " "	Fine –
"	30/5/17	"	" " " " " Moved to Camp on POPERINGHE – WEST OUTRE Road –	Fine –
L 29.C.9.1. map 27.	31/5/17	7 A.M.	" " " RENNINGHELST "	Fine –

2449 Wt. W14957/M90 750,000 1/16 J.B.C. & A. Forms/C.2118/12.

Confidential

Vol 22

War Diary

of

O. C. 24th Divisional Train

From June 1st to June 30th 1917.

Army Form C. 2118. 24

WAR DIARY
or
INTELLIGENCE SUMMARY
(Erase heading not required.)

Instructions regarding War Diaries and Intelligence Summaries are contained in F. S. Regs., Part II. and the Staff Manual respectively. Title Pages will be prepared in manuscript.

R. Blakeway Major 194 Coy A.S.C.

Place	Date	Hour	Summary of Events and Information	Remarks and references to Appendices
L.24.c.9.1. Sheet 27.	1/6/17	9.A.M.	Supply wagons refilled at RENNINGHELST Siding – Assisted in putting out fire at Farm & saving cattle & effects	Fine –
"	2/6/17	10.A.M	" " " "	Fine –
"	3/6/17	8-30	" " " " " POPERINGHE & area heavily shelled –	Fine –
"	4/6/17	9-30	" " " " " Back area on Railway line shelled –	Fine –
"	5/6/17	8-30	" " " " " CAPT. PEARSON returned from leave –	Fine –
"	6/6/17	"	" " " " " German aeroplane brought down about 12 midnight near POP.	Fine –
"	7/6/17	"	" " " " " LT. PLUMPTRE promoted CAPTAIN –	Thunderstorm –
"	8/6/17	"	" " " " " CAPT. SAUNDERS went on leave –	Fine –
"	9/6/17	"	" " " " "	Fine –
"	10/6/17	"	" " " " "	Fine –
"	11/6/17	"	" " " " "	Some rain – Heavy thunderstorm
"	12/6/17	"	" " " " "	
"	13/6/17	"	" " " " " Move to new Camp on OUDERDOM – MILLEKRUISSE Road Cancelled.	Fine –
"	14/6/17	"	" " " " " Moved " " " " "	Fine –
N.2.c.2.2.	15/6/17	7-30	" " " OUDERDOM "	Fine –
"	16/6/17	10-AM	" " " " " LT. WILDBLOOD killed & several N.C.O's & men killed & wounded by shell fire, whilst refilling, also several horses –	Fine –
"	17/6/17	1-30p.m.	" " " on OUDERDOM – MILLEKRUISSE Road –	Fine –
"	18/6/17	10-30	" " " " " "	Thunderstorm.
"	19/6/17	10-0	" " " " " "	Rain & thunder

2449 Wt. W14957/M90 750,000 1/16 J.B.C. & A. Forms/C.2118/12.

Instructions regarding War Diaries and Intelligence Summaries are contained in F. S. Regs., Part II. and the Staff Manual respectively. Title Pages will be prepared in manuscript.

WAR DIARY
or
INTELLIGENCE SUMMARY
(Erase heading not required.)

Army Form C. 2118.

P Blakeway Lieut 194 Coy A.S.C.

Place	Date	Hour	Summary of Events and Information	Remarks and references to Appendices
N2.C.2.2.	20/6/17	10 A.M.	Supply wagons refilled on OUDERDOM – MILLEKREUSE Road – Capt. SAUNDERS returned from leave –	Showery –
"	21/6/17	"	" " " " " "	Showery –
"	22/6/17	"	" " " " " "	Rain –
"	23/6/17	"	" " " " " "	Fine –
"	24/6/17	9-30	" " " " " "	Fine –
"	25/6/17	9 A.M	" " " " " " LT BARNES went on leave –	Fine day – Rain night –
"	26/6/17	9-A.M	" " " " " "	Fine –
"	27/6/17	"	" " " " " "	Fine –
"	28/6/17	9-30	" " " " " " Train HQ. marched to LUMBRES, this Company attached to 23rd Div:	Heavy thunderstorm in evening –
"	29/6/17	4 p.m.	" " " " " "	Fine –
"	30/6/17	4 p.m.	" " " " " "	Heavy Rain –

2449 Wt. W14957/M90 750,000 1/16 J.B.C. & A. Forms/C.2118/12.

Instructions regarding War Diaries and Intelligence Summaries are contained in F. S. Regs., Part II. and the Staff Manual respectively. Title Pages will be prepared in manuscript.

WAR DIARY
or
INTELLIGENCE SUMMARY
(Erase heading not required.)

Army Form C. 2118.

Place	Date	Hour	Summary of Events and Information	Remarks and references to Appendices
HOPOUTRE	1/6/17		197 Coy H.Q. moved to K 34 c 4 8 (STEENVOORDE). Rations for "B" Group drawn by M.T. in bulk - distributed at K 34 c 4 8. Supply Train very late.	
"	2/6/17		Balance of 197 Coy moved to K 34 c 4 8. Rations for B & D Groups drawn by M.T. (assisted by 6 G.S. Wagons) in bulk - distributed at K 34 c 4 8. Supply Train 3 hours late.	
"	3/6/17		Pack Train 2 hours late. POPERINGHE heavily shelled all day - nothing near Train Camps.	
"	4/6/17		195 & 197 Coys moved to HOPOUTRE. At 2.30 pm heavy shelling commenced around the Camp L.17 d 7.6 occupied by Train H.Q. & 195 Coy. Camp evacuated at 3 pm. - returned at 5.30 pm & shelling immediately recommenced. Camp cleared again, & reoccupied at 7.30 pm. No shells actually landed in Camp & no casualties in men or horses. Suspected case of communicating with enemy by extraordinary formation of clothes drying on the ground reported to & investigated by Intelligence, 2nd Army.	

2449 Wt. W14957/M90 750,000 1/16 J.B.C. & A. Forms/C.2118/12.

Instructions regarding War Diaries and Intelligence Summaries are contained in F. S. Regs., Part II. and the Staff Manual respectively. Title pages will be prepared in manuscript.

WAR DIARY
or
INTELLIGENCE SUMMARY.
(Erase heading not required.)

Army Form C. 2118.

Place	Date	Hour	Summary of Events and Information	Remarks and references to Appendices
HOPOUTRE	5/6/17		Lt. Col. F. B. Lord awarded D.S.O. (The Times 4.6.17). Capt. H. C. Pearson returned from leave.	
"	6/6/17		T/Lt. A. McCallum, E Kent Regt, formerly Adjt. 24 Div Train, awarded the M.C. (The Times 5.6.17). Temp. Lieuts. G. H. Hitch, R. F. Seddall, & K.M. Plumptre to be Temp Capts - date 5.6.17. (London Gazette 4.6.17). Capt. D. L. Dow, C.F. left Div Train for duty at ABBANCOURT	
"	7/6/17		Capt. D. Bottomley returned from leave	
"	8/6/17		Ordnance Stores delivered to Brigade Transport Lines by Div Train - in order to help Units with Pack Transport.	
"	9/6/17		Capt. F. A. R. Saunders proceeded on leave. Capt. R. T. Garrett proceeded to England to report to D of S. War Office & struck off strength from this date. 2/Lt. F. H. Pugh appointed S.O. 73 Inf Bde vice Capt Garrett & transferred from 195 to 197 Coy. A.S.C. 2Lieut. F. R. Nevill reported for duty from 1st Cav. Divl A.S.C. & posted to 195 Coy. A.S.C.	

Army Form C. 2118.

Instructions regarding War Diaries and Intelligence Summaries are contained in F. S. Regs., Part II. and the Staff Manual respectively. Title pages will be prepared in manuscript.

WAR DIARY
or
INTELLIGENCE SUMMARY.
(*Erase heading not required.*)

Place	Date	Hour	Summary of Events and Information	Remarks and references to Appendices
HOPOUTRE	10/6/17		Nothing of importance to report.	
"	11/6/17		Visited DDS&T 2nd Army.	
"	12/6/17		5 Reinforcements (4 Drivers + 1 Issuer) reported. Severe thunderstorm.	
OUDERDOM.	13/6/17		Train H.Q. 195. 196 + 197 Coys moved to G.36a.7.7 (Sheet 28) 194 Coy remained in old Camp.	
"	14/6/17		All Train Coys moved to new Camps at N.2 c 2.2.1 (Sheet 28) - Train H.Q. remained at G 36a 7.7.	
"	15/6/17		Railhead changed to OUDERDOM "B" - commenced 7 a.m.	
"	16/6/17		2/Lt. Neville proceeded on leave to PARIS for 4 days. Loading at Railhead commenced 10 a.m. Supplies for A + C Coys dumped in Yard - B + D issued in detail from the trucks. About 11 15 a.m. the enemy started shelling - the first two pitched 100-200 yards short. The third burst	

2353 Wt. W2544/1454 700,000 5/15 D. D. & L. A.D.S.S./Forms/C. 2118.

Instructions regarding War Diaries and Intelligence Summaries are contained in F. S. Regs., Part II. and the Staff Manual respectively. Title pages will be prepared in manuscript.

WAR DIARY
or
INTELLIGENCE SUMMARY.
(Erase heading not required.)

Army Form C. 2118.

Place	Date	Hour	Summary of Events and Information	Remarks and references to Appendices
OUDERDOM.	16/6/17		at the top end of the Yard. Considerable damage was done & horses started bolting. They were quickly got under control & the yard cleared in an orderly manner. Casualties in the Train were as follows:- Killed T/Lt. W.A. WILDBLOOD - wounded T/LT. L.G. BENNETT. O.R. 5 (1 at duty) - 1 man from 224 Employment Coy (attached D.T) wounded. Horses - killed - 2 H.D. (196) 1 Rider (195). Wounded 1 H.D. (196) 1 Rider (194). In addition 3 gunners were killed & 7 horses killed - about 12 others (men) wounded. Recommenced loading about 3pm - passed off without incident.	
			Lieut. Wildblood buried in RENINGHELST Military Cemetery at 8 p.m.	
MILLEKRUISSE	17/6/17		Railhead changed to WIPPENHOEK - Column on the road. Refilling took place about 1 pm. Train H.Q. moved to Camp at N2 C2.2 (Sheet 28)	
"	18/6/17		2/Lt A.N. Barnes transferred temp[orari]ly to 195 Coy A.S.C. Informed that Sgt Pritchett, S.J. (195 Coy) who had been wounded on the 16th inst died on admission to Hospital the same day, - buried at WIPPENHOEK. Stormy.	
"	19/6/17		Lieut. L.G. Bennett returned to duty. 1 O.R. (224 Employment Coy attached as loader) wounded by A.A. Shell - sent to hospital. Stormy - considerable rain.	

2353 Wt. W2544/1454 700,000 5/15 D. D. & L. A.D.S.S./Forms/C. 2118.

Instructions regarding War Diaries and Intelligence Summaries are contained in F. S. Regs., Part II. and the Staff Manual respectively. Title pages will be prepared in manuscript.

WAR DIARY
or
INTELLIGENCE SUMMARY.
(Erase heading not required.)

Army Form C. 2118.

Place	Date	Hour	Summary of Events and Information	Remarks and references to Appendices
MILLEKRUISE	20/6/17		Capt. F. A. R. Saunders returned from leave. Rain	
"	21/6/17		Visited D.D.S.&T. 2nd Army: G.Y. 308 received. Rain	
"	22/6/17		2/Lieut A. W. P. Le Sueur admitted 74 Field Ambulance - Rain.	
"	23/6/17		2/Lieut. F. R. Nevill returned from PARIS. Fine	
"	24/6/17		Visited LUMBRES & new area. March Order issued for Transport of 73 Inf Bde -	
"	25/6/17		2/Lt G. J. Motion reported for duty & posted to 195 Coy A.S.C. 197 Coy moved to BERTHEN Area. March Order No 2 issued for Transport of 17 Inf Bde	
"	26/6/17		197 Coy moved to BLARENGHEM Area. March Order No 3 issued for Transport of 72 Inf Bde 2/Lt. A. H. Barnes proceeded on leave.	
"	27/6/17		195 Coy moved to CAESTRE. 197 Coy to LUMBRES.	
CAESTRE	28/6/17		Train H.Q. & 196 Coy moved to CAESTRE. 195 Coy to RENESCURE.	

2353 Wt. W2544/1454 700,000 5/15 D. D. & L. A.D.S.S./Forms/C. 2118.

Instructions regarding War Diaries and Intelligence Summaries are contained in F. S. Regs., Part II. and the Staff Manual respectively. Title pages will be prepared in manuscript.

WAR DIARY
or
INTELLIGENCE SUMMARY.
(Erase heading not required.)

Army Form C. 2118.

Place	Date	Hour	Summary of Events and Information	Remarks and references to Appendices
RENESCURE	29/6/17		Train H.Q + 196 Coy moved to RENESCURE - 195 Coy moved to SELLES. 6 H.D. Remounts Collected by 196 Coy.	
LUMBRES	30/6/17		Train H.Q. + 196 Coy moved to LUMBRES. All in Rest area with exception of 194 Coy who are remaining behind with the Artillery.	
			1-7-17	
			J.B. Lord Lt Col Commd/ 24th Div! Train	

2353 Wt. W2544/1454 700,000 5/15 D. D. & L. A.D.S.S./Forms/C. 2118.

Vol 23

Confidential

War Diary

of

O C 24th Divisional Train

From July 1st 1917 To July 31st 1917

Army Form C. 2118.

Instructions regarding War Diaries and Intelligence Summaries are contained in F. S. Regs., Part II. and the Staff Manual respectively. Title pages will be prepared in manuscript.

WAR DIARY
or
INTELLIGENCE SUMMARY.
(Erase heading not required.)

Place	Date	Hour	Summary of Events and Information	Remarks and references to Appendices
LUMBRES	1/7/17		All Officers under 30 years of age medically examined, as instructed, with regard for fitness for duty with Infantry. Return sent to Div "A"	
"	2/7/17		Lt Col F.B. Lord & Capt S.H. Parslow proceeded on leave. Major T.W. Blakeway assumed command of the Train.	
"	3/7/17		Visited 74 Field Ambulance & 195 Coy. 194 Coy moved to ~~[illegible]~~ BORRE	
"	4/7/17		✓	
"	5/7/17		194 Coy moved to Rest area (Artillery) RACQUINGHEM.	
"	6/7/17		"H" Group on Div^l Feeding strength as from this date – first issue 7/7/17. 3 H.D. Remounts collected by 195 Coy (2 for 194 & 1 for 197 Coy.)	
"	7/7/17		2/Lt. A.H. Barnes returned from leave. Major Blakeway & Capt. J.P. Thompson acted as Judges at 72 Bde Transport Show. 2/Lt. A.W.P. Ledsam invalided to England 25/6/17 & struck off strength as from that date.	

Instructions regarding War Diaries and Intelligence Summaries are contained in F. S. Regs., Part II. and the Staff Manual respectively. Title pages will be prepared in manuscript.

WAR DIARY
or
INTELLIGENCE SUMMARY.
(Erase heading not required.)

Army Form C. 2118.

Place	Date	Hour	Summary of Events and Information	Remarks and references to Appendices
LUMBRES.	8/7/17		Dull.	
"	9/7/17		2/Lt. J.O. Tidy reported for duty & posted to 197 Coy A.S.C. 4 Reinforcements reported - posted as follows 194 Coy 1 Driver & 1 Issuer - 195 Coy 1 Sergt & 1 Driver.	
"	10/7/17		O.O. No 171 received.	
"	11/7/17		C.O. & S.S.O visited 5th Army Head Quarters	
"	12/7/17		Capt S.H. Paislee returned from leave. Capt R F Seddall proceeded on leave. Artillery Warning Order received.	
"	13/7/17		194 Coy moved to BORRE. All moves ordered in O.O 171 postponed 48 hours - Visited DDS&T 5th Army - arrangements made for move.	
"	14/7/17		194 Coy marched to new Area.	
"	15/7/17		Adjt. visited 194 Coy at new Camp. M.5 C 2 9 (Sheet 28) 194 Coy attached to 23rd Divn from this date inclusive	

2353 Wt. W2544/1454 700,000 5/15 D. D. & L. A.D.S.S./Forms/C. 2118.

Instructions regarding War Diaries and Intelligence Summaries are contained in F. S. Regs., Part II. and the Staff Manual respectively. Title pages will be prepared in manuscript.

WAR DIARY
or
INTELLIGENCE SUMMARY.
(Erase heading not required.)

Army Form C. 2118.

Place	Date	Hour	Summary of Events and Information	Remarks and references to Appendices
LUMBRES	16/7/17			
	17/7/17		196 Coy A.S.C. marched to RENESCURE – 195 Coy to LUMBRES. Major Blakeway visited 194 Coy. Informed by DAAG that Col Lord had been granted extension of leave to 19.7.17.	
"	18/7/17		196 Coy marched to CAESTRE, 197 Coy to RENESCURE	
STAPLE	19/7/17		Train H.Q. marched to STAPLE, 196 Coy to EECKE, 197 Coy to CAESTRE, 195 Coy to RENESCURE. Lt.Col. F.B. Lord returned from leave, having been granted 7 days extra leave by War Office to attend Investiture at Buckingham Palace on the 18th inst.	
"	20/7/17		196 Coy marched to RENINGHELST (Area "C") 197 Coy to EECKE, 195 Coy to CAESTRE. Major T.W. Blakeway rejoined 194 Coy.	
"	21/7/17		196 Coy moved to their new Camp at ZEVECOTEN. 197 Coy to RENINGHELST (Area "C") 195 Coy to EECKE. "A" Group rejoined 24 Div for rations &c	

Army Form C. 2118.

WAR DIARY
or
INTELLIGENCE SUMMARY
(Erase heading not required.)

Instructions regarding War Diaries and Intelligence Summaries are contained in F. S. Regs., Part II. and the Staff Manual respectively. Title Pages will be prepared in manuscript.

Place	Date	Hour	Summary of Events and Information	Remarks and references to Appendices
EECKE	22/7/17		Train H.Q. moved to EECKE. 195 Coy to STEENVOORDE. Supplies for 72nd Bde Group drawn from RENINGHELST Railhead by H.T.	
ZEVECOTEN	23/7/17		Train H.Q. moved to ZEVECOTEN. Capt. R.F. Seddall returned from leave.	
"	24/7/17		Convoy of 21 Wagons took Barrage Rations to Dumps as follows:- 12 Wagons from 194 Coy i/c of Capt. H.C. Pearson delivered 4600 rations to JACKSON'S DUMP (I 28 a 6.3.) Convoy left Camp at 2 30 am & returned at 8.0 am "Gas" Barrage encountered. One horse wounded. One Wagon knocked out. 9 Wagons from 196 Coy i/c of Lt. C.C. Gale delivered 3300 rations to VALLEY COTTAGES (I 23 d. 0.6). Convoy left Camp at 2 30 am & returned at 8.0 am No casualties. One Wagon slightly damaged by Shell fire. 197 Coy moved to new Camp - G35d central - Supplies for 73rd Bde Group drawn from RENINGHELST Railhead by H.T.	
"	25/7/17		195 Coy marched to new Camp - G35d central. Letter of appreciation received from AA&QMG on the conveyance of Barrage rations to JACKSON'S DUMP & VALLEY COTTAGES on the morning of the 24th. 5 Surplus Drivers returned to the Base.	

2449 Wt. W14957/M90 750,000 1/16 J.B.C. & A. Forms/C.2118/12.

Instructions regarding War Diaries and Intelligence Summaries are contained in F. S. Regs., Part II. and the Staff Manual respectively. Title Pages will be prepared in manuscript.

WAR DIARY
or
INTELLIGENCE SUMMARY
(Erase heading not required.)

Army Form C. 2118.

Place	Date	Hour	Summary of Events and Information	Remarks and references to Appendices
ZEVECOTEN	26/7/17		Supplies for 17th Bde group drawn from RENINGHELST Railhead by H.T.	
"	27/7/17		120 Barrage Rations delivered to Transport Lines - 73rd Inf Bde. Enemy aeroplanes bombed in vicinity at night.	
"	28/7/17		Temp. 2nd Lt. H. J. Lewis reported for duty pending absorption & attached to 196 Coy. Summary of evidence taken in case of Pte Hemington, A. by Major Hunter. Horses of the Train inspected by A.D.V.S. II Corps. Lieut. L. M. Fischer proceeded on leave.	
"	29/7/17		Convoy of 12 G.S. Wagons i/c Lt. Macnamara (197 Coy) transported R.E. Material from R.E. Dump VOORMEZEELE to JACKSON'S DUMP. Convoy left camp at 2.30 am. & returned to camp by 9.30 am. Gas barrage encountered - no casualties in men or horses. Capt. D. Bottomley assumed duties of S.O. 73rd Inf Bde & transferred to 197 Coy. 2Lieut. F. H. Pugh " " S.O. 17th " " " 195 Coy.	

2449 Wt. W14957/M90 750,000 1/16 J.B.C. & A. Forms/C.2118/12.

Instructions regarding War Diaries and Intelligence Summaries are contained in F. S. Regs., Part II. and the Staff Manual respectively. Title Pages will be prepared in manuscript.

WAR DIARY
or
INTELLIGENCE SUMMARY
(Erase heading not required.)

Army Form C. 2118.

Place	Date	Hour	Summary of Events and Information	Remarks and references to Appendices
ZEVECOTEN	30/7/17		Riding Horses of the Train inspected in view of the forthcoming reduction by 12.	
"	31/7/17		Lt. C. Macnamara proceeded on leave. Report on 2/Lt. F. R. Nevill sent to Div. as instructed by D.D.S.T. 2nd Army 2229 2/6/17. Big Offensive commenced 3.50 a.m.	
			1/8/17. [signature] Lieut. Col. Comnd'g. 24 Div Train	

2449 Wt. W14957/M90 750,000 1/16 J.B.C. & A. Forms/C.2118/12.

CONFIDENTIAL.

Vol

WAR DIARY.

OF.

194. Company - A.S.C.
24th Divisional Train -

from 1/7/17 to 31/7/17.

Instructions regarding War Diaries and Intelligence Summaries are contained in F. S. Regs., Part II. and the Staff Manual respectively. Title pages will be prepared in manuscript.

WAR DIARY
or
INTELLIGENCE SUMMARY.
(Erase heading not required.)

Army Form C. 2118.

R.B. Blakeway Major

Place	Date	Hour	Summary of Events and Information	Remarks and references to Appendices
		A.M.		
N2.C.22	1/7/17	8-30	Supply wagons refilled on OUDERDOM - MILLEKREUSE Road -	Dull -
"	2/7/17	"	" " " " " "Stand to" at 12.30 AM & MAJOR BLAKEWAY takes Command of Train Capt PEARSON of Coy.	fine
"	3/7/17	12 noon	" " " " " marched to BORRE after delivery	fine
BORRE	4/7/17	11 AM	" " " in BORRE	fine
"	5/7/17	11 AM	" " " " " marched to RACQUINGHEM lorries dumped twice	fine
RACQUINGHEM	6/7/17	9 AM	" " " ½ mile W.S.W. of RACQUINGHEM	fine
" "	7/7/17	10 AM	" " " " " "	fine
" "	8/7/17	9 AM	" " " " "	wet & thundery
" "	9/7/17	9 AM	" " " " " 2 RE Coys & 1 Sec. DAC left for the line	wet
" "	10/7/17	9 AM	" " " "	fine
" "	11/7/17	9 AM	" " " " " "	fine
" "	12/7/17	9 AM	" " " " " "	fine
" "	13/7/17	6.45 AM	S " " marched to BORRE & refilled in square	fine
BORRE	14/7/17	7.0 AM	" " refilled at BORRE & marched to camp at M.5.C.2.9. Map 28.	showery
RENINGHELST	15/7/17	9 AM	" " " on RENINGHELST - LOCRE Road	fine
" "	16/7/17	"	" " " " " " "	fine
" "	17/7/17	"	" " " " " " "	fine

2353 Wt. W2544/1454 700,000 5/15 D. D. & L. A.D.S.S. Forms/C. 2118.

Instructions regarding War Diaries and Intelligence Summaries are contained in F. S. Regs., Part II. and the Staff Manual respectively. Title pages will be prepared in manuscript.

WAR DIARY
or
INTELLIGENCE SUMMARY.
(Erase heading not required.)

Army Form C. 2118.

J. Blakeway – Major –

Place	Date	Hour	Summary of Events and Information	Remarks and references to Appendices
RENINGHELST.	18/7/17	9 AM	Supply wagons refilled on RENINGHELST – LOCRE road	wet
" "	19/7/17	"	" " " " " " " Col: LORD DS.O. returned from leave –	dull S.W. wind
" "	20/7/17	"	" " " " " " " MAJOR BLAKEWAY resumed command of Company –	fine
"	21/7/17	"	" " " " " " " moved to Camp on OUDERDOM – MALEKREUSE Rd.	fine –
OUDERDOM	22/7/17	1. pm.	" " " " " LA CLYTE " Shelled out of camp, moved to new Camp on RENINGHELST – LA CLYTE Road –	Fine –
RENINGHELST	23/7/17	2. pm	" " " " " " " Drew from Railhead by Horse Transport at 10-40 A.M._12 wagons delivered supplies under CAPT. PEARSON at SPOIL BANK., one horse wounded & wagon knocked [illegible]	Fine –
"	24/7/17	2. pm	" " " " " " " Drew from R. H at 10. A.M.	Fine –
"	25/7/17	9. AM	" " " " " " " " " " " " 6-50 A.M.	Rain –
"	26/7/17	9. A.M	" " " " " " " " " " " " "	Fine –
"	27/7/17	"	" " " " " " " " " " " " "	Fine –
"	28/7/17	"	" " " " " " " " " " " " "	Fine –
"	29/7/17	"	" " " " " " " " " " " " "	Rain
"	30/7/17	"	" " " " " " " " " " " " "	Dull & showery
"	31/7/17	"	" " " " " " " " " " " " "	Rain –

Vol 24

Confidential

War Diary

of

O. C. 24th Divisional Train

From 1 8/17 to 31 8/17

Instructions regarding War Diaries and Intelligence Summaries are contained in F. S. Regs., Part II. and the Staff Manual respectively. Title pages will be prepared in manuscript.

WAR DIARY
or
INTELLIGENCE SUMMARY.
(Erase heading not required.)

Army Form C. 2118.

Place	Date	Hour	Summary of Events and Information	Remarks and references to Appendices
ZEVECOTEN	1/8/17		Transport ordered to be at Railhead at 9 am, but loading did not commence until 11 am owing to delay caused by 25th Div loading in detail. CO visited D.D.S.T. Rained hard the whole day.	
"	2/8/17		Railhead 5 30 a.m. F.G. Court Martial assembled at Train H.Q. for the trial of S.S/85 Pte Hemington, A of 197 Coy. O.O. No. 177 received. Very wet	
"	3/8/17		Convoy of 8 G.S. Wagons i/c S.S.M. Lowrie (194 Coy) transported Trench boards from Div R.E. Dump to Observatory Ridge – started from Dump at 9 am. Heavy shelling encountered at Shrapnel Corner – no casualties. Wagons returned to Camp at 4 pm	
"	4/8/17		Similar details found for R.E. as yesterday. 2/Lt H. J. Lewis (196 Coy) i/c Convoy. Owing to shelling at Shrapnel Corner one Wagon fell off track & had to be unloaded. Load left & Wagon returned to Camp. 3 G.S. Wagons found for Pioneers for forward work. Sentence on S.S/85 Pte Hemington, A. promulgated. CO visited H.Q. II Corps & 23rd Div. Art.y Group. Wet.	
"	5/8/17		R.E. Convoy of 8 G.S. Wagons i/c of 2/Lt G. J. Morton (195 Coy) reported at Dump at 4.0 am. Returned to Camp at 9.30 am without incident. Fine.	

A6945 Wt. W11422/M1160 350,000 12/16 D. D. & L. Forms/C./2118/14.

Army Form C. 2118.

Instructions regarding War Diaries and Intelligence Summaries are contained in F. S. Regs., Part II, and the Staff Manual respectively. Title pages will be prepared in manuscript.

WAR DIARY
or
INTELLIGENCE SUMMARY.
(Erase heading not required.)

Place	Date	Hour	Summary of Events and Information	Remarks and references to Appendices
ZEVECOTEN	6/8/17		Major T. W. Blakeway proceeded on leave. R.E. Convoy of 8 G.S. Wagons i/c of Lt L.G. Blunnett (196 Coy) reported at Dump at 4 am. – 3 G.S. Wagons i/c of 2/Lt J.O. Tidy (197 Coy) reported at H.Q. Pioneers at 2.30 am. Trench boards carried to forward area. Wagons returned to Camp by 10 am without incident. Notification received from A.D.M.S. 24th Div. the M.O. i/c Div Train was to be withdrawn.	
"	7/8/17		23rd Div. Art. Group transferred to 18th Div. R.E. Convoy of 8 G.S. Wagons i/c 2/Lt A.H. Barnes (194 Coy) reported at Dump 4 am. – returned to Camp by 9.30 am without incident. Camp of 20th Aust. A.S.C. Coy shelled – 1 O.R. wounded – no horses. CO obtained permission from II Corps "Q" for this Coy to move to new Camp.	
"	8/8/17		R.E. Convoy of 8 G.S. Wagons i/c Capt. K.M. Plumptre (194 Coy) reported at Dump 4 am. – returned to camp by 10 am without incident. Lt. L.M. Mischer returned from leave. Lt C.C. Gale proceeded on leave. 20th Aust. A.S.C. Coy moved to M.5.C.2.9.	
"	9/8/17		R.E. Convoy of 8 G.S. Wagons i/c 2/Lt F.R. Nevill (195 Coy) reported at Dump 4 am. – returned to Camp by 10 am without incident. Instructed to feed 23rd Div. Art. Group as from 10/8/17 Noon	

Instructions regarding War Diaries and Intelligence Summaries are contained in F. S. Regs., Part II. and the Staff Manual respectively. Title pages will be prepared in manuscript.

WAR DIARY
or
INTELLIGENCE SUMMARY.
(Erase heading not required.)

Army Form C. 2118.

Place	Date	Hour	Summary of Events and Information	Remarks and references to Appendices
ZEVECOTEN	10/8/17		R.E. Convoy of 4 G.S. Wagons i/c Sgt. Heldon (194 Coy) reported at Dump 8 am - returned without incident. Fine	
"	11/8/17		Hostile Aeroplanes bombed in vicinity at 2 am. No bombs in Train Camps. One bomb in Wagon Park of H.Q. Coy 23rd Div Train (at present attached). 4 O.R. wounded & several Vehicles damaged. R.E. Convoy of 8 G.S. Wagons i/c 2/Lt G. J. Molton (195 Coy) reported at Dump 4 am. returned, without incident at 9.30 pm. Heavy rain at night.	
"	12/8/17		R.E. Convoy of 8 G.S. Wagons i/c 2/Lt H. J. Lewis (196 Coy) reported at Dump 7 am returned without incident at 1.30 pm. Visited 73rd Field Ambulance. Fine. Lt C. Macnamara returned from leave. 2 Remounts (HD) collected by 195 Coy - 1 for 195 1 for 197.	
"	13/8/17		3 Reinforcements reported 1 Sergt to 195 Coy. 2 Drivers to 194 Coy. R.E. Convoy of 8 G.S. Wagons i/c of Lt L. G. Bennett (196 Coy) reported at Dump at 7 am, two journeys made to forward areas. Wagons returned to Camp without incident. Lt C. Macnamara admitted to 74th Field Amb.	
"	14/8/17		Nothing of importance to report. Heavy thunderstorms.	

A6945 Wt. W11422/M1160 350,000 12/16 D. D. & L. Forms/C./2118/14.

Instructions regarding War Diaries and Intelligence Summaries are contained in F. S. Regs., Part II, and the Staff Manual respectively. Title pages will be prepared in manuscript.

WAR DIARY
or
INTELLIGENCE SUMMARY.
(Erase heading not required.)

Army Form C. 2118.

Place	Date	Hour	Summary of Events and Information	Remarks and references to Appendices
ZEVECOTEN	15/8/17		Convoy of 6 G.S. Wagons i/c of 2nd Lt J.O. Tealy reported at R.E. Dump & delivered fascines to forward dumps, returned to Camp 10.30 A.M without incident. Lt E.W.L. Martin given authority (G.H.Q) to wear Captains rank whilst holding the appointment of Adjutant pending notification in the Gazette. Proceeded on leave; 2nd Lt C.H. Barnes acting Adjutant during his absence.	
	16/8/17		Nothing of importance to report. Fine. Major T.W. Blakeway returned from leave	
	17/8/17		Convoy of 8 G.S. Wagons i/c of 2nd Lt F.R. Nevill reported at R.E. Dump 7 A.M delivered material to forward dumps, returned to Camp 1.30 P.M. without incident. Hostile aeroplanes dropped bombs in the vicinity between 9.30 & 10 P.M. No bombs in Train Camps.	
	18/8/17		Nothing of importance to report. Fine.	
	19/8/17		Convoy of 5 G.S. Wagons i/c of S.S.M. Cant (195 Coy) reported at R.E. Dump at 7 A.M. delivered material at forward dump & returned to Camp 12 Noon without incident. Convoy of 3 G.S. Wagons i/c of Sergt Ellwood (197 Coy) reported at R.E. Dump (Ouderdom) & conveyed Track Boards to Voormezeele returned to Camp 12 Noon without incident. Lt C.C. Gale returned from leave. Hostile aeroplanes dropped bombs in the vicinity between 9.15 & 10 P.M. No bombs in Train Camps. 2nd Lt F.R. Nevill proceeded on leave	

Instructions regarding War Diaries and Intelligence Summaries are contained in F. S. Regs., Part II. and the Staff Manual respectively. Title pages will be prepared in manuscript.

WAR DIARY
or
INTELLIGENCE SUMMARY.
(Erase heading not required.)

Army Form C. 2118.

Place	Date	Hour	Summary of Events and Information	Remarks and references to Appendices
ZEVECOTEN	20/8/17		Convoy of 8 G.S. Wagons in charge of Lt L. N. Fischer reported at R. E. Dump 7 A.M. delivered material to forward area, returned to Camp 11.30 A.M. without incident	
"	21/8/17		Convoy of 8 G.S. Wagons i/c Capt K. M. Plumptre reported at R. E. Dump 7 A.M. delivered material & returned to Camp without incident.	
"	22/8/17		Convoy of 8 G.S. Wagons i/c Capt W. J. Pearson ditto as above, returned to Camp 12.30 PM. Enemy aircraft dropped bombs in the vicinity between 9 & 10 P.M. one A.A. shell burst close to No 1 Corps Refilling Point, no damage.	
"	23/8/17		Convoy of 8 G.S. Wagons i/c 2nd Lt G. J. Holtom ditto as above.	
"	24/8/17		" " " " i/c Lt C. C. Gale " " " 23rd Div'l Art'y Group transferred	
"	25/8/17		Nothing of importance to report. Fine.	
"	26/8/17		Capt. E. W. L. Martin returned from leave	
"	27/8/17		Lieut. L. G. Bennett proceeded on leave. R.E. Convoy of 8 G.S. Wagons i/c 2/Lt. H. J. Lewis as above. Very wet all day.	
	28/8/17		24th Div'n transferred to Xth Corps 2nd Army as from 12 noon. Heavy gale blew all day. R.E. Convoy of 8 G.S. Wagons i/c 2nd Lt J. O. Tidy	
	29/8/17		R.E. Convoy of 8 G.S. Wagons i/c ~~Lt G. J. Holtom~~ Capt. K. M. Plumptre – Gale continued.	

A6945 Wt. W11422/M1160 350,000 12/16 D. D. & L. Forms/C./2118/14.

Instructions regarding War Diaries and Intelligence Summaries are contained in F. S. Regs., Part II. and the Staff Manual respectively. Title pages will be prepared in manuscript.

WAR DIARY
or
INTELLIGENCE SUMMARY.
(Erase heading not required.)

Army Form C. 2118.

Place	Date	Hour	Summary of Events and Information	Remarks and references to Appendices
ZEVECOTEN	30/8/17		R.E. Convoy of 8 G.S. Wagons i/c 2/Lt G. J. Motion. M.O. returned from 2nd Corps Main Dressing Station. The one days rations held by the Supply Column issued to	
"	~~31/8/17~~		Units in the afternoon. The days rations, therefore, will be held by Units instead of by the Train or Column.	
"	31/8/17		R.E. Convoy of 8 G.S. Wagons i/c Capt. H. C. Pearson. M.O. transferred to 74th Field Ambulance, a Divl Train no longer having one attached. 5 Surplus Riders transferred to other Units - a Div Train's Establishment having been reduced by 12 3 per Company - 1 for C.Q.M.S. & 2 for Farriers - bicycles substituted. 2/Lt. F. R. Nevill returned from leave.	

J. S. Shord Lt Col
Commdg 24th Div Train

A6945 Wt. W11422/M1160 350,000 12/16 D. D. & L. Forms/C./2118/14.

Instructions regarding War Diaries and Intelligence Summaries are contained in F. S. Regs., Part II. and the Staff Manual respectively. Title pages will be prepared in manuscript.

WAR DIARY
or
INTELLIGENCE SUMMARY.
(Erase heading not required.)

Army Form C. 2118.

A W Blakeway - Major -

Place	Date	Hour	Summary of Events and Information	Remarks and references to Appendices
RENINGHELST	1/8/17	P.M. 12-30	Supply wagons refilled on RENINGHELST - LA CLYTE Road. Drew from R. H at 11 AM	Rain -
„	2/8/17	A.M. 9-0	„ „ „ „ „ „ „ „ „ „ 6-45. A.M.	Rain -
„	3/8/17	9-0	„ „ „ „ „ „ „ „ „ „ „ „	Rain -
„	4/8/17	„	„ „ „ „ „ „ „ „ „ „ „ „	Rain -
„	5/8/17	„	„ „ „ „ „ „ „ „ „ „ „ „	fine
„	6/8/17	„	„ „ „ „ „ „ „ „ „ „ „ Major BLAKEWAY on leave. Capt PEARSON assumes Command of Coy.	fine
„	7/8/17	„	„ „ „ „ „ „ „ „ „ „ 6.30 AM	fine
„	8/8/17	„	„ „ „ „ „ „ „ „ „ „ „	fine to 6 PM. - rain
„	9/8/17	„	„ „ „ „ „ „ „ „ „ „ „	fine
„	10/8/17	„	„ „ „ „ „ „ „ „ „ „ „	fine
„	11/8/17	„	„ „ „ „ „ „ „ „ „ „ „	wet
„	12/8/17	„	„ „ „ „ „ „ „ „ „ „ „	fine to 6 PM. rain
„	13/8/17	„	„ „ „ „ „ „ „ „ „ „ „	~~fine~~ showery -
„	14/8/17	„	„ „ „ „ „ „ „ „ „ „ „	showery.
„	15/8/17	„	„ „ „ „ „ „ „ „ „ „ „	showery.
„	16/8/17	„	„ „ „ „ „ „ „ „ „ „ „ MAJOR BLAKEWAY returned from leave & assumed command of Company -	fine -

2353 Wt. W2544/1454 700,000 5/15 D. D. & L. A.D.S.S./Forms/C. 2118.

Instructions regarding War Diaries and Intelligence Summaries are contained in F. S. Regs., Part II. and the Staff Manual respectively. Title pages will be prepared in manuscript.

WAR DIARY
or
INTELLIGENCE SUMMARY.
(Erase heading not required.)

Army Form C. 2118.

R. Blakeway – Major –

Place	Date	Hour	Summary of Events and Information	Remarks and references to Appendices
RENINGHELST	17/8/17	9. A.M.	Supply wagons refilled on RENINGHELST – LA CLYTE Road – Drew from R.H. at 6-30 A.M. Bombed at night –	Fine –
"	18/8/17	"	" " " " " " " " " "	Fine, few showers.
"	19/8/17	"	" " " " " " " " " " " "	Fine –
"	20/8/17	"	" " " " " " " " " "	Fine –
"	21/8/17	"	" " " " " " " " " "	Fine –
"	22/8/17	"	" " " " " " " " " " " "	Fine –
"	23/8/17	"	" " " " " " " " " "	Showery –
"	24/8/17	"	" " " " " " " " " "	Showery –
"	25/8/17	"	" " " " " " " " " "	Fine –
"	26/8/17	"	" " " " " " " " " "	Heavy rain at night
"	27/8/17	"	" " " " " " " " " "	Heavy rain & gale –
"	28/8/17	"	" " " " " " " " " " Transferred to IX Corps – 2nd Army –	Rain & gale –
"	29/8/17	"	" " " " " " " " " " Camp shelled –	Showery & windy –
"	30/8/17	"	" " " " " " " " " "	Showery & windy –
"	"	2-30 p.m.	" " " " " "	
"	31/8/17	"	" " " " " " " " " "	Fine –

2353 Wt. W2544/1454 700,000 5/15 D. D. & L. A.D.S.S./Forms/C. 2118.

Vol 25

Confidential

War Diary

of

O C 24th Divisional Train

From 1 9/17 To 30 9/17

Instructions regarding War Diaries and Intelligence Summaries are contained in F. S. Regs., Part II. and the Staff Manual respectively. Title pages will be prepared in manuscript.

WAR DIARY
or
INTELLIGENCE SUMMARY.
(Erase heading not required.)

Army Form C. 2118.

Place	Date	Hour	Summary of Events and Information	Remarks and references to Appendices
DEVECOTEN	1/9/17		R.E. Convoy of 8 G.S. Wagons i/c Lt. C.C. Gale 196 Coy. Shelled heavily near Spoil bank – no casualties. By order of Xth Corps. 6 pairs H.D. Horses & Drivers (no Wagons) sent to be attached to O.C. 2° Army Workshop ABEELE – supplied by 194 Coy A.S.C. S.S.M. Lowrie i/c. 1 Complete turnout H.D. sent for duty with Area Sub-Commdt METEREN.	
"	2/9/17		C.O. visited detached H.D. Horses at ABEELE. From about 10 pm to 12 midnight the neighbourhood of Train H.Q. Coys was bombed by hostile aircraft. Windows of huts were broken, but there were no casualties in men or horses. Men from the Train assisted in extinguishing a big fire at D.A.D.O.S. Store caused by bombs from midnight to 1.30 am.	
"	3/9/17		Capt. W. A. Macgregor, O.C. i/c Train & 2/Lt. F. H. Pugh proceeded on leave – Lt. L. M. Mischer, (R.O.) to carry out duties as S.O. 17 Inf Bde during 2/Lt Pugh's absence. Commenced to ration 3 Field Coys, H.Q. R.E. & Pioneer Battn of 33rd Div.	
"			Hostile bombs dropped throughout the night in vicinity – commenced about 9.30 pm. last attack at 5 am.	
"	4/9/17		Hostile bombs dropped throughout the night. Two within about 100 yards of Train H.Q. no damage.	

A6945 Wt. W11422/M1160 350,000 12/16 D. D. & L. Forms/C./2118/14.

Instructions regarding War Diaries and Intelligence Summaries are contained in F. S. Regs., Part II. and the Staff Manual respectively. Title pages will be prepared in manuscript.

WAR DIARY
or
INTELLIGENCE SUMMARY.
(Erase heading not required.)

Army Form C. 2118.

Place	Date	Hour	Summary of Events and Information	Remarks and references to Appendices
ZEVECOTEN	5/9/17		2nd Aust Div Art[y] Group rationed by us for last time on transfer to 47th Div. Commenced to ration 242 A.F.A.B + 315 A.F.A.B from this date. CO visited DDS&T 2nd Army	
"	6/9/17		4 G.S. Wagons supplied for R.E. work. On order from "Q" 2 complete 'turnouts' sent for duty with 30 Labour Group - VIERSTRAAT. CO visited O.C. of this Unit - the turnouts to live with Unit.	
"	7/9/17		Rations issued to 298 A.F.A.B for last time. Commenced to ration 190 Bde R.F.A. CO visited D.D.S.&T 2nd Army. Lt L.G. Bennett returned from leave.	
"	8/9/17		Commenced to ration 1st Squadron Field Coy R.E. 3 Category "A" Supply Clerks sent to Base for transfer to fighting Units - replaced by Cat. "B" men - 2 Surplus Cat "B" Clerks returned to Base. 4 Drivers Reinforcements reported - 2 posted to 194 Coy + 2 to 74 Field Amb.	
"	9/9/17		113th A.F.A.B. rationed by us for the last time	
"	10/9/17		52nd A.F.A.B do. Commenced to ration 102 Field Coy R.E +9th S Staffs. The two G.S. Wagons - complete turnouts - returned from 30th Labour Group.	
"	11/9/17		Capt J.P. Thompson proceeded on 30 days leave - 197 Coy to be commanded by Capt. K.M. Plumpton	

A6945 Wt. W11422/M1160 350,000 12/16 D. D. & L. Forms/C./2118/14.

Army Form C. 2118.

Instructions regarding War Diaries and Intelligence Summaries are contained in F. S. Regs., Part II. and the Staff Manual respectively. Title pages will be prepared in manuscript.

WAR DIARY
or
INTELLIGENCE SUMMARY.
(Erase heading not required.)

Place	Date	Hour	Summary of Events and Information	Remarks and references to Appendices
ZEVECOTEN	11/9/17		(194 Coy). 2/Lieut. G J Motion proceeded on leave. 24 D.A. Operation Order received.	
"	12/9/17		O.O No. 200 received. Visited new area. Train horses inspected by C.R.A. who expressed great admiration.	
"	13/9/17		Visited new area & selected Refilling Points. Supplies for 107 Bde drawn by M.T. Supply Wagons of ~~106~~, 107 & D.A.C. marched to new area.	
"	14/9/17		Lorries on road for A. C & D Groups. Rations for 106 dumped at BOESCHEPPE,	
MERRIS			107 at PRADELLES. - D.A.C. & remainder of "A" Group at STEENVOORDE. 194 Coy moved to STEENVOORDE. 196 Coy moved to MERIS. 197 Coy moved to WESTOUTRE. Train H.Q. moved to MERRIS at 3pm. arriving 6.30pm	
"	15/9/17		197 Coy moved to BERQUIN area. 2/Lt F.H. Pugh & Capt W.A. MacGregor returned from leave.	
"	16/9/17		195 Coy moved to MERRIS. 194 Coy entrained at GODWAERSVELDE for new area - Baggage & Supply Wagons with Units. 194 Coy under orders of C.R.A. until the Division gets together again.	
"	17/9/17		Entraining Orders for the Div (less Artillery) received	

A6945 Wt. W11422/M1160 350,000 12/16 D. D. & L. Forms/C./2118/14.

Instructions regarding War Diaries and Intelligence Summaries are contained in F. S. Regs., Part II. and the Staff Manual respectively. Title pages will be prepared in manuscript.

WAR DIARY
or
INTELLIGENCE SUMMARY.
(*Erase heading not required.*)

Army Form C. 2118.

Place	Date	Hour	Summary of Events and Information	Remarks and references to Appendices
MERRIS	18/9/17		Nothing of importance to report	
"	19/9/17		2/Lt. L.A. Dennis reported for duty & attached pending absorbtion - posted to 195 Coy.	
"	20/9/17		195, 196 & 197 Coys entrained & proceeded to new area. CO & SSO proceeded to new area	
ROCQUIGNY	21/9/17		Train H.Q. established at ROCQUIGNY. No accommodation - tents borrowed from O.C. Reinforcement Camp. Railhead BAPAUME III Corps 3rd Army.	
"	22/9/17		2/Lt G. J. McLean returned from leave. CO visited new Area with AA & QMG	
"	23/9/17		2/Lt A.C. Corby reported for Duty from HT&S Depot, HAVRE - attached pending absorption - posted to 197 Coy for Supply duties.	
"	24/9/17		197 Coy moved to HAUT ALLAINS. Two Reinforcements (Drivers) reported.	
"	25/9/17		197 Coy moved to ROISEL, 196 to HAUT ALLAINES, 194 to DOINGT.	
"	26/9/17		73rd Inf Bde Group (197 Coy) rationed by 34th Div at ROISEL. Railhead for remainder of Div PERONNE LA CHAPELLETTE. Lieut L.G. Bennett proceeded to England on being transferred to Infantry.	
PERONNE	27/9/17		Train H.Q. moved to PERONNE. 196 Coy moved to ROISEL. 195 Coy to HAUT ALLAINES.	
"	28/9/17		Visited new area.	

A6945 Wt. W11422/M1160 350,000 12/16 D. D. & L. Forms/C./2118/14.

Instructions regarding War Diaries and Intelligence Summaries are contained in F. S. Regs., Part II, and the Staff Manual respectively. Title pages will be prepared in manuscript.

WAR DIARY
or
INTELLIGENCE SUMMARY.
(*Erase heading not required.*)

Army Form C. 2118.

Place	Date	Hour	Summary of Events and Information	Remarks and references to Appendices
ROISEL.	29/9/17		Train H.Q. 194 & 195 Coys moved to ROISEL – Division now complete in new Area. 2/Lt. H.W. Bradley reported for duty & posted to 196 Coy vice Lt. C.G. Barrett (to England 26/9/17)	
"	30/9/17		Supplies taken from Railhead – ROISEL, to Refilling Points by Light Railway & thence to Units by 1st Line transport in certain cases. Train wagons deliver rations to those who were unable to send their own transport. Ordered by Div to leave the supply wagons with the 106th & 107th Bdes, R.F.A. Units attached to Supply Groups of Div amounting to abt 4,800 men & 1700 horses.	

J. Ward McCol
Commdg 24 Div Train

A6945 Wt. W11422/M1160 350,000 12/16 D. D. & L. Forms/C./2118/14.

CONFIDENTIAL.

WAR DIARY.

OF

194. Comp: A.S.C. 24th Div: Train.

from 1/9/17 to 30/9/17.

Instructions regarding War Diaries and Intelligence Summaries are contained in F. S. Regs., Part II. and the Staff Manual respectively. Title pages will be prepared in manuscript.

WAR DIARY
or
INTELLIGENCE SUMMARY.
(Erase heading not required.)

Army Form C. 2118.

R. Blakeway - Major -

Place	Date	Hour	Summary of Events and Information	Remarks and references to Appendices
RENINGHELST	1/9/17	A.M. 9-30	Supply wagons refilled on RENINGHELST - LA CLYTE Road - Drew from R.H. at 6-30 A.M.	Showery -
"	2/9/17	"	" " " " " " " " " " Camp bombed at night -	Showery -
"	3/9/17	"	" " " " " " " " " " Bombs & shells round Camp at night.	Fine -
"	4/9/17	"	" " " " " " " " " " Bombs all round Camp at night.	Fine -
"	5/9/17	"	" " " " " " " " " "	Fine day - Thunderstorm at night
"	6/9/17	"	" " " " " " " " " "	Fine day - Thunderstorm in evening -
"	7/9/17	"	" " " " " " " " " "	Fine -
"	8/9/17	"	" " " " " " " " " "	Fine -
"	9/9/17	"	" " " " " " " " " 7. A.M.	Fine -
"	10/9/17	"	" " " " " " " " " 7-30 A.M.	Fine -
"	11/9/17	"	" " " " " " " " " 7. A.M.	Fine -
"	12/9/17	"	" " " " " " " " " " Supply wagons 107th detached to BRIG:	Fine -
"	13/9/17	"	" " " " " " " " " " " " 106th " " "	Fine, Wind at night
"	14/9/17	A.M. 6-30	Moved from Camp to STEENVOORDE, arrived 10.A.M. Supply wagons of D.A.C & COMP: refilled on STEENVOORDE - HAAZEBROOK Road at 2. p.m.	Fine -
STEENVOORDE	15/9/17	2. p.m.	Supply wagons of D.A.C & COMP: refilled on STEENVOORDE - HAAZEBROOK Road & formed the D.A.C -	Fine -
"	16/9/17	5-30 p.m.	Marched to GODERSKEDE Railway Siding for entraining - Entrained 2-30 A.M 17/9/17 -	Fine -

23530 Wt W2514/1454 700,000 5/15 D. D. & L. A.D.S.S. Forms/C. 2118.

Instructions regarding War Diaries and Intelligence Summaries are contained in F. S. Regs., Part II. and the Staff Manual respectively. Title pages will be prepared in manuscript.

WAR DIARY
or
INTELLIGENCE SUMMARY.
(Erase heading not required.)

Army Form C. 2118.

R Blakeway – Major

Place	Date	Hour	Summary of Events and Information	Remarks and references to Appendices
MAP. 57c				
N. 11. a. 2. 7.	17/9/17.	MIDDAY 12.	Arrived at BAPAUME Railway Siding, detrained & moved off to Camp at 12-45 pm, arrived 2-15 pm – Supply wagons refilled at 3-p.m., on BAPAUME – PERONNE Road – In 3rd Army & 4th CORPS –	Fine –
"	18/9/17	9. A.M.	" " " " " " "	Fine –
"	19/9/17	"	" " " " " " "	Fine –
"	20/9/17	"	" " " " " " "	Fine –
"	21/9/17	"	" " " " " " "	Fine –
"	22/9/17	"	" " " " " " "	Fine –
"	23/9/17	"	" " " " " " "	Fine –
"	24/9/17	"	" " " " " " "	Fine –
MAP. 62c	25/9/17	P.M. 4-30	" " " " PERONNE – ROISEL Road – Moved from Camp to new one –	Fine –
I. 36. b.	26/9/17	9. A.M.	" " " " " " " In 3rd CORPS –	Fine –
"	27/9/17	"	" " " " " " "	Rain early –
	28/9/17	"	" " " " " " "	Fine –
"	29/9/17	8-A.M.	" " " " " " " Moved into new Camp at ROISEL.	Fine –
ROISEL	30/9/17	11-A.M.	" " " K. 22. Only 107th BRIG: R.F.A. The remainder of R.A. rations sent up on Light Railways	Fine –

2353 Wt. W2544/1454 700,000 5/15 D. D. & L. A.D.S.S./Forms/C. 2118.

16

Vol 26

Confidential

War Diary

of

O. C 24th Divisional Train

from 1/10/1917 to 31/10/1917.

Instructions regarding War Diaries and Intelligence Summaries are contained in F. S. Regs., Part II, and the Staff Manual respectively. Title pages will be prepared in manuscript.

WAR DIARY
or
INTELLIGENCE SUMMARY.
(Erase heading not required.)

Army Form C. 2118.

Place	Date	Hour	Summary of Events and Information	Remarks and references to Appendices
VRAIGNES	1/10/17		Train H.Q moved to VRAIGNES. 2/Lt. A. C. Corby assumed duties of S.O. 72nd Inf Bde during Capt. R. F. Sedall's residence at H.Q. 2/Lt. L. A. Dennis assumed duties of S.O. 17th Inf Bde vice 2/Lt. F. H. Pugh (to 2nd Army). 43 G.S. Wagons + 1 H.D. Horse on various duties as detailed by Divn (Standing duties). War Estabt of 194 Coy reduced by 1 Sgt + 1 Rider	
"	2/10/17		Standing transport duties increased to 45 G.S. Wagons + 1 H.D. Horse.	
"	3/10/17		Hay at 5½ lbs only arrived at Railhead. Arrangements made to issue from Haystacks in Area. 10 G.S. Wagons employed on carting. 10 G.S. Wagons employed on carting ammunition to Dumps for 72nd Inf Bde	
"	4/10/17		Standing transport duties increased to 48 G.S. Wagons + 1 H.D. Horse. 30 G.S. Wagons on temporary duties. Major H. B. Hunter + Capt G. H. Hiltch proceeded on leave. F.G.C.M. assembled for trial of Sgt Pike + Cpl Saunders, both of 195 Coy. Fresh arrangements made by Div. to leave 5 Baggage Wagons with each Infantry Brigade	
"	5/10/17		13 G.S. Wagons on temporary duties. Very wet. D.D.S.&T. 3rd Army visited Dn Train & saw all the horses with the C.O.	
	6/10/17		Promulgation of F.G.C.M. of Sgt Pike + Cpl Saunders of 195 Coy. Both reduced to the	

A6945 Wt. W11422/M1160 350,000 12/16 D. D. & L. Forms/C./2118/14.

Instructions regarding War Diaries and Intelligence Summaries are contained in F. S. Regs., Part II. and the Staff Manual respectively. Title pages will be prepared in manuscript.

WAR DIARY
or
INTELLIGENCE SUMMARY.
(Erase heading not required.)

Army Form C. 2118.

Place	Date	Hour	Summary of Events and Information	Remarks and references to Appendices
VRAIGNES	6/10/17		ranks. 13 G.S. Wagons on temporary transport duties	
"	7/10/17		Very wet – nothing of importance to report. 6 Wagons on temp? duties	
"	8/10/17		1 Off. (2/Lt F R Nevile) 18 O.R. proceeded to III Army Rest Camp. 130 tons of Coal arrived at Railhead. 7 Wagons on temp? duties	
"	9/10/17		Very wet. 9 Wagons on temp? duties	
"	10/10/17		Stormy. S.S.O visited D.D.S.T. III Army. 14 Wagons on temp? duties.	
"	11/10/17		Do 12 Wagons on temp? duties	
"	12/10/17		Wet & windy. 14 Wagons on temp? duties.	
"	13/10/17		Wet. 23 Remounts (Riders) collected from PERONNE for Units in the Division – 1 for 190 Coy distributed same day. 6 Wagons on temp? duties.	
"	14/10/17		Capt S H Parslow proceeded on one month's leave. Capt J R Thompson returned from leave. Summary of evidence for F.G.C.M. on S/S Sgt Bolton (194 Coy) taken. 12 Wagons on casual duties	
"	[illegible]		Court of Enquiry on loss of certain commodities at Refilling Point held at 194 Coy's Camp (Pres? Capt H C Pearson). Lt. L M Mischer assumed command of 195 Coy during Capt Parslow's absence	
"	15/10/17		Court of Enquiry reassembled for further investigation. 11 G.S. Wagons on temp? duties. Capt. K. M. Plumptre proceeded on leave. Maj. H B Hunter & Capt G Hitch returned from leave	
"	16/10/17		C.S.M. Campbell, & 3 O.R. Reinforcements reported. Court of Enquiry assembled on cause of a fire in 195 Coy's lines (Presd? Capt F A R Saunders)	

A6945 Wt. W11422/M1160 350,000 12/16 D. D. & L. Forms/C.2118/14.

Instructions regarding War Diaries and Intelligence Summaries are contained in F. S. Regs., Part II. and the Staff Manual respectively. Title pages will be prepared in manuscript.

WAR DIARY
or
INTELLIGENCE SUMMARY.
(Erase heading not required.)

Army Form C. 2118.

Place	Date	Hour	Summary of Events and Information	Remarks and references to Appendices
VRAIGNES	16/10/17		Standing duties for Transport 53 - including 10 tip carts. Casual duties 10	
"	17/10/17		A/CSM Bayman (196 Coy) reduced to permanent rank of L Sgt for neglect of duty.	
			Casual duties 7	
"	18/10/17		Summary of evidence in case of Dr Dimmock (196 Coy) taken. Refilling groups changed	
			All "A" group at K22C "B" group at VRAIGNES (Decauville Railhead) Casual duties 10	
			2/Lt A N Barnes proceeded on leave. 5 French Vehicles salved from HARGICOURT handed to Area Commdt ROISEL	
"	19/10/17		Fine. Nothing of importance to report. Casual duties 5.	
"	20/10/17		Further evidence taken in the case of Staff Sgt Bolton. Standing duties for Transport	
			increased to 59. Casual duties 5.	
"	21/10/17		Nothing of importance to report. Casual duties 5.	
"	22/10/17		Standing Transport duties increased to 65. Casual duties 3 2/Lt F R Neville's party returned from 3rd Army Rest Camp. 6 O.R. proceeded to 3rd Army Rest Camp.	
"	23/10/17		Very wet. Casual details 5. Notification received for Lt F R Pugh to proceed to England for transfer to Infantry - replied that he had been attached to Chem. Adviser, 2nd Army since 18/9/17	
"	24/10/17		Lt Col T Blood, D.S.O. proceeded on special leave to England for 30 days. Major T W Blakeney	
			assumed command. Further evidence taken in case of CM. of Dr Dimmock 196 Coy.	
			Lieut O W Ball, Instructor at No 2 Cadet Coy. ASC attached to this Unit for a fortnight	
			to study the system of Supply & Transport in the field. Casual duties 5.	

A6945 Wt. W11422/M1160 350,000 12/16 D. D. & L. Forms/C./2118/14.

Instructions regarding War Diaries and Intelligence Summaries are contained in F. S. Regs., Part II. and the Staff Manual respectively. Title pages will be prepared in manuscript.

WAR DIARY
or
INTELLIGENCE SUMMARY.
(Erase heading not required.)

Army Form C. 2118.

Place	Date	Hour	Summary of Events and Information	Remarks and references to Appendices
VRAIGNES.	25/10/17		F.G.C.M. on Staff Sgt BOLTON, F.E held at H.Q. 72nd Bde. 2Lieut. F Channon reported for duty pending absorption – attached to 195 Coy. Heavy Gale Casual duties 5	
"	26/10/17		Very wet. Casual duties 5.	
"	27/10/17		Promulgation of F.G.C.M. Staff Sgt Bolton – reduced to Cpl. Casual duties 2	
"	28/10/17		Nothing of importance to report. Casual duties 2	
"	29/10/17		Lt L.M. Mischen proceeded to England on transfer to the Infantry. F.G.C.M. on Dr Dimmock 196 Coy held at H.Q. 24 D.A. Casual duties 3	
"	30/10/17		1 Corpl & 24 Drivers reinforcements arrived. Promulgation of F.G.C.M. Dr Dimmock – 21 days F.P. No 1. Casual duties 4.	
"	31/10/17		L Sgt Bazman & Cpl Bolton returned to Base – surplus to establishment. Casual duties 10. Advised that Capt K.M. Plumptre had been granted 4 days extension of leave by W.O	

R.H. Blakeway – Major
Commd. 24th Div Train

A6945 Wt. W11422/M1160 350,000 12/16 D. D. & L. Forms/C./2118/14.

Confidential

War Diary

of

194 Coy A.S.C

for

October 1917

Instructions regarding War Diaries and Intelligence Summaries are contained in F. S. Regs., Part II. and the Staff Manual respectively. Title pages will be prepared in manuscript.

WAR DIARY
or
INTELLIGENCE SUMMARY.
(Erase heading not required.)

194 Coy
Mtd Divl Train

Army Form C. 2118.

Place	Date	Hour	Summary of Events and Information	Remarks and references to Appendices
ROISEL.	1/10/17	A.M. 10-30	Supplies drawn from Light Railway at K.22 -	Fine -
"	2/10/17	9-0	" " " " " "	Fine - Showers in night -
"	3/10/17	9-30	" " " " " "	Dull -
"	4/10/17	10-0	" " " " " "	Rain -
"	5/10/17		All supplies drawn by Units at various Rail Heads on Light Railway -	Rain -
"	6/10/17		" " " " " " " " "	Rain -
"	7/10/17		" " " " " " " " " Summer time changed 1. A M. -	Rain -
"	8/10/17		" " " " " " " " "	Gale & Rain -
"	9/10/17		" " " " " " " "	Wind & showers.
"	10/10/17		" " " " " " " " "	Wind & showers.
"	11/10/17		" " " " " " " "	Fine -
"	12/10/17		" " " " " " " " " Corps Advisor on Horsemastership inspected Coy	Gale & rain -
"	13/10/17		" " " " " " " " " Lt. FRISCHER took over Command of 195 Coy	Showery & windy -
"	14/10/17		" " " " " " " " "	Showery -
"	15/10/17		" " " " " " " " " Capt. PLUMPTRE went on leave -	Fine -
"	16/10/17		" " " " " " " " "	Fine -

2353 Wt. W2544/1454 700,000 5/15 D. D. & L. A.D.S.S. Forms/C. 2118.

AHPearson Capt

Instructions regarding War Diaries and Intelligence Summaries are contained in F. S. Regs., Part II. and the Staff Manual respectively. Title pages will be prepared in manuscript.

WAR DIARY
or
INTELLIGENCE SUMMARY.
(Erase heading not required.)

194 Coy
24th Divl Train

Army Form C. 2118.

Place	Date	Hour	Summary of Events and Information	Remarks and references to Appendices
ROISEL.	17/10/17		All supplies drawn by Units at various Railheads on Light Railway – 2/Lt BARNES went on leave –	Fine –
"	18/10/17		" " " " " " " "	Rain morning – Fine after –
"	19/10/17		" " " " " " " "	Fine –
"	20/10/17		" " " " " " " "	Fine –
"	21/10/17		" " " " " " " "	Fine –
"	22/10/17		" " " " " " " "	Fine –
"	23/10/17		" " " " " " " "	Rain & Wind –
"	24/10/17		" " " " " " " " { Major T.W. BLAKEWAY assumes Command of Train Capt H.C. PEARSON — — 194 Coy.	fine
"	25/10/17		" " " " " " " " 2Lt O.W. Batt reported for instruction	rain strong SW. Wind
"	26/10/17		" " " " " " "	showery.
"	27/10/17		" " " " " " " "	fine
"	28/10/17		" " " " " " " "	fine
"	29/10/17		" " " " " " " "	fine
"	30/10/17		" " " " " " " "	fine
"	31/10/17		" " " " " " " "	fine

H.C. Pearson Capt

2353 Wt. W2544/1454 700,000 5/15 D. D. & L. A.D.S.S. Forms/C. 2118.

Vol 27

Confidential

War Diary

of

O.C. 24th Divisional Train

From Nov 1st to Nov 30th 1917

Instructions regarding War Diaries and Intelligence Summaries are contained in F. S. Regs., Part II. and the Staff Manual respectively. Title pages will be prepared in manuscript.

WAR DIARY
or
INTELLIGENCE SUMMARY.
(Erase heading not required.)

Army Form C. 2118.

Place	Date	Hour	Summary of Events and Information	Remarks and references to Appendices
YRAIGNES	1/11/17		Standing Transport duties 50 G.S Wagons & 10 Tip carts.	
"	2/11/17		Nothing of importance to report.	
"	3/11/17		CO visited D.D.S.&T at Army H.Q. T. Lieut O. W. Batt returned to Army H.Q. on completion of his visit. Capt K.M. Plumptre & 2/Lt A.H. Dawes returned from leave.	
"	4/11/17		Standing Transport duties reduced to 34 G.S. Wagons & 10 Tip carts from this date.	
"	5/11/17		S.S.O visited D.D.S.&T in connection with the rations handed over by 34 Div.	
"	6/11/17		1 OR Reinforcement arrives (Supply detail - Loader) W.E.T.	
"	7/11/17		✓	
"	8/11/17		7 Tip carts collected from 311 Road Construction Coy, VILLERS-FAUCON - also Harness - intended for use on Roads.	
"	9/11/17		Standing Transport duties 50 G.S Wagons - 17 tip carts	
"	10/11/17		Capt. H.C Pearson proceeded on leave	
"	11/11/17		Fine. 12 G.S Wagons handed over to 24 D.A.C by order of the Divn. Standing transport duties reduced to 41 Wagons, 1 H.D for broom & 17 tip carts	
"	12/11/17		Sharp frost early morning. Standing transport duties reduced to 35 Wagons, 1 H.D & 17 tip carts. 2/Lt. L.A Dennis admitted to 73rd Field Ambulance	
"	13/11/17		Foggy. Standing transport duties increased to 39 Wagons, 1 H.D & 17 tip carts	
"	14/11/17		A G.S. Wagon belonging to 195 Coy partially destroyed by Shell fire at L33b 8 8. It was	

Instructions regarding War Diaries and Intelligence Summaries are contained in F. S. Regs., Part II. and the Staff Manual respectively. Title pages will be prepared in manuscript.

WAR DIARY
or
INTELLIGENCE SUMMARY.
(Erase heading not required.)

Army Form C. 2118.

Place	Date	Hour	Summary of Events and Information	Remarks and references to Appendices
VRAIGNES	14/11/17		Carrying material for 180 Tunnelling Coy to the front line. The Driver & 2 H.D. escaped unhurt. Foggy & wet.	
"	15/11/17		Fine. The Wagon partially destroyed by Shell fire on 14/11/17 salved.	
"	16/11/17		Every available wagon detailed by the Division	
"	17/11/17		1 CSM for 196 Coy & 7 Drivers (3 for 194 & 4 for 197) reported from Base.	
"	18/11/17		Notification received that Army Commander has quashed proceedings of FGCM of S. Sgt BOLTON F.E. Capt. S.H. Pass be returned from leave. Lt L.A. Dennis discharged from Hospital	
"	19/11/17		2/Lt A.H. Barnes proceeded to ABBEVILLE to collect Remounts for the Div. All Baggage & Supply Wagons out with Units & on detached fatigue work collected & brought back to Coy's Camps. Fine	
"	20/11/17		No Standing transport duties performed this day. Supplies delivered to Units by Train Vehicles. The Wagons collected the previous day returned to Units - except Supply Wagons of 106 & 107 Bde R.F.A. III Army Offensive commenced.	
"	21/11/17		Standing Transport duties carried out, with exception of the 10 Tip carts. Rations taken away from Refilling Points by 1st Line transport except those for 106 & 107 Bde. R.F.A which were delivered in Train Vehicles - Supply Wagons less horses left with 106 & 107 2/Lt J.W. Duncan reported for duty & attached to 196 Coy pending absorption.	

A6945 Wt. W11422/M1160 350,000 12/16 D. D. & L. Forms/C./2118/14.

Instructions regarding War Diaries and Intelligence Summaries are contained in F. S. Regs., Part II. and the Staff Manual respectively. Title pages will be prepared in manuscript.

WAR DIARY
or
INTELLIGENCE SUMMARY.
(Erase heading not required.)

Army Form C. 2118.

Place	Date	Hour	Summary of Events and Information	Remarks and references to Appendices
VRAIGNES	22/11/17		Drill, inclined Drain. 2/Lt A H Barnes returned from ABBEVILLE with 56 Remounts which were handed over to D.A.C. 55 tons of Coal unloaded at Fuel Dump between 10 & 12 midnight	
"	23/11/17		1 Rider (195) & H.D. (196) Remounts collected. R.E. Officer i/c Stone work for which we supplied 15 Wagons killed by M.G. fire at HARBICOURT. One H.D. Horse slightly wounded. The Rev HOTCHCROFT, Non C of E attached to Train by G.O.C. & posted to 196 Coy.	
"	24/11/17		✓	
"	25/11/17		Heavy Gale. Lt C. McNamara returned from Hospital. Capt D Bottomley proceeded to England on transfer to Infantry. 2 G.S. Wagons handed over to 24 Div. Art[y] by 196 Coy.	
"	26/11/17		S.S.M. RENDER reported for duty & posted to 197 Coy A.S.C. Lt Col. F.B. Lord returned from leave	
"	27/11/17		Standing duties 42 G.S. Wagons - 16 Tip carts & 2 H.D. on Road Brown - Temp[y] duties 8 G.S. Wagons (7 for "G" Special Coy R.E.)	
"	28/11/17		Warning Order No G.Y. 2151 received. Supply & Transport arrangements issued. All Transport	

A6945 Wt. W11422/M1160 350,000 12/16 D. D. & L. Forms/C./2118/14.

Instructions regarding War Diaries and Intelligence Summaries are contained in F. S. Regs., Part II, and the Staff Manual respectively. Title pages will be prepared in manuscript.

WAR DIARY
or
INTELLIGENCE SUMMARY.
(Erase heading not required.)

Army Form C. 2118.

Place	Date	Hour	Summary of Events and Information	Remarks and references to Appendices
VRAIGNES	28/11/17		duties carried out except 13 Wagons on Stone. Lt. C.C. Gale transferred from 196 Coy to 195 Coy & appointed S.O. 17th Inf. Bde vice 2/Lt. F.N. Pugh (to America). 2/Lt. A.C. Corby attached in Establishment (197 Coy) & appointed S.O. 73rd Inf. Bde. vice Capt. D. Bottomley (to Infantry). 2/Lt. L.A. Dennis transferred from 195 to 196 Coy A.S.C. All Transport duties cancelled from 29th inst. inclusive.	
"	29/11/17		Capt. H.C. Pearson returned from leave. Baggage Wagons returned to Units of 72nd Inf. Bde & 3rd R.Bs & 13th Middlesex. Instructions for move issued.	
"	30/11/17		ROISEL Railhead shelled. 1 H.E. Shell in 196 Coy's Camp - ROISEL ~~[illegible]~~ Non Coff. Chaplain. Rev. HUTCHCROFT wounded in head - admitted No 5 C.C.S. 196 Coy marched out to proceed to HAUT ALLAINES. Shelled in road - no damage done. All orders for move cancelled at 10.30 am & 196 ordered back - returned to Camp about 6 pm. Supply wagons delivered rations to Units on return. Lorries which had been loaded to dump at HAUT ALLAINES dumped at K.22.c at 5 pm. All Baggage Wagons sent back to Units & all troops 'stood to' prepared for emergencies.	

J.K. Shord Lt Col
Comdg 24 Div Train

A6945 Wt. W11422/M1160 350,000 12/16 D. D. & L. Forms/C./2118/14.

CONFIDENTIAL

WAR DIARY

OF

194 Comp: A.S.C. 24th Div: Train

from 1/11/17 to 30/11/17

Instructions regarding War Diaries and Intelligence Summaries are contained in F. S. Regs., Part II. and the Staff Manual respectively. Title pages will be prepared in manuscript.

WAR DIARY
or
INTELLIGENCE SUMMARY.
(Erase heading not required.)

Army Form C. 2118.

W Blakeway – Major –

Place	Date	Hour	Summary of Events and Information	Remarks and references to Appendices
ROISEL	1/11/17		All supplies drawn by units at various Railheads on Light Railway	fine
" "	2/11/17		" " " " " " " "	showery
" "	3/11/17		" " " " " " " " {Lt O.W. BATT returned to Aldershot	dull
" "	4/11/17		" " " " " " " " Capt. K.H. PLUMPTRE returned from leave 2/Lt A.H. BARNES " " " }	dull
" "	5/11/17		" " " " " " " "	dull
" "	6/11/17		" " " " " " " "	wet
" "	7/11/17		" " " " " " " "	wet
" "	8/11/17		" " " " " " " "	fine to 8 PM.
" "	9/11/17		" " " " " " " "	stormy
" "	10/11/17		" " " " " " " " {Capt M.C. PEARSON proceeded on leave Capt. K.H. PLUMPTRE taken command	stormy
" "	11/11/17		" " " " " " " "	stormy
" "	12/11/17		" " " " " " " "	Clear
" "	13/11/17		" " " " " " " "	Foggy
" "	14/11/17		" " " " " " " "	Foggy
" "	15/11/17		" " " " " " " "	Clear
" "	16/11/17		" " " " " " " "	Dull
" "	17/11/17		" " " " " " " " 2nd Lt BARNES proceeded to	Dull
" "	18/11/17		" " " " " " " " ABBEVILLE to draw remounts.	Dull

2353 Wt. W2544/1454 700,000 5/15 D. D. & L. A.D.S.S./Forms/C. 2118.

Instructions regarding War Diaries and Intelligence Summaries are contained in F. S. Regs., Part II. and the Staff Manual respectively. Title pages will be prepared in manuscript.

WAR DIARY
or
INTELLIGENCE SUMMARY.
(Erase heading not required.)

Army Form C. 2118.

A B Blakeway – Major –

Place	Date	Hour	Summary of Events and Information	Remarks and references to Appendices
ROISEL	19/11/17		All supplies drawn by units at various Railheads or Light Railway	Fair
"			All Baggage & Supply Waggons with units recalled as per instruction from F.H.Q. (T94)	
"	20/11/17		Supplies delivered to 106 Bde R.H.A. & 117 Bde R.H.A. by Company Waggons – 8 Supply Waggons sent to D.A.C. (T94 cancelled by T95)	Bad
"	21/11/17		" " " " which remained with units	"
"	22/11/17		All supplies drawn by units at various Railheads or Light Railway	"
"	23/11/17		" " " " "	"
"	24/11/17		" " " " "	"
"	25/11/17		" " " " "	"
"	26/11/17		" " " " " Major Blakeway resumed command of Company.	Fair
"	27/11/17		" " " " "	Rain & snow –
"	28/11/17		" " " " "	Fine –
"	29/11/17		" " " " " Capt PEARSON returned from leave –	Fine –
"	30/11/17		" " " " " Camp shelled, ordered to [Company] Stand to, owing to GERMAN Counter attacks on DIVISION'S left flank –	Dull –

2353 Wt. W2544/1454 700,000 5/15 D. D. & L. A.D.S.S./Forms/C. 2118.

Confidential.

Vol 28

War Diary

of

Officer Commanding 24th Divisional Train

From 1 12/14. To 31 12/14.

Instructions regarding War Diaries and Intelligence Summaries are contained in F. S. Regs., Part II. and the Staff Manual respectively. Title pages will be prepared in manuscript.

WAR DIARY
or
INTELLIGENCE SUMMARY.
(Erase heading not required.)

Army Form C. 2118.

Place	Date	Hour	Summary of Events and Information	Remarks and references to Appendices
VRAIGNES	1/12/17		Rations delivered to all Units by Supply Wagons. All Companies prepared to move at 3 hours notice. CO visited D.D.S.&T. 3rd Army	
"	2/12/17		Temp. Lieut (Acting Capt) & Adjutant E.W.L. Martin to be Temp. Capt. as from 1/12/17 – London Gazette 30/11/17 ("Times" 1/12/17). 1 OR (Staff Sgt Sower) reinforcement reported.	
"	3/12/17		Capt. S.H. Paslow proceeded to England on transfer to Infantry. Capt. K.M. Clempton assumed command of 195 Coy. ASC vice Capt S.H. Paslow. 6 G.S. Wagons found for R.E. work	
"	4/12/17		Supplies drawn from Refilling Points by 1st Line transport – Baggage Wagons remain with Units. 30 G.S. Wagons detailed by Div. 2/Lt F. Channon transferred from 195 Coy to 194 Coy (pending absorption) Hard frost	
"	5/12/17		a/Whr Sgt Penis reported – posted to 194 Coy ASC. 25 G.S. Wagons detailed by Div. Letter received from G.O.C. 9th Cav. Bde desiring that his thanks should be given to all ranks in the Train for the kindness & hospitality shown to all ranks of the Bedford Yeomanry – copy of the letter sent to all Coys. Frost.	
"	6/12/17		Standing transport duties 6 – casual duties 33. Frost.	
"	7/12/17		Do 11 do 43 Milder – some rain	

Instructions regarding War Diaries and Intelligence Summaries are contained in F. S. Regs., Part II. and the Staff Manual respectively. Title pages will be prepared in manuscript.

WAR DIARY
or
INTELLIGENCE SUMMARY.
(*Erase heading not required.*)

Army Form C. 2118.

Place	Date	Hour	Summary of Events and Information	Remarks and references to Appendices
VRAIGNES	8/12/17		24th Divn came under the Command of Cavalry Corps at 10 am this day. A.D.S.&T. & CO went round Refilling Points & area together. Thaw set in - roads in very bad state. All available wagons detailed for Road work by the Div.	
"	9/12/17		Thaw scheme in force. In addition to Standing transport duties, 20 wagons detailed to deliver rations from ROISEL Railhead to Units of VII Corps Troops - 15 Wagons on Roadwork. Every available wagon in use.	
"	10/12/17		Major Blakeway proceeded on leave. All available wagons in use - thaw scheme still in force. 1 H.D. Horse (193 Coy) wounded by hostile bomb.	
"	11/12/17		Capt R.F. Seddall proceeded on leave. All available wagons in use. 2 pairs H.D. & 1 Baggage Wagon per Battn returned from 72nd & 73rd Bdes. Capt J.P. Thompson distributed Remounts for the Division at PERONNE. 6 collected by Train Coys 195 1 H.D. 196 4 H.D. 197 1 L.D.	
"	12/12/17		Remounts inspected by CO. Standing transport duties 28 G.S. Wagons 24 H.D. for tip carts & brooms & 5 Dump Wagons	
"	13/12/17		F.G.C.M. for trial of Dr Holden attd 73rd Field Ambulance assembled at these H.Qrs. CO presided acquitted.	
"	14/12/17		Nothing of importance to report	

A6945 Wt. W11422/M1160 350,000 12/16 D. D. & L. Forms/C./2118/14.

Instructions regarding War Diaries and Intelligence Summaries are contained in F. S. Regs., Part II. and the Staff Manual respectively. Title pages will be prepared in manuscript.

WAR DIARY
or
INTELLIGENCE SUMMARY.
(Erase heading not required.)

Army Form C. 2118.

Place	Date	Hour	Summary of Events and Information	Remarks and references to Appendices
VRAIGNES	15/12/17		CO visited ADST Car Corps. 2/Lt. J O Tidy proceeded on leave.	
"	16/12/17		Standing transport duties 39 GS Wagons. 20 HD for leg carts – 4 for Brown. 2/Lt. H W Bradley 196 Coy arrives at HQ.	
"	17/12/17		Heavy snow during night. Nothing of importance to report.	
"	18/12/17		Capt & Adjt E W L Marten proceeded on leave to England. Lieut H W Bradley took over duties of Acting Adjt. Convoy with RE material shelled between TEMPLEUX and HARGICOURT. No casualties. All available transport working.	
"	19/12/17		Capt H A R Saunders proceeded on leave to England. All available transport working.	
"	20/12/17		Capt C E Pasmore reported for duty with this unit from 12th Div Train and posted to 194 Coy pending absorption. All available transport working.	
"	21/12/17		Lieut C Wallis reported for duty and was posted to 196 Coy ASC pending absorption. Lieut Colonel Ford to Hospital.	
"	22/12/17		All available transport working	
"	23/12/17		" " " "	
"	24/12/17		" " " "	

A6945 Wt. W11422/M1160 350,000 12/16 D. D. & L. Forms/C./2118/14.

Instructions regarding War Diaries and Intelligence Summaries are contained in F. S. Regs., Part II. and the Staff Manual respectively. Title pages will be prepared in manuscript.

WAR DIARY
or
INTELLIGENCE SUMMARY.
(Erase heading not required.)

Army Form C. 2118.

Place	Date	Hour	Summary of Events and Information	Remarks and references to Appendices
VRAIGNES	25/12/17		Lieut C McNamara transferred to England for Infantry. One convoy	
"			of G.S. wagons only provided.	
"	26/12/17		Capt Seddall granted 4 days extension of leave. All available	
"			transport working	
"	27/12/17		Lieut Mathion proceeded on leave to PARIS. All available transport	
"			working	
"	28/12/17		Major T W Blakeway, Major A B Hunter, 1/c S.S.M. Fowree and Sergeant	
"			Clarke F A mentioned in Despatches. All available transport	
"			working	
"	29/12/17		All available transport working	
"	30/12/17		" " " "	
"	31/12/17		" " " "	

A B Hunter Major
Commdg. 24 Divisional Train

A6945 Wt. W11422/M1160 350,000 12/16 D. D. & L. Forms/C./2118/14.

194 Coy ASC

Instructions regarding War Diaries and Intelligence Summaries are contained in F. S. Regs., Part II. and the Staff Manual respectively. Title pages will be prepared in manuscript.

WAR DIARY
or
INTELLIGENCE SUMMARY.
(Erase heading not required.)

Army Form C. 2118.

T.W. Blakeway – Major –

Place	Date	Hour	Summary of Events and Information	Remarks and references to Appendices
ROISEL	1/12/17		All supplies drawn by Company at various R.H.Qs on D.RY.	Dull & windy –
"	2/12/17		" " " " " " " " " "	Fine & cold wind –
"	3/12/17		" " " " " " " " " " CAPT. PLUMPTRE transferred to 195 Comp:	Fine & frosty –
"	4/12/17		" " " Works " " " " " LT CHAPMAN joined Company from 195. Comp:	Fine & frosty –
"	5/12/17		" " " " " " " " " "	Fine & frosty –
"	6/12/17		" " " " " " " " " "	Fine & frosty –
"	7/12/17		" " " " " " " " " "	Dull & frosty during day Rain at night.
"	8/12/17		" " " " " " " " " "	Rain –
"	9/12/17		" " " " " " " " " "	Rain
"	10/12/17		" " " " " " " " " " {Major T.W. BLAKEWAY on leave / Capt H.C. PEARSON assumes command of Coy.	fine
"	11/12/17		" " " " " " " " " "	strong N. Wind
"	12/12/17		" " " " " " " " " "	fine
"	13/12/17		" " " " " " " " " "	fine
"	14/12/17		" " " " " " " " " "	dull
"	15/12/17		" " " " " " " " " "	fine
"	16/12/17		" " " " " " " " " "	fine to 8 PM – Snow.

H.C. Pearson Capt

194 Coy ASC

Instructions regarding War Diaries and Intelligence Summaries are contained in F. S. Regs., Part II. and the Staff Manual respectively. Title pages will be prepared in manuscript.

WAR DIARY
or
INTELLIGENCE SUMMARY.
(Erase heading not required.)

Army Form C. 2118.

Place	Date	Hour	Summary of Events and Information	Remarks and references to Appendices
ROISEL	17/12/17		All supplies drawn by units at various Railheads on Decauville Ry	heavy snow
"	18/12/17		" " " " " " " "	cold N.E wind
"	19/12/17		" " " " " " " "	frost
"	20/12/17		" " " " " " " " Capt. F.A.R. SAUNDERS on leave. Lt F.R. NEVILL took over Supplies	frost
"	21/12/17		" " " " " " " " Capt. C.E. PASSMORE reported for duty	frost
"	22/12/17		" " " " " " " "	frost,
"	23/12/17		" " " " " " " "	frost NE wind
"	24/12/17		" " " " " " " "	frost. rain in evening
"	25/12/17		" " " " " " " "	snow N.W wind
"	26/12/17		" " " " " " " "	frost fine
"	27/12/17		" " " " " " " " 2nd Lt A.H. BARNES temporarily transferred to 195 Coy.	frost NE wind
"	28/12/17		" " " " " " " "	very cold NE wind snow
"	29/12/17		" " " " " " " "	hard frost fine
"	30/12/17		" " " " " " " "	dull slight thaw
"	31/12/17		" " " " " " " "	frost.

H.L. Renson Capt
O.C. 194 Coy
3rd Divl Train

2353 Wt. W2544/1454 700,000 5/15 D. D. & L. A.D.S.S./Forms/C. 2118.

1.

Instructions regarding War Diaries and Intelligence Summaries are contained in F. S. Regs., Part II. and the Staff Manual respectively. Title pages will be prepared in manuscript.

WAR DIARY
or
~~INTELLIGENCE SUMMARY~~.
(Erase heading not required.)

24th Divisional Train
1st to 31st January 1918.

Army Form C. 2118.

V8 29

Page. I.

Place	Date 1918	Hour	Summary of Events and Information	Remarks and references to Appendices
	Jany.			
VRAIGNES	1		Captain R. F. SEDDALL and 2nd Lieut. J. O. TIDY returned from leave. One reinforcement - Sergeant Issuer - arrived for duty.	
"	2.		Major H. B. HUNTER awarded D. S. O. (London Gazette "Times" dated 2/1/18)	
"	3		2nd Lieut. L. A. DENNIS transferred to D. D. S., Investigation Department ABBEVILLE for duty.	
"	4		2nd Lieut. A. H. BARNES assumed duties of Supply Officer 17th Infantry Brigade, vice Lieut. C. C. GAIN on leave to PARIS from Jany 8th to 13th 1918.	
"	5		Capt. & Adjt. E. W. L. MARTIN awarded Military Cross (London Gazette "Times" dated 5/1/18).	
"	6		No. 2 Company struck off all transport duties, except Company Rations and Forage for one day only. Lieut-Col. A. G. GALLOWAY, D. S. O. reported for duty with 24th Divisional Train. 2nd Lieut. F. CHANNON admitted 73rd Field Ambulance.	
"	7		No. 3 Company struck off all transport duties (except Company Rations and Forage) for one day only 2 reinforcements - drivers - arrived for duty with 24th Divisional Train. Lieut. Col. A. G. GALLOWAY, D. S. O. took over command of 24th Divisional Train. Capt. F. A. R. SAUNDERS returned from leave.	
"	8		No. 4 Company struck off all transport duties (except Company Rations and Forage) for one day	
"	9		All available transport working on R. E. material to forward area. Nothing of importance to report	

A G Galloway ~~Lieut-Colonel~~
O. C. 24th Divisional Train.

(Contd)

A6945 Wt. W11422/M1160 350,000 12/16 D. D. & L. Forms/C./2118/14.

Instructions regarding War Diaries and Intelligence Summaries are contained in F. S. Regs., Part II. and the Staff Manual respectively. Title pages will be prepared in manuscript.

WAR DIARY
or
INTELLIGENCE SUMMARY.
(Erase heading not required.)

24th Divisional Train
Ist to 3Ist January I918

Army Form C. 2118.

Place	Date 1918	Hour	Summary of Events and Information	Remarks and references to Appendices
	Jany			
VRAIGNES	IO		All available transport working on R. E. material to forward area. 2nd Lieut. E. WALLIS admitted 73rd Field Ambulance.	
"	II		Thaw Scheme in operation from I2 mid-night. All available transport working on R. E. material to forward area. S. S. O. visited D. D. S. T. Fifth Army.	
"	I2		No transport working on account of Thaw Scheme.	
"	I3		Part Standing Transport duties resumed. Passes supplied by A. P. M.	
"	I4		Lieut. C. C. GALE returned from PARIS. All Standing Transport duties resumed. Passes supplied by A. P. M. Major T. W. BLAKEWAY granted extension of leave on medical certificate, from I2th Jan. I918	
"	I5		Lieut. NEVILL proceeded on leave to PARIS. Thaw Scheme in force from 6 p. m. this day. Horse Transport to carry half loads. Lt. Col. A. G. GALLOWAY, D. S. O. proceeded to MANANCOURT in connection with supply of Fuel Wood.	
"	I6		Standing Transport duties continued carrying half loads.	
"	I7		4 reinforcements (drivers) reported for duty. Lt. Col. A. G. GALLOWAY, D. S. O. visited 56th Divisional Train. Notified that Thaw precautions would continue I8th & I9th but full loads carried.	
"	I8		2nd Lieut. E. WALLIS returned for duty (light) from 73rd Field Ambulance.	
"	I9		Capt. E. W. L. MARTIN returned from leave.	

A G Galloway
Lieut-Colonel
O. C. 24th Divisional Train.

(Contd)

A6945 Wt. W11422/M1160 350,000 12/16 D. D. & L. Forms/C./2118/14.

Instructions regarding War Diaries and Intelligence Summaries are contained in F. S. Regs., Part II. and the Staff Manual respectively. Title pages will be prepared in manuscript.

WAR DIARY
or
INTELLIGENCE SUMMARY.
(*Erase heading not required.*)

24th Divisional Train
Ist to 3Ist January 1918

Army Form C. 2118.

Place	1918 Date Jany	Hour	Summary of Events and Information	Remarks and references to Appendices
VRAIGNES	20		Capt. THOMPSON proceeded on leave to PARIS. Capt. C. E. PASMORE assumed command of No. 4 Company during Capt. THOMPSON'S absence.	
"	2I		C. O. and A. A. Q. M. G. and Colonel SMITH of the U. S. A. Army inspected Train Coys and great satisfaction expressed. Wet. Capt. R. F. SEDDALL attached to Train Headquarters for temporary duty. 2nd Lieut. J. W. DUNCAN assumed duties of S. O. 72nd Inf. Brigade during Capt. SEDDALL'S absence at Train Headquarters	
"	22		Wet.	
"	23		2nd Lieut. A. H. BARNES proceeded on leave to PARIS. 2nd Lt. W. H. BRADLEY returned to No. 3 Coy.	
"	24		Major H. B. HUNTER, D. S. O. and Capt. G. H. HITCH proceeded to England on leave for one month.	
			Capt. R. F. SEDDALL assumed duties of S. S. O. during Major H. B. HUNTER'S absence on leave.	
			2nd Lt. BRADLEY assumed duties of O. C. No. 3 Coy during Capt. HITCH'S absence on leave. C. O. visited D. D. S. & T., Fifth Army. Lt. NEVILL returned from PARIS and proceeded to PERONNE for Sanitation Course. 2nd Lt. J. O. TIDY and 3 N. C. Os. proceeded to PERONNE to attend Gas Course lasting until 28-I-I8. 2nd Lt. H. J. LEWIS returned from leave from England.	
"	25		2nd Lieut. E. WALLIS proceeded on leave to England.	

[signature] Lieut-Colonel
O. C. 24th Divisional Train.

(Contd)

Army Form C. 2118.

Instructions regarding War Diaries and Intelligence Summaries are contained in F. S. Regs., Part II. and the Staff Manual respectively. Title pages will be prepared in manuscript.

WAR DIARY
or
~~INTELLIGENCE SUMMARY~~.
(Erase heading not required.)

24th Divisional Train
Ist to 3Ist January I918.

Place	I918 Date Jany	Hour	Summary of Events and Information	Remarks and references to Appendices
VRAIGNES	26		C. O. visited Cavalry Corps Hd. Qrs. and took Pte. JOSLIN (No. 2 Coy) for interview by D. A. D. S. & T. in connection with his application for a Commission. C. O. also saw D. A. Q. M. G., Cav Corps.	
			C. O. visited General STONE, B. G. C., I7th Inf. Brigade.	
"	27		Lieut. F. R. NEVILL returned from Sanitation Course. C. O. attended Divisional Canteen Committee at D. H. Q. Major T. W. BLAKEWAY struck off the strength of this unit from 22-I-I8 (Authority 24th Division A. 89/354 27/1 and G. H. Q., A. S. C./I9279 dated 22-I-I8) Oat Ration reduced by 2 lbs for all classes of animals.	
"	28		Capt. J. P. THOMPSON returned from PARIS leave. 2nd Lt. J. O. TIDY returned from Gas Course at PERONNE Fine frost at night.	
"	29		Fine. - Nothing of importance to report.	
"	30		Capt. K. M. PLUMPTRE and 2 N. C. Os proceeded to a Veterinary Course at No. 7 Vet. Hospital at FORGES-le-EAUX. Capt. C. F. PASMORE assumed command of No. 2 Coy during Capt. PLUMPTRE'S absence	
			C. O. attended meeting of Divisional Canteen Committee at D. H. Q.	
"	3I		2nd Lt. A. H. BARNES returned from PARIS leave. 4 complete turnouts from No. 4 Coy joined 2nd Leinster Regt. on being transferred to I6th Division. 2nd Lt. F. CHANNON invalided to England and struck off the strength 2I-I-I8 ((authy A. Q. M. G., G. H. Q. No. ASC/I9292/I2 dated 27-I-I8)	

A. Galloway
Lieut-Colonel
O. C. 24th Divisional Train

(Contd)

A6945 Wt. W11422/M1160 350,000 12/16 D. D. & L. Forms/C./2118/14.

Instructions regarding War Diaries and Intelligence Summaries are contained in F. S. Regs., Part II. and the Staff Manual respectively. Title pages will be prepared in manuscript.

WAR DIARY
or
~~INTELLIGENCE SUMMARY~~.
(Erase heading not required.)

24th Divisional Train
Ist to 3Ist January I9I8

Army Form C. 2118.

Page. 5.

Place	1918 Date Jany	Hour	Summary of Events and Information	Remarks and references to Appendices
VRAIGNES	3I		i/c S. S. M. T. H. LOWRIE awarded Belgian CROIX-de-GUERRE (D. R. O. 3370 dated 3I-I-I8)	
			2nd Lieut. E. WALLIS transferred from No. 3 Coy to No. 2 Coy from this date.	

24TH DIVISIONAL TRAIN
3 - FEB. 1918
No.
A. S. C.

3/2/18.

O. Galloway
LIEUT. COLONEL.
O.C. 24th DIVISIONAL TRAIN.

~~Lieut-Colonel.~~
~~O. C. 24th Divisional Train.~~

194 Coy ASC

Army Form C. 2118.

Instructions regarding War Diaries and Intelligence Summaries are contained in F. S. Regs., Part II. and the Staff Manual respectively. Title Pages will be prepared in manuscript.

WAR DIARY
or
INTELLIGENCE SUMMARY
(Erase heading not required.)

Place	Date	Hour	Summary of Events and Information	Remarks and references to Appendices
ROISEL	1/1/18		All supplies drawn by units at various railheads on Decauville Ry	hard frost NE wind
" "	2/1/18		" " " " " " " " "	frost
" "	3/1/18		" " " " " " " " "	frost
" "	4/1/18		" " " " " " "	hard frost
" "	5/1/18		" " " " " " "	slight thaw
" "	6/1/18		" " " " " " " bombs dropped near camp 4.30 AM. Lt Col A G GALLOWAY assumes command of Train. Capt. F.A.R. SAUNDERS returned from leave.	hard frost rain 10 PM rain
" "	7/1/18		" " " " " " " " "	frost
" "	8/1/18		" " " " " " " "	frost rain 10 PM
" "	9/1/18		" " " " " " " " "	thaw
" "	10/1/18		" " ~~Train Transport~~ " " " " "	dull slight drizzle
" "	11/1/18		" " " " " " "	dull, snow in evening
" "	12/1/18		" " " " " " "	
" "	13/1/18		" " " " " " " "	frost, slight snow
" "	14/1/18		" " " " " " " Lt F.R. NEVILL on PARIS leave	frost
" "	15/1/18		" " " " " " " 2nd Lt A.H. BARNES returned to duty	thaw
" "	16/1/18		" " " " " " " "	strong S.W. gale
" "	17/1/18		" " " " " " " "	rain
" "	18/1/18		" " " " " " " "	dull
" "	19/1/18		" " " " " " " Capt C.E. PASMORE temporarily attached to 197 Coy	fine
" "	20/1/18		" " " " " " "	fine
" "	21/1/18		" " " " " " "	rain
" "	22/1/18		" " " " " " Major T.W. BLAKEWAY struck off strength of Coy. 2nd Lt A.H. BARNES on PARIS leave	fine
" "	23/1/18		" " " "	wet

2449 Wt. W14957/M90 750,000 1/16 J.B.C. & A. Forms/C.2118/12.

[signature] Capt. O.C. 194 Coy ASC

194 Coy ASC.

Instructions regarding War Diaries and Intelligence Summaries are contained in F. S. Regs., Part II. and the Staff Manual respectively. Title pages will be prepared in manuscript.

WAR DIARY
or
INTELLIGENCE SUMMARY.
(Erase heading not required.)

Army Form C. 2118.

Place	Date	Hour	Summary of Events and Information	Remarks and references to Appendices
ROISEL	24/1/18		All supplies drawn by units at various railheads on Decauville Ry. Lt F.R. NEVILL returned from PARIS leave & proceeded to PERONNE to Sanitary school.	fine
"	25/1/18		" " " " " " " " "	fine
"	26/1/18		" " " " " " " " " Lt F.R. NEVILL returned from Sanitary school	misty
"	27/1/18		" " " " " " " " "	misty
"	28/1/18		" " " " " " " " "	fine
"	29/1/18		" " " Train transport " " " " Capt C.E. PASMORE temporarily transferred to 195 Coy.	fine
"	30/1/18		" " " " " " " " "	fine
"	31/1/18		" " " " " " " " "	misty

A.C. Pearson Capt.
O.C. 194 Coy
[illegible] Divl Train

ORIGINAL

Vol 30

Confidential War Diary

of

O.C. 24th Divisional Train

From 1st Feby 1918 to 28th Feby 1918

1

Instructions regarding War Diaries and Intelligence Summaries are contained in F. S. Regs., Part II. and the Staff Manual respectively. Title Pages will be prepared in manuscript.

WAR DIARY

or

~~INTELLIGENCE SUMMARY~~

(Erase heading not required.)

24th Divisional Train.
Ist to 28th February 1918.

Army Form C. 2118.

Place	Feby. Date 1918	Hour	Summary of Events and Information	Remarks and references to Appendices
VRAIGNES	Ist		2nd Batt. Leinster Regt., accompanied by Train transport, left the Division on transfer to I6th Divn.	
	2nd		2nd Lieut. E. R. A. HODGMAN reported for duty with this unit and posted ~~to me~~ for duty with No. 3 Coy. S. S. O. visited D. A. D. S., 5th Army. C. O. attended G. O. C's conference at "A" Mess D. H. Q.	
	3rd		C. O. visited G. O. C. at D. H. Q. Standing transport duties :- 45 G. S. wagons, 5 Tip Carts, I5 H. D. Horses on roadwork. Additional duties 7 G. S. wagons.	
	4th		Nothing of importance to report.	
	5th		C. O. addressed all ranks of Train in Canteen - subject "propaganda".	
	6th		The 4 complete turnouts sent with 2nd Leinsters to I6th Division returned to No. 4 Company by I6th Divisional Train. G. O. C. attended Concert held in Div'l Train Canteen.	
	7th		Sergeant reinforcement reported for duty and posted to No. I Company. 6 Remounts collected, (No. I Coy 2 H. D., No. 2 Coy I Rider I L. D., No. 3 Coy 2 H. D.)	
	8th		Notification received from W. O. that 2nd Lieut. E. WALLIS had been granted extension of leave on Medical Certificate (Q. M. G., A. S. C. I956I/2 dated 3-2-18).	
	9th		Capt. W. A. MACGREGER, V. O. i/c Div'l Train proceeded on leave to England.	
	I0th		C. O. visited A. D. S. & T., Cav. Corps. Interviewed A. A. & Q. M. G. re new camp for Train H. Q.	
	IIth		C. O. and C. R. E. inspected proposed sites for new camp for Train H. Q. C. O. attended as member of G. C. M. assembled at 2-30 p.m. at MONTIGNY. 4 reinforcements (2 Drivers & 2 Wheelers) reported for duty.	
	I2th		Capt. K. M. PLUMPTRE returned from Veterinary Course. Dr. NATHAM No. I Coy, absented, brought back under escort.	

LIEUT. COLONEL.
O.C. 24th DIVISIONAL TRAIN.

2449 Wt. W14957/M90 750,000 1/16 J.B.C. & A. Forms/C.2118/12.

2

Instructions regarding War Diaries and Intelligence Summaries are contained in F. S. Regs., Part II. and the Staff Manual respectively. Title pages will be prepared in manuscript.

WAR DIARY
or
~~INTELLIGENCE SUMMARY.~~

(Erase heading not required.)

24th Divisional Train.
Ist to 28th February 1918.

Army Form C. 2118.

Place	Date Feby 1918	Hour	Summary of Events and Information	Remarks and references to Appendices
VRIAGNES	I3th		Nothing of importance to report	
	I4th		Nothing of importance to report	
	I5th		Capt. K. M. PLUMPTRE and Lieut. C. C. GALE proceeded on leave to England.	
	I6th		Hard frost.	
	I7th		C. O. and S. S. O. visited D. D. S. & T., 5th Army. Tempy. Major H. C. ROBINSON reported for duty from 36th Divisional Train.	
	I8th		Major H. C. ROBINSON took over command of No. I Company from Capt. H. C. PEARSON.	
	I9th		Capt. H. C. PEARSON left to report to 62nd Divisional Train (Authority for transfer Q. M. G., ASC/I9269 dated II-2-I8) 2nd Lieut. H. J. LEWIS and 3 O. R. proceeded to ABBEVILLE with party from the Division to collect remounts.	
	20th		C. O. visited D. D. S. & T., 5th Army	
	2Ist		C. O. 66th Div'l Train and S. S. O. visited Train H. Q. S. S. O. taken round Dumps and Refilling Points by Capt. SEDDALL. C. O. taken round Train Camps by Adjutant.	
	22nd		C. O. and S. S. O. visited new area and selected Refilling Points. 24th Division Order No. 234 received.	
	23rd		Capt. W. A. MACGREGOR, A. V. C. returned from leave.	
	24th		2nd Lieut. H. J. LEWIS returned with Remounts from ABBEVILLE. Remounts distributed by D. A. C. No. 4 Company collected I Rider and 2 H. D. C. O. visited new area and made alterations in Refilling Points. All Transport duties performed by No. 3 Coy cancelled from this date inclusive.	
	25th		24th Div'l Train Order No. 22 issued at IO a.m. 24th Div'l Train No. 23 issued at 2-30 p.m. Major H. B. HUNTER, D. S. O. and Capt. G. H. HITCH returned from leave.	A. & B.

A E Galloway
LIEUT. COLONEL.
O.C. 24th DIVISIONAL TRAIN.

A5834 Wt. W4973 M687 750,000 8/16 D. D. & L. Ltd. Forms/C.2118/13.

3

Instructions regarding War Diaries and Intelligence Summaries are contained in F. S. Regs., Part II. and the Staff Manual respectively. Title pages will be prepared in manuscript.

WAR DIARY
or
~~INTELLIGENCE~~ ~~SUMMARY~~.
(Erase heading not required.)

24th Divisional Train.
Ist to 28th February 1918.

Army Form C. 2118.

Place	Feby 1918 Date	Hour	Summary of Events and Information	Remarks and references to Appendices
VRAIGNES	26th		24th Div'l Train Order No. 24 issued at 10 a.m. Lieut. F. R. NEVILL and 2nd Lieut. A. C. CORBY proceeded on leave. No. 3 Company marched with 72nd Brigade Road party to FRAMERVILLE. Inspected by G.O.C. on the road, who commented as follows :- "The wagons of 196 Coy A.S.C. marching with units were not clean, but those marching with the Company were smart and well turned out". The C.O. inspected the whole road party at VRAIGNES. Supply Group Table No. 3 issued.	C.
VILLERS BRETONNEUX	27th		Train H.Q. moved to Chateau du Bois l'Abbe. No. 3 Coy continued their march to CORBIE. I Saddler Sergt and 3 O.R. (B.I.) reinforcements reported for duty	
	28th		No. 2 Company marched with 17th Bde road party. Railhead changed to VILLERS BRETONNEUX. C.O. went to VRAIGNES to inspect the transport of the 17th Infantry Brigade on its march to rest area. The turnout of No. 2 Coy was very good. Orders received at 5 p.m. that Division would be concentrated in another area. Orders received for the return of the 72nd Brigade. Informed that Railhead on 1-3-18 would be LA CHAPELLETTE. Major H. B. HUNTER took over duties of S.S.O. on return from leave. 2nd Lieut. E. WALLIS struck off strength of this unit from 23-2-18 (Authy Q.M.G. No. ASC/1956I/2 dated 23-2-18, 24th Division A.84/122 dated 28-2-18). 24th Divl Train Order No. 25 issued.	D.

A E Galloway
Lieut-Colonel
O.C. 24th Divisional Train.

A5834 Wt. W4973 M687 750,000 8/16 D. D. & L. Ltd. Forms/C.2118/13.

Appendix "A"

SECRET. Copy No. 9.

24TH DIVISIONAL TRAIN ORDER NO. 22.

25th February 1918.

I. The 24th Division, accompanied by 24th Div. Supply Column, Ammunition Sub-park, and 3IIth Army Brigade R.F.A., on relief by 66th Division, is being transferred from Cavalry Corps to XIX Corps, BOVES Area.

2. (a) Personnel of 72nd Infantry Brigade Group will entrain at ROISEL on 27th February.
Personnel of I7th Infantry Brigade Group will entrain at ROISEL on Ist March.
Personnel of 73rd Infantry Brigade Group and Divisional Headquarters will entrain at ROISEL on 3rd March.

(b) Transport of 72nd Infantry Brigade Group will move by Road on 26th February.
Transport of I7th Infantry Brigade Group will move by Road on 28th February.
Transport of 73rd Infantry Brigade Group and Divisional Headquarters will move by Road on 2nd March.

Moves of Transport to BOVES Area are given in attached Table "B" (Appendix "A" to copies Nos. 2 to 7)

3. The relief of 24th Div. Arty and 3IIth Army F.A. Bde commences about 4th March.

4. The groups of Transport in Serials 3, 5 and 7, will include all animals and vehicles of the units named, less any small detachments made by Brigadiers, which will march the following day by the same routes.

5. Advanced Billeting Parties, not to exceed 40 all ranks per Brigade Group will proceed as follows:-

72nd Brigade Group, February 25th by rail from ROISEL

I7th Brigade Group, February 27th by rail from ROISEL.

73rd Brigade Group, February 28th by lorry from HERVILLY.

Parties for rail will report to R.T.O. ROISEL at 9 am. with movement order for each complete party to be issued by Brigade Headquarters.

6. All units and detachments whether proceeding by rail or road will carry with them the rations and forage for consumption up to and for the day of arrival in the Back Area.

7. Supplies for consumption on day after arrival and subsequent days will be drawn in the Back Area.

Two days rations for Advance Party of 72nd Infantry Brigade for consumption on 26th & 27th instants will be delivered to Town Major CORBIE on 25th instant by 66th Div. Supply Column.
Rations and forage for Ist Line Transport of I2th Royal Fusiliers, strength 30 A.R. 8 H.D. and 45 L.D. for consumption on 27th instant will be delivered to Town Major CORBIE on 26th instant by 66th Div. Supply Column.
Rations and Forage for this Transport for consumption 28th instant will be dumped with the Bde Group and must be delivered with those of Brigade Headquarters.

8. The attention of S.S.O., Os.C. Companies and Supply Officers is directed to Supply Group Tables Nos. I & 2 (Appendices B & C attached to Copies Nos. I to 8, and also issued direct to Group and Supply Column Supply Officers.

9. (a) The attention of S.S.O., Os.C. Companies and Supply Officers is directed to 24th Division No. C.384/12 (Appendices D, E & E.I. attached to Copies 2 to 8)

(b) Re para.4, Supply Officers will send at least I N.C.O. and 3 Men (Supply Details) to report to O.C. 24th Divnl. Supply Column by 2 p.m. on the day on which they issue for the last time to their group at DECAUVILLE Refilling Point. They will send with these details all the Sail Covers or Tarpaulins in their possession.

Os. C. Companies will arrange transport to convey the above to the Headquarters of the 24th Divnl. Supply Column, CARTIGNY.

(c) Appendix E shows the final grouping after the move into the New Area is complete.

IO. Baggage wagons will be sent out to units as follows :-

72nd Bde. Group,	by I2 midday	25.2.I8.
I7th - do -	- do -	27.2.I8.
73rd - do -	- do -	I.3.I8.

Os. C. Companies will send three G.S. Wagons to each Battalion for Baggage, the 3rd wagon being one of the four Train Vehicles rendered surplus by the recent re-organisation of Brigades.

BRIGADE

II. Train H.Q. will close at VRAIGNES at IO a.m. on 27.2.I8 and open at VILLERS BRETONNEUX at 3 p.m. same day.

I2. ACKNOWLEDGE.

C. E. Galloway

Lieut. Colonel.
O.C. 24th Divisional Train.

Copies to :-

No. I - A.& Q., 24th Division (for information)
2 - O.C. Train.
3 - S.S.O.
4 - O.C. No. I Coy & S.O. Div. Troops.
5 - O.C. No. 2 Coy & S.O. I7th Bde.
6 - O.C. No. 3 Coy & S.O. 72nd Bde.
7 - O.C. No. 4 Coy & S.O. 73rd Bde.
8 - O.C. 24th Div. Supply Column (for information)
9 - War Diary.
IO - File.

SUPPLY GROUP TABLE NO. I. to take effect (On A. Fs. 3316 & 3317. 25 & 26. 2. 18.
(At Railhead. 26 & 27. 2. 18.
(Consumption. 28. 2. 18 & 1. 3. 18.

GROUP "A".	GROUP "B".	GROUP "C" (a)	GROUP "D".
Railhead. R O I S E L. R. P. (DECAUVILLE RY. (26 & 27. 2. 18.	Railhead. R O I S E L. R. P. (DECAUVILLE RY. (26 & 27. 2. 18.	Railhead. VILLERS BRETONNEUX. R. P. CORBIE 27 & 28. 2. 18.	Railhead. R O I S E L. R. P. (DECAUVILLE RY. (26 & 27. 2. 18.
C. R. A. 106th Bde R. F. A. 107th Bde R. F. A. 24th Div. T. M. Bs. (H. & M.) No. 1 Coy. Train. No. 2 Coy. Train. No. 4 Coy. Train. 129th Field Coy R. E. Divisional H. Q. 24th Div. Signal Coy. C. R. E. D. A. D. O. S. 12th Sherwood Foresters. Divisional Baths.	17th Inf. Bde H. Q. 17th Inf. Bde M. G. Coy. 17th Inf. Bde T. M. B. 1st Royal Fusiliers. 8th Queens. 3rd Rifle Brigade. 8th Buffs. (Tpt only) 104 Field Coy R. E. 73rd Field Ambulance. 74th Field Ambulance. 24th D. A. C. 36th M. V. S.	72nd Inf. Bde H. Q. 72nd Inf. Bde T. M. Bs. 72nd Inf. Bde M. G. Coy. 9th E. Surreys. 8th R. W. Kents. 1st N. Staffs. 103rd Field Coy R. E. 72nd Field Ambulance. No. 3 Coy Train. 12th R. Fusiliers. (Tpt only) 191 M. G. Coy. Train H. Q.	73rd Inf. Bde H. Q. 73rd Inf. Bde M. G. Coy. 73rd Bde T. M. B. 9th R. Sussex. 7th Northants. 13th Middlesex. 10th R. D. Fus (Transport only)
Attached. 14th Kite Balloon Sec. Cav Corps. T. M. Batty. Y. M. C. A. HAMELET. 162 Labour Coy. 16A. A. Searchlight Sec. Area Commdt. [illegible].	Attached. 258 Tunnelling Coy R. E. Area Commdt. [illegible]. Area Commdt. [illegible]. (attchd. 24th D. A. C.) Y. M. C. A. [illegible]. Y. M. C. A. HANCOURT.	N. B. (a) By 66th Divn.	

A. G. Galloway

LIEUT, COLONEL.
C.O. 24th DIVISIONAL TRAIN.

SUPPLY GROUP TABLE NO. 2. to take effect { On A. F. 3316 & 3317. 27 & 28. 2. 18.
{ At Railhead on 28. 2. 18 & 1. 3. 18
{ Consumption. 2 & 3. 3. 18.

GROUP "A" (a)	GROUP "B" (b)	GROUP "C" (b)	GROUP "D" (a)
Railhead. R O I S E L. R. P. { DECAUVILLE RY { 28. 2. 18 & 1. 3. 18.	Railhead. VILLERS BRETONNEUX. R. P. { VILLERS BRETONNEUX { 1 & 2. 3. 18.	Railhead. VILLERS BRETONNEUX. R. P. CORBIE 1 & 2. 3. 18.	Railhead. R O I S E L. R. P. { DECAUVILLE RY { 28. 2. 18 & 1. 3. 18.
C. R. A. …6th Bde R. F. A. …7th Bde R. F. A. …th Div. T. M. Bs. (H. & M) … 1 Coy. Train. … 4 Coy. Train. 129th Field Coy R. E. Divisional H. Q. 24th Div. Signal Coy. C. R. E. D. A. D. O. S. 12th Sherwood Foresters. Divisional Baths. 24th D. A. C. 36th M. V. S. 8th Buffs (Transport only)	17th Inf. Bde. H. Q. 17th Inf. Bde. T. M. B. 1st R. Fusiliers. 8th Queens. 3rd Rifle Brigade. 104th Field Coy R. E. 74th Field Ambulance. No. 2 Coy Train. Train Headquarters. 10th R. D. Fus (Transport only)	72nd Inf. Bde H. Q. 72nd Inf. Bde T. M. B. 72nd Inf. Bde M. G. Coy. 9th E. Surreys. 8th R. W. Kents. 1st N. Staffs. 103 Field Coy R. E. 72nd Field Ambulance. No. 3 Coy Train. 12th R. Fusiliers (Tpt only) 191 M. G. Coy. 17th M. G. Coy.	73rd Inf. Bde. H. Q. 73rd Inf. Bde M. G. Coy. 73rd Bde T. M. B. 9th R. Sussex. 7th Northants. 13th Middlesex. 73rd Field Ambulance.
Attached. 14th Kite Balloon Sec. Cav. Corps. T. M. Batty. Y. M. C. A. HAMELET. 162 Labour Coy. 1… A. A. Searchlight Sec. Area Commdt. ROISEL. Area Commdt. VRAIGNES. (attchd 24th D. A. C.	Units hitherto attached to this Group, less Area Commdt. VRAIGNES, transferred to 66th Division for Rations for consumption 2. 3. 18, et sequitur.		

24. 2. 18.

N. B. (a) By 66th Division.
(b) By 24th Division.

Appendix C

A G Galloway
LIEUT. COLONEL.
O.C. 24th DIVISIONAL TRAIN.

Appendix "B"

S E C R E T. Copy No....9...

24th DIVISIONAL TRAIN ORDER NO. 23.

(In continuation of No. 22.)

25th February 1918.

I. Reference Appendix A to Train Order No. 22 and Footnote 2 on Page 2, the 17th Bde Group Transport will be commanded by the 17th Brigade Transport Officer and not by O. C. No. 2 Train Company.

2. Os. C. Companies will send to Units by 4 p.m. on the undermentioned days sufficient supply vehicles to carry the supplies of the Road Parties for consumption on the 2nd day's march. These vehicles will be collected early on the morning of the 1st day's march and will march as a section with the Headquarters of the Coy concerned.

The supplies will be delivered to Units on termination of the 1st day's march, the vehicles returning to and billeting with Train Companies that night.

Serial No. 3. Appendix "A". 25.2.18.
Serial No. 5. - do - 27.2.18.
Serial No. 7. - do - 1.3.18.

3. On the 2nd day's march the Supply Sections will march one hour in advance of the remainder of the Column. They will proceed direct to Refilling Points, refill with supplies (for consumption the following day) and deliver such supplies immediately after refilling, the vehicles returning to their Companies after delivery.

4. The exact sites of Refilling Points will now be as follows :- (24th Division C.384/18)

R.F.A. Group. The triangle of ground between the HANGARD - AUBERCOURT & HANGARD - MARCELCAVE roads at V.25.a. central (Sheet 66D.)

17th Bde. Group. The triangle of ground 100 yards from VILLERS BRETONNEUX Passenger Station at O.36.c. central. (Sheet 66D.)

72nd Bde. Group. CORBIE -RUE DU CALVAIRE off RUE GAMBETTA.

73rd Bde. Group. Near CASTEL. B.13.c.8.4.(Sheet 66E.)

A. R. Galloway
Lieut. Colonel.
O. C. 24th Divisional Train.

Copies to :-
No. 1. A. & Q. 24th Division (for information)
2. O. C. Train.
3. S. S. O.
4. O. C. No. 1 Coy & S. O. Div. Troops.
5. O. C. No. 2 Coy & S. O. 17th Bde.
6. O. C. No. 3 Coy & S. O. 72nd Bde.
7. O. C. No. 4 Coy & S. O. 73rd Bde.
8. O. C. 24th Div. Supply Column.
✓ 9. War Diary.
10. File.

Appendix "C". 9

SECRET.

24th DIVISIONAL TRAIN ORDER NO. 24.

(In continuation of No. 22.)

25th February 1918.

I. The Machine Gun Coys cannot be accommodated in VAIRE until March 6th. As a temporary measure they will be accommodated in BERTEAUCOURT and THENNES. Accommodation is not yet allotted for the various Coys. Transport proceeding on 26th and personnel 27th and subsequently will report BERTEAUCOURT.

2. Consequent on the above the O.C. No. 3 Coy will send the Supply Wagons of the 72nd & 191st M.G. Coys to BERTEAUCOURT after refilling at CORBIE on the 27th instant.

He will instruct the Drivers to :-

(a) Remain with the Units for the Nights of the 27 & 28.2.18.

(b) To draw Supplies from the "C" Group Refilling Point on 28.2.18.

(c) To draw Supplies from the "B" Group Refilling Point on 1.3.18 and to report to O.C. No. 2 Coy after delivering supplies on that date

3. The following alterations will be made by all concerned on Supply Group Table No. 2 (Appendix C to Train Order No. 22)

C Group. Delete 17th 72nd and 191st M.G. Coys.

B Group. Add 17th 72nd and 191st M.G. Coys.

4. O.C. 2 Coy will retain the Supply Wagon of 191st M.G. Coy but will note that Supplies are to be delivered to the unit at BERTEAUCOURT from 1.3.18 inclusive.

5. Acknowledge.

A. G. Galloway
Lieut. Colonel.
O.C. 24th Divisional Train.

Issued to:-

All Recipients of 24th Div. Train Orders Nos. 22 & 23.

Appendix "D"

Copy No. 7....

SECRET

24th DIVISIONAL TRAIN ORDER NO. 25.

28th February 1918.

I. The following are the arrangements for supplies for consumption Ist and 2nd March for 72nd Brigade Group.

2. Troops travelling by Train will carry supplies for consumption Ist March only. Road Parties will carry supplies for consumption Ist and 2nd March. Balance of the supplies at present on the Dump, i.e. :- rations for consumption for Train Parties 2nd March, will be picked up by Lorry to-morrow and carried through to New Area.

3. Figures of road and rail parties will be taken to be the same as for move to this rest Area.

4. Brigades have instructed Units to send two men per Battalion and one man per other unit, to travel with the supplies by lorry to the New Area.

5. All supply details will go by lorry to the new Area. Kit and Batman of Captain SEDDALL will be sent to you early to-morrow morning to be put on the lorries to go to New Area. I will take Captain SEDDALL through by car to meet lorries in New Area and witness distribution for consumption 2nd March for parties proceeding by rail.

6. 2nd Lieut. DUNCAN will return to duty as Transport Officer.

A. G. Galloway
Lieut-Colonel.
O.C. 24th Divisional Train.

Copies to :-
No. I. O.C. Train.
2. S.S.O.
3. O.C. No. 3 Coy & S.O. 72nd Bde.
4. Staff Captain 72nd Brigade.
5. O.C. 24th D.S.C. and S.O.
6. D.A.Q.M.G., 24th Division.
7. War Diary.
8. File.

1

Vol 31

Confidential

War Diary

of

O. C. 24th Divisional Train

From 1 3/18 To 31 3/18

No. 1...
Army Form C. 2118.

Instructions regarding War Diaries and Intelligence Summaries are contained in F. S. Regs., Part II. and the Staff Manual respectively. Title pages will be prepared in manuscript.

WAR DIARY or ~~INTELLIGENCE SUMMARY.~~

24th Divisional Train.

(Erase heading not required.)

Place	1918 Date Mch.	Hour	Summary of Events and Information	Remarks and references to Appendices
VILLERS BRETONNEUX	1st		Railhead - LA CHAPELLETTE. 24th Division Order No. 236 received at 8 a.m. Capt. R. F. SEDDALL returned to No. 3 Coy. and took over duties of S. O., 72nd Inf. Bde. No. 3 Coy. marched back from CORBIE to FRAMERVILLE. C. O. visited new area and arranged R. Ps. for 72nd & 17th Brigade Groups for this date and for 73rd Bde, Group for issue 2-3-18.	
PERONNE	2nd		Refilling Points 17th Bde. - Sheet 62c., V.4.d.9.1., 72nd Bde. - DEVISE, 73rd Bde. - BERNES, Divl Troops - ROISEL (opp. No. 1 Coy's Camp). 2nd Lieut. H. W. BRADLEY proceeded on leave to England. Div'l. Hd. Qrs. moved from NOBESCOURT Farm to MERAUCOURT. Train Hd. Qrs. moved to PERONNE (Rear Div. Hd. Qrs.). No. 3 Coy marched to new camp at DEVISE, No. 2 Coy to MONTECOURT, No. 4 Coy to BERNES. Heavy gale of wind and snow.	
"	3rd		Lieut. C. C. GALE returned from leave. 2nd Lt. H. ALPE, A. S. C. reported for duty and posted to No. 2 Coy., (Authority :- Q. M. G., A. S. C./19734 dated 25-2-18). 2nd Lt. E. R. A. HODGMAN transferred from No. 3 Coy to No. 1 Coy from this date.	
"	4th		24th Divl. Train Order No. 26 issued. Supply Group Table No. 4 issued.	"A" & "B"
"	5th		No. 1 Coy marched to MONTECOURT. All Groups refilled at P.30.d. central from this day owing to Cav. Corps instructions that no Lorries were to proceed South of BRIE - VERMAND Road or East of ESTREES Cross Roads (24th Div. Q2020 dated 3-3-18). 6 complete turnsout and 1 Sergt. attached to 64 Field Coy R. E. from this date (3 from No. 2 Coy and 3 from No. 3 Coy).	
"	6th		----	
"	7th		D. A. A. G. seen with reference to move of Train Hd. Qrs. to MERAUCOURT. 3 H. D. Remounts collected from LA CHAPELLETTE (No. 1 Coy 1 and No. 2 Coy 2).	
"	8th		Fine.	
"	9th		24th Division transferred to XIX Corps at 11 a.m. to-day. C. O. judged in Transport Show of 1st N. Staffs. "Summer Time" came in force at 11 p.m. this day. 24th Division Warning Order No. G. Y. 510 received 11 a.m.	
"	10th		24th Division Order No. 237 received 11 a.m. C. O. judged at 17th Bde. Horse Show held this day.	

A. L. Galloway
LIEUT. COLONEL.
O.C. 24th DIVISIONAL TRAIN.

(A7092). Wt. W12839/M1293. 750,000. 1/17. D. D. & L., Ltd. Forms/C.2118/14.

No. 2

Army Form C. 2118.

Instructions regarding War Diaries and Intelligence Summaries are contained in F. S. Regs., Part II. and the Staff Manual respectively. Title pages will be prepared in manuscript.

WAR DIARY
or
~~INTELLIGENCE SUMMARY~~.
(Erase heading not required.)

24th Divisional Train.

Place	1918 Date Mch	Hour	Summary of Events and Information	Remarks and references to Appendices
PERONNE	11th		C. O. saw D. A. A. G. re move and afterwards saw A. C. TREFCON re new camps for Train Hd. Qrs and Coys. Capt. R. F. SEDDALL proceeded to Hd. Qrs. FIFTH Army to be attached to D. D. S. & T.	
~~TERTRY~~ PERONNE	12th		C. O. and Adjt. met Company Officers and allotted new camps at TERTRY.	
TERTRY	13th		Train Hd. Qrs. and all four Coys moved to camps at CAUVIGNY Farm TERTRY. Lieut. NEVILL and 2nd Lt. A. C. CORBY returned from leave. Supply Groups Table No. 5 issued.	"C"
"	14th		Capt. J. P. THOMPSON and 2nd Lieut. G. J. MOTION proceeded on leave to England. C. O. visited 74th Field Ambulance. Railhead - TINCOURT. Supplies taken to R. Ps. by DECAUVILLE. R. Ps., "A" Group Q. 30. b. (sheet 62. c.) "B" & "D" VRAIGNES. "C" Group Q. 30. b. (sheet 62. c.) Supplies delivered to Units by Divl Train from R. Ps.	
"	15th		S. S. O. reported at 11-45 a.m. by message from Railhead that no lorries had arrived for transhipping Supplies from Broad Gauge to DECAUVILLE. O. C. Train proceeded at once to Railhead. In the meanwhile D. A. Q. M. G., XIX Corps had visited Railhead and on being informed as to the situation, had phoned for lorries. C. O. phoned to D. D. S. & T. FIFTH Army from Railhead reporting that no lorries had been sent by S. M. T. O., XIX Corps. O. C. Train visited D. H. Q. and reported what had occurred. O. C. Train and S. S. O. visited D. H. Q. at 6 p.m. O. C. 24th Div. M. T. Coy. was present. D. A. A. G. enquired into the whole matter, and found as follows :- "On arrival at Railhead at 10.5 a.m. S. S. O. found that no lorries had arrived and that nothing had been done. He found [illegible] the 2 lorries which had brought the 24th Division M. T. Coy's Supply Details to Railhead and the Supply Lorry of that Coy immediately and started the work of transferring the Pack Train to the DECAUVILLE. There was no Officer of the M. T. Coy at Railhead until Capt. KELLY arrived about 10-30 a.m. 6 lorries (phoned for by D. A. Q. M. G. XIX Corps) arrived about 12-45 p.m. No notification had been received from XIX Corps that lorries would not be supplied for transferring the supplies". D. A. A. G., 24th Division accompanied by O. C. Train visited XIX Corps Hd. Qrs. XIX Corps approved of 6 - 30 cwt. lorries being detailed daily, in addition to the 2 - 3 ton lorries already detailed for S. S. O. for transferring Supplies from Pack Train to DECAUVILLE	

A. L. Galloway
LIEUT. COLONEL,
O.C. 24th DIVISIONAL TRAIN.

A5834 Wt. W4973 M687 750,000 8/16 D. D. & L. Ltd. Forms/C.2118/13.

Instructions regarding War Diaries and Intelligence Summaries are contained in F. S. Regs., Part II. and the Staff Manual respectively. Title pages will be prepared in manuscript.

No. 3.
Army Form C. 2118.

WAR DIARY
or
INTELLIGENCE ~~SUMMARY~~.
(Erase heading not required.)

24th Divisional Train.

Place	Date 1918 Mch.	Hour	Summary of Events and Information	Remarks and references to Appendices
TERTRY.	16th		O. C. Train visited 23rd Army R. F. A. Bde. and arranged to inspect 2nd Line Transport on 17th instant. 2nd Lieut. J. O. TIDY sent on leave specially to England owing to domestic troubles (approved by D. A. A. G.) Meeting of Committees of Div'l Train Canteens held at Train Hd. Qrs.	
"	17th		S. S. O. found on arrival at Railhead that the 6 - 30 cwt. lorries had not arrived. He phoned S. M. T. O who at once ordered the lorries, which arrived at 11 a.m. O. C. Train accompanies by the Adjutant inspected the 2nd Line Transport of the 23rd Army R. F. A. Bde., which he found, on the whole, satisfactory. Arrangements were made for the repair of certain vehicles.	
"	18th		2nd Lieut. H. W. BRADLEY returned from leave. 2nd Lieut. A. H. BARNES proceeded on leave to England.	
"	19th		Capt. K. M. PLUMPTRE returned from leave.	
"	20th		Capt. C. E. PASMORE returned to No. 1 Company having handed over command of No. 2 Coy to Captain K. M. PLUMPTRE. In accordance with instructions from XIX Corps 10 wagons were detailed for 73rd Brigade - 2 to convey Supplies to Redoubts under 1 N. C. O. guide supplied by Brigade Hd. Qrs. These wagons wandered round the country all night and eventually parked at 72nd Brigade Hd. Qrs VERMAND. 8 G. S. wagons under 2nd Lieut. E. R. A. HODGMAN conveyed S. A. A. etc. to Redoubts. No guide provided by B. T. O., 73rd Brigade. Much difficulty experienced in locating the redoubts in dark and mist. One wagon left behind partially overturned.	
"	21st		Enemy bombardment commenced 4-45 a.m. All Companies aroused at 5-30 a.m. on account of heavy hostile shelling in neighbourhood - Gas shells being suspected. 2nd Lieut. HODGMAN endeavoured to retrieve wagon left behind in forward area, ~~[illegible]~~ but without success. XIX Corps issued instructions that Supplies would be drawn from TINCOURT Railhead by M. T. Coy's lorries instead of "DECAUVILLE". O. C. Train visited D. H. Q. at noon. Adjutant visited D. H. Q. at 4 p.m. and returned with written orders for Train to move at once to BRIE ((24th Divn Q. 2819 dated 21-3-18). Supply wagons refilled at Cross Roads P. 30. d. central. (62. c.) en route and delivered to Units. C. O. and Adjutant visited D. H. Q. at 6-30 p.m. and then proceeded to BRIE where accommodation was found in 17th Lancers Camp. Train arrived in camp between 11 p.m. and midnight.	
BRIE.	22nd		Railhead MARCHELEPOT. All leave stopped until further notice. 10 G. S. wagons proceeded to	

A5834 Wt. W4973 M687 750,000 8/16 D. D. & L. Ltd. Forms/C.2118/13.

W. E. Galloway
LIEUT. COLONEL,
O.C. 24th DIVISIONAL TRAIN.

No. 4.
Army Form C. 2118.

Instructions regarding War Diaries and Intelligence Summaries are contained in F. S. Regs., Part II. and the Staff Manual respectively. Title pages will be prepared in manuscript.

WAR DIARY
or
INTELLIGENCE SUMMARY.
(Erase heading not required.)

24th Divisional Train.

Place	1918. Date Mch.	Hour	Summary of Events and Information	Remarks and references to Appendices
			ROISEL R. E. Dump in accordance with instructions received from D. H. Q. to convey R. E. material forward. The wagons were stopped en route as it was ascertained that the enemy were approaching that town. All baggage wagons returned to R. A. Units. Divl. Hd. Qrs. arrived BRIE and took over Train camp. Train moved to VILLERS CARBONNEL - R. P. :- N. 30. b. central (62. c.) Supply wagons refilled on arrival at VILLERS CARBONNEL.	
VILLERS CARBON-NEL	23rd		Railhead LA FLAQUE. Orders received at 5 a.m. (Q. 2892 dated 23-3-18) for Train to move forthwith to ABLAINCOURT. C. O. and Adjutant started in car at 6-15 a.m. Train proceeded at 6-30 a.m. C. O. met D. A. A. G. at MARCHELEPOT at 8 a.m. and received verbal orders to place the Train ½ mile West of CHAULNES on North of Road. Train was blocked in MARCHELEPOT - CHAULNES Road. Ground West of CHAULNES unsuitable for Train camp. At 4 p.m. O. C. Train received verbal orders from D. A. A. G. to camp Train at P. of W. Camp on FOUCOUCOURT - CHAULNES Road ¼ mile West of "P" in PRESSOIRE (Amiens 17)	
P. of W Camp CHAULNES	23rd	5-30 p.m.	Train proceeded thither - last wagon arriving 5-30 p.m.	
"	24th	9-30 a.m.	Railhead LA FLAQUE. Train received verbal orders from D. A. Q. M. G. to move at short notice. At 10-45 a.m. Train moved via VERMANDOVILLERS - FOUCAUCOURT, RAINECOURT, FRAMERVILLE and camp in Field by Windmill midway between FRAMERVILLE & VANVILLERS. 1-30 p.m. orders received to move Train to LIHONS. 3-45 p.m. Train proceeded to LIHONS via FRAMERVILLE arriving at 5-30 p.m.	
LIHONS	"	5-30 p.m.	O. C. Train and Adjutant visited D. H. Q. at 6-30 p.m. and received orders to move the four Companies to HARBONNIERES and Train Hd. Qrs. to ROSIERES-EN-SANTERRE. The Companies moved from LIHONS at 10-30 p.m. and arrived at HARBONNIERES at 12 mid-night. Train Hd. Qrs. arrived ROSIERES same hour.	
ROSIER-ES	25th		Railhead MARCELCAVE. Supplies delivered to units between mid-day and 2 p.m. and immediately refilled. At 5 p.m. orders received to move Train forthwith to THENNES. [illegible] Supply Wagons with rations for consumption 27-3-18. C. O. proceeded to HARBONNIERES to advise Companies accordingly. Train Hd. Qrs. Transport and Adjutant proceeded at 5-25 p.m. and arrived DEMUIN at 8-30 p.m. where S. S. O. was met, who brought orders to wait there pending arrival of O. C. Train. O. C. Train having seen all Companies march off from HARBONNIERES proceeded to THENNES and selected a field for Companies to camp in. He guided the Companies in and then proceeded to DEMUIN arriving at 10-50 p.m.. He gave orders for Train Hd. Qrs. to proceed to THENNES. Marched off at 11 p.m.	

W. G. Galloway
LIEUT. COLONEL.
O.C. 24th DIVISIONAL TRAIN.

A5834 Wt. W4973 M687 750,000 8/16 D. D. & L. Ltd. Forms/C.2118/13.

No. 5.

Army Form C. 2118.

WAR DIARY or ~~INTELLIGENCE SUMMARY~~.

24th Divisional Train.

(*Erase heading not required.*)

Instructions regarding War Diaries and Intelligence Summaries are contained in F. S. Regs., Part II. and the Staff Manual respectively. Title pages will be prepared in manuscript.

Place	Date 1918 Mch	Hour	Summary of Events and Information	Remarks and references to Appendices
THENNES	26th		Train Hd. Qrs. arrived I2-30 a.m. Railhead BOVES.	
THENNES DEMUIN	27th "	IO am	Railhead SALEUX. Train Hd. Qrs. moved to DEMUIN arriving IO a.m. Train Companies moved to BOVES arriving 7 p.m. Train Hd. Qrs. marched to DOMART at 5 p.m. but returned to DEMUIN on verbal instructions given to Adjutant by A. A. & Q. M. G. - arriving at 9 p.m.	
DEMUIN	28th		Railhead AILLY-sur-SOMME. At 3 p.m. orders received for Train Hd. Qrs. to move to CASTEL.	
CASTEL	"	5 pm	Train Hd. Qrs. arrived. At 6 p.m. O. C. Train left to move Train Companies to West side of River at BOVES. Train Companies marched into new camp at LE PARACLET at IO p.m. O. C. Train arrived CASTEL I2 mid-night.	
"	29th		I a.m. O. C. Train left to move Train Companies to NAMPTY. Companies marched at 5-30 a.m. arriving at new camp at II a.m. O. C. Train visited Column at 8 a.m. re Railhead at LOEUILLY. O. C. Train went to Railhead 9 a.m. At 3 a.m. Train Hd. Qrs. marched out from CASTEL about 2 miles to BOIS de SENCAT and then halted till 7-I5 a.m. when they proceeded to COTTENCHY arriving at IO a.m. O. C. Train arrived COTTENCHY from NAMPTY at 3 p.m.	
COTTEN-CHY	"		Adjutant left COTTENCHY [illegible] to give instructions to Companies re delivery of Supplies.	
"	30th		Railhead LOEUILLY. O. C. Train left at 5 p.m. to move Train Companies to BUYON.	
"	3Ist		Railhead ST. ROCHE.	

A G Galloway

Lieut-Colonel.
O. C. 24th Divisional Train.

A5834 Wt. W4973 M687 750,000 8/16 D. D. & L. Ltd. Forms/C.2118/13.

A

SECRET Copy No. 6

24th DIVISIONAL TRAIN ORDER NO. 26.

(In continuation of No. 22)

3rd March. 1918.

With reference to 24th Divisional Artillery Operation Order No. 50/5.

I. The Sections and Ammunition Wagons marching to the New Area on 4th instant are carrying rations and forage for consumption on 5th instant.

2. The Supply Wagons of No. I Train Company will carry on 5th instant the supplies for consumption on the 6th instant for the whole Divisional Artillery, less the T.M.Bs (H.&.M.) which will be delivered on 4th instant.

3. Supplies for the whole of Group "A" for consumption on 7th instant will be dumped on the ESTREES Cross Roads at P.30.d.4.6. (sheet 62c) on the 5th instant at IO a.m. The Supply Officer, Divisional Troops and his Supply Details must be at the new Refilling Point by that hour to take delivery of the Supplies.

These supplies may either be left on the Dump for the night 5th/6th, or loaded on the Supply Wagons on the afternoon of 5th instant, kept on the Supply Wagons overnight, and delivered to Units on the 6th instant. This is left to the discretion of the O.C. No. I Coy and Supply Officer, Divisional Troops.

4. ACKNOWLEDGE.

Lieut-Colonel.
O.C. 24th Divisional Train.

Copies to :-
I. "Q" 24th Division.
2. O.C. Divl Train.
3. S.S.O.
4. O.C. No. I Coy & S.O. Div. Troops.
5. O.C. 24th D.S.C. & S.C.S.O.
6. War Diary.
7. File.

B

SUPPLY GROUP TABLE NO. 4 to take effect (On A. F. 33I6 & 33I7 4-3-I8) (At Railhead on 5-3-I8) (Consumption. 7-3-I8) Until further orders

Group "A"	Group "B"	Group "C"	Group "D".
R. P. P. 30. d. 4. 5. 5-3-I8 et. seq.	R. P. P. 30. d. 4. 6. 5-3-I8 et. seq.	R. P. P. 30. d. 4. 6. 5-3-I8 et. seq.	R. P. P. 30. d. 4. 6. 5-3-I8 et. seq.
C. R. A.	I7th Inf. Bde. H. Q.	72nd Inf. Bde. H. Q.	73rd Inf. Bde H. Q.
I06 Bde R. F. A.	I7th M. G. Coy.	72nd M. G. Coy.	73rd Inf. Bde. M. G. Coy.
I07 Bde R. F. A.	8th Buffs (Trp. only)	72nd Inf. Bde. T. M. Bs.	73rd Bde. T. M. B.
24th Div. T. M. Bs. (H. & M.)	Ist R. Fusiliers.	9th E. Surreys.	9th R. Sussex.
24th D. A. C.	8th Queens.	8th R. W. Kents.	7th Northants.
36th M. V. S.	3rd Rifle Brigade.	Ist N. Staffs.	I3th Middlesex.
No. I Coy Train.	I04 Field Coy R. E.	I03 Field Coy R. E.	I0th R. D. Fus. (Trp only)
	74th Field Ambulance.	72nd Fd. Ambulance.	73rd Fd. Ambulance.
	No. 2 Coy Train.	No. 3 Coy Train.	I29 Field Coy R. E.
	Train Headquarters.	I2th R. Fusiliers (Trp only)	No. 4 Coy Train.
	24th Div'l Headquarters.		I2th Sherwood Foresters.
	C. R. E.		
	D. A. D. O. S.		
	24th Signal Coy R. E.		
	I9I M. G. Coy.		

A. G. Galloway
Lieut-Colonel.
O. C. 24th Divisional Train.

6-3-I8

Distributed as per reverse.

1. A.&.Q., 24th Division.
2. O.C. Train.
3. S.S.O.
4. O.C. No.I Coy & S.O. Div Troops.
5. O.C. No.2 Coy and S.O. 17th Inf.Bde.
6. O.C. No.3 Coy and S.O. 72nd Inf.Bde.
7. O.C. No.4 Coy and S.O. 73rd Inf.Bde.
8. 24th D.S.C. and Supply Col.S.O.
9. R.T.O. Railhead.
IO. War Diary.
II. File.

Copy No....4..

SUPPLY GROUP TABLE NO. 5 (On A. Fs. W. 3317 & 3316 I3-3-I8.
(At Railhead. I4-3-I8.
(Consumption. I6-3-I8.

GROUP "A".	GROUP "B"	GROUP "C".	GROUP "D".
Railhead TINCOURT. R. P. (DECAUVILLE RLY) Q. 30. b.	Railhead TINCOURT. R. P. (DECAUVILLE RLY) VRAIGNES.	Railhead TINCOURT. R. P. (DECAUVILLE RLY) Q. 30. b.	Railhead TINCOURT. R. P. (DECAUVILLE RLY) VRAIGNES.
I06th Brigade R. F. A. I07th Brigade R. F. A. 24th D. A. C. 24th T. M. Bs. Train Hd. Qrs. No. I Coy Train. No. 2 Coy Train. No. 3 Coy Train. No. 4 Coy Train. 73rd Field Ambulance. 36th Mob. Vet. Section.	I7th Brigade Hd. Qrs. I7th T. M. Batty. Ist Royal Fusiliers. 8th Queens. 3rd Rifle Brigade. 8th Buffs (Tpt. only) 74th Field Ambulance. 24th Division Hd. Qrs. 24th Signal Coy R. E. A. O. D. C. R. A. C. R. E. I04 Field Coy R. E. 24th Div'l M. G. Batt.	72nd Brigade Hd. Qrs. 9th E. Surreys. 8th R. W. Kents. Ist North Staffs. 72nd T. M. Bs. I03rd Field Coy R. E. 72nd Field Ambulance. I2th R. Fusiliers (Tpt. only) I2th Sherwood Foresters.	73rd Brigade Hd. Qrs. 73rd T. M. Batty. 7th Northants. 9th R. Sussex. I3th Middlesex. I29 Field Coy R. E.
Attached. Hd. Qrs.) "A" Batty. } R. C. H. A. "B" Batty. } (Q. 33. d.)		GROUP "E" rationed direct from Railhead. 86th A. F. A. B.	Attached. R. H. A. "N" "U" "Q" Batteries. "A"

Distributed to all recipients of
Group Table No. 4.

I3-3-I8.

Lieut-Colonel.
O. C. 24th Divisional Train.

19

Instructions regarding War Diaries and Intelligence Summaries are contained in F. S. Regs., Part II. and the Staff Manual respectively. Title pages will be prepared in manuscript.

Army Form C. 2118.

WAR DIARY or ~~INTELLIGENCE SUMMARY~~. 24th Divisional Train.

(Erase heading not required.)

Vol 32

Place	1918 Date April	Hour	Summary of Events and Information	Remarks and references to Appendices
COTTENCHY	Ist		Railhead AMIENS Main Station. Nothing of importance to report.	
"	2nd		Railhead AILLY-SUR-SOMME. Nothing of importance to report	
"	3rd		Railhead AILLY-SUR-SOMME. No.I Coy.,66th Divisional Train attached to 24th Division for rations, arrived CAGNY.	
"	4th		Railhead AILLY-SUR-SOMME. Train Companies marched to VERS 8 a.m. Train Hd.Qrs. left COTTENCHY at 8 a.m. and proceeded to BOVES arriving at 9-30 a.m. Transport halted outside owing to town being shelled. Adjutant met C.O. in BOVES at I2-30 p.m. and at 2 p.m. both proceeded to CAGNY in search of quarters, returning to BOVES at 3-45 p.m. Transport marched off at 4 p.m. arriving	
CAGNY	"	5 pm.	CAGNY at 5 p.m. Capt. R.F. SEDDALL returned to duty from D.D.S.&.T.,5th Army and assumed duties of S.O. 72nd Infantry Brigade.	
"	5th		Railhead AILLY-SUR-SOMME. Orders received at midnight (G. 292) that Division was being relieved and would march to ST.VALERY area. Troops by rail, transport by road. O.C.Train to be in command of road party.	
LEGARD Farm Nr. PICQUIGNY	6th		Train Headquarters Transport marched out from CAGNY at 8 a.m. and proceeded to starting point AMIENS. All D.H.Q. Transport marched with B.T.O.,I7th Brigade's Convoy which started at I-45 p.m. O.C.Train gave instructions to B.T.Os. I7th, 72nd and 73rd Brigades at starting point. 72nd & 73rd Brigades followed I7th Brigade. Adjutant proceeded with O.C.Train to arrange accommodation at LEGARD. I7th Brigade Group arrived at 6 p.m. 72nd Brigade Group at 7-30 p.m. and 73rd Brigade Group at I0 p.m. Heavy rain from 9 p.m. onwards. Instructions issued to B.T.Os for following day's march. S.S.O. proceeded direct to ST.VALERY. D.H.Q. proceeded to ST.VALERY. No.I Company left behind with Divisional Artillery - to draw from 58th Division Pack. No.I Company moved to PETITE CAGNY. Artillery Group Railhead AMIENS.	
"	7th		Railhead AILLY-SUR-SOMME. All Supply wagons refilled at 7 a.m. at LEGARD. March continued, I7th Brigade Group started at 8 a.m. 72nd Brigade ½ hour after last wagon of I7th Brigade - 73rd Brigade ½ hour after last wagon of 72nd Brigade. Mid-day halt with head of I7th Brigade Transport at X Roads at BRAYLES MAREUIL. Following Brigades halted with head of column I mile in rear of tail of preceding column. 2 hours halt. No.I Company moved to CLAIRY. Artillery Group Railhead AILLY.	

J. Galloway
LIEUT. COLONEL.
O.C. 24th DIVISIONAL TRAIN.

Instructions regarding War Diaries and Intelligence Summaries are contained in F. S. Regs., Part II. and the Staff Manual respectively. Title pages will be prepared in manuscript.

WAR DIARY
or
~~INTELLIGENCE SUMMARY~~.
(Erase heading not required.)

24th Divisional Train.

Place	1918. Date April	Hour	Summary of Events and Information	Remarks and references to Appendices
CAMBRON	7th	5 pm	I7th Brigade group arrived 5 p.m., 72nd Brigade 6-30 p.m., 73rd Bde. 8-30 p.m. O.C. Train and Adjutant proceeded to ST. VALERY arriving at II a.m. Saw S.S.O. and "Q" and arranged accommodation for Divisional Transport for night 7th/8th at CAMBRON on return journey.	
"	8th		I7th Brigade Group marched out at 8 a.m. i/c B.T.O. to their new area round CAYEUX. 73rd " " " " " 8 a.m. " " " " " " FRIVILLE D.H.Q. " " " " 8-40 a.m. " acting A.P.M. " " ST VALERY 72nd " " " " " 9 a.m. " B.T.O. to their " " ARREST Field Coys. R.E. " " " 9-30 a.m. " Lieut. FORD " " " QUESNOY Train Hd. Qrs. Tpt. " " " IO a.m. " Adjutant " " ST VALERY, arriving I2-30 p.m. O.C. Train proceeded at IO a.m. to ST. VALERY. No. I Company moved to ANDAINVILLE. Artillery Group Railhead AMIENS.	
ST. VALERY	8th	I2-30 p.m.	Location of Train Companies :- No. 2, WATHIECOURT, No. 3, ARREST, No. 4, SAUCOURT. Railhead ST. VALERY. 2nd Lieuts. TIDY, MOTION, and BARNES & 35 O.R. rejoined from leave.	
"	9th		Informed that Capt. J. P. THOMPSON had been granted extension of leave for 2I days from 28-3-18 on Medical certificate (Q.M.G., A.S.C., G.H.Q. No. ASC/I9794/27 dated 30-3-18). Artillery Group R'head SALEUX.	
"	IOth		Nothing of importance to report.	
"	IIth		No. I Company moved to WANEL. Artillery Group Railhead LONGPRÉ.	
"	I2th		Supply group Table No. 6 issued by 24th Division "Q" (Q2/202). S.M.T.O. XVIII Corps visited O.C. Train re 2nd Lieut. H. W. BRADLEY as H.T. Adjutant.	"A"
"	I3th		2nd Lieut. H. W. BRADLEY proceeded to XVIII Corps H.Q. to act as H.T. Adjutant to S.M.T.O. 4 H.D. Remounts collected by No. 4 Company from IOth Dublin Fusiliers.	
"	I4th		Supplies for the 3 Bde. Groups drawn from ST. VALERY R'head by H.T. from this date. Arty. Group Railhead AIRAINES.	
"	I5th		O.C. Train & Adjt. visited No. I Coy. at WANEL. Lt. HODGMAN and party proceeded by lorry to Remount Depot ABBEVILLE at II p.m. to collect 40 Remounts for Division. Remounts distributed at FRESSENNVILLE Church at 8 a.m. I6-4-18. No. 2 Coy. received 3 H.D., No. 3 Coy 3 Rdg. & 7 H.D., No. 4 Coy 7 H.D.	

A Galloway
LIEUT. COLONEL
O.C. 24th DIVISIONAL TRAIN.

Army Form C. 2118.

Instructions regarding War Diaries and Intelligence Summaries are contained in F. S. Regs., Part II. and the Staff Manual respectively. Title pages will be prepared in manuscript.

WAR DIARY
or
~~INTELLIGENCE SUMMARY.~~
(*Erase heading not required.*)

24th Divisional Train.

Place	Date 1918 April	Hour	Summary of Events and Information	Remarks and references to Appendices
ST. VALERY	I6th		Entrainment orders, 24th Division "Q" C425 received at 3 a.m. Lorries drew supplies from Railhead. Supply wagons refilled immediately and sent out to units to entrain with them.	
"	I7th		O.C. Train and S.S.O. proceeded to D.H.Q. at LA THIEULOYE. Train Hd. Qrs. Transport marched out at 9 a.m. and proceeded to Entraining Station WOINCOURT arriving I p.m. Entrained at 6 p.m. Train left at 7-30 p.m. (3½ hours late). No. 3 Company entrained 9-I9 a.m. at FEUQUIERES. No. 4 Company entrained I-04 a.m. at WOINCOURT. Railhead DIEVAL. No. I Company moved to BUIGNY L'ABBE.	
VALHUON	I8th		No. I Company moved to BEAVOR-WAVANS. Artillery Group Railhead ST RIQIER. Railhead DIEVAL. Train Hd. Qrs. Transport detrained at PERNES at IO a.m. Met O.C. Train on arrival. Marched to VALHUON arriving I2 noon. No. 2 Company entrained FEUQUIERES 6 a.m. No. 4 Company detrained at PERNES and proceeded to BAJUS. No. 3 " " " BRYAS " " " VALHUON No. 2 " " " BRYAS " " " ROCOURT Supply wagons refilled on arrival and delivered to units and then returned to Train Companies.	
"	I9th		No. I Company marched with 24th Divisional Artillery to Divisional Area and arrived RAMECOURT at 5 p.m. C.O. and Adjutant visited No. I Company at 6 p.m. O.C. Train informed at D.H.Q. at 7 p.m. that Train Headquarters would have to leave VALHUON by noon 20-4-I8 and go to DIVION. Artillery Group Railhead FREVENT.	
"	20th		O.C. Train and Adjutant searched Divisional Area for billets from 9 a.m. to noon - eventually arranged billets at DIVION. 24th Divl. Artillery drew from 24th Division Pack Train. R'head DIEVAL.	
DIVION	20th	5 p.m	Train Headquarters marched out from VALHUON at 2 p.m. and arrived DIVION 5 p.m. O.C. Train visited No. I Company at RAMECOURT.	
"	2Ist		Supplies for I7th, 72nd and 73rd Brigade groups drawn from DIEVAL Railhead by Horse Transport, those for Divl. Artillery by M.T. from this day onwards.	
BAJUS	2Ist		Train Headquarters marched from DIVION at 4 p.m. and arrived BAJUS at 6 p.m. Supply Group Table No. 7 issued by 24th Division "Q" (Q2/208).	"B"
"	22nd		O.C. Train visited No. I Company at LE CAUROY.	

[signature] LIEUT. COLONEL
O.C. 24th DIVISIONAL TRAIN.

A5834 Wt. W4973/M687 750,000 8/16 D. D. & L. Ltd. Forms/C.2118/13.

Army Form C. 2118.

Instructions regarding War Diaries and Intelligence Summaries are contained in F. S. Regs., Part II. and the Staff Manual respectively. Title pages will be prepared in manuscript.

WAR DIARY
or
~~INTELLIGENCE SUMMARY~~

24th Divisional Train.

(Erase heading not required.)

Place	1918 Date April	Hour	Summary of Events and Information	Remarks and references to Appendices
BAJUS	23rd		Nothing of importance to report.	
"	24th		Information received that Capt. J. P. THOMPSON, absent on leave in U.K., had been granted extension of leave on Medical certificate (Q.M.G., A.S.C., G.H.Q. No. ASC/20097/2 dated 16-4-18.) I N.C.O. and 6 O.R., each from No. 2 and 4 Companies, proceeded to Canadian Light Horse at CARENCY for instructions in the use of Hotchkiss Guns.	
"	25th		Nothing of importance to report.	
"	26th		A.A.&.Q.M.G. and D.A.Q.M.G., 24th Division accompanied by O.C. Train visited No. 2, 3 and 4 Train Companies. Great satisfaction was expressed at the condition of the Horses and Vehicles.	
"	27th		A.A.&.Q.M.G., accompanied by O.C. Train, visited No. I Company at LE CAUROY and was most pleased with all he saw.	
"	28th		Verbal message received re move of 73rd Infantry Brigade on 29-4-18.	
"	29th		No. 4 Company marched out from BAJUS at 9-30 a.m. with 73rd Inf. Bde. Movement of 73rd Inf. Bde. cancelled at II a.m., and No. 4 Company returned to BAJUS at 12-30 p.m. O.C. Train presided at a F.G.C.M. which assembled at Hd. Qrs., 24th Battn. M.G.C. at CONTEVILLE. O.C. Train accompanied by O.C. No. 4 Company inspected Ist Line Transport of Pioneer Battn. (12th Sherwood Foresters) which he found excellent in every respect. Supplies for 73rd Brigade Group drawn from Railhead by M.T. 2 N.C.Os. and 12 other ranks returned from M.G. Course at CARENCY. Informed that Capt. J. P. THOMPSON had been boarded in England and found unfit for General Service. Struck off the strength from 27-4-18 (Authy :- Q.M.G., A.S.C., G.H.Q. No. ASC/20097/2 dated 27-4-18).	
"	30th		Warning order to move (24th Divn. G.477) received 8 a.m. No. 4 Company marched from BAJUS at 2 p.m. with 73rd Infantry Brigade. Arrived FOSSE 10 at 7-30 p.m. 24th Divn. order No. 239 received 7-30 p.m. Adjutant proceeded to FOSSE 10 with I Officer from No. 4 Company to arrange billets for No. 4 Company and afterwards visited 3rd Canadian Divisional Train at BARLIN re taking over their Headquarters.	

A G Galloway
LIEUT. COLONEL
O.C. 24th DIVISIONAL TRAIN.

A5834 Wt. W4973/M687 750,000 8/16 D. D. & L. Ltd. Forms/C.2118/13.

24th Division No. Q.2/202.

"A"

The following are the Supply Groups and Refilling Points until further notice:-

No.6.

SUPPLY GROUP TABLE to take effect (On A.Fs.3316 & 3317 8-4-18)
(At Railhead on 9-4-18)
(Consumption on 11-4-18)

GROUP "A". R.P.	GROUP "B". R.P. WATHIE HURT.	GROUP "C". R.P. ARREST.	GROUP "D". R.P. On ABBEVILLE - EU Road South of SAUCOURT.
C.R.A.	17th Inf.Bde.Hd.Qrs.	72nd Inf.Bde.Hd.Qrs.	73rd Inf.Bde.Hd.Qrs.
106th Bde.R.F.A.	3rd Rifle Bde.	9th E.Surreys.	73rd T.M.Batty.
107th Bde.R.F.A.	1st R.Fusiliers.	8th R.W.Kents.	9th R.Sussex.
24th D.A.C.(Hd.Qrs.& 2 Sects).	8th Queens.	1st N.Staffs.	7th Northants.
24th Divl.T.M.Batty.	17th T.M.Batty.	72nd T.M.Batty.	13th Middlesex.
No.1 Coy. Train.	74th Field Ambulance.	103rd Field Coy.R.E.	73rd Field Ambulance.
33th Mobile Vet.Section.	No.2 Coy. Train.	104th Field Coy.R.E.	24th D.A.C. (S.A.A.Section.)
	24th Divl.M.G.Battn.	129th Field Coy.R.E.	No.4 Coy. Train.
	Hd.Qrs.24th Division.	72nd Field Ambulance.	Details 24th Divl.Artillery.
	Hd.Qrs.R.E.	12th Sher.Foresters.	
	24th Signal Coy.R.E.	No.3 Coy.Train.	
	Hd.Qrs.24th Div.Train.		
	D.A.D.O.S.		

RAILHEAD. Groups "B", "C", & "D" ST.VALERY-SUR-SOMME.

E. Mason
Major,
D.A.Q.M.G., 24th Division.

12th April 1918.

Camp Commdt.	17th Inf.Bde.	D.A.D.O.S.
24th Signal Co.	72nd Inf.Bde.	36th Mob.Vet.Sect.
C.R.A.	73rd Inf.Bde.	A.D.M.S.
C.R.E.	12th Sher.Fors.	Div.Train.
D.A.D.V.S.	24th M.G.Battn.	
A.P.M.		24th D.A.C (S.A.A. Sect.)

24th Division No. Q.2/208. "B"

No. 7.

The following Supply Group Table is published for information :-

SUPPLY GROUP TABLE

On A.F. B.3316 dated 19/4/1918.
On A.F. 3317 dated do.
At Railhead on 20-4-1918.

Group "A". R.P.	GROUP "B". R.P. ROCOURT.	GROUP "C". R.P. VALHUON.	GROUP "D". R.P. BAJUS.
Headquarters R.A.	17th Inf.Bde. Hd.Qrs.	72nd Inf.Bde.Hd.Qrs.	73rd Inf.Bde.Hd.Qrs.
106th Bde.R.F.A.	3rd Rifle Bde.	9th East Surreys.	73rd L.T.M.Btty.
107th Bde.R.F.A.	1st R.Fusiliers.	8th R.W.Kents.	9th R.Sussex.
24th D.A.C.	8th Queens.	1st North Staffs.	7th Northants.
24th T.M.Btty.	17th T.M.Batty.	72nd T.M.Batty.	13th Middlesex.
36th Mobile Vet.Sect.	104th Field Co.R.E.	103rd Field Co.R.E.	73rd Field Ambce.
No. 1 Coy.Train.	74th Field Ambce.	No.3 Coy. Train.	129th Field Co.R.E.
	No.2 Coy. Train.	24th Machine Gun Battn.	24th D.A.C.(S.A.A. Sect.)
	Headquarters,24th Division.		12th Sherwood Foresters.
	C.R.E.		No.4 Coy.Train.
	24th Signal Coy.R.E.		72nd Field Ambce.
	Army O.Dept.		24th Div.Train Hd.Qrs.

Area Commandant MAGNICOURT.

E. Mason. Major,
D.A.Q.M.G.,24th Division.

21st April 1918.

Copies to :-

C.R.A. 36th Mob.Vet.Sect.
Div.Train. 17th Inf.Bde.
C.R.E. Camp Commandant.
D.A.D.O.S. 72nd Inf.Bde.
73rd Inf.Bde.
12th Sher.Fors.
D.A.D.V.S.
A.D.M.S.
24th Sig.Coy.
24th M.G.Bn.
24th D.A.C.(S.A.A.Sect.)
Area Commdt.MAGNICOURT.

Vol 2

CONFIDENTIAL

WAR DIARY,

of the

24th DIVISIONAL M.T. COMPANY.

From 1st April 1918 to 30th April 1918.

oooooooooooooooooooooooooooooooo

Instructions regarding War Diaries and Intelligence Summaries are contained in F. S. Regs., Part II. and the Staff Manual respectively. Title pages will be prepared in manuscript.

Army Form C. 2118.

WAR DIARY or ~~INTELLIGENCE SUMMARY.~~

(Erase heading not required.)

24th Divisional Train.

Vol 33

Place	Date 1918 May	Hour	Summary of Events and Information	Remarks and references to Appendices
BAJUS	Ist		No. 3 Company marched with 72nd Inf. Bde. from VALHUON to FOSSE IO - arriving there at 7 p.m. S. S. O. and Adjutant visited 3rd Can. Divl. Train re taking over attached Units and afterwards proceeded to FOSSE IO	
"	2nd		Railhead BARLIN. C. O. visited No. I Company at LE CAUROY. No. 3 & 4 Coys marched from FOSSE IO to BARLIN to new quarters.	
BARLIN	"	4 pm	Train Headquarters marched from BAJUS to new Headquarters at BARLIN arriving 4 p.m. No. 2 Company marched with I7th Brigade from ROCOURT to BARLIN arriving 8 p.m. Nos. 2, 3, & 4 Companies took over lines and billets previously occupied by 3 & 4 Companies 3rd Canadian Divl. Train.	
"	3rd		D. H. Q. moved to new Headquarters at SAINS-EN-GOHELLE at IO a.m. Refilling for "B", "C" & "D" Groups took place at SAINS BOUVIGNY Station, (R. 8. c. 0. 5.) Sheet 36B. 24 G. S. wagons turned out by 3 & 4 Companies to assist M. T. Company in drawing Supplies from BARLIN Railhead - Supplies conveyed to Refilling Points at SAINS-BOUVIGNY. O. C. Train and Adjutant visited D. H. Q. at I2 noon. 24th Divisional Train Order No. 27 issued II wagons turned out by No. 2 Company to assist M. T. Company in conveying II tons Fuel wood from Railhead to Coal Dump at R. I3. b. 8. IO.	"A"
BARLIN.	4th		Supplies for consumption 6-5-I8 for "B", "C" & "D" Groups drawn from Railhead by H. T. and conveyed to Refilling Points as yesterday - Route taken from Railhead in accordance with (map issued with) 24th Divl. Train Order No. 27. From this date Supplies drawn from Refilling Points by Ist Line Transport. No Hay on Pack Train and M. T. Company sent lorries to PERNES for it. I4 wagons turned out by Train to assist M. T. Company in transporting Fuel from Railhead. I Sergt., 6 Drivers and I Farrier reinforcement reported for duty. No. I Company marched from LE CAUROY to new lines at FOSSE IO. Addendum to 24th Divl. Train Order No. 27 issued.	"B"
"	5th		T. Capt. F. E. L. PHILP, A. S. C. reported for duty with this unit at 6 p.m., (Authy :- G. H. Q., Q. M. G., A. S. C. No. 20313/2 dated 30-4-18). Was placed under arrest for being "Drunk". Was, at his own request, seen by a M. O. (Capt. WHITE, No. 2 Fd Ambulance) as he stated he was ill.	
"	6th		O. C. Train visited D. D. S. & T., Ist Army and O. C. 56th Divl. Train. 24th Divisional Train Order No. 28 issued. Supply Group Table No. 8 issued. TI/SR/90, S. S. M. BAMPTON F. S. reported for duty and posted to No. 3 Coy., vice T/I424I. S. S. M. HUXFORD G. C. transferred to 4th Reserve Park.	
"	"	6 pm	O. C. Train interviewed T. Capt. F. E. L. PHILP, A. S. C.	

A. S. Galloway
LIEUT. COLONEL
O.C. 24th DIVISIONAL TRAIN.

A5834 Wt. W4973/M687 750,000 8/16 D. D. & L. Ltd. Forms/C.2118/13.

Army Form C. 2118.

Instructions regarding War Diaries and Intelligence Summaries are contained in F. S. Regs., Part II. and the Staff Manual respectively. Title pages will be prepared in manuscript.

WAR DIARY

or

~~INTELLIGENCE SUMMARY~~.

(Erase heading not required.)

24th Divisional Train.

Place	1918 Date May	Hour	Summary of Events and Information	Remarks and references to Appendices
BARLIN	7th		Summary of evidence in the case of T. Capt. F. E. L. PHILP, A. S. C., taken at IO a.m. by Major H. C. ROBINSON. Witnesses :- Major (Temp. Lt. Col.) A. G. GALLOWAY, D. S. O., O. C. Train, T. Major H. B. HUNTER, D. S. O., S. S. O. 24th Division, T. Capt. E. W. L. MARTIN, M. C., Adjutant, 24th Divisional Train, T. Capt. K. M. PLUMPTRE, O. C. No. 2 Company, 24th Divisional Train, the last named being witness for Defence.	
"	8th		T. Capt. F. E. L. PHILP admitted 73rd Field Ambulance.	
"	9th		Lieut. W. A. WATTS, A. S. C., T. F., reported for duty and given acting rank of Captain from this date - Authority :- G. H. Q., Q. M. G., ASC/20289 dated 28-4-I8. a/Capt. W. A. WATTS, A. S. C., T. F., took over the command of No. 4 Company from 2/Lieut. J. O. TIDY, A. S. C. as from this date. All baggage wagons sent out to units. No. I Company moved from FOSSE IO to BARLIN arriving midnight.	
"	IOth		Refilling Points from this date at Companies lines, BARLIN. Supplies drawn from Railhead by H. T. and immediately dumped. Rations for consumption next day delivered to units by Supply Wagons. No. I Company moved to new Camp near FOSSE 9, Q. 2. d., Sheet 36 B. Summary of evidence taken in the case of No. T3/02795I. Dr. GWATKIN F., No. 4 Company.	
"	IIth		O. C. Train presided at F. G. C. M. assembled at IO a.m. at Hd. Qrs. 24th Battn. M. G. C. at FOSSE 2 de BETHUNE, LES BREBIS.	
"	I2th		Normal Routine.	
"	I3th		I2 G. S. Wagons used daily from this date to collect extra forage (unbaled straw) from Purchase Board Dump at RUITZ.	
"	I4th		Permission granted to 2/Lieut. A. H. BARNES, A. S. C. to wear the badges of rank of Lieut. pending appearance of his promotion in "London Gazette". Authy :- 24th Divn. A. 90/277 dated I2-5-I8.	
"	I5th		Supplies for consumption I6-5-I8 delivered to units of 3 Infantry Brigades in the early morning. Supplies for consumption I7-5-I8 drawn as usual from Railhead. Supplies for consumption I7-5-I8 delivered to units of 3 Infantry Brigades in the afternoon. 2/Lieut. J. O. TIDY, A. S. C., I N. C. O. and 6 O. R. each from No. 2 & 4 Companies practised with Hotchkiss Guns on Rifle Range LES BREBIS from 9 a.m. to I p.m. Party of 24 O. R. i/c 2/Lt. G. J. MOTION, A. S. C. collected 48 Remounts for the Division from MARLES LES MINES. The Remounts remained in No. 2 Coy's lines for the night.	

A5834 Wt. W4973/M687 750,000 8/16 D. D. & L. Ltd. Forms/C.2118/13.

A G Galloway
LIEUT. COLONEL.
O.C. 24th DIVISIONAL TRAIN.

Instructions regarding War Diaries and Intelligence Summaries are contained in F. S. Regs., Part II. and the Staff Manual respectively. Title pages will be prepared in manuscript.

WAR DIARY
or
~~INTELLIGENCE SUMMARY.~~
(Erase heading not required.)

Place	Date 1918 May	Hour	Summary of Events and Information	Remarks and references to Appendices
BARLIN	I6th		2/Lieut. G. J. MOTION, A. S. C. distributed Remounts to Units of Division in accordance with 24th Division Q. I5/II6 dated I4-5-I8, 3 H. D. for Train (I to No. 2 Coy., 3 to No. 3 Coy.). No. T3/02795I. Dr. GWATKIN F. (No. 4 Company) tried by F. G. C. M. which assembled at Train Headquarters.	
"	I7th		Normal Routine.	
"	I8th		3 Reinforcements (Drivers) reported for duty and posted as follows :- 2 to No. 2 Company (the Company to post 2 Drivers to 74th Field Ambulance), 1 to No. 4 Company for posting to 73rd Field Ambulance. 2/Lieut. J. W. DUNCAN, A. S. C. proceeded on I4 days special leave to England, Authy :- XVIII Corps No. AI/I57I/64 dated I5-5-I8.	
"	I9th		I Reinforcement (Wheeler) reported for duty and posted to No. 1 Company. 2/Lt. J. O. TIDY, A. S. C., 1 N. C. O. and 6 O. R. from No. 1 Company and 1 N. C. O. and 6 O. R. from No. 3 Company proceeded to Canadian Light Horse at OLHAIN for a course on Hotchkiss Guns.	
"	20th		O. C. Train presided at a Court of Enquiry into the loss of public funds by Divl. Railhead Disbursing Officer held at Train Headquarters at I0 a.m. Sentence in case of F. G. C. M. on No. T3/02795I. Dr. GWATKIN F. promulgated by Adjutant at full parade of No. 4 Company.	
"	2Ist		Train Headquarters moved from BARLIN to VERDREL arriving 3-30 p.m.	
VERDREL	"	3-30 p.m.	Bombs dropped at BARLIN by E. A. One, which did not explode, in No. 2 Coy's Horse Lines. One 30 yards from No. 4 Coy's lines. One horse very slightly wounded in Chest.	
"	22nd		2/Lieut. G. J. MOTION, A. S. C. proceeded on 30 days special leave to England - Authy :- XVIII Corps No. AI/I57I/II3 dated 20-5-I8.	
"	23rd		Very wet.	

[signature]
LIEUT. COLONEL,
O.C. 24th DIVISIONAL TRAIN.

A5834 Wt. W4973/M687 750,000 8/16 D. D & L. Ltd. Forms/C.2118/13.

Army Form C. 2118.

Instructions regarding War Diaries and Intelligence Summaries are contained in F. S. Regs., Part II. and the Staff Manual respectively. Title pages will be prepared in manuscript.

WAR DIARY
or
~~INTELLIGENCE SUMMARY~~
(Erase heading not required.)

24th Divisional Train.

Place	1918 Date May	Hour	Summary of Events and Information	Remarks and references to Appendices
VERDREL	24th		According to orders received from Corps "Q"transport proceeded to Railhead to draw from Pack Train as follows :- "B" Group 6-0 a.m.,"C" Group 6-20,"D" Group 6-40,"A" Group 7-0 a.m. Pack Train was not available till 7-30 a.m. Orders received that all four Train Companies were to move to BOIS d'OLHAIN,Q.I4.a.9.5. by noon 25-5-I8. Very wet all day. Court of Enquiry assembled at No.3 Company to investigate and report on loss of Supplies from No.3 Coy's Cookhouse on night 23/24th May I9I8.	
"	25th		Times of drawing at Railhead altered as follows :- "B" Group 7-30 a.m. "C" Group 7-50 a.m. "D" Group 8-I0 a.m.,"A" Group 8-30 a.m. All Train Companies moved from BARLIN to camps about Q.I4.a.9.5., Sheet 36 B. Move completed by I p.m.	
"	26th		I H.D.Remount collected by No.I Company.	
"	27th		Inspection of horses for casting held at SAINS-EN-GOHELLE. No.2 Company paraded 3 H.D.,No.3 Coy 4 H.D.,No.4 Coy.I Rider.	
"	28th		"Mentioned in Dispatches" :- Major T.W.BLAKEWAY,Capt.F.A.R.SAUNDERS,Capt.J.P.THOMPSON,No.T4/055899. Dr.CLUBB T.,London Gazette 25-5-I8"Times"27-5-I8. Instructions received that the I2 G.S.Wagons which had become surplus to Establishment,owing to the disbandment of 3 Battalions,were to be evacuated to A.H.T.D.,ABBEVILLE. 2/Lt.J.O.TIDY and party returned from Hotchkiss Gun Course at Canadian Light Horse at OLHAIN.	
"	29th		The following changes in postings and duties of Officers took place as from this date :- a/Capt.W.A.WATTS,A.S.C.from command of No.4 Company to No.I Company as Transport Captain. T/Capt.C.E.PASMORE,A.S.C.,from Transport Captain No.I Company to No.4 Company in command. T/Lieut.F.R.NEVILL,A.S.C.from Train Headquarters as Requisitioning Officer (Subaltern) to No.I Company as Transport Subaltern. T2/Lieut.J.O.TIDY,A.S.C.from Transport Subaltern No.4 Coy.to Train Headquarters as Requisitioning Officer (Subaltern). ✗ T/2/Lieut.H.W.BRADLEY,A.S.C.from Transport Subaltern No.3 Coy.to Transport Subaltern No.4 Coy. T/2/Lieut.E.R.A.HODGMAN,A.S.C.from Transport Subaltern No.I Coy.to Transport Subaltern No.3 Coy. Lieut.A.H.BARNES assumed duties of S.O.,Divl.Troops vice Capt.SAUNDERS whilst on temporary duty as Assistant to S.S.O.at Train Headquarters. ✗ This Officer to remain with S.M.T.O.,XVIII Corps as H.T.Adjutant.	

A5834 Wt. W4973/M687 750,000 8/16 D. D. & L. Ltd. Forms/C.2118/13.

[signature]
LIEUT, COLONEL,
O.C. 24th DIVISIONAL TRAIN.

Army Form C. 2118.

WAR DIARY
or
~~INTELLIGENCE SUMMARY~~. 24th Divisional Train.

(Erase heading not required.)

Instructions regarding War Diaries and Intelligence Summaries are contained in F. S. Regs., Part II. and the Staff Manual respectively. Title pages will be prepared in manuscript.

Place	Date 1918 May	Hour	Summary of Events and Information	Remarks and references to Appendices
VERDREL	30th		2/Lieut. E. R. A. HODGMAN proceeded to A. H. T. D. ABBEVILLE i/c of I2 G. S. Wagons, 9 Drivers and 9 pairs H. D. Horses, which had become surplus owing to disbandment of 3 Battalions. (Authy :- S.& T., First Army wire ST/470 dated 28th May and 24th Division wire Q. I638 dated 28th May 1918. Instructions received (Q. I722) at 7-30 p.m. that 3 more Drivers and 3 pairs H. D. were to follow the above transport as soon as possible to make up complete turnsout.	
"	3Ist		3 Drivers and 3 pairs H. D. proceeded to A. H. T. D., ABBEVILLE, i/c No. T4/237548. a/Sergt. TURNER A., No. I Company, to make I2 complete turnsout. O. C. Train visited No. 8 C. C. S. re T/Capt. F. E. L. PHILP.	

[signature]
LIEUT. COLONEL,
O.C. 24th DIVISIONAL TRAIN.

A5834 Wt. W4973/M687 750,000 8/16 D. D. & L. Ltd. Forms/C.2118/13.

"A"

S E C R E T. Copy No 9...

24th DIVISIONAL TRAIN ORDER NO. 27.

May 3rd 1918.

I. Commencing the 4th instant, Supplies will be drawn for "B", "C" and "D" Groups from BARLIN Railhead by Horse Transport.

2. Times of drawing will be as under :-

"B" Group	10 a.m.
"C" Group	10-20 a.m.
"D" Group	10-40 a.m.

3. Os. C. Companies will be informed by S. Os concerned as to the strengths of their respective groups. Rations for attached A.F.A.Bs. will be drawn direct at Railhead by their own transport.

4. The Supplies will be conveyed to Refilling points at SAINS-BOUVIGNY Station, R.6.c.I.3. (sheet 36 B.)

5. Route to be taken by wagons from Railhead to Refilling Points will be as per attached map (issued to recipients of copies I, 2, 4, 5, 6 & 8).

6. Supplies will remain at Refilling Points over night and be issued the following day as ~~under~~ follows :-

9 a.m.	Units of 24th Division.
10 a.m.	Attached units.

7. Commencing on the 4th instant, Supplies will be drawn from Refilling Points by Ist Line Transport.

8. To enable the following units to draw their Supplies from Refilling Points the baggage vehicles will remain with them :-

D.H.Q.	2 G.S. wagons
C.R.E.	I L.G.S.
Pioneers	2 G.S. wagons.

9. Os. C. 2, 3 and 4 Companies to acknowledge.

A. Galloway
Lieut-Colonel.
O.C. 24th Divisional Train.

Copies to :-
I. 24th Divn. "Q".
2. O.C. Train.
3. S.S.O.
4. O.C. No. 2 Coy.
5. O.C. No. 3 Coy.
6. O.C. No. 4 Coy.
7. O.C. M.T. Company
8. File.
9. War Diary
10. " "
11. " "

"B"

S E C R E T.   Copy No..9....

ADDENDUM TO
24th DIVISIONAL TRAIN ORDER NO. 27.

May 4th 1918.

Para. 2 is cancelled and the following substituted :-

As the time of drawing at Railhead is uncertain owing to irregularity in the arrival of the Pack Train, an Orderly will be ~~xxxx~~ sent by each Company to report to the S.O., 24th Divl. M.T. Coy., at Railhead, at 9 a.m. daily. When the Train has arrived the Orderly will return to his Company Officer who will order his Transport to proceed to Railhead as under :-

"B" Group (No. 2 Coy) immediately.
"C" Group (No. 3 Coy) 20 minutes after No. 2 Coy.
"D" Group (No. 4 Coy) 20 minutes after No. 3 Coy.

A. Galloway
Lieut-Colonel.
O. C. 24th Divisional Train.

Distributed to all recipients of Order No. 27.

"C"

Copy No..11..

24th DIVISIONAL TRAIN ORDER NO. 28.

6th May 1918.

I. 24th Divisional Train Order No. 27 is cancelled.

2. Commencing the 7th instant, Supplies will be drawn for all Groups from Railhead by Horse Transport.

3. The order and times of drawing will be as under :-

"A" Group 9 a.m.
"B" Group 9-30 a.m.
"C" Group 9-45 a.m.
"D" Group 10-0 a.m.

4. Os.C.Companies will be informed by S.Os. concerned as to the strengths of their respective groups. Rations for attached A.F.A.Bdes. will be drawn direct at Railhead by their own transport.

5. The Supplies will be conveyed to Refilling Points as under :-

"A" Group to FOSSE 10
"B" " }
"C" " } to SAINS BOUVIGNY Station
"D" " } R.8.c.1.3., sheet 36B.

6. No restrictions as to route from Railhead to Refilling Points

7. Supplies will remain at Refilling Points over night and be issued the following day as follows :-

9 a.m. Units of 24th Division.
10 a.m. Attached units.

8. Supplies will be drawn from Refilling Points by 1st Line Transport except in the case of the 24th Divisional Artillery whose rations will be delivered to them as usual.

9. To enable the following units to draw their Supplies from Refilling Points the baggage vehicles will remain with them :-

D.H.Q. 2 G.S.wagons
C.R.E. 1 L.G.S.
Pioneers 2 G.S.wagons.

10. Os.C.Train Companies to acknowledge.

A.G. Galloway

Lieut-Colonel.
O.C. 24th Divisional Train.

Copies to :-

1. 24th Division "Q".
2. O.C.Train.
3. S.S.O.
4. O.C.No.1 Company.
5. O.C.No.2 Company.
6. O.C.No.3 Company.
7. O.C.No.4 Company.
8. O.C.,M.T.Company.
9. File.
10. War Diary.
11. " "
12. " "

"1"

SUPPLY GROUP TABLE NO. 8 (To take effect on A.F.W. 3316 & 3317 dated 6-5-18. At Railhead 7-5-18. For consumption 9-5-18 & until further notice.)

Copy No. 11.

GROUP "A" R.P. FOSSE IO.	GROUP "B" R.P. SAINS BOUVIGNY Station.	GROUP "C" R.P. SAINS BOUVIGNY Station.	GROUP "D" R.P. SAINS BOUVIGNY Station.
C. R. A. IO6th Bde. R.F.A. IO7th Bde. R.F.A. 24th D. A. C. 24th Div. T.M. Batty. 36th Mobile Vet. Sect. No. I Company Train.	I7th Inf. Bde. Hd. Qrs. 3rd Rifle Brigade. Ist R. Fusiliers. 8th Queens. I7th Trench M. Batty. IO4th Field Coy. R.E. 74th Field Ambulance. No. 2 Company, Train. Headquarters, 24th Divn. " R. E. 24th Signal Coy. R.E. I2th Sherwood Foresters. Army Ordnance Dept. H.Q. 24th Divl. Train.	72nd Inf. Bde. Hd. Qrs. 9th East Surreys. 8th R.W. Kents. Ist North Staffs. 72nd T.M. Batty. IO3rd Field Coy. R.E. 72nd Field Ambulance. No. 3 Company, Train. 24th Divl. M.G. Battn.	73rd Inf. Bde. Hd. Qrs. 73rd L.T.M. Batty 9th R. Sussex. 7th Northants. I3th Middlesex. 73rd Field Ambulance. I29 Field Company R.E. No. 4 Company, Train.
	"Y" Special Coy. R.E. No. 2 Balloon Company. 33Ist Coy. Road Troops R.E. Town Major, LES BREBIS. Town Major, MAROC.	Town Major, BULLY GRENAY. Town Major, BOUVIGNY. Town Major, BRACQUEMONT. ~~"Y" Special Coy. R.E.~~ "C" Dump Ist Army. "J" Section F.S.C. I26th A.F.A. Brigade. No. 4 Area Signal Party. Town Major, CITE ST PIERRE.	No. 3 Special Coy. R.E. No. 4 " " " "Z" " " " No. 9 Group Ist F.S.C. No. 9 " Isaac Section. 2nd Tramway Company R.E. Town Major, LOOS. Hd. Qrs. Special Company R.E. No. 4 Canadian Sanitary Section. No. IO Group Ist F.S.C.

Distributed as per reverse.

6th May I9I8.

Lieut-Colonel.
O.C. 24th Divisional Train.

Distribution :-

Copy No. I. HQ. 24th Division.
2. O. C. Train.
3. R. S. O.
4. O. C. No. I Company.
5. O. C. No. 2 Company.
6. O. C. No. 3 Company.
7. O. C. No. 4 Company.
8. O. C. H. T. Company.
9. R. T. O.
IO. File.
II. War Diary —
I2. War Diary.

Instructions regarding War Diaries and Intelligence Summaries are contained in F. S. Regs., Part II. and the Staff Manual respectively. Title pages will be prepared in manuscript.

WAR DIARY
or
~~INTELLIGENCE SUMMARY.~~

(Erase heading not required.)

24th Divisional Train.

Army Form C. 2118.

Vol 34

Place	Date 1918 June	Hour	Summary of Events and Information	Remarks and references to Appendices
VERDREL.	1st		Normal routine.	
"	2nd		O. C. Train proceeded on leave to United Kingdom for 14 days. Major H. B. HUNTER, D. S. O., to command during his absence. 6 Reinforcements reported for duty - 1 Sergt. (No. 4 Coy), 3 B. ii Drivers (73rd Field Amb.), 2 B. Drivers (No. 2 Coy.), No. 2 Company to send 1 Driver to 74th Field Ambulance Informed by wire that Railhead from 4-6-18, inclusive, would be SAVY-BERLETTE and that Light Railway would be used between Railhead and Refilling Points.	
"	3rd		Major H. B. HUNTER, D. S. O., presided at meeting of Board to Audit Accounts of 24th Divisional institute. A. A. & Q. M. G., 24th Division, accompanied by Adjutant made tour of inspection of Light Railway system to select Refilling Points for 4-6-18. Old Amm. Refilling Point at BOYEFFLES Sidings, R. 13. b. 6. 7. (Sheet 44B.) selected for all groups. 24th Divisional Train Order No. 29 issued. 2/Lieut. E. R. A. HODGMAN returned from ABBEVILLE.	A.
"	4th		Railhead SAVY-BERLETTE. Dumps allotted to Supply Officers at BOYEFFLES Siding, by a/O. C. Train. Instructed by Division that only rations for consumption following day to be in the hands of all Units (Authy :- XVIII Corps wire Q. 530 dated 3-6-18) No supplies delivered to Units of 72 & 73rd Brigades or attached units. Major T. W. BLAKEWAY late O. C. No. 1 Coy., awarded D. S. O. ("London Gazette" Supplement 3-6-18) and "Times" dated 3-6-18).	
"	5th		Hotchkiss Gun teams of No. 1 & 3 Companies i/c 2/Lieut. J. O. TIDY practised on Range at LES BREBIS	
"	"	9 pm.	Informed by 24th Division "Q" that two days rations were to be in possession of units in forward area. Lorries would be available at Railhead owing to the uncertainty of the running of the Light Railway. Refilling took place at BOYEFFLES Siding as follows :- "B" & "D" Groups 8 a. m., "C" Group 9 a. m., "A" Group 9-30 a. m.	
"	6th		Refilling at usual hours. Lorries arrived Refilling Point with rations for consumption 8-6-18 for the 3 Infantry Brigades, 3 Field Companies, Pioneers, and M. G. Battn. at 1 p. m. These were immediately delivered to units by Supply Wagons which had remained at Refilling Point after first delivery. 2/Lt. J. W. DUNCAN returned from leave. a/O. C. Train visited D. D. S. & T., 1st Army. G. O. C., 24th Division attended by A. A. & Q. M. G. walked round the horse lines of the Train Companies at 6-15 p. m. He expressed satisfaction with all he saw.	

[signature]

LIEUT. COLONEL.
O.C. 24th DIVISIONAL TRAIN.

Page 2.
Army Form C. 2118.

Instructions regarding War Diaries and Intelligence Summaries are contained in F. S. Regs., Part II. and the Staff Manual respectively. Title pages will be prepared in manuscript.

WAR DIARY
or
~~INTELLIGENCE SUMMARY~~.
24th Divisional Train.
(Erase heading not required.)

Place	Date 1918 June	Hour	Summary of Events and Information	Remarks and references to Appendices
VERDREL	7th		Instructed by "Q" that the holding of two days supplies by Units as mentioned yesterday would continue until further orders. Capt. C. E. PASMORE proceeded on leave to United Kingdom for 14 days.	
"	8th		Normal routine.	
"	9th		Normal routine.	
"	10th		Instructions received from 24th Division "Q" (Q.342 dated 10-6-18) that normal supply arrangements would be resumed as from 11-6-18 inclusive.	
"	11th		No supplies delivered to those units who were already in possession of two days rations (see 6-6-18).	
"	12th		1 Reinforcement (Clerk) reported for duty - posted to No. 1 Company.	
"	13th		Normal routine.	
"	14th		Application received from 2/Lt. G. J. MOTION for extension of leave for 2 months without pay and allowances. Case referred to Division "A" who stated application must be made direct to War Office. 2/Lieut. MOTION wired accordingly.	
"	15th		2/Lt. E. R. A. HODGMAN proceeded on leave to United Kingdom for 14 days. Two days rations delivered to following Units of 17th Inf. Bde. :- Bde. H. Q., 3 Battns., T. M. Batty., and Field Coy. R. E. for special reasons.	
"	16th		Capt. F. E. L. PHILP discharged from No. 1 C. C. S. and conducted to this unit by Capt. K. M. PLUMPTRE. One day's rations delivered to units of 17th Inf. Bde. mentioned above.	
"	17th		One day's rations delivered to Units of 17th Brigade mentioned above.	
"	18th		No supplies delivered to those Units of 17th Inf. Bde who were already in possession of 2 days rations.	

A. Galloway
LIEUT, COLONEL
O.C. 24th DIVISIONAL TRAIN.

A5834 Wt. W4973 M687 750,000 8/16 D. D. & L. Ltd. Forms/C.2118/13.

Army Form C. 2118.

Instructions regarding War Diaries and Intelligence Summaries are contained in F. S. Regs., Part II. and the Staff Manual respectively. Title pages will be prepared in manuscript.

WAR DIARY
or
~~INTELLIGENCE SUMMARY.~~
(*Erase heading not required.*)

24th Divisional Train.

Place	1918. Date June.	Hour	Summary of Events and Information	Remarks and references to Appendices
VERDREL	19th		No. T2/017861 i/c S. S. M. G. W. CANT, and No. T4/040986 Sergt. F. CLARKE awarded Meritorious Service Medals, "London Gazette" dated 17-6-18, "Times" dated 18-6-18.	
"	20th		T/2/Lt. A. H. BARNES promoted to T/Lieut. as from 13-5-18 (Authy :- "London Gazette" 18-6-18 "Times" 19-6-18. Capt. R. F. SEDDALL proceeded on leave to United Kingdom for 14 days.	
"	21st		T4/092989, Whlr. Staff Sergt. TAYLOR P. H. awarded Meritorious Service Medal ("London Gazette" 17-6-18 and "Times" 20-6-18. Informed by D. D. S. & T., 1st Army that Lieut-Colonel A. G. GALLOWAY, D. S. O., had been granted an extension of leave for period of 7 days from 16-6-18 (Authy :- Q. M. G. 5/344, dated 15-6-18)	
"	22nd		Normal routine.	
"	23rd		Lieut. Colonel A. G. GALLOWAY, D. S. O., and Capt. C. E. PASMORE returned from leave.	
"	24th		Notification received that 2/Lt. G. J. MOTION had been granted 3 days extension of leave from 21-6-18 (Authy :- Q. M. G. 5/350 dated 18-6-18).	
"	25th		Major H. C. ROBINSON proceeded on leave. G. C. M. for trial of T/Capt. F. E. L. PHILP assembled at Divl. Train Hd. Qrs - accused acquitted.	
"	26th		O. C. Train and S. S. O. visited D. D. S. & T., 1st Army.	
"	27th		Permission granted to 2/Lt. J. O. TIDY, A. S. C., to wear the badges of rank of Lieut., pending appearance of his promotion in "London Gazette" - Authy :- 24th Division A. 90/298 dated 26-6-18. 1 Staff Sergt. Issuer and 2 B. ii Drivers R. F. A., reinforcements reported for duty. Instructions received by O. C. Train from A. A. & Q. M. G. that the Train was to undertake and carry out the manufacture of Coal Dust Briquettes.	
"	28th		Briquette Factory started by Capt. F. A. R. SAUNDERS at Div'l. Coal Dump.	

A. G. Galloway
LIEUT, COLONEL,
O.C. 24th DIVISIONAL TRAIN.

A5834 Wt. W4973 M687 750,000 8/16 D. D. & L. Ltd. Forms/C.2118/13.

Army Form C. 2118.

Instructions regarding War Diaries and Intelligence Summaries are contained in F. S. Regs., Part II. and the Staff Manual respectively. Title pages will be prepared in manuscript.

WAR DIARY
or
~~INTELLIGENCE SUMMARY~~. 24th Divisional Train.

(Erase heading not required.)

Place	1918. Date June.	Hour	Summary of Events and Information	Remarks and references to Appendices
VERDREL	29th		Normal routine.	
"	30th		Capt. F. E. L. PHILP admitted 74th Field Ambulance. Informed that 2/Lieut. G. J. MOTION had been granted extension of leave, without pay and allowances for one month from 21-6-18 (Authy :- Q. M. G., G. H. Q., A. S. C./20592/14 dated 28-6-18).	

C. G. Galloway

Lieut-Colonel.
O. C. 24th Divisional Train.

"A."

Copy No. 10

24th DIVISIONAL TRAIN ORDER NO. 29.

3rd June 1918.

I. Railhead from the 4th instant inclusive will be SAVY-BERLETTE.

2. Supplies will be conveyed from Railhead by Light Railway to Refilling Points which will be at BOYEFFLES Sidings, R.13.b.6.7., Sheet 44B., for all Groups.

3. The 24th Div. M.T. Coy. will be responsible for the safe custody of the supplies until they are handed over to S.Os. at Refilling Pts.

4. Refilling will take place on arrival of the L.R. Train at about II a.m.

5. S.Os. will be responsible for informing Units attached to their Group of the time of drawing at the new Refilling Point.

6. Supplies will be delivered by Train Vehicles from R.Ps. to Unit's lines exactly as at present.

7. Supply Officers will arrange for Supply Details to live at R.P. from the 4th instant inclusive.

8. All rations drawn at Railhead this morning for delivery to Units to-morrow will be sent out at 7 a.m., 4th instant.

H. B. Hunter.
Major.
O.C. 24th Divisional Train.

Copies :-
I. 24th Divn. "Q".
2. O.C. Train.
3. S.S.O.
4. O.C. No. I Coy.
5. O.C. No. 2 Coy.
6. O.C. No. 3 Coy.
7. O.C. No. 4 Coy.
8. O.C. M.T. Coy.
9. File.
✓IO. War Diary
II " "
I2. " "

24TH DIVISIONAL TRAIN
2 AUG. 1918
No. B1770
A. S. C.

CONFIDENTIAL.

Headquarters,
24th Division.

Herewith Confidential War Diary of O. C., 24th Divisional Train for month of July 1918.

2-8-18.

[signature]
Lieut. Colonel.
O. C. 24th Divisional Train.

Army Form C. 2118.

Instructions regarding War Diaries and Intelligence Summaries are contained in F. S. Regs., Part II. and the Staff Manual respectively. Title pages will be prepared in manuscript.

WAR DIARY
or
~~INTELLIGENCE SUMMARY~~
(Erase heading not required.)

24th Divisional Train.

VR 35

Place	1918. JULY	Hour	Summary of Events and Information	Remarks and references to Appendices
VERDREL	1st		3 Reinforcements reported for duty - posted as follows :- 1 Sergt. and 1 Supply Detail to No. 4 Coy., 1 Dr. Farrier to No. 2 Coy for duty with 74th Field Ambulance. 2/Lieut. E. R. A. HODGMAN, A. S. C., returned from leave. Rev. H. KIDMAN, S. C. F. Non C. of E., attached to No. 3 Company, proceeded to England on termination of contract.	
"	2nd		Order received for T/Lieut. F. R. NEVILL, A. S. C., to report to O. C. 55th Divisional Train for duty (Authy :- Q. M. G., ASC/20803 dated 28-6-18) Rev. W. S. COOPER, C. F., non C. of E., reported to Train Headquarters and was attached to No. 3 Company.	
"	3rd		Normal routine.	
"	4th		T/Capt. F. W. L. MARTIN, M. C., A. S. C., and T/Capt. F. A. R. SAUNDERS, A. S. C., proceeded to England on 14 days leave. T/Lieut. F. R. NEVILL, A. S. C., left to join the 55th Divisional Train and was struck off the strength of No. 1 Company from 5-7-18. Sergt. TURNER A. (No. T4/237548) being surplus to establishment was ordered to proceed to A. S. C. Base Depot (H. T. & S.) HAVRE. Notice received that T/Capt. H. C. BOYS, A. S. C., 56th Divisional Train was reporting to 24th Divisional Train for duty. T/Lieut. J. O. TIDY, A. S. C., assumed duties of Adjutant during the absence of T/Capt. F. W. L. MARTIN, M. C., A. S. C., on leave to England.	
"	5th		O. C. Train visited D. A. D. T., First Army and was informed verbally that T/Capt. H. C. BOYS's. orders to join the Train had been cancelled.	
"	6th		Five Reinforcements reported for duty, 2 Bi Drivers were posted to No. 1 Company, 1 Bi Driver posted to No. 2 Company, 1 Corporal and 1 L/Corpl. were attached to No. 1 Company until further orders.	
"	7th		Normal routine.	
"	8th		L/Cpl. WRIGHT proceeded on one months re-engagement leave to England. 24th Divisional Train Fund Audit held at Train Headquarters.	
"	9th		O. C. Train visited D. D. S. & T. Major H. B. HUNTER, D. S. O., A. S. C. attended 24th Divisional Institute Audit.	

J. G. Galloway
LIEUT. COLONEL,
O.C. 24th DIVISIONAL TRAIN.

A5834 Wt. W4973 M687 750,000 8/16 D. D. & L. Ltd. Forms/C.2118/13.

Instructions regarding War Diaries and Intelligence Summaries are contained in F. S. Regs., Part II. and the Staff Manual respectively. Title pages will be prepared in manuscript.

WAR DIARY 24th Divisional Train.

or

~~INTELLIGENCE SUMMARY.~~

(*Erase heading not required.*)

Army Form C. 2118.

Place	1918. Date. JULY	Hour	Summary of Events and Information	Remarks and references to Appendices
VERDREL.	10th		Normal routine.	
"	11th		O. C. Train visited Corps M. T. Supply Column. 2/Lieut. H. ALPE, A. S. C., applied for special leave to England.	
"	12th		2/Lieut. ALPE's 14 days leave approved from July 17th to July 31st 1918.	
"	13th		24th Division Rear Headquarters moved to SAINS-en-GOHELLE from GOUY SERVINS. Corpl. DEATH C. S. (reinforcement) attached to No. 1 Coy., posted to No. 2 Company and taken on the strength. O. C. Train asked by "Q" to take over rear Headquarters.	
GOUY SERVINS	14th		Train Headquarters moved to rear Headquarters GOUY SERVINS. O. C. Train visited 56th Div. Train.	
"	15th		2/Lieut. H. W. BRADLEY 'phoned to say he had been granted special leave to England from 15-7-18. [illegible]. Received information that Major H. C. ROBINSON, A. S. C., had been granted an extension of leave on Medical Certificate pending further instructions. (Authy :- R. O./121 (Q. M. G. 5) dated 9-7-18.)	
"	16th		Normal routine.	
"	17th		O. C. Train attended Divl. Headquarters on committee re Brigade, Divisional and Corps Horse Shows. 2/Lieut. H. ALPE, A. S. C., proceeded to England on leave.	
"	18th		O. C. Train visited Railhead with A. A. & Q. M. G. O. C. Train visited D. D. S. T. with A. A. & Q. M. G. T/Capt. F. A. R. SAUNDERS, A. S. C., & T/Capt. E. W. L. MARTIN, M. C., A. S. C., returned from leave.	
"	19th		Normal routine. O. C. Train attended Horse Show Committee. Instructions received that the 3 Brigade Coys would have to move by 9 a.m., 20-7-18 from present camps. O. C. Train met A. A. & Q. M. G. and D. A. Q. M. G. at BOIS d'OLHAIN and selected new sites for camps. O. C. Train obtained permission from Corps "Q" later that Companies need not move until further instructions.	

LIEUT. COLONEL,
O.C. 24th DIVISIONAL TRAIN.

Army Form C. 2118.

Instructions regarding War Diaries and Intelligence Summaries are contained in F. S. Regs., Part II. and the Staff Manual respectively. Title pages will be prepared in manuscript.

WAR DIARY
or
~~INTELLIGENCE SUMMARY~~.

24th Divisional Train.

(*Erase heading not required.*)

Place	1918. Date JULY	Hour	Summary of Events and Information	Remarks and references to Appendices
GOUY SERVINS	20th		The wagons on North side of Road in BOIS d'OLHAIN ordered to be removed to South side by 12 noon. No. 4 Companys' wagons parked with No. 1 Company. No. 3 Companys' wagons moved to No. 4 Companys' old park. O. C. Train attended Horse Show Committee.	
"	21st		O. C. Train visited D. D. S. T., First Army re Divisional Horse Show. O. C. Train attended Divisional Horse Show Committee. 3 Reinforcements reported (1 Issuer to No. 2 Coy., 1 Driver to No. 3 Company and 1 to No. 4 Company). Informed that Major H. C. ROBINSON, A. S. C., had been granted further extension of leave on Medical grounds and that he would be boarded at an early date (Q. M. G., G. H. Q. No. ASC/20846/10 dated 18-7-18)	
"	22nd		O. C. Train visited D. D. S. T., First Army re Divisional Horse Show. O. C. Train attended Divisional Horse Show Committee. Instructions issued for Train Eliminating Horse Show to be held 23-7-18.	
"	23rd		Very wet all day. Train Show postponed. Informed by D. D. S. T., that T/2/Lt. W. SCARISBRICK, A. S. C., had been ordered to report for duty to this unit vice T/Capt. F. E. L. PHILP, A. S. C., (reported invalided) Q. M. G., G. H. Q. No. ASC/20967 dated 19-7-18. T/2/Lieut. E. R. A. HODGMAN, A. S. C. and party of 21 O. Rs. proceeded to No. 4 Base Remount Depot to collect remounts for the Division. 24th Divisional Train Order No. 30 issued.	A
"	24th		Railhead BARLIN. Supplies conveyed to Refilling Points by Horse Transport. Rations carried from Refilling Points by 1st Line Transport. Major NUSSY, South African Union Forces, attached to Division, studying administrative arrangements, attached to Train for 2 days. Visited Refilling Points and Railhead with S. S. O. and spent the afternoon with O. C. Train. T/2/Lieut. W. SCARISBRICK, A. S. C., reported for duty with this unit and posted to No. 3 Company. T/2/Lieut. E. R. A. HODGMAN, A. S. C. transferred to No. 1 Company from this date.	
"	25th		T/Capt. F. E. L. PHILP, A. S. C., reported invalided, struck off the strength of this unit as from 19-7-18. (Authy :- Q. M. G., G. H. Q. No. ASC/20967 dated 19-7-18). T/2/Lieut. G. J. MOTION, A. S. C., returned to duty after two months special leave. Major NUSSY continued his programme with this unit. Enemy aircraft active; - many bombs dropped in vicinity of Train Headquarters.	
"	26th		Wet. Normal routine.	

A. G. Galloway
LIEUT. COLONEL.
~~O.C.~~ 24th DIVISIONAL TRAIN.

A5834 Wt. W4973 M687 750,000 8/16 D. D. & L. Ltd. Forms/C.2118/13.

Army Form C. 2118.

Instructions regarding War Diaries and Intelligence Summaries are contained in F. S. Regs., Part II. and the Staff Manual respectively. Title pages will be prepared in manuscript.

WAR DIARY
or
~~INTELLIGENCE SUMMARY.~~

24th Divisional Train.

(Erase heading not required.)

Place	1918. Date JULY	Hour	Summary of Events and Information	Remarks and references to Appendices
GOUY SERVINS	27th		Informed that T/Capt. F. R. L. PHILP, A. S. C. was transferred to England 9-7-18 and should be struck off strength from that date. (Authy :- VIII Corps No. A1/1187/106 dated 22-7-18). T/2/Lieut. E. R. A. HODGMAN, A. S. C. i/c Remount party returned with 23 Remounts for the Division. Very wet & stormy. 24th Divisional Train Order No. 31 issued.	B
"	28th		Remounts distributed by T/2/Lieut. E. R. A. HODGMAN, A. S. C., at 10 a.m. (No. 1 Coy 6 H.D., No. 2 - 3 H.D., No. 3 - 4 H.D.)	
"	29th		O. C. Train attended Divisional Horse Show Committee meeting.	
"	30th		O. C. Train visited D. D. S. T., First Army. An Eliminating Show was held at VERDREL to select pairs for the Divisional Horse Show. Judges:- Brig-General E. S. HOARE-NAIRNE, C.B., C.M.G., R.A., Major ASCOTT, D.A.D.V.S., 56th Division, Capt. N. ZAMBRA, M.C., 24th D.A.C., and Capt. W. A. MACGREGER, A.V.C. Best universal turnout for a Company was awarded to No. 1 Company, No. 3 Company being second. D.D.S.T., First Army, O.C. 25th Divl. Train and Major NUSSY, S. African Forces were present.	
"	31st		O. C. Train visited Secretary First Army Horse Show.	

A G Galloway
LIEUT. COLONEL
O.C. 24th DIVISIONAL TRAIN.

A5834 Wt. W4973 M687 750,000 8/16 D. D. & L. Ltd. Forms/C.2118/13.

A

Copy No. 10

24th DIVISIONAL TRAIN ORDER NO. 30.

23rd JULY 1918.

1. Commencing to-morrow the 24th instant, Supplies will be drawn for all Groups from Railhead by Horse Transport. Railhead BARLIN.

2. The order and times of drawing will be as under :-

"B"	Group	9.00 a.m.
"C"	"	9.15 a.m.
"D"	"	9.30 a.m.
"A"	"	9.45 a.m.

3. Os.C. Companies will be informed by S.Os. concerned as to the strengths of their respective groups.

4. Supplies will be conveyed to present Refilling Points.

5. No restrictions as to route from Railhead to Refilling Points.

6. Supplies will remain at Refilling Points over night and be issued the following days as follows :-

"B"	Group	8.00 a.m.
"C"	"	8.00 a.m.
"D"	"	9.00 a.m.
"A"	"	9.30 a.m.

7. Supplies will be drawn from Refilling Point by units with their own transport.

8. Os.C. Train Companies to acknowledge.

A. Galloway

Lieut. Colonel.
O.C. 24th Divisional Train.

Copies to :-
1. 24th Division "Q".
2. O.C. Train.
3. S.S.O.
4. O.C. No. 1 Company.
5. O.C. No. 2 Company.
6. O.C. No. 3 Company.
7. O.C. No. 4 Company.
8. O.C., M.T. Company.
9. File.
10. War Diary.
11. " "
12. " "

"A1."

Copy No. 10.......

Amendment to
24th DIVISIONAL TRAIN ORDER NO. 29 dated 23-7-18.

The No. of the above Order will be amended to read :- "NO. 30".

A. G. Galloway
Lieut. Colonel.
O. C. 24th Divisional Train

Copies to :-
1. 24th Division "Q"
2. O. C. Train.
3. S. S. O.
4. O. C. No. 1 Company.
5. O. C. No. 2 Company.
6. O. C. No. 3 Company.
7. O. C. No. 4 Company.
8. O. C., M. T. Company.
9. File.
10. War Diary
11. " "
12. " "

B

Copy No. 10

24th DIVISIONAL TRAIN ORDER NO. 31.

-:-:-:-:-:-:-:-:-:-:-:-:-:-:-:-:-:-

27th JULY 1918.

1. Para. 2 of 24th Divisional Train Order No. 30 dated 23rd July 1918, is cancelled and the following substituted :-

"The order and times of drawing, from to-morrow the 28th July 1918, inclusive, will be as under :-

"B" Group	9-30 a.m.	
"C" "	9-45 a.m.	
"D" "	10-00 a.m.	
"A" "	10-15 a.m. "	

2. Os. C. Train Companies to acknowledge.

A E Galloway

Lieut. Colonel.
O. C. 24th Divisional Train.

Copies to :-
1. 24th Division "Q".
2. O. C. Train.
3. S. S. O.
4. O. C. No. 1 Company.
5. O. C. No. 2 Company.
6. O. C. No. 3 Company.
7. O. C. No. 4 Company.
8. O. C., M.T. Company.
9. File
10. War Diary
11. " "
12. " "

VR 36

C O N F I D E N T I A L.

W A R   D I A R Y.

O F

24th Divisional Train.

From:-   1st August 1918.   To:-   30th August 1918.

Instructions regarding War Diaries and Intelligence Summaries are contained in F. S. Regs., Part II. and the Staff Manual respectively. Title pages will be prepared in manuscript.

WAR DIARY
or
~~INTELLIGENCE SUMMARY~~.
(Erase heading not required.)

24th Divisional Train

Army Form C. 2118.

Place	1918 Date Aug.	Hour	Summary of Events and Information	Remarks and references to Appendices
GOUY SERVINS.	1st		A. D. M. S., 24th Division, accompanied by O. C. Train inspected the Train Camps in BOIS d'OLHAIN. O. C. Train acted as Judge at D. A. C., Horse Show. 2/Lieut. H. ALPE returned from leave. Owing to an accident on the line, the Pack Train did not arrive at Railhead. Oats drawn from HOUDAIN by H. T. Mens rations and hay drawn by M. T. from PERNES.	
"	2nd		Very wet. Normal routine.	
"	3rd		Lieut. C. C. GALE proceeded on 8 days leave to TOURS (France). 2/Lieut. H. ALPE acting as S. O., 17th Inf. Bde. during Lieut. GALE's absence. O. C. Train acted as Chief Judge at 73rd Brigade Horse Show and afterwards presented the prizes in the absence of the Brigadier General Commanding.	
"	4th		O. C. Train visited proposed Horse Show Ground with C. R. A. Informed that T/Major H. C. ROBINSON appeared before a Medical Board on 25-7-18 and was pronounced to be unfit for General Service for a period of 3 months and should be struck off strength (Authy :- Q. M. G., G. H. Q., A. S. C. No. 20846/10 dated 1-8-18)	
"	5th		O. C. Train visited 1st Division re Divisional Horse Show.	
"	6th		Horse Show business.	
"	7th		Horse Show business.	
"	8th		Horse Show business. 2/Lieut. J. T. COPPOCK, A. S. C., reported for duty, vice T/Major H. C. ROBINSON, and posted to No. 1 Company (Authy :- Q. M. G., G. H. Q., A. S. C. No. 21086/1 dated 2-8-18).	
"	9th		Divisional Horse Show held. A. S. C. turnsout won by No. 1 Company, 1st & 2nd. H. D. Horse stripped No. 1 Company 1st & 2nd. Open G. S. turnout with H. D. Horses, No. 1 Coy., 1st, No. 2 Coy. 2nd.	
"	10th		Normal routine.	

A G Galloway
LIEUT. COLONEL.
O.C. 24th DIVISIONAL TRAIN.

D. D. & L., London, E.C.
(10340) Wt W5300/P713 750,000 3/18 E 2688 Forms/C2118/16.

Army Form C. 2118.

Instructions regarding War Diaries and Intelligence Summaries are contained in F. S. Regs., Part II. and the Staff Manual respectively. Title pages will be prepared in manuscript.

WAR DIARY 24th Divisional Train.
or
~~INTELLIGENCE SUMMARY~~.
(Erase heading not required.)

Place	1918. Date Aug.	Hour	Summary of Events and Information	Remarks and references to Appendices
GOUY SERVINS.	11th		Normal routine. 1 H.D.Horse killed and 1 H.D.Horse wounded by bomb from E.A. (Baggage horses of No.4 Company, attached 9th R.Sussex) 2 H.D.Horses killed & 2 H.D.Horses wounded by bomb from E.A.) No.3 Company - attached 1st N.Staffs)	
"	12th		O.C.Train visited XIII Corps Horse Show at FERFAY.	
"	13th		Conference, which was attended by Os.C.Companies, held at Train Headquarters with the Divisional Education Officer. Prizes presented by G.O.C., at Div'l Headquarters, to winners at Divisional Horse Show. Tea for 200 men arranged by Divisional Train.	
"	14th		O.C.Train judged at VIII Corps Troops Horse Show held this day. Lieut. C.C.GALE returned from leave to TOURS. Vicinity of Refilling Point shelled - no damage or casualties.	
"	15th		Normal routine.	
"	16th		Supply vehicles of 52nd A.F.A.Bde. returned to unit from No.1 Company.	
"	17th		All attached units which had been rationed by this Division were handed over to Corps Troops rationed up to consumption 18-8-18 inclusive.	
"	18th		Normal routine. 15 G.S.Wagons turned out to collect green forage from LES BREBIS.	
"	19th		O.C.Train visited D.D.S.&T., and Camp Commandant, 1st Army.	
"	20th		Normal routine. 3 Reinforcements reported for duty and posted 1 driver to each Nos.1,2 & 3 Companies.	
"	21st		Normal routine. 2/Lt. J.T.COPPOCK attached to S.O., Divl.Troops from this date to be instructed in S.O's duties. Hostile aircraft active at night. Bombs dropped in vivinity of Train Hd.Qrs and Companies Camps. O.C.Train & Company Officers inspected model standings at No.10 Army Aux.Horse Coy. at OLHAIN at 11 a.m. under instructions of G.O.C., 24th Division. O.C.Train attended lecture by Corps Commander at 3 p.m., subject :- Repulse of German attack on 15-7-18, East of RHEIMS by 4th French Army.	

A.G.Galloway
LIEUT. COLONEL
O.C. 24th DIVISIONAL TRAIN.

D. D. & L., London, E.C.
(10340) Wt W5300/P713 750,000 3/18 E 2688 Forms/C2118/16.

Army Form C. 2118.

WAR DIARY

or

INTELLIGENCE SUMMARY.

24th Divisional Train.

(*Erase heading not required.*)

Instructions regarding War Diaries and Intelligence Summaries are contained in F. S. Regs., Part II. and the Staff Manual respectively. Title pages will be prepared in manuscript.

Place	1918. Date Aug.	Hour	Summary of Events and Information	Remarks and references to Appendices
GOUY SERVINS	22nd		Lieut. J. O. TIDY transferred from Train Headquarters to No. 4 Company, but to remain attached to Train Headquarters as Guns & Gas Officer. 2/Lieut. H. W. BRADLEY transferred from No. 4 Company to No. 1 Company, but to remain attached to S. M. T. O. VIII Corps. 2/Lt. J. T. COPPOCK transferred from No. 1 Company to Train Headquarters as Requisition Officer (Subaltern) but to remain attached to No. 1 Company A. A. & Q. M. G., O. C. Train, D. A. & Q. M. G., and Adjutant visited OLHAIN for the purpose of finding winter quarters for the Train Companies.	
"	23rd		O. C. Train assisted by Capt. G. E. PASMORE and Lt. J. O. TIDY judged 1st Line Transport of 73rd Inf. Bde at BULLY GRENAY to eliminate for Corps Commander's Cup. 2/Lt. H. J. LEWIS proceeded on leave to United Kingdom.	
"	24th		2/Lieut. E. R. A. HODGMAN proceeded i/c party to THEROUANNE to collect remounts for this Division. Capt. O. A. TUNNICLIFFE attached to the Train from this date for general instructions in connection with his Staff Course. VIII Corps Horse Show took place. Divisional Train entered for the three events open to it. H. D. Horse stripped - 1st prize No. 1 Company (Dr. BEAUMONT) 2nd-8th Divisional Train. G. S. turnout with N. C. O. - 1st prize No. 1 Coy. (Sgt. HILDON & Dr. EGGAR with pair of Greys), 2nd 20th Div'l. Train. Open G. S. turnout (open to all unit in Corps with H. D. Horses) 1st prize No. 1 Coy. (Dr. BEAUMONT) 2nd No. 2 Coy. (Dr. HANLIN) The prize winners now eligible to compete in the Army Horse Show. Enemy aircraft dropped 2 bombs in No. 3 Coy's lines at 10-30 p. m. one failed to explode. casualties 1 O. R. killed, 1 O. R. wounded.	
"	25th		Normal routine. No. T/33764, Dr. STANTON W., No. 3 Coy, killed by enemy bomb on 24-8-18 buried at BARLIN Military Cemetery.	
"	26th		Brig. General R. W. MORGAN, D. S. O., acting Divisional Commander, accompanied by A. A. & Q. M. G. inspected Train Camps in BOIS d'OLHAIN at 6 p. m. He expressed satisfaction. 2/Lt. E. R. A. HODGMAN returned with Remount Collecting Party conducting 22 Rdg., 7 L. D., 8 Mules and 6 H. D. for the Divn. Remounts distributed. Nos. 1 & 2 Coys 1 Rider each. Nos. 1 & 3 Coys 2 H. D. each.	

A G Galloway

LIEUT. COLONEL.
D.S. 24th DIVISIONAL TRAIN.

D. D. & L., London, E.C.
(10340) Wt W5300/P713 750,000 3/18 E 2688 Forms/C2118/16.

Instructions regarding War Diaries and Intelligence Summaries are contained in F. S. Regs., Part II. and the Staff Manual respectively. Title pages will be prepared in manuscript.

WAR DIARY 24th Divisional Train.

or

~~INTELLIGENCE SUMMARY~~.

(Erase heading not required.)

Army Form C. 2118.

Place	1918. Date Aug.	Hour	Summary of Events and Information	Remarks and references to Appendices
GOUY SERVINS.	27th		2/Lt. G. J. MOTION and batman and 1 Clerk detached to VIII Corps M. T. Coy. for supply duties from this date (Authy :- 24th Divn. No. Q. 2/299 dated 19-8-18) Lieut. J. B. STURGES, 8th Bn. Queens attached to Train (No. 4 Coy.) for instructional purposes from this date at the request of O. C. 8th Bn. Queens. Train Sports held at VERDREL at 2-15 p.m. Prizes presented by the Actg. Divisional Commander, Brig. General R. W. MORGAN, D. S. O.	
"	28th		O. C. Train accompanied by Capt. O. A. TUNNICLIFFE (under instructions) inspected 1st Line Transport of 1st Bn. R. Fusiliers. All baggage wagons returned to Train Companies from units.	
"	29th		Capt. O. A. TUNNICLIFFE returned to Div'l Headquarters his Course with Divisional Train having terminated. Both Sections of Train working - Baggage Section from Railhead to Refilling Point - Supply Section from Refilling Point to Units in normal manner.	
"	30th		Normal routine.	
"	31st		Capt. G. H. HITCH and a/Sergt COLE S. A. (No. 1 Coy) proceeded to No. 12 & 13 Veterinary Hospitals, NEUFCHATEL for 10 days to attend a Course in Veterinary work.	

O. G. Galloway
Lieut. Colonel.
O. C. 24th Divisional Train.

D. D. & L., London, E.C.
(10340) Wt W5300/P713 750,000 3/18 E 2688 Forms/C2118/16.

21

Instructions regarding War Diaries and Intelligence Summaries are contained in F. S. Regs., Part II. and the Staff Manual respectively. Title pages will be prepared in manuscript.

WAR DIARY or ~~INTELLIGENCE SUMMARY~~

(Erase heading not required.)

24th Divisional Train.

Army Form C. 2118.

Vol 37

Place	Date 1918 Sept.	Hour	Summary of Events and Information	Remarks and references to Appendices
GOUY SERVINS.	1st.		Lieut. STURGIS, 8th Queens returned to his Battalion from No. 4 Company.	
"	2nd		O. C. Train visited D. D. S. & T., First Army.	
"	3rd		O. C. Train assisted by Capt. K. M. PLUMPTRE and Lieut. J. O. TIDY judged 1st Line Transport of 17th Infantry Brigade in connection with competition for the Corps Commander's Cup. Results attached. 2/Lieut. J. O. TIDY promoted to be Lieut. to date from 21-6-18. 2/Lieut. H. W. BRADLEY promoted to be Lieut. to date from 1-7-18. (Authy :- "London Gazette Supplement" dated 31-8-18 and "Times" dated 2-9-18.	A
"	4th		Lecture delivered to all Companies on Traffic Control by D.A.P.M., 24th Division.	
"	5th		O. C. Train assisted by Lieut. TIDY and 2/Lt. DUNCAN judged 1st Line Transport of 72nd Infantry Brigade in connection with the Competition for the Corps Commander's Cup. Results attached. Audit Board assembled at Train Hd. Qrs at 2-30 p.m. to examine Canteen Accounts for July and August. President :- Major H. B. HUNTER, D. S. O. Members :- 2/Lt. A. C. CORBY and 2/Lt. E. P. A. HODGMAN.	A
"	6th		Normal routine.	
"	7th		O. C. Train assisted by Capt. K. M. PLUMPTRE inspected Transport of Divisional Hd. Qrs. Captain F. A. R. SAUNDERS arrived at Train Hd. Qrs. to understudy S. S. O.	
"	8th		O. C. Train attended meeting of Judges for Corps Commander's Cup held at "Q" Office at 6 p.m. 2/Lt. R. J. LEWIS returned from leave.	
"	9th		O. C. Train (Senior Judge & Referee), Capt. K. M. PLUMPTRE and Lieut. J. O. TIDY attended the judging of 3rd Rifle Brigade and M. G. Battalion transport in connection with Corps Commander's Cup.	
"	10th		Major H. B. HUNTER, D. S. O. proceeded on 14 days leave to U.K. Capt. F. A. R. SAUNDERS to be acting S. S. O. in his place. O. C. Train (Senior Judge & Referee), 2/Lt. J. W. DUNCAN, and Lt. J. O. TIDY attended judging of the 8th R. W. Kents and Pioneers Battn Transport in connection with the Corps Commander's Cup.	

A. Holloway
LIEUT. COLONEL.
O.C. 24th DIVISIONAL TRAIN.

D. D. & L., London, E.C. (10340) Wt W5300/P713 750,000 3/18 E 1688 Forms/C2118/16.

Instructions regarding War Diaries and Intelligence Summaries are contained in F. S. Regs., Part II. and the Staff Manual respectively. Title pages will be prepared in manuscript.

WAR DIARY 24th Divisional Train.

or

~~INTELLIGENCE SUMMARY~~.

(Erase heading not required.)

Army Form C. 2118.

Place	1918. Date Sept.	Hour	Summary of Events and Information	Remarks and references to Appendices
GOUY SERVINS.	10th		Capt. (a/Major) D. L. McCARRISON, A. S. C. (T. F.) reported for duty (Q. M. G., G. H. Q. No. ASC/21361/2 dated 4-9-18).	
"	11th		O. C. Train (Senior Judge & Referee), Capt. C. F. PASMORE and Lieut. J. O. TIDY attended the judging of the 9th R. Sussex and 104 Field Company R. Es. in connection with the Corps Commander's Cup. a/Major D. L. McCARRISON assumed command of No. 1 Company vice T/Major H. C. ROBINSON (invalided).	
"	12th		T/2/Lt. J. T. COPPOCK transferred to 1st Divisional Train from this date. (Authy Q. M. G., G. H. Q. No. ASC/21361/2 dated 4-9-18. Supplies for Infantry Battns of 17th Infantry Bde and 72nd Inf. Bde drawn by 1st Line Transport from Refilling Point from this date. 9 G. S. Wagons detailed daily from Nos. 2 & 3 Coys for No. 2 Canadian Forestry Coy, BOIS d'OLHAIN from this date.	
"	13th		A second day's rations delivered to 73rd Bde. Hd. Qrs., T. M. Batty and 3 Battns. of 73rd Brigade this date - two days rations will be held at the Q. M. Stores of these Units until further notice. Train wagons deliver the supplies immediately after they have been conveyed from Railhead to Refilling Point. Nos. 2 & 3 Coys moved to billets in OLHAIN (Authy :- Q. 326 dated 12-9-18).	
"	14th		a/Major D. L. McCARRISON admitted Hospital this day. The following changes in the duties of Officers took place as from this day. :- Capt. R. A. R. SAUNDERS to be in command of No. 1 Company temporarily, vice a/Major D. L. McCARRISON to hospital 14-9-18 - a/Capt. W. A. WATTS to be attached to S. O., 17th Inf. Bde under instruction in the duties of a Supply Officer. Lieut. A. H. BARNES to be acting S. O. Divl. Troops. - 2/Lt. E. R. A. HODGMAN to return to duty as a Transport Officer - Capt. R. F. SEDDALL to be acting S. S. O. vice Capt. R. A. R. SAUNDERS, during the absence on leave of Major H. B. HUNTER, D. S. O. - 2/Lt. W. SCARISBRICK to be acting S. O. 72nd Inf. Bde. during Capt. R. F. SEDDALL's absence at Train Hd. Qrs. Pack Train did not arrive until 3 p.m. Capt. G. H. HITCH returned from Veterinary Course.	
"	15th		A second day's rations delivered to 17th Bde. H. Q., T. M. Batty., and 3 Battns this date - two days rations will be held at the Q. M. Stores of these Units until further notice.	
"	16th		Conference of O. C. Train and Company Commanders held at No. 1 Company.	
"	17th		Normal routine.	

[signature]
LIEUT. COLONEL,
O.C. 24th DIVISIONAL TRAIN.

D. D. & L., London, E.C.
(10340) Wt W5300/P713 750,000 3/18 E 2688 Forms/C2118/16.

24th Divisional Train.

WAR DIARY
or
~~INTELLIGENCE SUMMARY.~~
(Erase heading not required.)

Army Form C. 2118.

Instructions regarding War Diaries and Intelligence Summaries are contained in F. S. Regs., Part II. and the Staff Manual respectively. Title pages will be prepared in manuscript.

Place	Date 1918 Sept.	Hour	Summary of Events and Information	Remarks and references to Appendices
GOUY SERVINS	18th		Normal routine.	
"	19th		Normal routine.	
"	20th		O. C. Train attended the final judging of 8th R.W.Kents and 9th R.Sussex 1st Line Transport by the Corps Commander's Judges. Capt. G.H.HITCH proceeded on leave to U.K. for 14 days.	
"	21st		Remounts 1 L.D. & 6 H.D. collected (No.3 Coy 2 H.D.,No.4 Coy 1 L.D.& 4 H.D.)	
"	22nd		3 Reinforcements B1 reported for duty and posted to No.4 Company.	
"	23rd		O. C. Train visited D.D.S.&.T.,1st Army accompanied by Adjutant.	
"	24th		Normal routine.	
"	25th		24th Division Warning Order No.2 received at 11 a.m.	
"	26th		24th Division Order No.247 received at 10-15 a.m. 24th Divl.Train Order No.32 issued at 6 p.m. Copy attached. Major H.B.HUNTER,D.S.O. returned from leave.	"B"
27th	27th		Normal routine.	
"	28th		The following changes in the duties of Officers took place as from this date :- 2/Lt. A.C.CORBY to be S.O.,Divl.Troops and to be transferred to No.1 Company - Lieut. A.H.BARNES to return to duty as a Transport Officer - a/Capt.W.A.WATTS to be S.O.,73rd Inf.Bde vice 2/Lt. A.C.CORBY,and to be transferred to No.4 Company. - Capt.R.R.SEDDALL to resume duties of S.O. 72nd Inf.Bde. - 2/Lt.W.SCARISBRICK to return to duty as a Transport Officer. 24th Divl.Train Orders Nos.33 & 34 and Supply Group Table No.9 issued this day. O.C.58th Divl. Train and S.S.O. visited Train Hd.Qrs.re taking over.	"C" "D" & "E"

A.J.Galloway
Lieut. Colonel,
O.C. 24th Divisional Train.

D. D. & L., London, E.C.
(10340) Wt W5300/P713 750,000 3/18 E 2688 Forms/C2118/16.

WAR DIARY 24th Divisional Train.

Army Form C. 2118.

or

~~INTELLIGENCE SUMMARY~~

(Erase heading not required.)

Instructions regarding War Diaries and Intelligence Summaries are contained in F. S. Regs., Part II. and the Staff Manual respectively. Title pages will be prepared in manuscript.

Place	1918. Date Sept.	Hour	Summary of Events and Information	Remarks and references to Appendices
GOUY SERVINS.	29th.		O. C. Train went round New area and selected billets for Divisional Transport in Staging area and Refilling Points in Rest Area. Lt. G. J. MOTION returned to Train from VIII Corps M. T. Coy. and attached to No. 2 Company for duty. Rations for consumption 30th instant and 1st prox by Train Parties, were delivered to all units except the Divisional Artillery. For those units who entrained on 30th instant, rations for consumption by Train Party on 1st prox were delivered by lorry in new area. Rations for consumption on the 1st prox by Road Parties were loaded on Supply Sections and taken to Company Lines.	
"	30th		24th Divl. Train Order No. 35 and Orders for March of Division Transport issued this day (copy attached) Train Headquarters marched out at 8 a.m. All Division Transport (with exception of	F G
ETREE WAMIN	30th	4 pm.	Divl. Artillery) marched to Staging area under command of O. C. Train. Train H. Q. & Nos. 2, 3 & 4 Coys proceeded to ETREE WAMIN arriving between 3-30 & 4-30 p.m. 17th Inf. Bde. Transport staged in PENIN area, 72nd Bde. BERLENCOURT, 73rd Bde. IZEL & MANIN. Supplies delivered to Road parties at termination of march. Supplies for consumption 1-10-18 dumped by lorry at new Refilling Point vide Train Order No. 35. No. 1 Company left behind with 24th Divl. Artillery and will draw from 58th Div. Pack.	

Lieut. Colonel.
O. C. 24th Divisional Train.

D. D. & L., London, E.C.
(10340) Wt W5300/P713 750,000 3/18 E 2688 Forms/C2118/16.

24th D I V I S I O N.

Result of Inspection of First Line Transport
for Corps Commander's Cup.

"A"

14th Sept. 1918.

U N I T.	HARNESS. Draught.	HARNESS. Pack.	HARNESS. Riders.	ANIMALS. Draught.	ANIMALS. Pack.	ANIMALS. Riders.	VEHICLES. Vehicles.	VEHICLES. Water Carts.	VEHICLES. Cookers or Pontoons.	MEN. Mounted.	MEN. Dis-mounted.	TOTALS.	Order.
Maximum.	180.	60.	30.	420.	140.	70.	300.	300.	300.	100.	100.	2000.	
8th R. W. Kents.	137.46.	47.83.	19.	397.57.	129.14.	64.	275.62.	254.5.	227.5.	92.70.	94.13.	1739.45	1st
9th Royal Sussex.	123.22.	46.83.	2[illegible].	393.82.	130.83.	56.50.	280.83.	211.	245.75.	95.73.	97.75.	1703.43.	2nd
3rd Rifle Bde.	145.59.	54.83.	23.50.	382.14.	120.	59.	278.24.	227.	197.25.	90.63.	89.44.	1667.62.	3rd
104th Fld. Coy. R. E.	124.93.	31.50.	14.	394.50.	133.25.	61.83.	284.30.	136.	278.	95.91.	94.08.	1648.30.	4th
12th Sher. Foresters.	134.45.	50.54.	24.50.	394.47.	129.08.	60.	233.5.	142.5.	233.6.	94.00.	94.64.	1591.28.	5th
24th M. G. Battn.	100.*		19.6.	495.69.*		57.25.	233.05.	112.75.	10.2.	90.01.	97.00.	1215.55.	6th

* As pack animals were shown in draught and pack saddlery shown with other harness, draught and pack animals and draught and pack harness were marked collectively, and not separately as in the case of other units.

A. Galloway.
Lieut. Colonel.
O.C. 24th Divisional Train.
Senior Judge & Referee.

"B"

S E C R E T.

Copy No. 9....

24TH DIVISIONAL TRAIN ORDER NO.32.

26th September 1918.

1. It is anticipated that there will be considerable hostile retaliation possible extending to the rearward parts of the Divisional area, and probably including the use of gas shell, during to-morrow the 27th instant.

2. All personnel proceeding forward of Refilling Point will wear Box Respirators in the alert position. Officers and W.Os. in charge of convoys will be responsible that Box Respirators are adjusted in the alert position before any personnel or turnsout leave Refilling Point.

3. Company Gas N.C.Os., will inspect the Box Respirators of all personnel going forward of Refilling Point.

4. Company Commanders will see that all horses proceeding forward of Refilling Point carry Gas Respirators, so far as the numbers in possession will permit. The horses going farthest forward will be given preference.

A. Galloway
Lieut. Colonel.
O.C. 24th Divisional Train.

Issued at 6 p.m.

Copies to :-

1. O.C. Train.
2. S.S.O.
3. O.C. No.1 Company.
4. O.C. No.2 Company.
5. O.C. No.3 Company.
6. O.C. No.4 Company.
7. Orderly S.O. (for information of all S.Os.)
8. File.
9. War Diary.
10. War Diary.
11. War Diary.

S E C R E T. "C" Copy No. 11

24th DIVISIONAL TRAIN ORDER NO. 33.

28th SEPTEMBER 1918.

1. Baggage Wagons will be sent out to all Units, except Divisional Artillery, but including S. A. A. Section of the D. A. C., at 7 a.m. to-morrow the 29th instant.

2. Supplies will be drawn from Railhead to-morrow for "B", "C", and "D" Groups by the 24th Divl. M. T. Company. Supplies for "A" Group will be drawn by horse transport as usual.

3. Supplies for consumption 30th instant will be delivered to units in the normal manner to-morrow the 29th instant.

4. Supplies for consumption 1st October will also be delivered to-morrow. Detailed instructions as to these supplies will be issued later.

A G Galloway
Lieut-Colonel.
O. C. 24th Divisional Train.

Copies to :-
1. 24th Division "Q".
2. O. C. Train.
3. S. S. O.
4. O. C. No. 1 Company.
5. O. C. No. 2 Company.
6. O. C. No. 3 Company.
7. O. C. No. 4 Company.
8. Orderly S. O. (for information of all S. Os.)
9. O. C. 24th M. T. Coy. & S. O., 24th M. T. Coy.
10. File.
11. War Diary
12. War Diary
13. War Diary.

S E C R E T.   "D"   Copy No. 11...

24th DIVISIONAL TRAIN ORDER NO. 34.

28th SEPTEMBER 1918.

1. The 24th Division, less Artillery, is being relieved in the line by the 58th Division on 28th, 29th, and 30th instants.
On relief 24th Division is being transferred to the Third Army by tactical train and road on September 30th and October 1st., and will be accommodated in the HUMBERCOURT area (East of DOULLENS), with Divisional Headquarters at LUCHEUX.

2. Extracts from Relief Table are attached hereto. (Enclosure "A" with Copies 2, 4, 5, 6, 7, & 8.)

3. (a) Transport is marching on September 30th to FREVIN sub-area.

(b) Route :- BOYEFFLES - BOUVIGNY - PETIT SERVINS - GRAND SERVINS - VILLERS CAMBLIGNEUL - AUBIGNY - SAVY - FREVIN.

(c) Billets from sub-area Commandant FREVIN.

(d) Baggage wagons will accompany 1st line transport of units.

(e) Normal halts and intervals will be observed.

(f) After passing LES 4 VENTS the whole column will be under the command of O. C., Divisional Train.

(g) The march will be resumed on October 1st to the HUMBERCOURT area under orders of Third Army to be sent c/o sub-area Commandant, FREVIN.

(h) Transport of Divisional Headquarters will march direct to LUCHEUX on September 30th under command of the Camp Commandant.

4. Train Headquarters and Heads of Train Coys will pass the Starting Point at LES 4 VENTS (W.G. Central. Sheet 36b) as follows :-

Train Headquarters.	8-40 a.m.	30.9.18.
No. 2 Coy.	8-45 a.m.	"
No. 3 Coy.	8-55 a.m.	"
No. 4 Coy.	9 a.m.	"

5. No. 36 M.V.S. will march in rear of No. 2 Coy. passing the starting point at 8-53 a.m.

6. Nos. 2 & 3 Coys will proceed to the Starting Point via :- GAUCHIN - LEGAL and ESTREE CAUCHIE. No. 4 Coy via VERDREL and GRAND SERVINS.

7. Supplies.
(a) Units have been instructed to inform their Group Supply Officers the respective strengths of the ROAD and RAIL Parties at Refilling Points tomorrow morning, 29th instant.
(b) The Supplies drawn from Railhead to-morrow the 29th instant for consumption 1st prox., will be immediately dumped at present Refilling Points and split up into the requirements of ROAD and RAIL Parties. The Rations for consumption on 1st prox. by RAIL Parties of the following Units will be taken to-morrow, 29th instant, by Lorries to Billets in the New Area. These Lorries will be loaded immediately the above splitting up has been completed and will proceed to FREVIN, where they will be met by O. C. Train at the Area Commandant's Office and given their final destinations. S.S.O. will arrange to send one Supply Detail with each lorry to guard supplies when dumped.

H.Q. 73rd Brigade.	103 Field Coy R.E.	Pioneer Bn.
3 Bns. " "	~~[illegible]~~	H.Q., 24th Division.
	73rd Field Ambulance.	24th Bn. M.G.C.

(c) The Rations for consumption on 1st prox. by RAIL Parties of all other units of the Division will be delivered to Units as early as possible after dumping to-morrow, 29th instant.

(d) The Rations for consumption on 1st prox. by ROAD Parties will be loaded on the Supply Wagons to-morrow afternoon, 29th inst, and the loaded wagons parked in Train Coy lines, except Divl H.Q. Supply Wagon which will be sent to Divl. H.Q. Supply Officers of "B" and "D" Groups will, however, bear in mind that a few turnsout of their Brigades may be left behind on 30th inst to march straight through on 1st prox. The Rations of these turnsout must be delivered to Units to-morrow, 29th inst, with those of the RAIL Parties. The numbers of such Turnsout and their Ration Strengths will be notified from this office as soon as known, but Supply Officers concerned must also ascertain Ration Strengths direct from Brigades and Units concerned.

(e) Rations for consumption by all Units on 2nd prox. will be picked up at Refilling Points in the New Area on termination of march on 1st prox. and at once delivered to Units. Locations of Refilling Points will be notified later.

8. Copies of Administrative Instructions are attached hereto. (Enclosures "B" & "C" with Copies 2, 4, 5, 6, 7, & 8.)

9. Supply Group Table No. 9 issued herewith.

10. Recipients of Copies Nos. 4, 5, 6, 7, & 8 to acknowledge.

C G Galloway
Lieut. Colonel.
O.C. 24th Divisional Train.

Copies to :-
1. 24th Division "Q".
2. O.C. Train.
3. S.S.O.
4. O.C. No. 1 Company.
5. O.C. No. 2 Company.
6. O.C. No. 3 Company.
7. O.C. No. 4 Company.
8. Orderly S.O. (for information of all S.Os)
9. O.C. & S.O., 24th M.T. Coy (for information)
10. File.
11. War Diary.
12. War Diary.
13. War Diary.

E

SUPPLY GROUP TABLE NO. 9.

(To take effect on A.R.V. 3316 and 3317 - 29-9-18
(At Railhead 30-9-18.
(For consumption 2-10-18.

GROUP "A" R.P. :- As at present.	GROUP "B" R.P. :-	GROUP "C" R.P. :-	GROUP "D". R.P. :-
C. R. A. 106th Bde., R.F.A. 107th Bde., R.F.A. D.A.C. (less S.A.A. Sect.) 24th T.M. Battery. No. 1 Company, Train.	H.Q. 17th Inf. Bde. 17th T.M. Battery 3rd Rifle Bde. 1st R. Fusiliers. 8th Queens. No. 2 Company, Train. 74th Field Ambulance. 104th Field Coy. R.E. H.Q., 24th Division. C. R. E. 24th Signal Coy. R.E. A. O. D. H.Q., Divl. Train. 36th M.V. Section.	H.Q. 72nd Inf. Bde. 72nd T.M. Battery. 9th E. SURREYs. 8th R.W. Kents. 1st North Staffs. No. 3 Company, Train. 72nd Field Ambulance. 103rd Field Coy. R.E. 24th M.G. Battn. S.A.A. Section D.A.C.	H.Q. 73rd Inf. Bde. 73rd T.M. Battery. 9th R. Sussex. 7th Northants. 13th Middlesex. No. 4 Company, Train. 12th Sherwood Foresters. 73rd Field Ambulance. 129th Field Coy. R.E.
10th Aux. H.T. Company. Town Major, SAINS-en-GOHELLE " " BULLY GRENAY. " " LES BREBIS. Y.M.C.A. SAINS. " MARQUEFFLES.			

G. K. Galloway (signature)

Lieut. Colonel.
O.C. 24th Divisional Train.

SECRET

"F"

Copy No. 7.

24th Divisional Train Order No 35

29th September 1918.

1. Refilling Points for Supplies for consumption 2nd and 3rd October, which will be dumped on the 30th and 1st, will be as follows:–

"B" GROUP. On South side of road, beneath high wall just East of Church at BREVILLERS.

"C" GROUP. On East side of road running South from BEAUDRICOURT but North of the IVERGNY – SUS-ST-LEGER Cross-roads.

"D" GROUP On the MONDICOURT – GRINCOURT Road, 400 yards east of the MONDICOURT – PAS Road

2. Company Commanders in conjunction with Supply Officers will send one senior supply N.C.O. and at least 3 supply details (more if desired) to join the 24th M.T. Coy at VERDREL by 8-30 am tomorrow the 30th instant to proceed with the Column & guard the supplies that will be dumped at the above places on the above dates

No 4 Company will drop the above supply details on passing through VERDREL.

No 1 Company will provide a Limber at OLHAIN at 7-30 am to take the kits of the supply details of Nos 2 & 3 Coys to VERDREL.

A. G. Galloway

Lieut-Colonel

OC 24th Divisional Train

Copies to:-

1. OC Train
2. OC No 1 Coy
3. OC No 2 Coy
4. OC No 3 Coy
5. OC No 4 Coy
6. 24th M.T. Coy
7. War Diary
8. War Diary

"G"

Copy No.......11

MARCH ORDERS FOR 24th DIVISION TRANSPORT
BY
Lieut-Col. A. G. GALLOWAY, D. S. O., O. C., 24th Divl. Train.

Sent

29th SEPT. 1918.

1. Halts and Distances will be as follows :-

HALTS.

9.50 a.m. - 10 a.m.
10.50 a.m. - 11 a.m.
11.50 a.m. - 1.30 a.m.

and from 10 minutes to every half hour to the half hour, commencing with halt at 2.20 p.m.

DISTANCES.

In accordance with S.S. 724, viz :-

Between Brigade Groups	500 yards
" Units	100 "
" each Section of 12 Vehicles	50 "
Between Train & S. A. A. Section D. A. C. and between S. A. A. Section D. A. C. and 72nd Brigade Group	200 "

2. Cross Roads and ~~Cross~~ Road Junctions must be left clear at all Halts. No Halts will be made in the main streets of Towns or Villages or on Bridges.

3. From AUBIGNY to SAVY the road North of the Railway will be taken.

4. Billeting Areas will be as follows :-

17th Inf. Bde. Group	PENIN. FERME DOFFINE. VILLERS-SIR-SIMON
72nd Inf. Bde. Group including Pioneer Bn.	BERLENCOURT.
73rd Inf. Bde. Group including 24th M. G. Bn.	~~HAMEAU~~ IZEL-LEZ-HAMEAU. GIVENCHY-LE-NOBLE. WAMIN.
Train H. Q., and 3 Coys. S. A. A. Section, D. A. C.	ETREE-WAMIN.

5. (a) B. T. Os. 17th and 73rd Brigades will send Billeting Parties of one Officer from the Group and 1 N. C. O. from each Unit in advance to Sub-Area Commandant, PENIN Area, whose office is at VILLERS-SIR-SIMON, to take over and allot billets.

(b) B. T. O., 72nd Brigade will send Billeting Party of one Officer from the Group and 1 N. C. O. from each Unit, in advance, to Sub-Area Commandant BERLENCOURT to take over and allot billets.

(c) The Divisional Train will send the Interpreter and one Officer from the Train and 1 N. C. O. from each Company, in advance, to Town Major ETREE WAMIN, to take over and allot billets for the Train and S. A. A. Section D. A. C. The latter unit will send one senior N. C. O. to take over billets from the Officer of the Train.

6. B. T. Os. 17th and 73rd Brigades will report their exact locations to the Sub-Area Commandant PENIN, for the information of O. C. 24th Divisional Train.

B. T. O., 72nd Brigade will report his exact location to O. C. Train.

7. The march to the New Area will be continued on 1st prox. as follows :-

Group.	Starting Point.	Time.	Route.
(a) S. A. A. Section.	ETREE-WAMIN.	8 a.m.	BEAUDRICOURT. SUS-ST-LEGER.
(b) 17th Brigade.	AMBRINES.	8.30 a.m.	ETREE-WAMIN. BEAUDRICOURT. IVERGNY.
(c) 72nd Brigade.	ETREE-WAMIN.	8.30 a.m.	ETREE-WAMIN. BEAUDRICOURT.
(d) 73rd Brigade.	WAMIN.	8 a.m.	AVESNES-LE-COMTE. BARLY. + SAULTY.
(e) Train. 4 Coy.	ETREE-WAMIN.	8.15 a.m.	ETREE-WAMIN. BEAUDRICOURT. IVERGNY. LUCHEUX.
(f) " 3 Coy.	"	To follow 72nd Bde. Group.	
(g) " 2 Coy.	"	To follow 17th Bde Group.	

8. B.T.Os. will synchronise watches with O.C. Train at Starting Point (Les 4 Vents)

9. Train Headquarters will be at ETREE-WAMIN on night of 30th inst/1st prox.

A.G. Galloway
Lieut. Colonel.
O.C. 24th Divisional Train.

Copies to:-

1. 24th Division "Q".
2. O.C. Train.
3. B.T.O., 17th Inf. Bde.
4. B.T.O., 72nd Inf. Bde.
5. B.T.O. 73rd Inf. Bde.
6. O.C. No. 2 Train Coy.
7. O.C. No. 3 Train Coy.
8. O.C. No. 4 Train Coy.
9. O.C. S.A.A. Section D.A.C.
10. File.
11. War Diary.
12. War Diary.

Issued at Starting Point on 30.9.18.

7

Instructions regarding War Diaries and Intelligence Summaries are contained in F. S. Regs., Part II. and the Staff Manual respectively. Title pages will be prepared in manuscript.

WAR DIARY 24th Divisional Train.
or
~~INTELLIGENCE SUMMARY.~~
(Erase heading not required.)

Army Form C. 2118.

Vol 38

Place	Date 1918 October	Hour	Summary of Events and Information	Remarks and references to Appendices
ETREE-WAMIN. LUCHEUX.	1st	08.45 11.30	Train Headquarters marched to new area. Train Headquarters arrived LUCHEUX. Divisional Transport resumed its march and proceeded under instructions given by O. C. Train to B. T. Os. of Brigades. No. 2 Company marched to LE SUICH. No. 3 Company to WARLUZEL. No. 3 Company to BOUT DES PRES. Railhead SAULTY. Refilling took place in new area and supplies for consumption 2nd instant immediately delivered to units.	
LUCHEUX	2nd		Normal routine.	
"	3rd		Normal routine. 24th Division Warning Order No. 1 received. The Division (less Divl. Artillery) transferred to XVII Corps, Third Army.	
"	4th		24th Division Order No. 250 received. 24th Divisional Train Order No. 36 issued at 13.30. Supplies for consumption 6th instant by rail parties issued this afternoon - those for road parties to be conveyed by supply wagons. X 24th Divisional Train Order No. 37 issued at 1930. * March Orders for 24th Division Transport issued at 23.00.	A X B * B1
"	5th		Railhead SAULTY. Train Headquarters marched from LUCHEUX at 09.30. 1st Line Transport of the Division (less Divl. Artillery) and Train Transport marched under orders of the O. C. Train from the LUCHEUX Rest Area to Staging area at BOISLEUX AU MONT. Route from X Roads S. E. of COUTURELLE - LAHERLIE, X Roads N. W. of RIVIERE - RIVIERE, BRETENCOURT - FICHEUX. Supply wagons carried rations for road party. O. C. Train and Adjutant proceeded to BOISLEUX and arranged with Town Major for bivouacing for the night. 1st transport (73rd Brigade) started to arrive at 17.00 and last transport of 17th Brigade pulled in at 20.00.	
BOISLEUX-AU-MONT	"	18.00	O. C. Train returned to 24th Divisional Headquarters at LUCHEUX in the afternoon for further orders. Verbal orders issued to B. T. Os. for continuation of march on the 6th instant.	

W. G. Galloway
LIEUT. COLONEL.
O.C. 24th DIVISIONAL TRAIN.

D. D. & L., London, E.C.
(10340) Wt W5300/P713 750,000 3/18 E 2683 Forms/C2118/16.

Instructions regarding War Diaries and Intelligence Summaries are contained in F. S. Regs., Part II. and the Staff Manual respectively. Title pages will be prepared in manuscript.

WAR DIARY or ~~INTELLIGENCE SUMMARY~~. 24th Divisional Train.

Army Form C. 2118.

(Erase heading not required.)

Place	Date 1918. October	Hour	Summary of Events and Information	Remarks and references to Appendices
BOISLEUX-AU-MONT.	6th		Winter time commenced at 01.00 hours this day. Railhead VAULX-VRAUCOURT - Supplies dumped at Refilling Point on VAULX-VRAUCOURT - MORCHIES Road. Supply Sections marched off at 07.00 and proceeded direct to Refilling Point as above. The Division transport continued the march - pulling out after the Supply Sections of the Train in the order of 73rd Brigade, 17th Brigade, 72nd Brigade, and proceeded via BOISLEUX St. Marc - BOYELLES - ERVILLERS - MORY - VAULX-VRAUCOURT to LAGNICOURT. The head of column reached latter place at 11.15 hours, mid-day halt took place.	
		09.00	O.C. Train and Adjutant proceeded direct to MOEUVRES and met Capt. HEATON of "Q" Staff. Ground for camping about E.19 and 25 (sheet 57c) arranged and allotted to Brigades representatives.	
		11.45	O.C. Train returned to the transport column and informed B.T.Os. Brigades of the location of their camps. He then proceeded to Refilling Point and gave the same instructions to Officers i/c Supply Sections. Train Headquarters marched into MOEUVRES at 17.00 hours. Capt. HITCH returned from leave.	
MOEUVRES	7th		Refilling Point same as for 6/10/18. Supply wagons arrived at Refilling Point at noon - watered and fed and proceeded to units Q.M. Stores. Supplies for consumption 9th instant conveyed from Railhead VAULX-VRAUCOURT by Decauville to Refilling Point, D.30.b. (sheet 57c.). 9 G.S. Wagons proceeded to Corps Headquarters to collect and convey Battle Stores to D.A.D.O.S. at E.19.d.8.0. Train Companies locations as follows :- No. 2 Company D.29.b.5.3.) No. 3 Company D.30.c.5.5.) Sheet 57c. No. 4 Company D.30.central)	
"	8th		Refilling took place at 09.00 hours at Decauville Railhead, D.30.b., and supplies immediately delivered to Units. Supplies for consumption 10th instant delivered in the late afternoon to 73rd Brigade Headquarters, T.M. Batty. and 3 Battalions.	
"	~~9th~~			

[signature]
LIEUT. COLONEL.
O.C. 24th DIVISIONAL TRAIN.

D. D. & L., London, E.C.
(10340) Wt W5300/P713 750,000 3/18 E 2688 Forms/C2118/16.

Army Form C. 2118.

WAR DIARY
or
~~INTELLIGENCE SUMMARY.~~

24th Divisional Train.

Instructions regarding War Diaries and Intelligence Summaries are contained in F. S. Regs., Part II. and the Staff Manual respectively. Title pages will be prepared in manuscript.

(*Erase heading not required.*)

Place	Date 1918 October	Hour	Summary of Events and Information	Remarks and references to Appendices
MOEUVRES	9th		Refilling Point D. 30. b. (sheet 57c.). Train Companies ordered to move at 14. 30 hours. Company H. Q. marched off at 16. 30 hours to FONTAINE. Supply wagons refilled and followed on. O. C. Train left MOEUVRES at 15. 45 hours and proceeded to Divisional Headquarters at Quarries near RUMILLY and returned to FONTAINE where he met the Adjutant and Company Commanders O. C. Train and Adjutant at Advanced Train H. Q., FONTAINE. S. S. O. and Gas Officer remained at MOEUVRES. Divisional Canteen Officer billeted with rear Train H. Q. this night.	
FONTAINE	10th		O. C. Train and Adjutant proceeded to Div'l H. Q. at 08. 30 and 12. 30 hours. Rear Train Headquarters marched into FONTAINE at 09. 30. Supply wagons left at 15. 30 to deliver to units at B. 4. a. & c. (sheet 57b), and got back to camps at midnight. O. C. Train, Adjutant and	
AWOINGT	"		Company Commanders proceeded to AWOINGT to select camps for Companies. Supplies conveyed from Railhead VAULX-VRAUCOURT to F. 22. b. (sheet 57b) by Decauville. Div'l H. Q. "Q" located at A. 18. b. 5. 4. (sheet 57b) in CAMBRAI.	
"	11th		Supplies conveyed from Decauville Railhead at F. 22. b. to Refilling Point, B. 25. b. (sheet 57b) by Lorry - Supply wagons refilled at 10. 30 hours and stood by for orders. Orders issued at 14. 00 for supply wagons to deliver to Units. Railhead MARCOING. Canteen Stores for distribution to units arrived 23. 00 hours. O. C. Train visited "Q" at 09. 00 hours. S. S. O. visited "Q" at 14. 00 hours. O. C. Train visited "Q" at 18. 00 hours.	
"	12th		Lorries dumped supplies at Refilling Point at B. 25. b. (sheet 57b). Supplies delivered to units in late afternoon and evening. Canteen stores sent up to units on supply wagons. O. C. Train & S. S. O. visited "Q" at 09. 00. S. S. O. and Adjutant visited "Q" at 14. 00 hours and brought back free gift of Cigarettes and Chocolates for Train. O. C. Train visited "Q" at 16. 00 hours. Adjutant visited "Q" at 18. 00 hours.	
"	13th		Lorries dumped supplies at Refilling Point at B. 25. b. (sheet 57b). Supplies delivered to units of 73rd Brigade immediately - to other units in afternoon. O. C. Train and Adjutant visited "Q" at 10. 00 hours and arranged Refilling Point for lorries to dump in afternoon at U. 25. b. 3. 0. (sheet 51A) O. C. Train and Adjutant visited "Q" at AVESNES at 13. 30 hours. S. S. O. visited "Q" at AVESNES at 16. 00 hours.	

LIEUT. COLONEL.
O.C. 24th DIVISIONAL TRAIN.

(10340) Wt W5300/P713 750,000 3/18 E 2688 Forms/C2118/16. D. D. & L., London, E.C.

WAR DIARY 24th Divisional Train. Army Form C. 2118.

or

~~INTELLIGENCE SUMMARY~~.

(Erase heading not required.)

Instructions regarding War Diaries and Intelligence Summaries are contained in F. S. Regs., Part II. and the Staff Manual respectively. Title pages will be prepared in manuscript.

Place	Date 1918 October	Hour	Summary of Events and Information	Remarks and references to Appendices
AWOINGT.	14th		Capt. R. R. SEDDALL proceeded on 14 days special leave to U.K. 15-10-18 to 29-10-18. Supply wagons refilled at U.25.b.3.0. (sheet 51a), at 08.00 and supplies delivered to Units in the morning. O.C. Train and Adjutant visited "Q" at 10.00 hours. S.S.O. and Adjutant visited "Q" at 15.30 hours. Capt. C. C. GALE proceeded on 14 days leave to U.K. 16-10-18 to 30-10-18.	
"	15th		Refilling Point as for 14-10-18. Adjutant visited "Q" at 09.00 hours. 24th Division Order No. 258 received 09.30 hours. O.C. Train visited "Q" at 14.00 hours. 2 O.R. wounded, 1 by partially buried shell which exploded and 1 by detonator. 2 H.D. Horses killed and 1 wounded (since died) by same shell. S.S.O. visited "Q" at 6 p.m. and handed rations to French Mission for civilians liberated from HAUSSY. Orders received at 22.15 hours that supplies would be drawn from Railhead ~~xxxxx~~ from 16th instant and until further orders by H.T.	
"	16th		Railhead CAMBRAI ANNEXE. O.C. Train and Adjutant visited "Q" at 10.00 hours. 100 British rations sent up to French Mission for civilians liberated from HAUSSY. Capt. K. M. PLUMPTRE proceeded on leave to U.K. for 14 days, 18-10-18 to 1-11-18. S.S.O. visited "Q" at 16.00 hours. Instructions received that supplies would be drawn from Railhead by H.T. As Pack Train did not arrive at Railhead until late, arrangements made to off-load it at 07.00 hours 17-10-18. 1 Driver and 2 H.D. Horses of No. 2 Company wounded by shell fire at RIEUX whilst attached to 1st Royal Fusiliers.	
"	17th		Supplies for consumption 18th instant drawn from Railhead by H.T. in following order :- 17th Bde. Group 07.00, 72nd Bde. Group 07.15, 73rd Bde. Group 07.30, Divl. Troops (by M.T.) 07.40 hours. Supplies conveyed to new Refilling Point, B.8.a.6.8. (sheet 57b) - distributed immediately and delivered to units. S.S.O. and Adjutant visited "Q" at 10.30 hours. Owing to breakdown on Railway supplies for consumption 19th instant drawn from Pack Train at VELU by M.T. O.C. Train got into touch with No. 1 Company at CAMBRAI and later sent written instructions to O.C. No. 1 Company to move on 18-10-18 to West of AVESNES. O.C. Train visited "Q" at 15.00 hours.	
"	18th		S.S.O. ascertained that the Pack Train would be very late. Refilling took place at 08.30 hours. No. 1 Company marched from CAMBRAI to billets at CAUROIR. O.C. Train & Adjutant visited Railhead and Divl. H.Q. at CAMBRAI at 15.00 hours. S.S.O. visited Railhead at 18.00 hours and arranged that Pack Train on this day should be cleared at 06.30 hours, 19-10-18. Lieut. J. O. TIDY proceeded i/c Remount Collecting Party to HAVRINCOURT.	

O. Galloway
LIEUT. COLONEL,
O.C. 24th DIVISIONAL TRAIN.

Army Form C. 2118.

Instructions regarding War Diaries and Intelligence Summaries are contained in F. S. Regs., Part II. and the Staff Manual respectively. Title pages will be prepared in manuscript.

WAR DIARY 24th Divisional Train.

or

~~INTELLIGENCE SUMMARY~~.

(Erase heading not required.)

Place	1918 October Date	Hour	Summary of Events and Information	Remarks and references to Appendices
AWOINGT.	19th		Pack Train due 18-10-18 cleared at 06.30 hours and supplies delivered to units. O.C. Train visited "Q" at 11.00 hours. O.C. Train & Adjutant visited B.G.C., 73rd Inf. Bde. in afternoon. S.S.O. visited "Q" at 14.00 hours.	
"	"	14.00	Lieut. J.O. TIDY returned from HAVRINCOURT where Remounts had been distributed at 10.00 hours. Pack Train arrived too late to be cleared to-day.	
"	20th		Pack Train due 19-10-18 cleared by H.T. at 11.00 hours. Informed that no vegetables would be sent up on Pack Train arriving 21-10-18 and subsequently. All vegetables would be obtained locally from captured territory under Army arrangements. 2 G.S. complete turnsout & 3 loaders (all No. 1 Coy.) sent to 3rd Army Farm, FRESNOY. Lieut. G.J. MOTION and batman, and Pte. JOSLIN attached to XVIIth Corps Troops M.T. Company from this date. (Authy :- Third Army No. S/1128/1 dated 18-10-18).	
"	21st		O.C. Train & Adjutant visited "Q" at 09.00 hours. Pack Train due 20-10-18 cleared at 10.00 hours. Supplies for Divl. Artillery Group drawn by M.T. and conveyed to Refilling Point at U.25.b.3.0. Informed that Pack Train due this day would be cleared by M.T. for all Groups. No. 1 Company moved to AVESNES in afternoon. S.S.O. visited "Q" at 16.00 hours.	
"	22nd		Refilling took place at 08.30 hours. O.C. Train & Adjutant visited "Q" at 11.00 hours. S.S.O. visited "Q" at 16.00 hours. Pack Train due this day to be cleared by M.T.	
"	23rd		Refilling took place at 15.00 hours, as Pack Train due 22-10-18 was not cleared till this morning. Notification received that Lieut. (a/Capt.) W.A. WATTS, A.S.C. (T.F.) was to be transferred forthwith to England for duty. This Officer proceeded this day - to cross on the 25-10-18, and struck off the strength of this unit from that date (Authy :- Q.M.G., G.H.Q. No. ASC/21558 dated 17-10-18). No Pack Train arrived this day.	
"	24th		Lt. J.O. TIDY proceeded on leave to U.K. for 14 days from 25-10-18. Pack Train due 23-10-18 cleared by H.T. at 10.00 hours and supplies immediately delivered to units. O.C. Train, accompanied by B.G.C., 73rd Inf. Bde and Capt. C.E. PASMORE, inspected 1st Line transport of 73rd Brigade, as follows :- B.H.Q., 09.30 hrs., 9th R. Sussex 10.00 hrs., 7th Northants 10.45 hrs., 13th Middlesex 11.30 hrs., He found everything to be in a very satisfactory state.	

A. Galloway

LIEUT. COLONEL,
O.C. 24th DIVISIONAL TRAIN.

D. D. & L., London, E.C.
(10340) Wt W5300/P713 750,000 3/18 E 2688 Forms/C2118/10.

Army Form C. 2118.

Instructions regarding War Diaries and Intelligence Summaries are contained in F. S. Regs., Part II. and the Staff Manual respectively. Title pages will be prepared in manuscript.

WAR DIARY or ~~INTELLIGENCE SUMMARY.~~

24th Divisional Train

(Erase heading not required.)

Place	Date 1918 October	Hour	Summary of Events and Information	Remarks and references to Appendices
AWOINGT.	25th		Pack Train due 24-10-18 arrived 15.00 hours and cleared by H.T. Supplies immediately delivered to units. Pack Train due this day arrived and cleared by M.T. at 19.00 hours. Supplies immediately dumped at Refilling Points. O.C. Train visited "Q" at 11.00 hours. O.C. Train attended Conference at "G" Office at 18.00 hours. 24th Division Order No. 260 received at 21.00 hrs. 24th Divl. Train Order No. 38 issued at 23.00 hrs.	C
"	26th		2/Lieut. W. SCARISBRICK proceeded to MASNIERES i/c Remount collecting party and distributed Remounts, 5 H.D. for Train (3 to No. 1 Coy., 2 to No. 2 Coy) Refilling took place at 07.00 hrs. Supply Sections marched at 11.00 hrs., and delivered to units in new area. Train H.Q. and 3	
AVESNES	"	13.30	Brigade Companies marched from AWOINGT at 10.30 hrs and arrived AVESNES LEZ AUBERT at 13.30 hours. No. 1 Company marched to SAULZOIR. Informed that M.T. will clear Pack Train until further orders. O.C. Train visited "Q" at 10.00 hours. O.C. Train visited "Q" at ST. AUBERT at 16.00 hrs.	
"	27th		Refilling Points as follows :- Divl. Troops P.34.c.5.3. (sheet 57b), 17th Bde. Group and 73rd Bde. Group U.23.d.9.7. (sheet 57b), 72nd Bde. Group C.4.a.5.3. (sheet 51a). O.C. Train & Adjutant visited "Q" at 10.00 hours. O.C. Train instructed to make his Headquarters with Divisional Headquarters at ST. AUBERT. Train H.Q. marched from AVESNES at 14.00 hours and	
ST. AUBERT	"	15.00	arrived ST. AUBERT at 15.00 hours.	
"	28th		Owing to Pack Train due 27-10-18 not being placed in position for off-loading supplies were not dumped at Refilling Points until 15.00 hours. Supplies immediately delivered to units. 3 Reinforcements (drivers) reported for duty and posted to No. 1 Company. Refilling Points as for 27th instant except that 72nd Bde. Group refilled with 17th and 73rd Brigade Groups at U.23.d.9.7. (sheet 51a.)	
"	29th		2/Lieut. J.W. DUNCAN proceeded on leave to U.K. for 14 days from 31-10-18. Lorries dumped at Refilling Points at 10.00 hours. Supplies delivered immediately to units. O.C. Train acted as Judge at 73rd Brigade Sports held this day.	

A. G. Galloway
LIEUT, COLONEL.
O.C. 24th DIVISIONAL TRAIN.

D. D. & L., London, E.C.
(10340) Wt W5300/P713 750,000 3/18 E 2688 Forms/C2118/16.

Army Form C. 2118.

Instructions regarding War Diaries and Intelligence Summaries are contained in F. S. Regs., Part II. and the Staff Manual respectively. Title pages will be prepared in manuscript.

WAR DIARY
or
~~INTELLIGENCE SUMMARY~~.
(*Erase heading not required.*)

24th Divisional Train.

Place	1918 Date October	Hour	Summary of Events and Information	Remarks and references to Appendices
ST. AUBERT	30th		Capt. C. E. PASMORE detailed as Member of F. G. C. M. assembled this day at 17th Bde. H. Q. Supplies dumped at 08.00 hours. Refilling took place immediately and supplies delivered to units. O. C. Train saw Company Commanders with reference to 24th Division Confidential letter. The following changes in the duties of Officers take place as from this day :- 2/Lt. J. W. DUNCAN from Transport Officer No. 3 Coy to Train Hd. Qrs. as Requisition Officer Lt. J. O. TIDY from Transport Officer No. 4 Coy to Transport Officer No. 1 Company. Lt. H. W. BRADLEY from Transport Officer No. 2 Coy to Transport Officer No. 1 Coy. 2/Lt. G. J. MOTION from Requisition Officer Train H. Q. to Transport Officer No. 2 Coy. 2/Lt. A. C. CORBY from S. O., Divl. Troops to S. O., 73rd Bde, vice Lt. (a/Capt.) W. A. WATTE to England. Lieut. A. H. BARNES from Transport Officer No. 1 Coy to S. O., Divl. Troops.	
"	31st		Lorries dumped at 08.00 hours and supplies delivered immediately to units. Lieut. G. J. MOTION rejoined from Corps Troops M. T. Company and assumed command of No. 2 Company pending Capt. K. M. PLUMPTRE's return. 24th Division Order No. 261 received 20.30 hours. Capt. R. F. SEDDALL rejoined from leave.	

A. H. Galloway
Lieut. Colonel.
O. C. 24th Divisional Train.

COLONEL,
O.C. 24th Div...

D. D. & L., London, E.C.
(10340) Wt W5300/P713 750,000 3/18 E 2688 Forms/C2118/16.

A

SECRET. Copy No...10...

24th DIVISIONAL TRAIN ORDER 36.

4th OCTOBER 1918.

1. The Division is moving towards the line, the Infantry and portion of the 1st Line Transport, as per attached* table marked "A" by Tactical Train on the 6th, the 1st and 2nd Line Transport by Road on the 5th and 6th instants.

* Issued in advance to Commanding Officer, 2, 3, & 4 Companies, and S.Os., 17th, 72nd and 73rd Brigades.

2. Orders for the move of Transport will be issued later.

3. Supplies for consumption 6th instant are being dumped immediately. Refilling will take place at 3 p.m. this afternoon, supplies for Rail Parties being delivered immediately afterwards, and supplies for Road Parties being loaded on the Supply Wagons and taken to Train Companies parks. These latter supplies will be delivered in the normal manner on termination of the march on the 5th instant.

4. Supply Officers will send this afternoon to 24th M.T. Coy, at least one S. Sergt or Sergt and at least 4 Rank and File, immediately after Refilling, to travel with the M.T. Company, and to guard the supplies for consumption 7th instant, which will be dumped in the forward Refilling Points to-morrow 5th instant.

All tarpaulins, sail covers, etc., in possession of Supply Officers will be sent with the Supply Details to be conveyed by the lorries to the New Area.

5. Rations for consumption on the 7th instant by all parties will be dumped in the New Area, and picked up and delivered by Supply Sections on termination of the march on the 6th instant, in the normal manner.

6. A Store for surplus kits etc is being found by the Division. Its location will be notified later. Company Commanders will notify this office by 6 p.m. to-day of the quantities of stores they are leaving behind, and where, (nil returns will be rendered) so that these may be collected by lorries at a later date.

Each Company will leave one man to guard the Stores left behind.

7. Any alterations in the Supply Groups will be notified later.

8. ACKNOWLEDGE.

A G Galloway

Lieut. Colonel.
O.C. 24th Divisional Train.

Copies to :-

1. 24th Division "Q".
2. O.C. Train.
3. S.S.O.
4. O.C. No. 1 Company.
5. O.C. No. 2 Company.
6. O.C. No. 3 Company.
7. O.C. No. 4 Company.
8. O.C. 24th M.T. Coy.
9. File.
10. War Diary
11. War Diary.

Issued at 13.30 hrs.

"B"

SECRET.

Copy No......9.....

24th DIVISIONAL TRAIN ORDER NO. 37.

4th OCTOBER 1918.

1. The 24th Division (less Divisional Artillery) is moving by tactical trains to XVII Corps area (West of CAMBRAI) on 6th instant.

2. Para. 3 of 24th Division Order No. 250, reads as follows :-

Transport, other than that proceeding by train (vide 24th Division No. C/512/2 of 4-10-18, paras. 2 and 4.) will proceed by march route on 5th instant to BOISLEUX-AU-MONT - BOIRY BEQUERELLE area in accordance with attached table. Accommodation night 5/6th October from Town Major BOISLEUX-AU-MONT.

Route main DOULLENS - ARRAS Road to BEAUMETZ LES LOGES thence via BRETENCOURT and FICHEUX.

After passing the starting point the whole column will be under the orders of Lt. Col. GALLOWAY, O. C. 24th Divisional Train.

The march will be resumed on 6th instant under orders to be issued to Lt. Col. GALLOWAY.

3. Train Companies will move under the orders of the Brigade to which they are affiliated.

4. Recipients of copies Nos. 4, 5 and 6 to acknowledge.

A. G. Galloway

Lieut. Colonel.
O. C. 24th Divisional Train.

Copies to :-

1. 24th Division "Q".
2. O. C. Train.
3. S. S. O.
4. O. C. No. 2 Company.
5. O. C. No. 3 Company.
6. O. C. No. 4 Company.
7. O. C. 24th M. T. Coy.
8. File.
9. War Diary.
10. War Diary.

Issued at 19.30 hrs.

Table to accompany 24th Divn. Order No. 250.

Serial No.	Date.	Unit.	Starting point.	Route to starting point.	Time Head to pass starting Point.	Remarks.
1.	1918. Oct. 5th	73rd I. Bde. Group incl. Pioneer Bn.	Cross roads U. 18. d. 2. 0.	Any.	11. 00.	(a). Bde. group includes transport of Bde. H. Q. Battns, Fd. Coy. R. E. Field Amb. and Coy. Divl. Train.
2.	" "	24th Bn. M. G. C.	ditto.	COUTURELLE.	11. 45.	
3.	" "	S. A. A. Section, D. A. C.	ditto.	Any.	11. 50.	
4.	" "	24th Div. Sig. Coy.	ditto.	Any.	11. 55.	(b). Divn. H. Q. will move under orders to be issued by 24th Divn. "Q".
5.	" "	H. Q., Divl. Train and M. V. S.	ditto.	Any.	12. 05.	
6.	" "	72nd I. Bde. group.	ditto.	COUTURELLE.	12. 10.	(c). Baggage wagons will accompany transport of units.
7.	" "	17th I. Bde. group	ditto.	Any.	12. 50.	(d). Normal halts and intervals will be observed.

B1 13

Copy No. 13.

MARCH ORDERS FOR 24th DIVISION TRANSPORT
BY
Lieut. Col. A. C. GALLOWAY, D.S.O., S.T.O., 24th Division.

---

1. Para. 3 of 24th Division Order No. 200 reads as follows :-

Transport other than that proceeding by train (vide 24th Divn. No. G/513/2 of 4.10.18, paras. 2 and 4.) will proceed by march route on 8th instant to BOISLEUX-AU-MONT - BOIRY BECQUERELLE area in accordance with attached table. Accommodation night 8/9th October from Town Major BOISLEUX-AU-MONT.

Route main DOULLENS - ARRAS Road to BEAUMETZ LES LOGES thence via BRETENCOURT and FICHEUX.

After passing the starting point the whole column will be under the orders of Lt. Col. GALLOWAY, C.O., 24th Divisional Train.

The march will be resumed on 9th instant under orders to be issued to Lt. Col. GALLOWAY.

2. Halts and Distances will be as follows :-

HALTS.

The mid-day halt will be from 11.50 to 13.15. After mid-day halt all halts will be from 5 minutes past every clock hour to ¼ past every clock hour commencing with halt at 14.05.

DISTANCES.

In accordance with S.S. 724, viz :-

Between Brigade Groups.	200 yards.
" Units.	100 "
" each Section of 12 vehicles	50 "
Between Train & S.A.A. Section, D.A.C. and between S.A.A. Section, D.A.C. and 72nd Brigade group	200 "

3. Cross Roads and ~~Road~~ ROAD Junctions must be left clear of all halts. No halts will be made in the main streets of Towns or Villages or on Bridges.

4. Billeting Parties of one Officer from each Brigade Group and one Senior N.C.O. from each Unit will report at the Town Major's Office BOISLEUX-AU-MONT at 14.00 hours. There they will receive the orders of the S.T.O., 24th Division, regarding billeting areas.

A representative from the 24th Bn. M.G.C. and S.A.A. Section, D.A.C., (Senior N.C.O. in each case) will report to the billeting Officer of the 73rd Brigade Group and receive their billets from him.

B.T.Os. will receive intimation as to the areas in which they are billeting from the S.T.O. on the line of march, either during or after the mid-day halt.

5. B.T.Os. will report their exact locations to the Town Major BOISLEUX-AU-MONT for the information of the S.T.O.

6. Orders for the march on the 9th instant will be issued to B.T.Os. later.

A C Galloway
Lieut. Colonel.
C.C. 24th Divisional Train.

Copies to :-
1. 24th Division "Q".
2. O.C. Train.
3. B.T.O., 17th Inf. Bde.
4. B.T.O., 72nd Inf. Bde.
5. B.T.O., 73rd Inf. Bde.
6. T.O., 24th Bn. M.G.C.
7. O.C., S.A.A. Section, D.A.C.
8. T.O., 24th Divl. Signals.
9. O.C. No. 2 Company.
10. O.C. No. 3 Company.
11. O.C. No. 4 Company.
12. File.
13. War Diary
14. War Diary

SECRET. C Copy No........7..

24th DIVISIONAL TRAIN ORDER NO. 38.

25th OCTOBER 1918.

1. The 24th Division is moving from its present area to the following Area, to-morrow 26th October :- Area East of a line through C. 3. central - U. 27. central - U. 21. central - U. 15. central.

2. Refilling will take place at 07.00 hours. All supply wagons will have passed through CAUROIR on their way to Refilling Point by that hour. After refilling, supply sections will water and feed.

3. Supply Sections in the following order, viz :- 4 Company, 2 Company, and 3 Company will be ready to follow the 12th Sherwood Foresters who will pass Refilling Point at 11.00 hours.
The head of No. 4 Company supply section will pass the cross roads at B. 4. d. 1. 1. at 11.30 hours. 100 yards will be kept between supply sections. Company Commanders will, however, ~~will~~ arrange to collect their own Company supply wagons in CAUROIR as their Headquarters pass through there. These wagons will not march with the supply sections.
Supply sections will continue to march to their Brigade Group Area, deliver supplies to units, and then return to AVESNES-LEZ AUBERT.

4. Train Headquarters and Brigade Companies Headquarters will move in the same order as the supply sections, Train Headquarters moving with No. 4 Company H. Qrs.
No. 4 Company Headquarters will leave AWOINGT at 10.30 hours and will pass the Cross Roads as above after the supply section of No. 3 Company, leaving 100 yards interval.
The remaining Companies will follow No. 4 Company at 50 yards interval.

5. Time and place of the next refilling will be notified later.

6. Division will be distributed in the new area as follows :-

24th Divn. H. Q.	ST. AUBERT.
73rd Inf. Bde. Group	HAUSSY and MONTRECOURT.
17th Bde. Group	ST. AUBERT.
24th Bn. M. G. C.	ST. AUBERT.
72nd Bde. Group	AVESNES-LEZ-AUBERT.
12th Sherwoods.	AVESNES.
Divl. Train (less 1 Coy.)	AVESNES.

7. The route to be followed will be CAMBRAI - SOLESMES Road - AVESNES - ST. AUBERT.

8. Train Headquarters will close at AWOINGT at 09.30 hours and open AVESNES at 15.00 hours.

9. ACKNOWLEDGE.

C. G. Galloway
Lieut. Colonel.
O. C. 24th Divisional Train.

Copies to :-
1. 24th Division "Q" (for information).
2. O. C. Train.
3. O. C. No. 1 Company.
4. O. C. No. 2 Company.
5. O. C. No. 3 Company.
6. O. C. No. 4 Company.
7. War Diary
8. War Diary
9. File.

1

Instructions regarding War Diaries and Intelligence Summaries are contained in F. S. Regs., Part II. and the Staff Manual respectively. Title pages will be prepared in manuscript.

WAR DIARY
or
~~INTELLIGENCE~~ SUMMARY.
(Erase heading not required.)

24th DIVISIONAL TRAIN.

Army Form C. 2118.

WD 39

Place	1918 Date NOV.	Hour	Summary of Events and Information	Remarks and references to Appendices
ST. AUBERT	1st.		24th Divisional Train Order No. 39 issued at 07.00 hours this day. Capt. C. C. GALE rejoined from leave. 24th Divisional Train Order No. 40 issued at 2000 hours this day.	A B
"	2nd		Hd. Qrs. of Nos. 2, 3, & 4 Companies marched from AVESNES to HAUSSY. Refilling took place at 0900 hours and supplies delivered to units in new area. S. S. O. and Adjutant visited BERMERAIN re billets for Train Headquarters. Lorries dumped supplies for consumption 4-11-18 at Refilling Points at 1600 hours as follows :- Divl. Troops - no change, Brigade Groups V. 4. b. (sheet 51a).	
" BERMERAIN.	3rd "	1400	Train Headquarters marched from ST. AUBERT at 1000 hours and arrived BERMERAIN at 1400 hours. Refilling took place at 0900 hours, supplies being immediately delivered to units. O. C. Train visited Train Companies and arrived at BERMERAIN at 1430 hours & visited "Q" with S. S. O. O. C. Train ~~visited~~ proceeded on leave to U. K. for 14 days from 5-11-18. Major H. B. HUNTER, D. S. O. assumed command of Train during absence on leave of Lt. Col. A. G. GALLOWAY, D. S. O. Information received that Lieut. H. W. BRADLEY would rejoin on 4-11-18.	
BERMERAIN.	4th		a/O. C. Train and Adjutant visited "Q" at 0900 hours. Orders sent to Brigade Companies at 0930 hrs that Companies would move forthwith to Q. 25. b. & d. Supplies to be delivered immediately to units	
SEPMERIES	4th	1430	Train Headquarters marched from BERMERAIN 1300 hours and arrived SEPMERIES at 1430 hours a/O. C. Train visited Companies at Q. 25. b. & d, returned to Hd. Qrs. at 1530 hours and Companies instructed that Refilling Point would be at Q. 25. b. and that lorries would dump immediately the Pack Train was cleared to-day.	
"	5th		Railhead ST. AUBERT, U. 29. b. (sheet 51a). a/O. C. Train visited "Q" at 0900 hours. A. A. & Q. M. G. gone to Report Centre. Refilling took place at dawn at Q. 25. b., and Brigade Companies marched off at 0730 hours and proceeded to the Rendezvous at Q. 6. c., arriving at 08.30 hours. Guides reported at Q. 6. c. at 11.00 hours and wagons proceeded to units and delivered rations. Returning Supply Wagons to Rendezous at L. 23. b. & 9. a/O. C. Train saw A. A. & Q. M. G. at 1200 hours re Move of Companies to JENLAIN. Hd. Qrs. of Companies marched from Q. 6. c. at 1300 hours and proceeded to L. 23. central. Train Headquarters marched from SEPMERIES at 13.30 hours and	
WARGNIES LE-GRAND	5th	1600.	proceeded to WARGNIES LE GRAND, arriving at 1600 hours. a/O. C. Train proceeded at 1300 hours to visit M. T. Coy to arrange Refilling Points for 6-11-18 on N. and S. Road at L. 23. b. & d. He visited Brigade Coys and returned to Train Hd. Qrs. at 1700 hours and visited "Q" on arrival.	

A. G. Galloway
LIEUT. COLONEL
O.C. 24th DIVISIONAL TRAIN.

A5834 Wt. W4973/M687 750,000 8/16 D. D. & L. Ltd. Forms/C.2118/13.

Army Form C. 2118.

WAR DIARY
or
~~INTELLIGENCE~~ SUMMARY.
(Erase heading not required.)

24th DIVISIONAL TRAIN.

Instructions regarding War Diaries and Intelligence Summaries are contained in F. S. Regs., Part II. and the Staff Manual respectively. Title pages will be prepared in manuscript.

Place	Date 1918 NOV.	Hour	Summary of Events and Information	Remarks and references to Appendices
WARGNIES LE GRAND	5th		No. 1 Company marched from SAULZOIR this day and arrived at Q.6.a.2.9. at 1100 hours. 3 reinforcements reported for duty (No. 1 Coy 1 driver, No. 4 - 1 driver and No. 2 - 1 wheeler). a/O.C. Train visited "Q" at 1900 hours, nothing further required. Information received that Lieut. H.W. BRADLEY unable to report owing to illness, but would rejoin as soon as possible. Adjutant visited "Q" at 2200 hours. Considerable enemy shelling in vicinity of Brigade Coy's Camps and Train Hd. Qrs, no casualties.	
"	6th		a/O.C. Train and Adjutant visited "Q" at 0900 hours. Refilling took place at 1130 hours, N. and S. Road L.23.b.&.d. (sheet 51a). Lorries took 4 and 1/2 hours to reach Refilling Point owing to bridges having been broken. Supply Sections proceeded to rendezvous west of X Roads, G.20.a. (sheet 51a). Guides met wagons and supplies delivered to units. Informed that Railhead from 8th instant would be SOLESMES. Letter dated 1-11-18 received from 2/Lt. A.C. CORBY stating that he was ill with influenza and would be some days late in returning from leave to U.K. Orders sent to No. 1 Company to move 7-11-18 to vicinity of Train Companies about L.23.central. Information received at 1900 hours that supplies had been delivered to all units this day. a/O.C. Train and Adjutant visited "Q" at 2100 hours and rendezvous fixed for 7-11-18 at G.20.a. (sheet 51). Considerable enemy shelling throughout the day in vicinity of Train Headquarters, particularly after 2100 hours.	
"	7th		Lorries dumped for all Groups at L.23.b.&.d. (sheet 51a) at 09.30 hours and refilling took place immediately. Supply wagons proceeded to rendezvous W. of X Roads G.20.a. (sheet 51) where guides met them and supplies delivered to units. a/O.C. Train and Adjutant visited "Q" at 0900 hours. a/O.C. Train visited M.T. Company re Railheads and Supplies. No. 1 Company marched from SEPMERIES to JENLAIN arriving at 1200 hours. A.A.& Q.M.G., accompanied by a/O.C. Train selected camps for Companies at G.30.a. and Refilling Points for 8-11-18 at G.29.b.d.8. Orders sent to Brigade Companies at 1700 hours to march forthwith to G.30.a. Orders sent to No. 1 Company to march at 0700 hours, 8-11-18 to G.30.a. Divisional Troops to refill with Brigade Groups at G.29.b.6.8. Informed by Division that Railhead for 8-11-18 would be ST. AUBERT and not SOLESMES as previously stated. Nos. 2, 3, & 4 Companies arrived LE BOIS CRETTE (G.30.a.) between 2000 & 2100 hours.	

A. G. Galloway
LIEUT. COLONEL.
O.C. 24th DIVISIONAL TRAIN.

A5834 Wt. W4973/M687 750,000 8/16 D. D. & L. Ltd. Forms/C.2118/13.

Army Form C. 2118.

Instructions regarding War Diaries and Intelligence Summaries are contained in F. S. Regs., Part II. and the Staff Manual respectively. Title pages will be prepared in manuscript.

WAR DIARY
or
INTELLIGENCE SUMMARY.
(Erase heading not required.)

24th DIVISIONAL TRAIN.

Place	Date 1918 NOV.	Hour	Summary of Events and Information	Remarks and references to Appendices
WARGNIES LE GRAND.	8th		No. 1 Company marched from JENLAIN at 0700 hours arriving LE BOIS CRETTE(G. 30. a.) at 0900 hours a/O. C. Train and Adjutant saw A. A. & Q. M. G. at 0900 hours. Lorries dumped at G. 29. b. 6. 8. at 0900 hours. Supply Sections proceeded to rendezvous at W. of X Roads in H. 20. c. (sheet 51) where guides met them. a/O. C. Train and Adjutant visited ST. WAAST to select Refilling Point for 9-11-18, but could find no place owing to there being no bridges for lorries to go over. "Q" informed of this at 1830 hours, arranged with "Q" that Companies would move to neighbourhood W. of BAVAY on 9-11-18. Informed that Railhead 9-11-18 would be SOLESMES. Orders for Companies to move on 9-11-18 sent out at 22. 15 hours.	
" BAVAY	9th 9th	1200	Train Headquarters marched out from WARGNIES and proceeded to BAVAY, arriving at 12. 00 hours. Refilling took place at G. 29. b. 6. 8. and Supply Sections proceeded to Brigade rendezvous at H. 24. c. (sheet 51). H. Q. of Companies marched from G. 30. a. at 0900 hours and arrived at billets west of BAVAY at H. 24. c. central at 1100 hours. Supplies delivered to units. Wagons returned to camp very late. Supply Section of No. 4 Company remained with 73rd Brigade overnight owing to long distance they had to do and the animals being exhausted. 24th Division order No. 264/5 received at 23. 00 hours.	
BAVAY.	10th		24th Division relieved this day by 20th Division. Refilling for all Groups took place at 11. 00 hours in vicinity of H. 24. c. The lorry containing groceries for 17th Brigade Supply Group broke down and as it had not arrived by 1800 hours, supplies, less groceries were sent out to units who were informed of the fact and told, if necessary, to use their Iron Rations (grocery portion). Nos. 2, 3, & 4 Companies vacated billets at H. 24. c. in order to make room for part of D. H. Q. and marched at 1600 hours to old billets at LA BOIS CRETTE (G. 30. c.). On verbal instructions to a/O. C. Train by "Q", Train Headquarters marched from BAVAY at 1500 hours and arrived at H. 24. c. at 16. 00 hours. Lorry with groceries for 17th Brigade arrived at 20. 00 hours.	
" H. 24. c. 8. 5.	11th		Refilling Points this day :- Divl. Troops H. 23. d. 8. 8., 17th, 72nd and 73rd Brigade Groups G. 29. b. 6. 8. Information received from Division at 08. 30 hours that hostilities would cease at 11. 00 hours (24th Division G. 655 dated 11-11-18) Companies informed immediately. Lieut. H. W. BRADLEY rejoined from VIII Corps, appointed S. O., Divl. Troops, vice Lieut. A. H. BARNES to Transport duties. 2/Lieut. E. R. A. HODGMAN proceeded on 14 days leave to U. K. 13-11-18 to 27-11-18.	

A. Galloway
LIEUT. COLONEL.
O.C. 24th DIVISIONAL TRAIN.

 Army Form C. 2118.

Instructions regarding War Diaries and Intelligence Summaries are contained in F. S. Regs., Part II. and the Staff Manual respectively. Title pages will be prepared in manuscript.

WAR DIARY 24th DIVISIONAL TRAIN.
or
INTELLIGENCE SUMMARY.
(Erase heading not required.)

Place	Date 1918 NOV.	Hour	Summary of Events and Information	Remarks and references to Appendices
BAVAY H. 24. c.	12th		Supply Group Table No. 10 issued this day. Lieut. J. O. TIDY rejoined from leave. Major H. B. HUNTER D. S. O. attended as witness at enquiry into Divisional Regimental Institute. Adjutant and O. C. No. 1 Company selected new billets for No. 1 Company at I. 29. d.	C
"	13th		No. 1 Company marched to new billets at I. 29. d. arriving at 11.30 hours. Lorries did not dump at Refilling Points until afternoon owing to non-arrival of Pack Train due 12-11-18 until the morning. "A" Group refilled at I. 29. d. a/O. C. Train attended Conference on Educational and Recreational Training, held at Divl. Hd. Qrs. at 1430 hours	
"	14th		a/O. C. Train, Adjutant and 1 Officer per Company and 2 O. Rs per Company attended Thanksgiving Service, held at the request of the G. O. C. 17th Corps at 10.30 hours at Theatre at BAVAY. Warning Order (24th Division G. 691 dated 14-11-18) that 24th Division will march to First Army on 16-11-18, received at 20.00 hours.	
"	15th		Informed at 12.00 hours that move to First Army was postponed (24th Division G. 697 dated 15-11-18). Warning order received at 16.00 hours that 24th Division will move to First Army, DENAIN Area on 18-11-18 (24th Divn. G. 699 dated 15-11-18) Telegram received from Capt. K. M. PLUMPTRE stating that he had been granted extension of leave to 15-11-18 on medical grounds.	
"	16th		19 H. D. Horses and 6 Riders handed over to VI Corps (1 Coy 8 H. D. and 3 Riders, Nos. 2, 3, 4 Coys 4 H. D. and 1 Rider each) These transfers necessitated by imminent transfer of VI Corps to Germany. Owing to previous deficiencies these transfers made the Train immobile. The situation was met by certain Artillery units horsing their baggage wagons with L. D. teams, the H. D. horses thus freed being used for Supply Wagons.	
"	17th		From this date Companies informed they would march under orders of the Formations to which affiliated. No. 3 Company marched to MARESCHES, No. 2 Company to JENLAIN. Refilling Points for these Groups was at L. 23. d. (sheet 51a). Divl. Troops and 73rd Brigade refilled at LA BOIS CRETTE. 8 H. D. Horses, remounts, collected from 61st Division and distributed as follows :- 1 Coy 4, 2 Coy 2, and 4 Coy 2 and 3 Coy 2, which latter were immediately evacuated by D. A. D. V. S. Capt. C. H. PASMORE rejoined from leave.	

A. L. Galloway
LIEUT. COLONEL,
O.C. 24th DIVISIONAL TRAIN.

A5834 Wt. W4973/M687 750,000 8/16 D. D. & L. Ltd. Forms/C.2118/13.

Army Form C. 2118.

Instructions regarding War Diaries and Intelligence Summaries are contained in F. S. Regs., Part II. and the Staff Manual respectively. Title pages will be prepared in manuscript.

WAR DIARY
or
INTELLIGENCE SUMMARY.
(*Erase heading not required.*)

24th DIVISIONAL TRAIN.

Place	1918 Date NOV.	Hour	Summary of Events and Information	Remarks and references to Appendices
BAVAY. MASNY	18th "	1400	Railhead ANICHE. Train Headquarters closed at BAVAY at 10.00 hours and opened at MASNY at 14.00 hours. No. 1 Company marched from LA BOIS CRETTE to ESCAUDAIN refilling on arrival. No. 2 Company marched from JENLAIN to BRILAING refilling at HERIN en route. No. 3 Company marched from MARESCHES to LOURCHES refilling on arrival. No. 4 Company marched from LA BOIS CRETTE to PROUVY refilling at ROUVIGNIES en route. Remounts for Division collected from CAUDRY. 2/Lieut. W. SCARISBRICK i/c Conducting party. No. 1 Coy 5 H. D. and Nos. 2 & 4 Coys 2 H. D. each.	
MASNY	19th		No. 1 Company marched to LEWARDE refilling on arrival. No. 2 " " " SOMAIN, " " " No. 3 " " " ECAILLON " " " No. 4 " " " ANICHE " " "	
"	20th		Lt. Col. A. G. GALLOWAY, D. S. O., rejoined from leave. Supplies for 73rd Brigade Group drawn from Railhead by H. T. commencing to-day.	
"	21st		Normal routine.	
"	22nd		Normal routine.	
"	23rd		Audit Board assembled at Train Hd. Qrs at 14.00 hours to examine Central and Company Canteen Accounts for Sept. and October. President :- Major H. B. HUNTER, D. S. O. Members :- Lieut. H. W. BRADLEY and 2/Lieut. W. SCARISBRICK. 24th Division Warning Order G. 759 received at 18.00 hours. 24th Division Order No. 268 received at 19.00 hours.	
"	24th		24th Division Order No. 269 received at 14.00 hours containing information that the Division would be transferred to I Corps and would move into I Corps area on 25/26th and 27-11-18. 24th Divisional Train Order No. 41 issued at 15.30 hours. 72nd and 73rd Brigades refilled in afternoon supplies for consumption 26-11-18.	D

A G Galloway
LIEUT. COLONEL.
O.C. 24th DIVISIONAL TRAIN.

A5834 Wt. W4973 M687 750,000 8/16 D. D. & L. Ltd. Forms/C.2118/13.

Army Form C. 2118.

Instructions regarding War Diaries and Intelligence Summaries are contained in F. S. Regs., Part II. and the Staff Manual respectively. Title pages will be prepared in manuscript.

WAR DIARY *or* INTELLIGENCE SUMMARY.

24th DIVISIONAL TRAIN.

(Erase heading not required.)

Place	Date 1918. NOV.	Hour	Summary of Events and Information	Remarks and references to Appendices
MASNY.	25th		No. 3 Company marched to LANDAS. No. 4 Company marched to RUMEGIES. O. C. Train and Capt. F. A. R. SAUNDERS visited D. D. S. & T., First Army. Lieut. A. H. BARNES proceeded on leave to U.K. for 14 days from 27-11-18. 2/Lieut. J. W. DUNCAN attached to No. 1 Company from this date. Pack Train arrived too late to be off-loaded this day.	
" SAMEON.	26th "	15.30	Train Headquarters marched from MASNY at 09..00 hours and arrived SAMEON at 15.30 hours. Divl. Headquarters closed at MASNY at 13.00 hours and opened at SAMEON at same hour. O. C. Train went on in advance. No. 2 Company marched to RUMEGIES. No. 3 Company marched to LE QUIMBERGE. No. 4 Company marched to MOUCHIN. Refilling in each case took place before commencement of march.	
SAMEON.	27th		Railhead SOMAIN. No. 1 Company marched to LANDAS arriving 15.00 hours. As the lorries were late in dumping at LE WARDE, supplies were carried by H. T. to LANDAS in bulk - refilling took place in LANDAS on arrival.	
"	28th		A Belgian Interpreter, Mon. Hector BUSSERS, attached to the Train from this date - to live with No. 3 Company. O. C. Train, President of Divisional Troops Educational Committee, visited by Education Officer. They both visited 12th Sherwood Foresters in connection with the scheme.	
"	29th		Railhead TOURNAI. O. C. Train and Adjutant visited 8th Divl. Train re taking over billets at TOURNAI. 2/Lieut. E. R. A. HODGMAN rejoined from leave. O. C. Train visited No. 2 Company at 22.00 hours re move and supply arrangements.	
"	30th		No. 2 Company marched from RUMEGIES with 17th Brigade to billets at GRUSON. Lorries dumped supplies for Brigade Group at SIN, map reference M. 23. c. 8. 9. (sheet 37). Supply Wagons of Brigade Group (less Field Company) marched empty to Refilling Point. Supplies for the units of "B" Group remaining in SAMEON area were dumped at Church SAMEON by lorry. Supply Wagons after delivering joined No. 1 Company at LANDAS. Supply Wagons of Field Coys ordered to remain with their units and march with them to TOURNAI on 1-12-18.	

A. Galloway
Lieut. Colonel.
O. C. 24th Divisional Train.

A5834 Wt. W4973 M687 750,000 8/16 D. D. & L. Ltd. Forms/C.2118/13.

"A"

S E C R E T.

Copy No...7...

24th DIVISIONAL TRAIN ORDER NO. 39.

1. The following moves are taking place to-morrow :-

73rd Bde. Group to ST. MARTIN - BERMERAIN.
17th Bde. Group to HAUSSY.
12th Sherwood Foresters to HAUSSY.
24th Bn. M. G. Corps (less 2 coys) to BERMERAIN.

2. Company Commanders will arrange direct with Staff Captains the times at which they desire supplies delivered in the New Area. In no case will refilling take place later than 12 mid-day.

3. O. C. No. 3 Company will deliver to 24th Bn. M. G. Corps at present location, but may lend one or more supply wagons to take supplies of the two Companies moving forward to the new location, should the unit ask for it.

4. Brigade Train Companies will move to HAUSSY on the 2nd instant, under detailed orders to be issued later.

5. The term "Brigade Group" as above includes the Infantry Bde., Field Coy., R. E., and Field Ambulance.

6. Refilling for "C" Group will take place at 09.00 hours, and supplies will be delivered immediately afterwards.

C. G. Galloway
Lieut. Colonel.
O. C. 24th Divisional Train.

Issued at 07.00 hours, 1-11-18.

Copies to :-
1. O. C. Train.
2. O. C. No. 1 Company.
3. O. C. No. 2 Company.
4. O. C. No. 3 Company.
5. O. C. No. 4 Company.
6. File.
7. War Diary
8. War Diary.

A

S E C R E T.   Copy No....7....

24th DIVISIONAL TRAIN ORDER NO. 40.

1st November 1918.

1. Headquarters Train Brigade Companies will move from AVESNES-LEZ-AUBERT to HAUSSY, tomorrow 2nd November, at the following times;-

No. 4 Company passes Starting Point at 09.00 hours.
No. 2 Company " " " at 09.10 hours.
No. 3 Company " " " at 09.20 hours.

Starting Point :- U.22.c.4.0.

Route :- ST. AUBERT - HAUSSY.

2. The Train will be camped between the road and the river at V.5.c. (Sheet 51a.)

3. Ground will be allotted by Captain G.H. HITCH, O.C. No. 3 Company, who has reconnoitred the ground.

4. Supply Sections will refill at 09.00 hours, but will not leave Refilling Point before 10.00 hours.
Supplies will be delivered and Supply Sections will follow Company Headquarters to the new camp, except Supply Section of No. 3 Company which will march full to the new camp, and deliver to Units after the 72nd Brigade has arrived at HAUSSY. O.C. No. 3 Company will arrange time of delivery with Staff Cap tain, 72nd Brigade.
Should it be convenient, 72nd Bde Supplies may be delivered to the Billetting Parties in the morning, to enable the empty Supply Wagons to be back in camp at 13.00 hours.

5. As far as possible all Train Transport must be off the road by 13.00 hours.

6. Refilling Point on the 3rd instant will be South of the road in V.4.b. (Sheet 51a.) Time of refilling will be notified later.

7. Train Headquarters does not move from present location until 3rd instant.

8. Acknowledge by bearer.

J. Galloway
Lieut. Colonel.
O.C. 24th Divisional Train.

Issued at 20.00 hours. 1.11.18.

Copies to :-

1. 24th Division " Q" (for information)
2. O.C. Train.
3. O.C. No. 1 Company.
4. O.C. No. 2 Company.
5. O.C. No. 3 Company.
6. O.C. No. 4 Company.
7. War Diary.
8. War Diary.
9 File.

B

Copy No 12 "C"

SUPPLY GROUP TABLE NO. 10.

On A. R. W. 3316 & 3317 Nov. 11th 1918.
At Railhead Nov. 12th 1918.
Consumption Nov. 14th 1918.

"A" Group R.P. H.23.c.5.8.(sheet 51)	"B" Group. R.P. ,C.29.b.6.8.(sheet 51)	"C" Group. R.P. ,C.29.d.4.8.(sheet 51)	"D" Group. R.P. ,C.9.b.4.4.(sheet 51)
C. R. A.	17th Bde. H. Qrs.	72nd Inf. Bde. H. Qrs.	73rd Inf. Bde. Hd. Qrs.
106th Brigade R. F. A.	3rd Rifle Brigade.	9th East Surreys.	73rd T. M. Batty
107th " "	1st R. Fusiliers.	8th R. W. Kents.	9th R. Sussex.
24th D. A. C. (all sections)	8th Queens.	1st North Staffs.	7th Northants.
24th T. M. Battery.	17th Trench M. Batty.	72nd T. M. Batty.	13th Middlesex.
No. 1 Company, Train.	74th Field Ambulance.	72nd Field Ambulance.	73rd Field Ambulance.
103rd Field Coy., R. E.	No. 2 Company, Train.	No. 3 Company, Train.	No. 4 Company, Train.
104th " " "		24th M. G. Battn.	
129th " " "			
H. Q. 24th Division			
24th Signal Coy. R. E.			
A. O. D.			
36th Mobile Vet. Section.			
H. Q. 24th Divl. Train.			
12th Sherwood Foresters.			

12-11-18.

H B Hunter
Major.
O. C. 24th Divisional Train.

Distribution :-

No. 1. "Q" 2.th Division
2. O. C. Train.
3. S. S. O.
4. O. C. No. 1 Company.
5. O. C. No. 2 Company.
6. O. C. No. 3 Company.
7. O. C. No. 4 Company
8. O. C. 2.th M. T. Coy.
9. R. T. O.
10. File.
11. War Diary
12. War Diary

Copy No.....9.....

24th DIVISIONAL TRAIN ORDER NO.41.

24th NOVEMBER 1918.

1. The 24th Division is being transferred to 1 Corps and will move into 1 Corps area on 25th, 26th and 27th instant.
Train Companies will move under the orders of the Formations to which they are affiliated.

2. The strictest march discipline and intervals will be maintained.

3. The following amendments will be made to the Supply Group Table issued on the 12th instant :-

Dates.	U N I T.	From	To.
Railhead 25th Nov.	Divl. Hd. Qrs.	"A" Group	"B" Group
Consumption 27th Nov.	24th Signal Coy.	"A" "	"B" "
et sequitur	Train Hd. Qrs.	"A" "	"B" "
except (a)	24th Bn. M. G. C.	"D" "	"B" "
	Pioneer Bn. (a)	"D" "	"B" "
Railhead 27th Nov. Consumption 29th Nov. et sequitur	Pioneer Bn.	"B" Group	"D" Group

4. Refilling Points will be as follows :-

Date of Dumping.	"A" Group	"B" Group.	"C" Group	"D" Group
25th Nov.	LEWARDE.	SOMAIN.	LANDAS.	RUMEGIES.
26th Nov.	LEWARDE.	RUMEGIES.	NOMAIN.	MOUCHIN.
27th Nov.	LANDAS.	RUMEGIES.	NOMAIN	MOUCHIN

Lorries will dump in the afternoon of the day on which they draw from Railhead. The actual refilling Point in each village will be in the vicinity of the Church.

5. "C" & "D" Groups will refill this afternoon with supplies for consumption on 26th.
The supply wagons of Pioneer Bn and M. G. Bn will deliver the above supplies to-morrow morning and then proceed to join No. 2 Coy at SOMAIN.
Refilling will, as far as possible, take place each afternoon immediately after the delivery of supplies for the following day's consumption.

6. Train Hd. Qrs. will close at MASNY at 0900 hours 26th instant and will open at SAMEON at 1500 hours same day.

7. Copies 3, 4, 5 & 6 to be acknowledged.

Copies to :- (issued at 15.30 hours)

A G Galloway
Lieut. Colonel.
O. C. 24th Divisional Train.

1. 24th Division "Q" (for information)
2. O. C. Train.
3. O. C. No. 1 Company.
4. O. C. No. 2 Company.
5. O. C. No. 3 Company.
6. O. C. No. 4 Company.
7. O. C. 24th M. T. Company.
8. War Diary
9. War Diary
10. File.

Army Form C. 2118.

Instructions regarding War Diaries and Intelligence Summaries are contained in F. S. Regs., Part II. and the Staff Manual respectively. Title pages will be prepared in manuscript.

WAR DIARY 24th DIVISIONAL TRAIN
or
~~INTELLIGENCE~~ SUMMARY.

(Erase heading not required.)

VR 40

Place	1918. Date Dec.	Hour	Summary of Events and Information	Remarks and references to Appendices
SAMEON.	1st		103, 104 and 129 Field Companies marched to TOURNAI this day. Supply Wagons marched with units and will remain with them until further orders. Arrangements made with Divl. M. T. Company to issue rations to these units pending the formation of a Supply Group in TOURNAI. Informed at 11.00 hours that 48th A. F. A. B. would be rationed by this Division on their arrival in Divisional Area. Informed at 23.00 hours that 48th A. F. A. B. would arrive at PERONNES 2-12-18 rationed to date of arrival only. Capt. C. E. PASMORE proceeded on special leave to U. K., 14 days - 3-12-18 to 17-12-18.	
"	2nd		Normal routine.	
"	3rd		O. C. Train and Adjutant proceeded to TOURNAI in search of billets for Train Headquarters.	
"	4th		Pioneer Battn. and Hd. Qrs. R. F. marched to TOURNAI. Supply Wagons delivered at TOURNAI and remain with Unit until further orders. These Units put on "E" Group for rations. 2/Lieut. W. SCARISBRICK proceeded on 14 days leave to U.K., from 6-12-18. O. C. Train and Adjutant proceeded to TOURNAI in search of billets for Train Headquarters.	
"	5th		Train Headquarters marched from SAMEON at 09.00 hours and opened at TOURNAI on arrival at	
TOURNAI	"	13.00	13.00 hours. No. 3 Company marched to new billets at GENECH.	
"	6th		2/Lieut. J. W. DUNCAN attached to Train Headquarters from this date to be in charge of "E" Group at TOURNAI - one Issuer supplied by each Company for duty with this Group.	
"	7th		2 Officers and 50 O. Rs. paraded with Troops from the Division on the occassion of the visit to TOURNAI of H. M. The King. Refilling Point for "C" Group at The Chateau, GENECH from this date.	
"	8th		O. C. Train visited all 4 Companies and Divisional Headquarters. Arrangements made to take over units at present rationed by III Corps Troops for consumption 11th instant.	
"	9th		O. C. Train visited Nos. 1 & 4 Coys., Divisional Headquarters and S. M. T. O., I Corps re lorries for supply duties. 5 reinforcements reported for duty - posted as follows :- No. 2 Coy 1 Sgt., 1 Cpl. and 1 Cpl. Issuer - No. 1 Coy. 1 Driver - No. 4 Coy 1 Driver.	

A. H. Galloway.
LIEUT. COLONEL
O.C. 24th DIVISIONAL TRAIN.

(A7092). Wt. W12839/M1293. 750,000. 1/17. D. D. & L., Ltd. Forms/C.2118/14.

WAR DIARY
or
INTELLIGENCE SUMMARY.
(Erase heading not required.)

24th DIVISIONAL TRAIN.

Instructions regarding War Diaries and Intelligence Summaries are contained in F. S. Regs., Part II. and the Staff Manual respectively. Title pages will be prepared in manuscript.

Place	1918. Date Decr.	Hour	Summary of Events and Information	Remarks and references to Appendices
TOURNAI.	10th		All units transferred from III Corps M. T. Company drew from "E" Group this day. 2/Lieut. A. C. CORBY reported at Train Headquarters having rejoined from sick leave in England - landed in FRANCE 7-12-18.	
"	11th		I Corps Race Meeting held at MOUCHIN. 24th Division won 4 Races out of the 7 - the Divisional Train won two races out of the 4 - 6 furlongs - open to I Corps, and 1 Mile Army Championship (open to First Army) with Capt. E. W. L. MARTIN's Chestnut Gelding "Phillip". Information received that Capt. K. M. PLUMPTRE (sick in England) has been granted further extension on Medical grounds - orders being issued for him to be boarded.	
"	12th		72nd Field Ambulance marched to TOURNAI - supply wagon to remain with unit till further orders. This unit to be rationed by "E" Group from 13th instant.	
"	13th		7 Coalminers proceeded to Corps Concentration Camp en route for CHISLEDON Dispersal Station for release. Lieut. H. W. BRADLEY attached Train Headquarters from this date to act for Adjutant whilst on leave.	"A"
"	14th		3 Coalminers proceeded to Corps Concentration Camp enroute for DUDDINGSTON Dispersal Station for release. Remounts collected for Division this day from RAISMES Railhead - Lieut. J. O. TIDY in charge Conducting Party. 13 H. D. Remounts for Divisional Train (No. 1 - 3, No. 2 - 4, No. 3 - 4, No. 4 - 2.	"A"
TOURNAI.	15th		Informed that Capt. A. C. BENDIT, Requisition Officer attached Central Purchase Board had been boarded in England and struck off strength of B. E. F. from 11-12-18. (Authy :- Q. M. G., G. H. Q. No. QP/ASC/21598/36 dated 11-12-18).	
"	16th		O. C. Train visited "Q" re move of Division. 24th Divisional Train Order No. 42 and Supply Group table Nos. 11, 12, & 13 issued this day. Lieut. A. H. BARNES rejoined this unit on return from leave.	B
"	17th		Capt. F. A. R. SAUNDERS and Capt. & Adjt. E. W. L. MARTIN, M. C. proceeded on leave for 14 days 19-12-18 to 2-1-19.	
"	18th		No. 2 Company marched from GRUSON to new billets at HERTAIN. No. 4 Coy marched from MOUCHIN to new billets at ESPLECHIN - refilling took place on arrival. No. 3 Coy marched from GENECH to billets in TOURNAI. Divl. Headquarters moved into TOURNAI this day.	

O. G. Galloway
LIEUT. COLONEL
O.C. 24th DIVISIONAL TRAIN.

Army Form C. 2118.

WAR DIARY
or
~~INTELLIGENCE SUMMARY.~~

24th DIVISIONAL TRAIN

(*Erase heading not required.*)

Instructions regarding War Diaries and Intelligence Summaries are contained in F. S. Regs., Part II. and the Staff Manual respectively. Title pages will be prepared in manuscript.

Place	Date 1918. Dec.	Hour	Summary of Events and Information	Remarks and references to Appendices
TOURNAI.	19th		No. 1 Company marched from LANDAS to billets in TOURNAI. Capt. C. R. PASMORE rejoined from leave. Lieut. J. O. TIDY attached to No. 2 Company from this date in temporary command. 2/Lt. H. ALPE attached to No. 1 Company, temporarily, from this date.	
"	20th		Lieut. H. W. BRADLEY, A/Adjt., proceeded to back area to purchase goods for Xmas Dinners. 24th Div. Train Order No. 43 issued this day. Lt. G. J. MOTION proceeded on leave to U. K., 22-12-18 to 5-1-19.	C
"	21st		Nos. 2 & 4 Companies marched to billets in TOURNAI. Pack Train cleared by H. T. from this date.	
"	22nd		5 Coalminers proceeded to Corps Concentration Camp en route for DUDDINGSTON Dispersal Station for release. 2/Lt. H. ALPE detailed for duty as Conducting Officer i/c men returning to U. K. for demobilization.	A
"	23rd		24th Divisional Train Order No. 44 issued this day.	"D"
"	24th		2 Coalminers proceeded to Corps Concentration Camp en route for SHORNCLIFFE Dispersal Station for release.	A
"	25th		Xmas Day.	
"	26th		Notification received that T/Capt. K. M. PLUMPTRE has been retained at home for duty & struck off strength of B. E. F. from 21-12-18. (Authy :- Q. M. G., G. H. Q. No. QP/ASC/21598/33 dated 21-12-18.	
"	27th		Normal routine.	
"	28th		Normal routine.	
"	29th		2/Lt. J. W. DUNCAN, Divl. Requisition Officer, attached to 1 Company from this date, temporarily, as S. O. Divl. Troops.	
"	30th		Normal routine.	
"	31st		For the first time since arriving in FRANCE the Officers of the Train dined together. Officers present :- Lt. Col. A. G. GALLOWAY, D. S. O., Major H. B. HUNTER, D. S. O., Captains HITCH, SEDDALL, PASMORE & GALE. Lieuts. TIDY, BARNES & BRADLEY. 2/Lieuts. LEWIS, CORBY, DUNCAN, HODGMAN & SCARISBRICK. Chaplain Rev. COOPER. Guests :- Lt. Col. MASSEY, A. A. & Q. M. G., Major YEO, M. C. and Capt. W. A. McGREGOR, R. A. V. C.	

A G Galloway
LIEUT. COLONEL,
O.C. 24th DIVISIONAL TRAIN.

(A7092). Wt. W12839/M1293. 750,000. 1/17. D. D. & L., Ltd. Forms/C.2118/14.

A

APPENDIX "A" - War Diary.

Nominal Roll of W.Os, N.C.Os, and Men demobilized during the month of Decr. 1918.

Regtl No.	Rank and Name.	Number Ind. Group	Code	Dispersal Stn	Date
T3/028565	Whr Cpl JAMES H C.	3	225	CHISLEDON	13-12-18
T3/030093	Dr. JAMES W	3	225	"	"
T3/027413.	Dr. KENDAL A J	3	225	"	"
T2/14939	Dr. WEIR R.	3	225	"	"
T4/109163	Dr. CRONIN. M J.	3	225	"	"
T4/144217	Dr. GRANFIELD J H	3	225	"	"
T3/023239	Dr. HOLE J H	3	225	"	"
T4/040840	Cpl. McLELLAND W	3	225	DUDDINGSTON	14-12-18.
T4/040844	Dr. ALEXANDER W.	3	225	"	"
T1/888	Dr. BONAR N	3	225	"	"
T4/040833	Dr. WILSON J T	3	225	"	22-12-18.
T3/026236	Dr. JONES W	3	225	"	"
T4/040879.	Dr. WILLIAMSON J G	3	225	"	"
T4/040919	Dr. BROWN J	3	225	"	"
T3/14509	Dr. GRAY J	3	225	"	"
T4/036577	Dr. WOODWARD E V	3	225	SHORNCLIFFE	24-12-18
T4/245511	a/Cpl. SHELTON W	3	225	"	"

A.G. Galloway

Lieut. Colonel,
O.C. 24th. Divl. Train.

Copy No. 8

24th DIVISIONAL TRAIN ORDER NO. 42.

16th DECEMBER 1918.

1. The Divl. Artillery, 72nd and 73rd Inf. Bdes., M.G. Bn., and Division H.Q. are moving to final areas on 18th, 19th and 20th instant. Train Coys will march under the orders of the Formations to which they are affiliated.

2. Supply Turnsout of Division H.Q. and 24th Bn. M.G.C. will remain with units after delivery 17th instant and will march empty with units on 18th and refill from "C" Group Refilling Point on arrival at TOURNAI, on that date.

3. Supply Turnsout of 106th & 48th Bde. R.F.A. will march with those units on 18th loaded with Supplies for consumption 19th. O.C. No. 1 Company will inform the drivers of the exact time and place of refilling at TOURNAI on 19th instant.

4. The Units transferred from "E" to "A" Group on Supply Group Table No. 14 will be so informed by O. i/c "E" Group. O.C. No. 1 Company will arrange for the Supply Turnsout to remain with his Company after delivery on 20-12-18.

5. Supply Turnsout of 7th Northants and 13th Middlesex will march with their units on 17th instant loaded with supplies for consumption 18th instant. O.C. No. 4 Company will inform Drivers of the exact time and place of refilling on 18th instant.

6. Supply Officers and Details of "C" & "D" Groups will move to the new Refilling Point immediately after refilling on 17th instant and take over supplies for consumption on 19th instant, which will be dumped early on 18th instant.

7. Supply Officer and Details of "A" Group will move to new Refilling point on 18th instant immediately after refilling to take over supplies for consumption on 20th instant which will be dumped early on 19th instant.

8. Supply Officers affected by paras 6 & 7 will be billeted by Train Headquarters for the nights in question if desired.

9. A lorry will be supplied to deliver rations to the two Batteries of 107 moving on 20th instant. This lorry will report to Supply Officer "A" Group at Refilling Point at 9 a.m. 19th instant.

10. Supply Group Tables Nos. 11. 12 & 13 are attached.

A. E. Galloway

Lieut. Colonel.
O.C. 24th Divisional Train.

Copies to :-
1. 24th Division "Q"
2. O.C. Train.
3. O.C. No. 1 Company.
4. O.C. No. 2 Company.
5. O.C. No. 3 Company.
6. O.C. No. 4 Company.
7. O.C. 24th M.T. Coy.
8. War Diary –
9. War Diary.
10. File.

B

Copy No. 8 B

SUPPLY GROUP TABLE NO. 11.

To take effect on A.F.W.3316 & 3317.
At Railhead 17-12-18. R.P. 18-12-18.
For consumption 19-12-18.

GROUP "A". R.P. :- LANDAS.	GROUP "B"	GROUP "C". ✻ R.P. :- TOURNAI.	GROUP "D". ✻ R.P. :- WILLEMEAU.
Hd. Qrs. R.A.	17th Bde. H.Q.	72nd Bde. H.Q.	73rd Bde. H.Q.
106th Bde. R.F.A.	8th Queens.	72nd T.M.Batty	73rd T.M.Batty
107th Bde. R.F.A.	1st R. Fusiliers.	9th R. Surreys.	9th R. Sussex.
24th D.A.C.(less detached.)	3rd Rifle. Bde.	8th R.W.Kents.	7th Northants.
24th T.M.Batty.	74th Field Amb.	1st N. Staffs.	13th Middlesex.
No. 1 Coy. Train.	No. 2 Coy. Train.	No. 3 Coy. Train.	73rd Field Amb.
36th M.V. Sect.		24th Divl. H.Q.	No. 4 Coy. Train.
		24th Bn. M.G.C.	
		72nd Field Amb.	
	109th Labour Coy.	48th A.F.A. Bde.	

✻ Supply Wagons to march empty & refill on arrival in new area.

A Galloway

Lieut. Colonel.
O.C. 24th Divisional Train.

Copies to :-
1. 24th Division "Q".
2. O. C. Train.
3. O. C. No. 1 Company.
4. O. C. No. 2 Company.
5. O. C. No. 3 Company.
6. O. C. No. 4 Company.
7. O. C. 24th M.T. Coy.
8. War Diary
9. War Diary
10. File.

SUPPLY GROUP TABLE NO. 12.

To take effect on A.R.W. 3316 and 3317.
At Railhead 18-12-18 R.P. :- 19-12-18
For consumption 20-12-18.

COPY NO....8....

B

GROUP "A". R.P. :- TOURNAI. ✳	GROUP "B" R.P. :-	GROUP "C" R.P. :- TOURNAI	GROUP "D". R.P :- WILLEMEAU
H. Qrs. R.A.	17th Bde. H.Q.	72nd Bde. H.Q.	73rd Bde. H.Q.
106th Bde. R.F.A.	8th Queens.	72nd Bde. L.T.M.B.	73rd T.M. Batty.
107th Bde. R.F.A.	1st R. Fusiliers.	9th E. Surreys.	9th R. Sussex.
24th D.A.C. (complete)	3rd Rifle Bde.	8th R.W. Kents.	7th Northants.
24th T.M. Batty.	74th Field Amb.	1st N. Staffs.	13th Middlesex.
No. 1 Coy. Divl. Train.	No. 2 Coy. Divl. Train.	72nd Field Amb.	73rd Field Amb.
36th M.V. Sect.		No. 3 Coy. Divl. Train.	No. 4 Coy. Divl. Train.
		24th Div. H.Q.	
		24th Bn. M.G.C.	
	109th Labour Coy.	46th A.A.A. Bde.	

✳ Supply Wagons to march empty & refill on arrival in new area.

Lieut. Colonel.
O.C. 24th Divisional Train.

Copies to :-

1. 24th Divison "Q".
2. O. C. Train.
3. O. C. No. 1 Company.
4. O. C. No. 2 Company.
5. O. C. No. 3 C mpany.
6. O. C. No. 4 Company.
7. O. C. 24th M. T. Coy.
8. War Diary
9. War Diary
10. File.

Copy No. 8.........

B

SUPPLY GROUP TABLE No. I3

To take effect on A.R.W. 33I6 & 33I7
At Railhead I9-I2-I8 et seq. R.P. :- 20-I2-I8 et seq
For consumption 2I-I2-I8 et seq.

GROUP "A" R.P. :- TOURNAI.	GROUP "B"	GROUP "C" R.P. :- TOURNAI	GROUP "D" R.P. :- WILLAMBAU
H.Qrs. R.A.	I7th Bde. H.Q.	72nd Bde. H.Q.	73rd Bde H.Q.
I06th Bde. R.F.A.	8th Queens.	72nd L.T.M. Batty.	73rd L.T.M. Batty
I07th Bde. R.F.A.	Ist. R. Fusiliers.	9th E Surreys.	9th R. Sussex
24th D.A.C.	3rd Rifle Bde.	8th R.W. Kents.	7th Northants.
24th T.M. Batty.	74th Field Amb.	Ist N. Staffs.	I3th Middlesex.
No. I Coy. Train	No. 2 Coy. Train.	72nd Field Amb.	73rd Field Amb.
36th M.V. Sect.		No. 3 Coy. Train.	No. 4 Coy Train.
24th Div. H.Q.			
24th Signal Co. R.E. ※			
24th Bn. M.G.C.			
I2th Sher. Foresters ※			
I03 Field Coy. R.E. ※			
I04 Field Coy. R.E. ※			
I29 Field Coy. R.E. ※			
Army Ord. Dept. ※			
48th A.F.A. Bde.	I09 Labour Coy.		

※ From "E" Group

A. G. Galloway
Lieut Colonel
O.C. 24th Divisional Train

Copy No. 13

24th DIVISIONAL TRAIN ORDER NO. 43.

20th DECEMBER 1918.

1. Nos. 2 & 4 Companies will move from their present billets to TOURNAI to-morrow the 21st instant. No restrictions as to time and route.

2. From to-morrow the 21st instant, inclusive, the Pack Train will be cleared by H.T. Supplies will be dumped by lorries to-morrow the 21st instant at 7 a.m. and will be issued immediately to units.

3. From tomorrow the 21st instant, inclusive, each Company will take it in turn commencing with No. 1 Company to have an Orderly at the R.S.O's Office at Railhead from 9 a.m. He should be relieved at 1 p.m. and again at 6 p.m. If the Train has not arrived at the latter hour the Orderly will be relieved by an Orderly who will take blankets and be prepared to sleep at the R.S.O's Office all night.

His duties will be as follows :-

(a) On being informed by the R.S.O. that the Pack Train has arrived the Orderly will proceed at once direct to T.H.Q.
(b) He will then proceed to the Office of the 24th Divl. M.T. Coy and inform them of the arrival of the Train in order that the M.T. Company Supply Officer and Supply Details may be warned.
(c) He will then proceed to his own Company with a message given him by T.H.Q.

4. The other 3 Companies will be warned of the arrival of the Train by an Orderly from this office.

5. All Companies will receive the notification that the Train has arrived at such and such an hour and will proceed to Railhead in the following order and the following times:-

No. 4 Coy.	One hour after the time given on the message from this office.
No. 1 Coy.	One hour & 15 minutes " " " " " " "
No. 3 Coy.	One hour & 45 " " " " " " " " "
No. 2 Coy.	2 Hours after the time " " " " " " "

6. The supplies may either be left on the wagons or dumped at the Refilling Point but in either case the Formation Supply Officer is responsible for the safety of the supplies, but the O.C. Company is responsible for finding the guard.

A. G. Galloway
Lieut. Colonel.
O.C. 24th Divisional Train.

Copies to :-
1. 24th Division "Q".
2. O.C. Train.
3. S.S.O.
4. Lt. J.W. DUNCAN, R.A.S.C.
5. O.C. No. 1 Company.
6. O.C. No. 2 Company.
7. O.C. No. 3 Company.
8. O.C. No. 4 Company.
9. O.C. 24th Div. M.T. Coy.
10. R.S.O., TOURNAI.
11. R.T.O., TOURNAI.
12. War Diary
13. War Diary ✓
14. File.

15

Copy No.....12...

24th DIVISIONAL TRAIN ORDER NO. 44.

23rd DECEMBER 1918.

1. Para. 5 of 24th Divisional Train Order No. 43 is cancelled and the following substituted :-

Train Companies will be notified in writing from this office. The message will be sent out as per pro forma attached.

Pack Train arrived. Zero hour
Train Companies will ARRIVE at Railhead at the following times :-

No. 4 Coy.	Zero	plus	1	hour
No. 2 Coy.	Zero	plus	1	hour 15 minutes
No. 1 Coy.	Zero	plus	1	hour 30 minutes
No. 3 Coy.	Zero	plus	2	hours.

The receipt slip will immediately be signed, timed and returned to the bearer, by either an Officer, W.O., or S.Q.M.S.

2. Para. 3 (c) will be cancelled and the following substituted :-

(a) When the Orderly (at the R.S.O's Office) is found by either 1 or 4 Companies he will take the message from Train Headquarters to these two Companies, proceeding first to No. 4 Company and second to No. 1 Company, and thence returning to Train Hd. Qrs with the receipts.

(b) When he is found by either 2 or 3 Coys he will take the message from Train Hd. Qrs. to these two Coys, proceeding first to No. 2 Company and second to No. 3 Company, thence returning to Train Hd. Qrs. with the receipts.

(c) The message to the two Companies not mentioned in either (a) or (b) above will be sent out by a Train Headquarter Orderly.

3. An Officer or W.O. from each Company will always be at Railhead while wagons are being loaded. The strictest Traffic Discipline will be maintained.

4. Recipients of copies 5, 6, 7, & 8 to acknowledge.

A. S. Galloway

Lieut. Colonel.
O. C. 24th Divisional Train.

Copies to :-

1. 24th Division "Q".
2. O.C. Train.
3. R.S.O.
4. 2/Lt. J. W. DUNCAN.
5. O.C. No. 1 Company.
6. O.C. No. 2 Company.
7. O.C. No. 3 Company.
8. O.C. No. 4 Company.
9. O.C. 24th Div. M. T. Coy.
10. R.S.O., TOURNAI.
11. R.T.O., TOURNAI.
12. War Diary
13. War Diary
14. File.

24/1/3

Instructions regarding War Diaries and Intelligence Summaries are contained in F. S. Regs., Part II. and the Staff Manual respectively. Title pages will be prepared in manuscript.

Army Form C. 2118.

WAR DIARY 24th DIVISIONAL TRAIN
or
~~INTELLIGENCE SUMMARY.~~
(Erase heading not required.)

Vol 41

Place	1919 JAN. Date	Hour	Summary of Events and Information	Remarks and references to Appendices
TOURNAI.	1st.		Normal routine.	
"	2nd		2/Lieut. H. J. LEWIS detailed for duty as Conducting Officer i/c men returning to U. K. for demobilization.	
"	3rd		Normal routine.	
"	4th		Capt. F. A. R. SAUNDERS & Capt. E. W. L. MARTIN, M. C. returned from leave. O. C. Train presided at F. G. C. M. held at Train Headquarters.	
"	5th		O. C. Train proceeded on 3 days leave to BRUSSELS.	
"	6th		2/Lieut. E. R. A. HODGMAN, on "Joe", ran second in the VIII Corps "All Comers" Steeplechase (open to B. E. F.), held at ORCHIES. Major H. B. HUNTER, D. S. O. proceeded on 14 days leave to U. K. 9-1-19 - 23-1-19. Capt. R. F. SEDDALL to act as S. S. O. during Major HUNTER's absence.	
"	7th		Normal routine.	
"	8th		O. C. Train returned from BRUSSELS.	
"	9th		Normal routine.	
"	10th		Lieut. H. W. BRADLEY proceeded on 14 days leave to U. K., 12-1-19 to 26-1-19.	
"	11th		Normal routine.	
"	12th		Notification received that Lt. G. J. MOTION had been granted 14 days extension of leave, pending demobilization as a Pivotal man. Authy :- W. O. Letter No. Q. M. G. 5/181059/3 dated 4-1-19 and G. H. Q., Q. M. G. QP/ASC/22151/18 dated 9-1-19.	
"	13th		Pack Train due 12-1-19 did not arrive till mid-day this day and was not in position for clearing until 16.15 hours. Capt. F. A. R. SAUNDERS detailed as member of G. C. M. which assembled this day at Hd. Qrs. 17th Inf. Bde. 1 C. S. M. reported for duty - posted to No. 4 Company.	

A. R. Galloway
LIEUT. COLONEL
O.C. 24th DIVISIONAL TRAIN.

Instructions regarding War Diaries and Intelligence Summaries are contained in F. S. Regs., Part II. and the Staff Manual respectively. Title pages will be prepared in manuscript.

WAR DIARY or ~~INTELLIGENCE SUMMARY~~.

24th DIVISIONAL TRAIN.

(Erase heading not required.)

Army Form C. 2118.

Place	1919. Date JAN.	Hour	Summary of Events and Information	Remarks and references to Appendices
TOURNAI.	14th		T/2/Lieut. H. WARNER, R. A. S. C. reported for duty this day - Authy :- G. H. Q., Q. M. G. No. QP/ASC 22174 dated 24-12-18. Posted to No. 1 Company, but to be attached for duty to No. 2 Company. O. C. Train visited D. D. S. & T., First Army. Two days rations of certain commodities arrived this Railhead this day. Advised that eventually 1 complete day's rations for the Division would be accumulated in order that serious inconveniences should not take place in the event of a Pack train being more than a day late.	
"	15th		Normal routine.	
"	16th		O. C. Train went round Refilling Points with A. A. & Q. M. G., and D. A. Q. M. G. 7 reinforcements reported for duty - No. 1 Coy 1 Whlr. Cpl. & 2 Drivers, No. 2 Coy 2 Drivers, No. 4 Coy 2 Drivers.	
"	17th		Normal routine.	
"	18th		Normal routine.	
"	19th		Pack Train due this day did not arrive.	
"	20th		1 S. S. M. reported for duty and posted to 72nd Field Amb. through No. 3 Coy. O. C. Train visited D. D. S. & T., First Army. Pack Train due 19-1-19 arrived this day.	
"	21st		Pack Trains due 20-1-19 and 21-1-19 arrived and off-loaded this day. Capt. E. W. L. MARTIN, M. C. on "Philip" won "The Valenciennes Cup" - 1 mile open to First Army - at 12th Division Race Meeting held at AUBERCHICOURT this day. 2/Lieut. E. R. A. HODGMAN and Lieut. J. O. TIDY ran in "The Victory Cup" 1/2 Mile Steeplechase open to First Army. 2/Lt. E. R. A. HODGMAN placed sixth. Capt. C. C. GALE detailed for duty as Conducting Officer i/c men returning to U. K. for demobilization.	
"	22nd		Notification received that 2/Lt. H. ALPE was granted an extension of leave on Medical Certificate pending receipt of further Medical Certificate. (Authy :- W. O. Letter No. QMG 5/AE/532 dated 14-1-19 and Q. M. G., R. A. S. C., G. H. Q. No. QP/ASC/22233/14 dated 17-1-19. Notification received by O. C. No. 2 Company from D. of S. & T., War Office, that Lt. G. J. MOTION (at home on leave) should be demobilized immediately.	

A E Galloway
LIEUT. COLONEL
O.C. 24th DIVISIONAL TRAIN

D. D. & L., London, E.C.
(10340) Wt W5300/P713 750,000 3/18 E 2688 Forms/C2118/10.

24th DIVISIONAL TRAIN.

WAR DIARY
or
~~INTELLIGENCE SUMMARY~~.
(Erase heading not required.)

Army Form C. 2118.

Instructions regarding War Diaries and Intelligence Summaries are contained in F. S. Regs., Part II. and the Staff Manual respectively. Title pages will be prepared in manuscript.

Place	1919 Date JAN.	Hour	Summary of Events and Information	Remarks and references to Appendices
TOURNAI.	23rd		No. T3/029311, T/S. S. M. BAGSHAW R. and No. T3/023166, Cpl. JAMES M. awarded Meritorious Service Medal (London Gazette Supplement Jan. 18th 1919).	
"	24th		Pack Train due this day did not arrive.	
"	25th		Pack Train due 24-1-19 cleared at 08.30 hours this day. Pack Train due to-day cleared at 14.00 hours. O. C. Train attended Conference at I Corps "Q" at which D. A. D. S. First Army was present.	
"	26th		O. C. Train proceeded on 24 hours leave to BRUSSELS. Pack Train did not arrive this day. Heavy fall of snow.	
"	27th		Pack Train due 26-1-19 arrived and off-loaded at 10.30 hours this day. Major H. B. HUNTER, D. S. O. rejoined from leave having been granted an extension to 26-1-19 inclusive. Lieut. J. O. TIDY detailed for duty as Conducting Officer i/c men returning to U. K. for demobilization. Notification received that 2/Lt. H. ALPE was granted an extension of leave on Medical Certificate for 3 weeks from 15-1-19 (Authy :- W. O. Letter No. QMG5/AE/532 dated 15-1-19 and G. H. Q., Q. M. G. No. QP/ASC/22233/14 dated 23-1-19) Capt. G. H. HITCH proceeded on leave to U. K. - 14 days from 28-1-19 to 11-12-19. 2/Lieut. H. J. LEWIS rejoined from leave.	
"	28th		Instructions received for Lieut. A. H. BARNES and 2/Lieut. J. W. DUNCAN to report at I Corps Concentration Camp 29-1-19 at 11.00 hours for demobilization - struck off strength from 29-1-19 (Authy :- 24th Division wire No. A. 700 dated 27-1-19) Lt. H. W. BRADLEY rejoined from leave. Lt. H. W. BRADLEY appointed Demobilization Officer and Assistant Adjt from this date.	
"	29th		4 Coalminers proceeded to I Corps Concent. Camp this day for demobilization.	A
"	30th		O. C. Train visited D. D. S. & T., First Army. 24th Divl. Train Order No. 45 issued this day.	B
"	31st		"B", "C", & "D" Groups amalgamated this day into one Group, to be known as "C" Group i/c Captain R. F. SEDDALL.	

A E Galloway
LIEUT. COLONEL
O.C. 24TH DIVISIONAL TRAIN

D. D. & L., London, E.C.
(10340) Wt W5300/P713 750,000 3/18 E 2688 Forms/C2118/16.

APPENDIX.....A.....

NOMINAL ROLL OF R. A. S. C. Personnel sent to
I CORPS Concent. Camp for DISPERSAL.

Regtl. No.	Rank & Name.	Dispersal Station.	Date.
T4/040722,	Farr. Dr. OUTRAM E.	CLIPSTONE.	29. 1. 19.
T2/14538,	Corpl. GATENBY T.	RIPON.	29. 1. 19.
T2/14537,	Dr. HANLON H.	"	29. 1. 19.
T2/14422,	Dr. SHUTT W.	"	29. 1. 19.

C E Galloway.
LIEUT. COLONEL
O.C. 24th DIVISIONAL

"B"

Copy No. 15

24th DIVISIONAL TRAIN ORDER NO. 45.

30th JANUARY 1919.

1. FROM to-morrow the 31st instant, inclusive the following Supply and Transport arrangements will come into force.

2. "B" "C" & "D" Supply Groups will amalgamate into one Supply Group under Capt. R. F. SEDDALL, R. A. S. C. and will be known as "C" Group.

3. THE Refilling Point of this new "C" Group will be the same as that of the old "B" Group, viz :- No. 2 Company's Refilling Point.

4. 2/Lieut. A. C. CORBY, Supply Officer, 73rd Brigade, will take over the duites of Supply Officer, Divl. Troops, and be attached to No. 1 Coy.

5. Nos. 2, 3, & 4 Companies will remain three separate and distinct Companies under their respective Company Commanders or Acting Company Commanders, but the turnsout of these three Companies will be pooled and detailed daily from this office by the Assistant Adjutant.

6. IN order that there may be no difficulty about Drivers finding the Unit to whom they are taking the Supplies, loaders will continue as at present to go out with the Supply Wagons of the Units for which they load.

7. THE detail from this office will state the number of turnsout, Officers, W. Os., N. C. Os., etc., to be provided by each of the Brigade Coys and the Units to which Supplies are to be delivered by the respective Companies vide attached Pro-formas "A" & "B".

8. ALL Company Commanders will render to this office by 14.00 hours to-morrow the 31st instant, and each day thereafter, the Availability Return as per attached pro-forma "C", of all transport available on the day following that of the Return.

9. NO. 1 Company will not be detailed to assist in the drawing and delivery of Supplies of "C" Group, but will be called upon to assist in the drawing of Fuel and Vegetables.

10. PARA. 1 of 24th Divisional Train Order No. 44 is cancelled as regards the times of arrival of Train Companies at Railhead, and the following substituted :-

Nos. 2, 3, & 4 Coys.	ZERO PLUS 1 Hour.
No. 1 Company.	ZERO PLUS 1 Hour & 30 minutes.

11. The Supply Details of Nos. 2, 3 & 4 Coys will be pooled for work under Capt. R. F. SEDDALL, Supply Officer "C" Group, but will continue to live with their Companies.

12. The Guard for "C" Group Refilling Point will be furnished by each of the Brigade Train Companies in turn as detailed from this office. The Guard will consist of 1 N. C. O. and 6 men and will be found from the Supply Details and Loaders of the Companies detailed.

A. E. Galloway

Lieut. Colonel.
O. C. 24th Divisional Train.

Copies to :-
1. 24th Division "Q") For information.
2. 17th Inf. Bde.)
3. 72nd Inf. Bde.)
4. 73rd Inf. Bde.)
5. O. C. Train.
6. S. S. O.
7. O. C. No. 1 Company.
8. O. C. No. 2 Company.
9. O. C. No. 3 Company.
10. O. C. No. 4 Company.
11. Capt. R. F. SEDDALL.
12. 2/Lieut. A. C. CORBY.
13. Assistant Adjutant.
14. Supply Officer, 24th Divl. M. T. Coy.
15. War Diary.
16. War Diary.
17. File.

Pro-forma "A".

Detail for Transport and Personnel for RAILHEAD ON ______

TIME - ZERO HOUR AS PUBLISHED.

Company.	Officers or W. Os.	N. C. Os.	G. S. Turnsout.	REMARKS.
No. 2.				
No. 3.				
No. 4.				
TOTALS				

Time.......

Date.......

Lieut.
Asst. Adjt., 24th Div'l. Train.

Pro-forma "B"

Detail for Transport & Personnel for REFILLING POINT ON...........
Time -

Company	Officers or W. Os.	N. C. Os.	G. S. Turnsout	Units to which Supplies are to be delivered.	GUARD	
					N. C. O.	Men
No. 2						
No. 3						
No. 4.						
TOTALS						

Time ....

Date ....

Lieut.
Asst. Adjt, 24th Divl. Train.

Pro-forma "C"

TRANSPORT STATE for - / - /19 .
No.... COMPANY, 24th. DIVISIONAL TRAIN

DETAIL	Wagons	Horses	REMARKS
(a) In Camp.			
(b) Sick & under repair. Required for Coy. duties.			
Total (b)			
Available for duty			

Date..........

O. C. Company.

Instructions regarding War Diaries and Intelligence Summaries are contained in F. S. Regs., Part II. and the Staff Manual respectively. Title pages will be prepared in manuscript.

WAR DIARY
or
INTELLIGENCE SUMMARY.
(Erase heading not required.)

24th DIVISIONAL TRAIN

V8 42

Place	1919. Date Feby.	Hour	Summary of Events and Information	Remarks and references to Appendices
TOURNAI.	1st		O. C. Train accompanied A. A. & Q. M. G round Refilling Points this day.	
"	2nd		Transport situation working satisfactorily under the Pool system.	
"	3rd		6 Other Ranks proceeded to 1 Corps Concentration Camp this day for dispersal. Supply Group Table No. 14 issued this day.	"A" "B"
"	4th		Notification received that 2/Lieut. H. ALPE had been demobilized whilst on leave in U. K. Struck off strength as from 15-1-19 (Authy :- D. of S. & T. W. O. letter dated 1-2-19.	
"	5th		Normal routine.	
"	6th		2/Lt. E. R. A. HODGMAN proceeded to 1 Corps Concentration Camp for ~~disperse~~ demobilization and struck off strength as from this date - Authy D. D. S. T., 1st Army No. ST/648 dated 31-1-19.	
"	7th		2 Other Ranks proceeded to 1 Corps Concentration Camp this day for demobilization.	"A"
"	8th		O. C. Train visited D. D. S. & T. First Army.	
"	9th		Divl. Horse Demob. Officer classified Horses of Nos. 1 & 2 Companies.	
"	10th		Normal routine. D. D. S. & T. First Army dined at Train Headquarters.	
"	11th		Normal routine.	
"	12th		Div. Horse Demob. Officer classified Horses of Nos. 3 & 4 Companies.	
"	13th		S. S. O. visited D. D. S. & T. First Army. 6 O. Rs. proceeded to 1 Corps Concent. Camp this day for demobilization.	"A"
"	14th		Lt. H. W. BRADLEY appointed Adjutant, 24th Divl. Train from this date, vice Capt. E. W. L. MARTIN, M. C. (resigned) to Regimental Duty. Notification received from H. BIRCH, Esq. (Trustee) that Capt. G. H. HITCH died from Pneumonia 8-2-19.	

H. B. Hunter.
Major
O. C. 24th Divisional Train.

D. D. & L., London, E.C.
(10340) Wt W5300/P713 750,000 3/18 E 2688 Forms C/2118/16.

Army Form C. 2118.

Instructions regarding War Diaries and Intelligence Summaries are contained in F. S. Regs., Part II. and the Staff Manual respectively. Title pages will be prepared in manuscript.

WAR DIARY
or
INTELLIGENCE SUMMARY

(Erase heading not required.)

24th DIVISIONAL TRAIN

Place	Date 1919. Feby.	Hour	Summary of Events and Information	Remarks and references to Appendices
TOURNAI.	15th		2/Lieut. A. C. CORBY proceeded to 1 Corps Concentration Camp for demobilization and struck off strength as from this date - Authy :- D. D. S. & T., First Army wire D. M. 57 dated 8-2-19.	
"	16th		Normal routine. 2 re-inforcements (Drivers) reported for duty and posted to No. 1 Company.	
"	17th		3 re-inforcements (Supply details) reported for duty and posted as follows :- 2 to 1 Coy - 1 to 4 Coy. The I Corps Commander accompanied by the D. A. Q. M. G., 1 Corps, the G. O. C., and A. A. Q. M. G., 24th Division inspected the four Companies of the Train in the following order :- No. 1 Company 14. 30 hours - No. 4 Company 15. 00 hours - No. 3 Company 15. 25 hours - No. 2 Company 16. 00 hours. Capt. C. E. PASMORE, R. A. S. C. detailed as member of F. G. C. M. which assembled on this day at 17th Inf. Bde. Hd. Qrs.	
"	18th		Authority given for T/Lieut. H. W. BRADLEY, R. A. S. C. to wear the badges of a/Captain pending the appearance of his appointment in the "London Gazette". Authy :- 24th Divn. A/1523 dated 18-2-19.	
"	19th		Nos. 2 & 4 Companies amalgamated under command of Capt. C. E. PASMORE with 2/Lt. H. WARNER as Subaltern.	
"	20th		Lt. Col. A. G. GALLOWAY, D. S. O., R. A. S. C. proceeded on 14 days leave to England from 21-2-19 to 7-3-19. Lt. J. O. TIDY, R. A. S. C. rejoined from leave. 1 W. O. and 3 O. Rs. proceeded to 1 Corps Concentration Camp this day for demobilization. Major H. B. HUNTER, D. S. O., R. A. S. C. took over temporary command of the Train during the absence on leave of Lt. Col. A. G. GALLOWAY, D. S. O., R. A. S. C.	A
"	21st		Normal routine.	
"	22nd		Capt. C. E. PASMORE, R. A. S. C. proceeded on four days special leave to England from 23-2-19 to 27-2-19. O. C. Train visited D. D. S. & T., First Army. 82 "Y" Horses demobilized.	
"	23rd		D. A. D. V. S. inspected "Z" class horses for sale.	

H. B. Hunter
Major.
O. C. 24th Divisional Train.

D. D. & L., London, E.C.
(10340) Wt W5300/P713 750,000 3/18 E 2688 Forms C/2118/16.

Instructions regarding War Diaries and Intelligence Summaries are contained in F. S. Regs., Part II. and the Staff Manual respectively. Title pages will be prepared in manuscript.

WAR DIARY
or
INTELLIGENCE SUMMARY.

24th DIVISIONAL TRAIN

Army Form C. 2118.

(Erase heading not required.)

Place	Date 1919 Feby.	Hour	Summary of Events and Information	Remarks and references to Appendices
TOURNAI.	24th		Normal routine.	
"	25th		Normal routine.	
"	26th		Horse Transport Detail curtailed from this date. Capt. E. W. L. MARTIN, M. C., R. A. S. C. on "Philip" won the Mile Flat Race open to Officers of the Allied Armies at XXII Corps Race Meeting at MONS.	
"	27th		Capt. E. W. L. MARTIN, M. C., R. A. S. C. on "Philip" won the Mile Flat Race open to Officers of the Allied Armies at 63rd (Royal Naval) Division Race Meeting held at MONS. A Silver Cup was presented for this Race.	
"	28th		Normal routine.	

H. B. Hunter
Major.
O. C. 24th Divisional Train.

D. D. & L., London, E.C.
(10340) Wt W5300/P713 750,000 3/18 E 2688 Forms/C2118/16.

Appendix "A".

NOMINAL ROLL OF R. A. S. C. PERSONNEL SENT TO CONCENTRATION CAMP FOR DISPERSAL

Regtl. No.	Rank	N A M E	Dispersal Station	Date Proceeded
T4/040738.	Dr.	KNIGHT, HERBERT	CLIPSTONE.	3-2-19.
T3/022732.	Dr.	JACKSON, ANDREW	GEORGETOWN.	3-2-19.
T2/SR/03364.	Dr.	EDGE GEORGE	THETFORD	3-2-19.
S4/158491.	Pte.	DOWELL CECIL ERNEST	FOVANT	3-2-19.
S4/064815.	S. Sgt.	CARTER WALTER THOMAS	SHORNCLIFFE	3-2-19.
T4/254222.	Dr.	FERGUSSON ERNEST	CHISLEDON	7-2-19.
T3/024789.	Dr.	BARNES FREDERICK WILLIAM	THETFORD	7-2-19.
T/28673.	a/Sgt.	DAVIES FREDERICK JAMES	CLIPSTONE	13-2-19.
CHT/231.	Dr.	GAUL ALBERT	CLIPSTONE	13-2-19.
T/19937.	Dr. Sadd	HOWARD JOHN	PREES HEATH	13-2-19.
T/21432.	a/L/Cpl	FROST HERBERT JAMES	PURFLEET	13-2-19.
S3/030801.	Sgt.	TIBBLE CHARLES GEORGE	SHORNCLIFFE	13-2-19.
T4/091473.	L/Cpl.	VEVERS JOSEPH MONTAGU WYATT	CHISLEDON	13-2-19.
T/18107.	i/c S. S. M.	LOWRIE THOMAS JOSEPH	CLIPSTONE	20-2-19.
S/256638.	Pte.	NICHOLSON CLAUD ALAN	CLIPSTONE	20-2-19.
T4/109381.	Cpl.	CULLEN JOHN DAVID	SHORNCLIFFE	20-2-19.
T/23983.	a/Cpl.	SVENSSON JOHN HJALMAR	PURFLEET	22-2-19.
T2/10975.	C. Q. M. S.	HARMAN JOHN RICHARD	CHISLEDON	27-2-19.
S4/064802.	Sergt.	CARMICHAEL WILLIAM	DUDDINGSTON	27-2-19.
T4/039044.	Wh. Dr.	ATKINSON HENRY	RIPON	27-2-19.
T3/024188.	Dr.	HUNT CHARLES GEORGE	THETFORD	27-2-19.

4

Copy No. 15

SUPPLY GROUP TABLE NO. 14.

On A. F. W. 3316 & 3317 Feby. 1st
At Railhead Feby. 1st
For issue Feby. 1st

B

Divisional Troops
R. P. :- Rue de ATH.

Hd. Qrs., 24th Division.
C. R. A.
106th Bde. R. F. A.
107th Bde. R. F. A.
24th D. A. C.
24th T. M. Batty.
No. 1 Company, Train.
36th M. V. Section.
H. Q., 24th Divl. Train.
24th Signal Company. R. E.
24th Battn. M. G. C.
12th Sherwood Fors.
103rd Field Coy. R. E.
104th Field Coy. R. E.
129th Field Coy. R. E.
24th Div. Recept. Camp.
Army O. Dept.

72nd Inf. Bde.
R. P. :- Boulevard Leopold.

Hd. Qrs. 17th Inf. Bde.
3rd Rifle Bde.
1st R. Fusiliers.
8th Queens.
74th Field Amb.
No. 2 Company, Train.
H. Q., 72nd Inf. Bde.
9th East Surreys.
8th R. W. Kents.
1st North Staffs.
72nd T. M. Batty.
No. 3 Company, Train.
72nd Field Amb.
Hd. Qrs. 73rd Inf. Bde.
9th R. Sussex.
7th Northants.
13th Middlesex.
73rd T. M. Batty. 73rd Field Amb.
No. 4 Company, Train.

48th A. F. A. Bde.
325 Quarry Company.
196 Land Dranage Coy.
" " " " Details.
III Corps Recept. Camp.
H. Q., 69 Labour Coy.
77th Labour Coy.
122nd Labour Coy.
109th Railway T. Coy.
12th M. A. C.
No. 5 Telegraph Coy.
61 Aux. Petrol Coy.

Church Army Hut, TAINTIGNIES.
77th Road Section.
66th Sanitary Section.
823 Area Empt. Coy.
3rd Aust. Tun. Coy.
C. R. E., VII Corps.
Town Major, TOURNAI.
" " B. R. C. S.
" " Y. M. C. A.
" " Armee Belge.
135th H. T. Coy., R. E.
58th Div. M. T. Coy.

R. Galloway

Lieut. Colonel.
O. C. 24th Divisional Train.

3-2-19.

Copies to :-
1. "Q" 24th Division.
2. O. C. Train.
3. S. S. O.
4. Adjutant.
5. Asst. Adjutant.
6. O. C. No. 1 Company.
7. O. C. No. 2 Company.
8. O. C. No. 3 Company.
9. O. C. No. 4 Company.
10. 2/Lt. A. C. CORBY.
11. Capt. R. F. SEDDALL.
12. S. O., 24th M. T. Coy.
13. R. T. O., TOURNAI.
14. R. S. O., TOURNAI.
15. War Diary.
16. War Diary.
17. File.

B

Army Form C. 2118.

Instructions regarding War Diaries and Intelligence Summaries are contained in F. S. Regs., Part II. and the Staff Manual respectively. Title pages will be prepared in manuscript.

WAR DIARY or INTELLIGENCE SUMMARY.

24th DIVISIONAL TRAIN

(Erase heading not required.)

WO 43

Place	Date 1919 Mch.	Hour	Summary of Events and Information	Remarks and references to Appendices
TOURNAI.	1st		66 "Z" Class horses inspected by D. A. D. V. S. Orders to send 100 "Z" Horses to ABBEVILLE.	
"	2nd		100 "Z" Class Horses despatched by Rail to ABBEVILLE this day.	
"	3rd		44 "Z" Class Horses sent for sale to Belgians this day.	
"	4th		Major H. B. HUNTER, D. S. O., R. A. S. C. visited D. D. S. & T. First Army this day. Orders received for 16 "Z" Class horses to be sent for sale.	
"	5th		16 "Z" Class Horses sent for sale this day. Infantrymen attached for temporary duty returned to their respective units this day. Increased allotment of men for demobilization received from D. D. S. & T., First Army.	
"	6th		Normal routine.	
"	7th		24 N. C. Os and men proceeded to I Corps Concent. Camp this day for demobilization.	"A"
"	8th		Lieut. Colonel A. G. GALLOWAY, D. S. O., R. A. S. C. returned from leave.	
"	9th		Orders received for draft of 14 Drivers, 1 Clerk and 2 Issuers to proceed to the Rhine,	
"	10th		Normal routine.	
"	11th		" "	
"	12th		4 "X" Class horses (R2.) transferred to 108th Bde. A. F. A.	
"	13th		4 "Y" Class R2 Horses transferred to England for sale (Officers' Chargers) 40 O. Rs. proceeded this day to I Corps Concent. Camp for demobilization.	"A"

H. B. Hunter
Major.
O. C. 24th Divisional Train.

D. D. & L., London, E.C.
(10340) Wt W5300/P713 750,000 3/18 E 2688 Forms/C2118/16.

Army Form C. 2118.

Instructions regarding War Diaries and Intelligence Summaries are contained in F. S. Regs., Part II. and the Staff Manual respectively. Title pages will be prepared in manuscript.

WAR DIARY
or
INTELLIGENCE SUMMARY.
(Erase heading not required.)

24th DIVISIONAL TRAIN

Place	1919. Mch. Date	Hour	Summary of Events and Information	Remarks and references to Appendices
TOURNAI.	14th		Commanding Officer & Adjutant visited D. D. S. & T. First Army.	
"	15th		Commanding Officer & Adjutant visited Vehicle Park at BAISIEUX.	
"	16th		Commanding Officer & Adjutant attended conference at "Q" 24th Division.	
"	17th		Draft of 12 O. Rs. proceeded this day to 1st Divisional Train.	
"	18th		8 H. D. Horses transferred to HAVRE.	
"	19th		Normal routine.	
"	20th		Capt. E. W. L. MARTIN, M. C., R. A. S. C. proceeded direct to England for demobilization and struck off strength as from this date. (Authy :- D. D. S. & T. First Army DM. 272 dated 15-3-19).	
"	21st		Lt. Col. A. G. GALLOWAY, D. S. O., R. A. S. C. proceeded to BRUSSELS on 48 hours leave of absence. Commanding Officer inspected 40 N. C. Os. and men proceeding on 22nd March for demobilization.	
"	22nd		Normal routine.	
"	23rd		Normal routine.	
"	24th		Major H. B. HUNTER, D. S. O., R. A. S. C. proceeded on 6 days Special leave to England. Rev. W. S. COOPER C. F. proceeded direct to England for demobilization. (Authy :- A. P. C. First Army No. 22/18 d-20-3-19)	
"	25th		86 H. T. W. Os., N. C. Os and men and 2 Supply Details proceeded this day for demobilization to I Corps Concent. Camp.	"A"
"	26th		Commanding Officer & Adjutant visited D. D. S. & T., First Army.	
"	27th		Commanding Officer & Adjutant visited D. D. S. & T. First Army.	
"	28th		Capt. & Adjt. H. W. BRADLEY and Lieut. M. J. LEWIS, R. A. S. C. granted 48 hours leave to BRUSSELS.	
"	29th		1 N. C. O. proceeded this day to 1st Divisional Train.	
"	30th		7 N. C. O.s and men proceeded this day to I Corps Concent Camp for demobilization.	"A"
"	31st		Lieut. Colonel A. G. GALLOWAY, D. S. O., R. A. S. C. struck off strength on taking over command of 32nd Divisional Train.	

H. B. Hunter
Major.
O. C. 24th Divisional Train.

D. D. & L., London, E.C.
(10340) Wt W5300/P713 750,000 3/18 E 1688 Forms/C2118/16.

"A"

Nominal Roll of R. A. S. C. Personnel who have proceeded to 1 Corps Concent. Camp for Dispersal on dates shewn.

Regtl. No.	Rank and Name.	Dispersal Station.	Date.
T4/040820.	Cpl. MARSHALL P.		7-3-1919
T2/14600.	Dr. HANLIN J.		"
T4/040817.	Dr TENNANT J.		"
T/36300.	Dr. CLAYTON R. P.		"
T4/058718.	Dr. COWLES G.		"
T2/14600.	Dr JOHNSON J.		"
T4/040586.	Cpl. RICHARDSON J.		"
T4/055535	Dr. DOMAN A. U.		"
T4/040132.	Dr. JEFFORD J.		"
T/330541.	Dr. CUSSEN H. M. E.		"
T4/085300.	~~Dr.~~ Cpl. DIXON F. W.		"
T/26238.	Cpl. BAILLIE W. J.		"
T4/040969.	Cpl. GORDON A.		"
T4/026883.	Dr. DARCY F.		"
T3/023360.	L/Cpl. HUGHES T.		"
T4/044333.	Dr. TRUEMAN F.		"
T/22063.	Farr. S. Sgt. WALKER W.		"
T4/036615.	Dr. WARKUP G. F.		"
T4/040805.	Dr. HOLMES S.		"
T4/084280.	Dr. GLISTER S. J.		"
T3/21445.	Sgt. INGRAMS G. T.		"
TS/7219.	Sadd. S. Sgt. VALLANCE A. E.		"
T/23689.	L/Cpl. THORNE W. J.		"

Nominal Roll of R. A. S. C. Personnel who have proceeded to I Corps Concent. Camp for Dispersal on dates shown

Regtl. No.	Rank & Name.	Dispersal Station.	Date.
T/384364,	Dr. WEBBER S.	FOVANT.	
T3/028951,	Cpl. GEDGE E. J.	THETFORD	13-3-1919.
T3/022725,	Dr. BELL H.	"	" "
T/17819,	Farr. Stf. Sgt. ABRAM J. C.	"	" "
T4/092989,	Whlr. Stf. Sgt. TAYLOR P. H.	PURFLEET	" "
T/32729,	Sadd. Cpl. SHARPE G. A.	SHORNCLIFFE	" "
T/15214,	Whlr. Stf. Sgt. FERRIS H.	"	" "
T3/024180,	Dr. ELMES H.	"	" "
T4/055799,	Dr. CLUBB T.	"	" "
TS/705,	Dr. BAULCH T. A.	"	" "
T4/071511,	Pte. ROBERTSON A. W. H.	"	" "
T/25333,	[illegible]r. HARDY J. A.	"	" "
T/22652,	Dr. CHANDLER C.	"	" "
T4/040275,	Dr. TYLER W. J.	"	" "
T3/029682,	Dr. JAMES F.	"	" "
T/30950,	Dr. ARNOLD J. C.	"	" "
T/32811,	Farr. [illegible]r. DARRACH J.	OSWESTRY	" "
T2/14595,	Dr. MARTIN J.	"	" "
T2/14460,	Dr. LINEHAM D.	"	" "
T/29066,	Dr. BUTCHART J.	KINROSS	" "
T4/040748,	Dr. HEALEY J.	GEORGETOWN	" "
T4/213222,	Whlr. Cpl. BROWN P. C.	"	" "
T3/029674,	Dr. HALL R.	PREES HEATH	" "
T1/333,	Dr. GIBBONS W.	"	" "
/25405,	Dr. FISHER J.	"	" "
4/173426,	Dr. ROGERS W. A. T.	"	" "
4/040696,	Dr. WILSON R.	RIPON	" "
4/040810,	Dr. WAITES J. W.	CLIPSTONE	" "
S/7867,	Dr. SHEPHERD H. G.	"	" "
4/040804,	Dr. ROBINSON G.	"	" "
4/040848,	Dr. MOSLEY G.	"	" "
HT/626,	Wgnr. KIRBY T.	"	" "
4/036819,	Dr. JOBSON A.	"	" "
3/023783,	Dr. HEWITT J.	"	" "
Wheeler)			
HT/575,	Whnr. APPLEBY R.	"	" "
1/250843,	Dr. ASPINALL W.	"	" "
4/041066,	Dr. BUST R. W.	"	" "
5/130,	Dr. NOCK W.	CHISLEDON	" "
/1104,	Dr. GATES H. W. J.	"	" "
3/017848,	Whlr. Cpl. BURNELL F.	"	" "

NOMINAL ROLL OF OTHER RANKS SENT FOR DISPERSAL ON -- -3-1919.

Regtl. No.	Rank.	Name.	Dispersal Station.
T1/586.	Dr.	Wills A.J.	Shorncliffe.
T4/058143.	Dr.	Biddle, E.J.	"
T4/058184	Dr.	Buckmaster B.	"
ET/4828?.	Dr.	Tuson A.	"
T1/481	Dr	Clark M.	"
T4/056073.	Dr.	Beaumont R.	"
T/15857.	Dr.	Geraldine W.	"
T2/567.	Dr.	Widgery W.	"
T2/014173.	Dr.	Hayter J.	"
T4/055792.	Dr.	Fullbrook H.	"
T4/148718	Dr.	Brankcom C.V.	"
T/25186.	Dr.	Baldwin A.J.	"
T/25014	Dr.	Kemp A.	"
T/27194.	Dr.	Barton R.A.	"
ET/48224.	Dr.	Funnell A.E.	"
T2/14485.	Dr	Garnham T.W.	Thetford.
T3/025214.	L/Cpl.	Buck W.W.	"
T2/13885.	Cpl.	Death G.S.	Purfleet.
T4/159928.	Dr.	Hodge A.	"
S/253987	Pte.	Reddan C.	"
TS/10095.	Whlr.	Clarke H.C.	Fovant
~~[illegible]~~	~~Dr~~	~~[illegible]~~	"
T/055344	Dr.	Goddard J.	"
T4/146771	Dr.	Fudge P.J.	"
T4/214112.	Dr.	Wiscock W.	"
T/20732.	Dr.	Connell G.W.	"
T4/040103	L/Cpl.	Glasspool S.	"
T3/029677.	Dr	Huson W.	Prees Heath.
T3/025?75.	Dr.	Langston J.A.	"
T/35139.	Dr.	Simpson T.	"
T4/0?2405	Dr.	Cain J.	"
TS/5450	Sadd. Cpl.	Ashworth	"
T4/083967	Dr.	Bamford J.	"
T3/029079.	Dr.	Hillier P.	"
T/24999.	Dr.	Porter C.	"
T4/0555??	Dr.	Nixon W.E.	"
T4/055917.	Whlr. Cpl.	Rowe. G.W.	"
T2/12272.	Whlr. Dr.	Hulme S.	"
T2/12199.	Dr.	Edwards T.	"
T4/055934.	Dr.	Gresty A.	"
T3/028553.	Dr.	Stoddart. A.	Duddingstone.
T4/040884	Farr. Cpl.	Rennie J.	"
T4/212273	C.S.M.	McCulloch D.	Hanorsby, Duddingstone
T4/040865.	Dr	McKenna M.	Georgetown.
T3/025775.	Dr.	Wilson A.	"
T4/010742.	Dr.	Henderson J.	Chisledon.
T3/023090	Dr.	Swain E.	"
T4/055896.	Dr.	Biggerstaffe J.	"
T2/12986.	Dr.	Mulliner J.	"
T3/025034.	Cpl.	Jenkins E.	"
T3/029502.	Dr.	Vernon F.W.	"
T4/185453.	Sadd. Dr.	Allen R.S.	"
T4/243314.	Dr.	Gibson A.	"
T4/058019.	Dr.	Shepherd C.	"
T3/D29351.	Dr.	Taylor H.	"
T4/040360.	Dr.	Lane A.H.	"
T4/055973.	Dr.	Harrison F.	"
~~T2/14128.~~	~~Dr.~~	~~Underwood W.~~	~~[illegible]~~
~~T4/040711.~~	~~Dr.~~	~~Sturrock J.G.~~	"
T4/041038.	Dr.	Cooper J.	"
T2/14536.	Dr.	Smith W.	"
T4/043323.	Dr.	Saint G.C.	"
T4/054196	Dr.	Cotton W.	"

NOMINAL ROLL OF OTHER RANKS SENT FOR DISPERSAL ON ~~22~~ 25-3-1919.

Regtl No.	Rank.	Name.	Dispersal Station.
T4/037850.	Dr.	Hook W.J.	Harrowby.
T/17194.	Dr.	Sears G.	"
T4/249585.	C.Q.M.S.	Andrew C.P.	Clipstone.
T4/253126.	S.S.M.	Bender E.B.	"
T/358666.	Dr	Bassett E.	"
T4/089558.	Dr.	Greenlees J.	"
T4/124066.	Dr.	Swaby L.	"
T4/040808.	Dr	Walker H.	"
~~T4/040992~~	~~Dr.~~	~~Micklethwaite J.W.~~	~~"~~
T4/040998.	Dr	Clark S.A.	"
T4/049716.	Farr. S Sgt.	Wolstenholme T.	"
T2/14310.	Dr.	Wilson R.	"
ET/48265.	Dr.	Exton J.	"
T/35703.	Dr.	Greenway W.	"
T4/042019.	Dr.	Allsop G.	"
T1/SR/971.	Whlr. Dr.	Power T.	Oswestry.

Nominal Roll of R. A. S. C. Personnel who have proceeded to 1 Corps Concent. Camp for Dispersal on date shewn.

Regtl. No.	Rank and Name.	Dispersal Station.	Date.
T1/SR/90.	S. S. M. BAMPTON F. J.	Shorncliffe	30-3-1919
ET/48364.	Dr. RICHARDSON W.	Harrowby	"
T4/092273.	Dr. MASTERS A. S.	Clipstone	"
T/29363.	Dr. PRIDDLE A. J.	Shorncliffe	"

Headquarters,
24th Div. Bde. Group.

Herewith Confidential War Diary of O. C. 24th Divisional Train for the month of April, 1919.
~~Please acknowledge~~.

H. Beasley
Capt. and Adjt.,
for O. C. 24th Divisional Train.

2-5-1919.

Army Form C. 2118.

Instructions regarding War Diaries and Intelligence Summaries are contained in F. S. Regs., Part II. and the Staff Manual respectively. Title pages will be prepared in manuscript.

WAR DIARY of O. C. 24th Divisional Train.

~~INTELLIGENCE SUMMARY.~~

(Erase heading not required.)

Vol 44

Place	Date	Hour	Summary of Events and Information	Remarks and references to Appendices
	April 1919.			
TOURNAI.	1st.		Major H. B. HUNTER, D. S. O., R. A. S. C., returned from leave of absence to England. Major H. B. HUNTER, D. S. O., R. A. S. C., took over command of 24th Divisional Train vice Lieut-Colonel A. G. GALLOWAY, D. S. O., R. A. S. C. to 32nd Divisional Train.	
	2nd.		9. O. R. Supply Details proceeded this day to CALAIS, (transferred for duty) Adjutant visited Vehicle Park, BAISSEUX.	"A"
	3rd.		Cadre of 36th M. V. S. taken over by 24th Divisional Train.	
	4th.		C. O. visited D. D. of S. & T. 1st Area. 5. O. R. Supply Details transferred to 56 R. S. D., TOURNAI. 1. O. R. transferred to 13th R. S. D., ANZIN.	
	5th.		Capt. R. F. SEDDALL, R. A. S. C., granted leave to PARIS.	
	6th.		Normal Routine.	
	7th.		Normal Routine.	
	8th.		C. O. visited D. D. of S. & T. 1st Area. 2 Supply Details transferred to 1st Divisional Train.	
	9th.		Normal Routine.	
	10th.		A. F. Z. 56 received for Major H. B. HUNTER, D. S. O., R. A. S. C. Capt. R. F. SEDDALL, R. A. S. C., returned from leave to PARIS.	
	11th.		Normal Routine.	
	12th.		Normal Routine.	
	13th.		Normal Routine.	
	14th.		Normal Routine.	
	15th.		Major H. B. HUNTER, D. S. O., R. A. S. C., granted leave to BRUSSELS for 72 hours.	

H. Bradley
Captain. 15/4/1
for O. C. 24th Divisional Train.

2353 Wt. W2514/1454 700,000 5/15 D. D. & L. A.D.S.S./Forms/C. 2118.

Army Form C. 2118.

Instructions regarding War Diaries and Intelligence Summaries are contained in F. S. Regs., Part II. and the Staff Manual respectively. Title pages will be prepared in manuscript.

WAR DIARY ~~or~~ of O. C. 24th Divisional Train.

~~INTELLIGENCE SUMMARY.~~

(Erase heading not required.)

Place	Date April 1919.	Hour	Summary of Events and Information	Remarks and references to Appendices
TOURNAI.	16th.		Nos. 194 and 196 Companies amalgamated with Nos. 195 and 197 Companies under command of Lieut. H. J. LEWIS, R. A. S. C. Capt. F. A. R. SAUNDERS and Capt. C. E. PASMOTE, R. A. S. C., proceeded to England independently for Demobilization.	
	17th.		Major H. E. HUNTER, D. S. O., R. A. S. C., proceeded to England independently for Demobilization. Capt. R. F. SEDDALL, R. A. S. C., assumed command of 24th Divisional Train Cadre.	
	18th.		Capt. R. F. SEDDALL, R. A. S. C., proceeded to England on 14 days leave of absence.	
	19th.		Captain H. W. BRADLEY, R. A. S. C., assumed temporary command of 24th Divisional Train Cadre during the absence on leave of Capt. R. F. SEDDALL, R. A. S. C.	
	20th.		Arrangements made for parties of 12 N. C. O's and men to visit YPRES every other day by motor lorry. First party proceeded today.	
	21st.		Orders received for Railhead to be changed from TOURNAI to TEMPLEUVE (FRANCE) from 25th instant inclusive.	
	22nd.		Second party proceeded to visit YPRES this day.	
	23rd.		Capt. W. A. MacGREGOR, R. A. V. C., proceeded this day to England for duty. Cadre of No. 1. V. E. S. taken over by 24th Divisional Train.	
	24th.		Third party proceeded this day to visit YPRES. ~~Capt. H. W. BRADLEY, R. A. S. C., visited Railhead at TEMPLEUVE this day.~~ Capt. H. W. BRADLEY, R. A. S. C., visited new Railhead at TEMPLEUVE.	
	25th.		Normal Routine.	
	26th.		Normal Routine.	
	27th.		Capt. H. W. BRADLEY, R. A. S. C., visited D. D. of S. & T., 1st Area. 2/Lieut. W. SCARISBRICK, R. A. S. C., admitted to 51st. C. C. S. Fourth party visited YPRES this day.	

H. W. Bradley Capt.
for Captain.
O. C. 24th Divisional Train.

2353 Wt. W2544/1454 700,000 5/15 D. D. & L. A.D.S.S./Forms/C. 2118.

Army Form C. 2118.

Instructions regarding War Diaries and Intelligence Summaries are contained in F. S. Regs., Part II. and the Staff Manual respectively. Title pages will be prepared in manuscript.

WAR DIARY of O. C. 24th Divisional Train.

~~INTELLIGENCE SUMMARY~~.

(*Erase heading not required.*)

Place	Date April 1919.	Hour	Summary of Events and Information	Remarks and references to Appendices
TOURNAI.	28th.		Capt. H. W. BRADLEY, R. A. S. C., visited Railhead TEMPLEUVE this day.	
	29th.		Normal Routine.	
	30th.		13. O. R's proceeded this day to, 1st Army H. T. Reception Camp for reposting. Allotment received for further demobilization of 20. O. R's week-ending 3-5-1919.	"B"

H. W. Bradley.
Captain. HWB
for O. C., 24th Divisional Train.

2353 Wt. W2544/1454 700,000 5/15 D. D. & L. A.D.S.S./Forms/C. 2118.

A

NOMINAL ROLL OF OTHER RANKS TRANSFERRED FROM
24TH DIVISIONAL TRAIN TO B. S. D. CALAIS ON 2-4-1919.

Supply Personnel.

No. S2/015393	Cpl.	WEBB A. R.
No. T4/096460.	Pte.	BROWN H.
No. S /388729.	Pte.	ELDRED C. E.
No. S /312111	Pte.	ROBINSON P. H.
No. S /393895	Pte.	JOSLIN F. W.
No. T4/216179.	Pte.	MORRIS W.
S2/016263.	Pte.	ROBERTS G. W.
No. S /31040.	Pte.	BARRETT S. G.
No. T /292689.	Pte.	EDWARDS A. G.

B

NOMINAL ROLL OF PERSONNEL PROCEEDING FROM 24TH DIVL. TRAIN TO 1ST ARMY H.T. RECEPTION PARK VALENCIENNES ON 30-4-1919.

H. T. Personnel.

No. T4/198129.	Dr. Sadd.	COPPING S. (For 7th Army Aux. Horse Co)
No. T /37765	Dr.	CORLESS E.
T4/144734	Dr.	ELLIS W.
No. T4/092087.	Dr.	HALLEY J.
No. T /356364.	Dr.	HOLCROFT F.
TS/10011	Dr. Whr.	LEWIS J.
No. T4/160023.	Dr.	McKINLEY A.
No. TS/9718.	Dr. Whr.	OSBORN M. A.
No. TS/9907.	Dr. Whr.	PADDISON W.
No. T4/144240.	Dr.	PARISH W. A.
No. T4/144777	Dr.	PARISH S.
No. T /37765.	Dr.	SAUNDERS L. F.
No. TS/8066	Dr. Whr.	SIMPKIN A.

Authy. :- A. D. S. & T. No. 1 Area wire No. TD. 327 dated 26-4-1919.

Instructions regarding War Diaries and Intelligence Summaries are contained in F. S. Regs., Part II. and the Staff Manual respectively. Title pages will be prepared in manuscript.

WAR DIARY of O. C. 24th Divisional Train, R. A. S. C.

or

INTELLIGENCE SUMMARY.

(Erase heading not required.)

Army Form C. 2118.

Page 1.

Place	Date	Hour	Summary of Events and Information	Remarks and references to Appendices
TOURNAI.	1/5/19.		Normal Routine.	
	2nd.		Normal Routine.	
	3rd.		Lieut. H. J. LEWIS, R. A. S. C. granted 14days leave to U. K. Lieut. J. O. TIDY, R. A. S. C., assumed temporary command of Train Cadre Coys.	
	4th.		Capt. R. F. SEDDALL, R. A. S. C. granted 7days extension of leave. Capt. H. W. BRADLEY, R. A. S. C. attended Conference at 24th Divisional Headquarters.	
	5th.		T/2/Lieut. H. WARNER, R. A. S. C. returned from leave of absence to U. K.	
	6th.		Fifth party of N. C. O's and Men visited YPRES.	
	7th.		Capt. H. W. BRADLEY, R. A. S. C. visited A. D. S. & T. No. 1. Area.	
	8th.		32 O. R's proceeded this day for Demobilization. Capt. H. W. BRADLEY, R. A. S. C. visited Railhead at TEMPLEUVE.	"A".
	9th.		T/2/Lieut. H. WARNER, R. A. S. C. transferred for duty to B. S. D., ROUEN.	
	10th.		Sixth party of N. C. O's visited BETHUNE. Lieut. G. F. B. GIBBS, R. A. S. C. joined from 58th Divisional Train for duty.	
	11th.		Seventh party of N. C. O's and Men visited WATERLOO. Capt. R. F. SEDDALL, R. A. S. C. returned from leave and assumed command of Train Cadre.	
	12th.		Lieut. N. W. GEDDES, R. A. S. C. joined for duty from 57th Divisional Train.	
	13th.		O. C. and Adjutant visited A. D. S. & T. No. 1. Area.	

R F Seddall

Captain,
O. C. 24th Divisional Train Cadre.

D. D. & L., London, E.C.
(10340) Wt W5300/P713 750,000 3/18 E 2688 Forms C/2118/15

Instructions regarding War Diaries and Intelligence Summaries are contained in F. S. Regs., Part II. and the Staff Manual respectively. Title pages will be prepared in manuscript.

WAR DIARY of O. C. 24th Divisional Train Cadre.
or
INTELLIGENCE SUMMARY.
(Erase heading not required.)

Army Form C. 2118.

Place	Date	Hour	Summary of Events and Information	Remarks and references to Appendices
TOURNAI.	14th.		Capt. R. F. SEDDALL, R. A. S. C. visited Railhead at TEMPLEUVE.	
	15th.		Capt. H. W. BRADLEY, R. A. S. C. visited Vehicle Park at BAISIEUX.	
	16th.		O. C. and Adjutant attended Conference at A. D. S. & T. No. 1. Area.	
	17th.		Normal Routine.	
	18th.		Normal Routine.	
	19th.		Capt. R. F. SEDDALL, R. A. S. C. visited Railhead.	
	20th.		28 O. R's proceeded this day for Demobilization.	"B".
	21st.		Normal Routine.	
	22nd.		Normal Routine.	
	23rd.		Lieut. H. J. LEWIS, R. A. S. C. rejoined from leave of absence.	
	24th.		O. C. and Adjutant visited A. D. S. & T. No. 1. Area. 19 O. R's proceeded for Demobilization.	"C".
	25th.		Lieut. J. O. TIDY, R. A. S. C. proceeded this day on leave of absence to U. K.	
	26th.		Normal Routine.	
	27th.		Normal Routine.	
	28th.		As from Railhead drawing 28/5/19, under instructions from A. D. S. & T. No. 1. Area, all Units of 24th Division Group were taken over by S. O. 1st Corps Troops M. T. Coy., for rations; all Supply and Transport work being carried out by 1st Corps Troops M. T. Coy.	
	29th.) 30th.) 31st.)		Normal Routine.	

R F Seddall
Captain,
O. C. 24th Divisional Train Cadre.

D. D. & L., London, E.C. (10340) Wt W5300/P713 750,000 3/18 E 2688 Forms/C/2118/16.

NOMINAL ROLL OF PERSONNEL WHO PROCEEDED FOR DISPERSAL ON

8th MAY, 1919. "A"

No. T2/016379	C. S. M.	BUTTRESS E. J.	No. T3/027219.	C. S. M.	CAMPBELL J.
No. T3/023364.	Farr. S. Sgt.	MILLWARD H.	No. T3/029566.	Cpl.	KNEEBONE W. G.
No. TS/13355.	Farr. Cpl.	MARTIN J.	No. T4/040783.	Dr.	NOTMAN W.
T4/040792.	Dr.	EAGLESHAM A.	No. T3/028029.	Dr.	CARROLL G.
No. T4/035645.	Dr.	CLARKE S.	No. T4/040674.	Dr.	STEVENSON J.
No. T /21298.	Dr.	TOMPKINS T.	No. T3/024210.	Dr.	HILTON A. G.
No. T2/14417.	Sgt.	GODDARD G. E.	No. T3/023918.	L. Cpl.	GAMBLES A.
No. T3/027344.	Dr.	MAJOR G.	No. T4/039702.	Dr.	WILLEY R.
No. T4/036929.	Dr.	JAKEMAN A.	No. T3/027343.	Dr.	MARDY E.
No. T3/029286.	CPL.	LESTER W.	No. T3/028492.	Dr.	LEEMING R.
No. T2/14427.	Cpl.	HOPE J.	No. T4/040394.	Dr.	BROADLEY D.
No. T2/14817.	Dr.	KEDDIE D.	No. T4/249149.	Dr.	HERBERT F.
No. T3/024195.	L. Cpl.	PIKE M.	No. T3/031053.	Dr.	REED A. E.

Capt. and Adjt.,

9-5-1919. for O. C. 24th Divisional Train.

"B"

NOMINAL ROLL OF PERSONNEL WHO PROCEEDED FOR DISPERSAL

ON 20 - 5 - 1919.

T4/084598.	Whr. Corpl.	Jones A. W.
T4/055593.	Dr.	Stevenson T.
T4/040871.	Dr.	Smith W. H.
S2/030[illegible]21.	Cpl.	Ruston R. W.
T4/040[illegible]67.	Whr. S. Sgt.	Taylor C. [illegible]
T4/055601.	Dr.	Jackson [illegible] J.
T2/10116.	Dr.	Holland W.
TS/550[illegible].	Sadd. Dr.	[illegible] A. W.
T4/055987.	Dr.	Catchesides A. R.
T4/056141.	Dr.	Bingham J.
T4/144626.	Dr.	Gastrell A.
T4/058921.	Dr.	Gray G.
T4/055921.	Driver.	Simpson J. W.
TS/6457.	Farr. Cpl.	Wilson A.
S2/018024.	Cpl.	Walker H.
T4/040760.	Dr.	Pattison W.
T4/[illegible]49360.	Sadd. Dr.	[illegible] W. R.
TS/6790.	Sadd. S. Sgt.	Thurmott.
T4/092568.	Dr.	Saunders T.
T4/059430.	Dr.	Ong R. W.
T4/056145.	Dr.	Butterfield
T4/056081.	Dr.	Scott J.
T4/056103.	Dr.	Robertson J.

"C"

NOMINAL ROLL OF PERSONNEL WHO PROCEEDED FOR DISPERSAL

ON 24 - 5 - 1919.

TS/7367.	Sadd. Cpl.	Triggs W.H.P.	T4/091357.	Dr.	Hannaford F.E.
T4/040711.	Dr.	Sturrock J.G.	T2/14529.	Dr.	Underwood W.
T4/040784.	Cpl.	Mennell W.G.	T4/040802.	Dr.	Micklethwaite J.W.
T2/[illegible].	Dr.	Sutcliffe H.	T /37736.	Dr.	McLoughlin W.T.
T4/055604.	Dr.	Sparrow E.L.	T3/022431.	C.S.M.	Alves R.
T2/017862.	Dr.	Wallard A.W.	T4/092673.	Dr.	James R.
T4/059943.	Sadd. Cpl.	Parfitt C.A.	T4/191353.	L. Cpl.	Hodges C.H.
T4/092836.	Dr.	Woolven F.E.	TS/6429.	Farr. Dr.	Gould R.B.
TS/7370.	Sadd. Dr.	Talbot R.H.	33597.	Pte.	Carmichael W.

Instructions regarding War Diaries and Intelligence Summaries are contained in F.S. Regs., Part II. and the Staff Manual respectively. Title pages will be prepared in manuscript.

WAR DIARY
or
INTELLIGENCE SUMMARY.
(Erase heading not required.)

Army Form C. 2118.

24 D Train

VR 46

Place	Date	Hour	Summary of Events and Information	Remarks and references to Appendices
TOURNAI	1-6-19.		Entrainment of Cadr es of Division commenced t o-day.-	Ceased
	2-6-19.		Lieut. C. F. B. Gibbs, R. A. S. C. transferred for Duty to 31st Divisional Train.-	
	3-6-19.		Entrainment of Cadres continued.-	
	4-6-19.			
	5-6-19.			
	6-6-19.		Entrainment of Cadres ordered to proceed to United Kingdom with Equipment ceased to-day.- Remaining Cadres standing by for breaking up in this Country. No Cadres of Train have so far been despatched to United Kingdom.-	
	7-6-19.		Lieut. N. W. Geddes R. A. S. C. granted 48 hours leave to Antwerp.	
	8-6-19.		Orders received all 1914 Men must be Demobilized by 15th June, 1919.	
	9-6-19.			
	10-6-19.		All Pool Horses transferred to No. 1 Ar ea Remount Squadron, Douai.- Proceeded this day by March Route via ORCHIES.-	
	11-6-19.		Orders received to hand all Equipment (except Vehicles) to I. C. S. Tournai, on 13th June.-	
	12-6-19.			
	13-6-19.		27 N. C. O's and Men proceeded this day to No 5 Concentration Camp for Demobilization.-	
	14-6-19.		Captain R. F. Seddall, Capt, H. W. Bradley, and Lieut N. W. Geddes R. A. S. C. granted 48 hours leave to Antwerp.-	
	15-6-19.			

R F Seddall Capt
O.C. 24th Div Train
24/6/19

2353 Wt. W2544/1454 700,000 5/15 D. D. & L. A.D.S.S./Forms/C. 2118.

Instructions regarding War Diaries and Intelligence Summaries are contained in F.S. Regs., Part II. and the Staff Manual respectively. Title pages will be prepared in manuscript.

WAR DIARY
or
INTELLIGENCE SUMMARY.
(Erase heading not required.)

Army Form C. 2118.

Place	Date	Hour	Summary of Events and Information	Remarks and references to Appendices
Tournai	16-6-19.		Entrainment of Vehicles commenced this to-day.-	
	17-6-19.		19 N.C.O's and Men proceeded this Day to No 5 Concentration Camp for Demobilization.-	
	18-6-19		O.C. and Adjutant visited A.D.S.&.T. No 1 Area to arrange final Demobilization of Personnel.	
	19-6-19.		All Equipment handed into I.C.S. Tournai, this day.-	
	20-6-19.			
	21-6-19.		Lieut H.J.Lewis R.A.S.C. proceeded this day for Duty to Rhine Reinforcement Camp, Cologne.-	
			Lieut, N.W.Geddes, R.A.S.C. proceeded this day for Duty to No 1 Army Aux.(Horse) Company.-	
			Lieut, J.O.Tidy, R.A.S.C. (at present on Leave in England ordered to report to No. 1 Army Aux. (Horse) Company for Duty.	
			Capt and Adjt. H.W.Bradley, R.A.S.C. granted Leave to United Kingdom.-	
			Capt. R. F. Seddall, R.A.S.C. proceeded for Demobilization.-	
	25.6.19		Final dispersal of 24th Div Train	

R F Seddall
Capt
O.C. 24th Div Train cadre
24/6/19

2353 Wt. W2514/1454 700,000 5/15 D. D. & L. A.D.S.S./Forms/C. 2118.

www.ingramcontent.com/pod-product-compliance
Lightning Source LLC
Chambersburg PA
CBHW080814010526
44111CB00015B/2557